Generative AI Unleashed

Other related titles:

You may also like

- PBPC080 | Karna | Prompt Engineering Techniques for Optimizing Generative AI | Contracted July 2024
- PBPC082 | Dalal | Generative AI in Multimedia Content Processing: Security and Privacy Perspectives | Contracted Sept 2024
- PBPC078 | Rajasekar | Generative AI for Sign Language Recognition and Translation | Contracted May 2024
- PBPC077 | Sharma | The Power of Large Language Models in the Digital Age: From technical aspects to applications, real-world examples, ethical and security concerns and future perspectives | Contracted April 2024

We also publish a wide range of books on the following topics:
Computing and Networks
Control, Robotics and Sensors
Electrical Regulations
Electromagnetics and Radar
Energy Engineering
Healthcare Technologies
History and Management of Technology
IET Codes and Guidance
Materials, Circuits and Devices
Model Forms
Nanomaterials and Nanotechnologies
Optics, Photonics and Lasers
Production, Design and Manufacturing
Security
Telecommunications
Transportation

All books are available in print via https://shop.theiet.org or as eBooks via our Digital Library https://digital-library.theiet.org.

IET COMPUTING SERIES 76

Generative AI Unleashed

Advancements, transformative applications and future frontiers

Edited by
Karthik Ramamurthy, Suganthi Kulanthaivelu,
Shajina Anand and Thangavel Murugan

The Institution of Engineering and Technology

About the IET

This book is published by the Institution of Engineering and Technology (The IET).

We inspire, inform and influence the global engineering community to engineer a better world. As a diverse home across engineering and technology, we share knowledge that helps make better sense of the world, to accelerate innovation and solve the global challenges that matter.

The IET is a not-for-profit organisation. The surplus we make from our books is used to support activities and products for the engineering community and promote the positive role of science, engineering and technology in the world. This includes education resources and outreach, scholarships and awards, events and courses, publications, professional development and mentoring, and advocacy to governments.

To discover more about the IET please visit https://www.theiet.org/.

About IET books

The IET publishes books across many engineering and technology disciplines. Our authors and editors offer fresh perspectives from universities and industry. Within our subject areas, we have several book series steered by editorial boards made up of leading subject experts.

We peer review each book at the proposal stage to ensure the quality and relevance of our publications.

Get involved

If you are interested in becoming an author, editor, series advisor, or peer reviewer please visit https://www.theiet.org/publishing/publishing-with-iet-books/ or contact author_support@theiet.org.

Discovering our electronic content

All of our books are available online via the IET's Digital Library. Our Digital Library is the home of technical documents, eBooks, conference publications, real-life case studies and journal articles. To find out more, please visit https://digital-library.theiet.org.

In collaboration with the United Nations and the International Publishers Association, the IET is a Signatory member of the SDG Publishers Compact. The Compact aims to accelerate progress to achieve the Sustainable Development Goals (SDGs) by 2030. Signatories aspire to develop sustainable practices and act as champions of the SDGs during the Decade of Action (2020–30), publishing books and journals that will help inform, develop, and inspire action in that direction.

In line with our sustainable goals, our UK printing partner has FSC accreditation, which is reducing our environmental impact to the planet. We use a print-on-demand model to further reduce our carbon footprint.

British Library Cataloguing in Publication Data

A catalogue record for this product is available from the British Library

ISBN 978-1-83724-099-9 (hardback)
ISBN 978-1-83724-100-2 (PDF)

Typeset in India by MPS Limited
Printed in the UK by CPI Group (UK) Ltd, Eastbourne

Cover image: Olemedia/E+ via Getty Images

Contents

5 **Generative AI in image synthesis: review and recent advancements**   **69**
   Vijayarajan Rajangam, Sangeetha Nagarajan and Alex Noel Joseph Raj

6 **Harnessing generative AI for enhanced brain tumor detection in**
   clinical trials   **83**
   MV Sujan Kumar, Ganesh Khekare, Shashi Kant Gupta and
   Sharnil Pandya

7   A systematic review of GAN-based models in data synthesis for privacy protection   **103**

M. Srimathi, B. Rajesh Kanna and Ulrich Furbach

8   Impact of generative AI on Industry 4.0 and digital transformation   **139**

Shanthababu Pandian and Shanthakumar Pandian

About the editors

Karthik Ramamurthy is an associate professor in the Research Centre for Cyber Physical Systems at the Vellore Institute of Technology, Chennai, India. His research interests include deep learning, computer vision, digital image processing, and medical image analysis. He has published 80+ papers in peer reviewed journals and conferences and is an active journal reviewer. He obtained his doctoral degree from the Vellore Institute of Technology and his master's degree from Anna University, India.

Suganthi Kulanthaivelu is an associate professor in the School of Electronics Engineering, Vellore Institute of Technology, Chennai, India. Her areas of research interest focus on artificial intelligence, wireless sensor networks, internet of things applications and industrial IoT, and image processing. She has published 20+ research papers in journals and at conferences. She holds a PhD degree in wireless sensor networks from Anna University, India.

Shajina Anand is an assistant professor and manager of the Cybersecurity Lab at Seton Hall University, NJ, USA. With over a decade of experience in both industry and academia, her research interests include artificial intelligence, data engineering, cloud computing security, and cybersecurity, including authentication, ethical hacking, cyberattacks, and cyber detection. She holds a PhD degree in cloud data security from Anna University, India.

Thangavel Murugan is an assistant professor in the Department of Information Systems and Security, College of Information Technology, United Arab Emirates University, UAE. He specializes in data science for cybersecurity, information security, ethical hacking, cyber forensics, blockchain, and high-performance computing (HPC). He has published in international journals and at conferences and authored 15+ book chapters. He is a senior member of the IEEE and a professional member of the ACM.

Chapter 1

Introduction to generative artificial intelligence

R. Karthik[1], K. Suganthi[2], Shajina Anand[3] and Thangavel Murugan[4]

Abstract

Generative artificial intelligence (GAI) is revolutionizing digital content creation across multiple domains, including text, speech, images, and scientific data. Leveraging advanced models such as generative adversarial networks, variational autoencoders, and transformer-based architectures, GAI mimics human-like creativity and generates highly realistic outputs. The evolution of these technologies has been driven by advancements in deep learning and computational power, enabling applications in natural language processing, speech synthesis, and image generation. Text generation models based on transformers enhance human-computer interactions, while speech synthesis models produce expressive and human-like voice outputs, reshaping industries like entertainment and customer service. In computer vision, GAI enables hyper-realistic image synthesis, benefiting artistic creation and scientific applications like tumor detection in clinical trials. Additionally, GAI facilitates data synthesis for privacy protection by generating synthetic datasets that retain statistical properties while safeguarding sensitive information. Its influence extends into Industry 4.0 and digital transformation, optimizing automation and smart systems. However, ethical concerns arise, particularly regarding deepfake technology, misinformation, and identity fraud. GAI's applications in unconventional fields, such as astronomy, further illustrate its expansive impact. Challenges such as bias, intellectual property rights, and content authenticity necessitate careful navigation for responsible AI deployment. As GAI continues to evolve, new applications and ethical considerations emerge, shaping the future regulatory landscape. This chapter explores GAI's transformative potential, providing a comprehensive understanding of its capabilities, challenges, and implications in the digital era.

Keywords: Generative artificial intelligence; generative adversarial networks; deep learning; transformer

[1]Centre for Cyber Physical Systems, Vellore Institute of Technology Chennai, India
[2]School of Electronics Engineering, Vellore Institute of Technology Chennai, India
[3]Department of Mathematics and Computer Science, Seton Hall University, USA
[4]Department of Information Systems and Security, College of Information Technology, United Arab Emirates University, United Arab Emirates

1.1 Introduction

Generative artificial intelligence (GAI) represents a revolutionary branch of artificial intelligence (AI) focused on creating new content, data, or solutions by leveraging machine learning (ML) approaches. The receptiveness of advanced GAI tools such as ChatGPT, Google Bard signifies a major shift, creating new opportunities for both learning and teaching [1]. On the contrary, traditional AI, which mainly performs tasks based on pre-defined rules or by analyzing actual data, GAI can produce original outputs that mimic or enhance human creativity and intelligence. This capability stems from sophisticated models that learn underlying patterns and structures in ample datasets, facilitating them to generate new, coherent, and contextually relevant content. The evolution of GAI has been marked by significant milestones, from the previous neural networks and probabilistic models to the progressive deep learning (DL) architectures and transformer models that monopolize the field today.

The bottom line of GAI lies in its use of neural networks, notably DL models, which have the scope to learn and replicate complex patterns in data. Among various generative models, generative adversarial networks (GANs) have gained significant familiarity in recent years. This model works on the principle of two adversaries continuously striving to outperform each other [2]. GANs, introduced by Ian Goodfellow in 2014, consist of two neural networks—a generator and a discriminator—that work in tandem to create highly pragmatic data. The generator creates new data instances, while the discriminator evaluates their authenticity, preeminent to progressively better outputs over this antagonistic process. Variational autoencoders (VAEs), on the other hand, overture a probabilistic approach to generating data by encoding input data into a latent space and then decoding it back into new data instances, indulgent for more control and variation in the generated outputs. VAE is an unsupervised generative model that can yield data with a probability distribution firmly matching that of the training dataset [3].

The applications of GAI are extensive and diverse, impacting diverse domains and industries. GAI technologies, like ChatGPT, present enormous potential applications across various sectors, including business, education, healthcare, and content creation [4]. This section examines examples of how GAI is being utilized in these fields. In the creative arts, GAI has permitted the generation of unique artworks, music compositions, and designs, providing artists and creators with powerful tools to enhance their innovative processes. In healthcare, GAI is being used to generate fabricated medical images for research and training, evolve new drug candidates through molecular generation, and even create customized treatment slate by analyzing patient data. Additionally, GAI plays a pivotal role in Industry 4.0 and digital transformation by streamlining automation and improving operational efficiency. In astronomy, it enables the synthesis of cosmic data, aiding in the analysis of celestial phenomena.

As GAI continues to evolve, its potential and influence are expected to grow even further. The ongoing advancements in computational power, algorithmic efficiency, and data availability are paving the way for more sophisticated and capable generative models. However, with this improvement come major ethical and practical scrutiny. Ensuring the responsible use of GAI, addressing biases in stemming content, and managing the societal brunt of widespread AI integration are critical challenges that must be addressed. AI developers should work toward establishing an accordance on comprehensive ethical standards that are universally acceptable and take into account cultural differences [5]. By fostering collaboration between AI researchers, industry professionals, and policymakers, the future of GAI can be directed toward escalating its benefits while mitigating potential risks, ultimately leading to a more innovative and equitable community.

1.2   Historical development and evolution of GAI

The development and evolution of GAI is an enthralling narrative that stretches several decades, recurrent by critical breakthroughs in computer science, neural networks, and ML. Generative models have been part of AI since the 1950s. Traditional models include hidden Markov models and Gaussian mixture models, which formed fundamental data. Significant advancements in generative models occurred with the advent of DL [6]. The journey began in the 1950s when Alan Turing laid the foundational concepts for AI by proposing the idea of a machine capable of inspiring human intelligence. This early period also saying the creation of the Perceptron by Frank Rosenblatt in 1957, one of the first artificial neural networks capable of learning from data. The 1970s carry the development of the backpropagation algorithm, a significant breakthrough that enabled the potent training of multi-layer neural networks and forward the restraint of single-layer perceptrons. These fresh upgrading set the stage for the eventual exploration and expansion of neural network capabilities.

The 1980s and 1990s decided the inflation of neural networks, driven by momentous grant from researchers such as John Hopfield and Geoffrey Hinton. Hopfield introduced networks capable of storing and retrieving memories, contributing to the understanding of neural dynamics. Hinton and Terry Sejnowski introduced Boltzmann Machines in 1985, utilizing stochastic processes to model distributions of inputs. During this period, probabilistic graphical models like Bayesian Networks emerged, laying the groundwork for structured generative modeling. The 2000s heralded the dawn of DL, with Geoffrey Hinton's deep belief networks (DBNs) demonstrating the ability to learn hierarchical data representations. DBNs are probabilistic generative models comprising of multiple layers of contingent latent variables, with restricted Boltzmann machines serving as their fundamental components. DBNs employ a greedy, layer-wise unsupervised learning algorithm for training, followed by a discriminative fine-tuning procedure to augment performance on classification tasks [7]. Additionally, advancements in reinforcement learning algorithms enabled AI to learn complex tasks through trial and error, further presuming the frontier of what AI could achieve.

Figure 1.1 illustrates the hierarchical structure and applications of GAI within the broader contexts of AI, ML, and DL. At the core is GAI, highlighting its

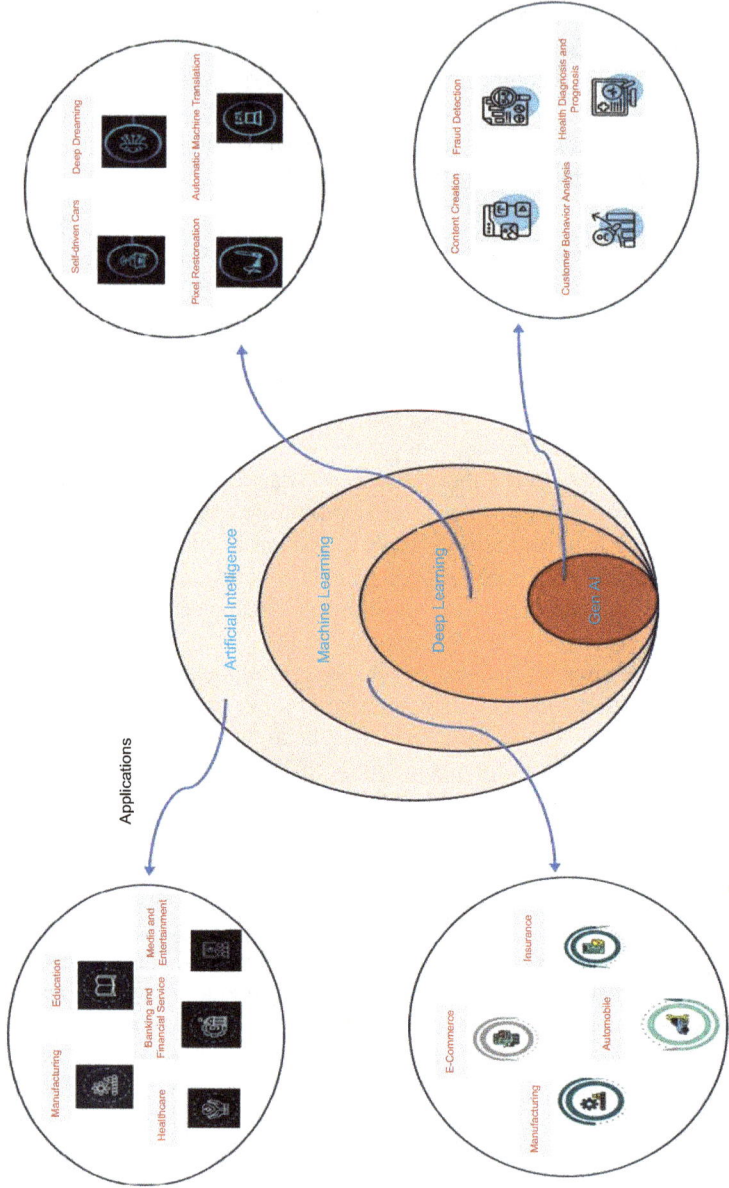

Figure 1.1 Structural evolution of generative artificial intelligence

position as a subset of DL, which itself is a subset of ML. ML is further nested within the broader domain of AI.

Figure 1.1 also showcases specific applications for each layer of this hierarchy. AI is applied across various industries, including manufacturing, education, healthcare, banking and financial services, and media and entertainment. ML finds uses in e-commerce, manufacturing, insurance, and the automobile industry. DL enables advancements such as self-driven cars, deep dreaming, pixel restoration, and automatic machine translation. At the core, GAI is utilized for content creation, fraud detection, customer behavior analysis, and health diagnosis and prognosis. The arrows connecting these layers to their applications emphasize the practical implementations and the interconnections between these technologies.

The 2010s brought about practical applications and significant breakthroughs in GAI. Ian Goodfellow's introduction of GANs in 2014 revolutionized the field by enabling two neural networks to compete, leading to the formation of pragmatic manufactured data. Around the same time, Kingma and Welling's VAEs provided a probabilistic way of data generation, enhancing the possibilities of generative models. In short, it can be stated that GANs and VAEs have enabled remarkable improvements in image generation. While developments in generative models took numerous paths, they ultimately converged with the introduction of transformers for natural language processing (NLP) in 2017. The 2020s have been dominated by the impact of transformer models, introduced by Vaswani *et al.* in 2017, revolutionizing NLP and leading to the development of powerful models like OpenAI's GPT-3. Transformers become pivotal in many generative models across various domains. In NLP, large models like Bidirectional Encoder Representations from Transformers (BERT) and Generative Pre-trained Transformer (GPT) grease transformers. In computer vision, models such as vision transformers and Swin transformers assimilate transformers with visual elements for image processing. Additionally, transformers have enhanced the creation of multimodal models like Contrastive Language–Image Pre-training (CLIP), which is trained on extensive text and image datasets and can generate images from text prompts. In addition, advances in multimodal AI, adorned by DALL-E and CLIP, have identified the likelihood of AI to understand and generate complex data across different modalities. Looking ahead, the center of attention is on scaling these models, assuring ethical and responsible AI development, and assimilating AI with emerging technologies such as quantum computing and advanced robotics, auspicious a future where AI continues to revamp society and technology profoundly.

1.3   Significance of generative AI in different domains

GAI has emerged as a transformative force across multiple domains, significantly impacting text generation, speech, and image synthesis. These techniques serve as a vital aid in sectors involving healthcare, security, industrial automation, and scientific discovery. The advancements in DL and neural network architectures have facilitated the development of highly sophisticated generative models, thereby enabling novel applications that enhance productivity, innovation, and efficiency in multiple sectors.

1.3.1   Text generation and speech synthesis

GAI has significantly improved NLP applications by enhancing machine comprehension and automated text generation. Transformer-based models, such as OpenAI's Generative Pre-trained Transformer series have redefined human-computer interactions by generating highly coherent, context-aware, and semantically rich textual content [8]. These models are widely used in content creation, automated customer support, and real-time language translation. Similarly, the evolution of generative models for speech synthesis, such as WaveNet [9] and Tacotron [10], has facilitated the production of highly expressive, natural-sounding synthetic voices. These technologies have found applications in assistive technologies for visually impaired individuals, audiobook production, virtual assistants, and entertainment.

1.3.2   Image synthesis and healthcare applications

GAI has enabled the synthesis of hyper-realistic images, a capability that has significant implications for both artistic creation and scientific research. Techniques such as GANs and diffusion models have demonstrated remarkable progress in generating high-quality, photorealistic images. In the healthcare sector, generative models are playing a crucial role in augmenting medical image datasets, thereby addressing the challenges of data scarcity and improving the training of diagnostic models. AI-generated synthetic medical images have been utilized to enhance the performance of DL models [11]. The ability of GAI to generate anatomically accurate and diverse datasets contributes to more robust and generalized diagnostic algorithms, ultimately improving patient outcomes.

1.3.3   Data privacy and security

The generation of synthetic data through GAI has proven to be an effective approach in mitigating privacy concerns associated with the sharing of sensitive information. By leveraging AI-driven data synthesis techniques, organizations can generate artificial datasets that preserve the statistical properties and distributions of real-world data while eliminating personally identifiable information. This approach ensures compliance with stringent data protection regulations while maintaining the integrity of ML models trained on such data [12]. The adoption of synthetic data in financial transactions, healthcare records, and user behavior analytics is instrumental in advancing AI-driven solutions without compromising privacy.

1.3.4   Industry 4.0 and digital transformation

GAI is at the forefront of Industry 4.0 and digital transformation, facilitating automation, predictive maintenance, and process optimization across various industrial sectors. The integration of AI-generated simulations in digital twin technology has enhanced manufacturing processes by enabling real-time performance monitoring and predictive analytics [13]. These AI-driven enhancements can contribute to increased operational efficiency, reduced downtime, and improved decision-making capabilities in industries such as aerospace, automotive, and logistics. By harnessing the power of generative models, organizations can simulate complex production environments, optimize resource allocation, and forecast potential system failures before they occur.

1.3.5   GAI in astronomy and scientific discovery

Beyond traditional applications, GAI is making noteworthy contributions to scientific research and discovery, particularly in the field of astronomy. AI-generated simulations of cosmic events can serve as a vital aid to astronomers in understanding complex celestial phenomena. Additionally, AI-powered image enhancement techniques have improved the analysis of astronomical observations, enabling researchers to extract valuable insights from vast datasets collected by space telescopes. These advancements underscore the expanding role of GAI in accelerating scientific exploration and expanding the boundaries of human knowledge.

By revolutionizing various fields, GAI continues to reshape the digital landscape, unlocking different opportunities for innovation and problem-solving. However, alongside its benefits, it is imperative to address the associated ethical, legal, and technical challenges to ensure responsible and trustworthy deployment. As research in GAI advances, interdisciplinary collaboration among policymakers, researchers, and industry stakeholders will be essential in maximizing its potential while mitigating risks.

1.4   Limitations of GAI

While GAI has shown remarkable potential across various industries, it also has several limitations and challenges that need to be addressed. Understanding these limitations is crucial for responsible development and deployment of GAI technologies. One such notable limitation is that GAI systems are highly dependent on large volumes of high-quality data to function effectively. The quality and quantity of the data used to train these models directly impact their performance. Inadequate or biased data can lead to poor model performance and unintended consequences. If the training data lacks diversity, the generated outputs may exhibit biases, reinforcing stereotypes and unfair practices. Moreover, the need for vast amounts of data raises privacy concerns. Collecting and utilizing personal data to train GAI models can infringe on individuals' privacy rights and lead to potential misuse of sensitive information [14]. Ensuring data privacy and security while obtaining sufficient and diverse datasets remains a significant challenge.

Training and deploying GAI models require substantial computational resources. These models often involve complex architectures and extensive training times, which demand powerful hardware and significant energy consumption [15]. This not only makes GAI development expensive but also raises concerns about its environmental impact. For many organizations, especially smaller ones with limited resources, the high computational requirements can be a barrier to entry. This creates a disparity where only well-funded entities can leverage the full potential of

GAI, potentially widening the gap between large tech companies and smaller businesses or researchers.

GAI has the potential to generate content that is indistinguishable from human-created content, raising ethical and social concerns [16]. For example, GAI can be used to create deepfakes, realistic but fake images or videos that can be employed to spread misinformation, manipulate public opinion, or damage reputations. The ease with which GAI can generate convincing fake content poses a significant threat to information integrity and societal trust. Additionally, GAI can perpetuate and amplify existing biases present in the training data. If not properly addressed, these biases can result in discriminatory outcomes in applications such as hiring, lending, and law enforcement. Ensuring fairness and accountability in GAI systems requires rigorous testing, validation, and ongoing monitoring to mitigate these ethical risks.

Many GAI models, particularly those based on DL, are often considered black boxes due to their complex and opaque nature. This lack of interpretability makes it challenging to understand how these models arrive at their outputs. In critical applications such as healthcare and finance, the inability to explain the decision-making process of GAI models can hinder their adoption and raise concerns about reliability and trustworthiness [17]. Researchers and developers are actively working on methods to improve the interpretability of GAI models, but it remains a significant challenge. Achieving a balance between model complexity, performance, and interpretability is essential for the broader acceptance and responsible use of GAI technologies.

While GAI can enhance cybersecurity, it also introduces new security risks. Adversarial attacks, where malicious actors manipulate the inputs to deceive GAI models, can lead to incorrect or harmful outputs. For example, slight modifications to input data can cause image recognition systems to misclassify objects or speech recognition systems to misunderstand commands. Moreover, GAI-generated content can be used to create sophisticated phishing attacks, spam, and other malicious activities that are difficult to detect with traditional security measures. Ensuring the robustness and security of GAI models against such adversarial attacks is a critical area of ongoing research. Fully autonomous GAI systems can make errors, exhibit unexpected behaviors, or generate inappropriate content. Human supervision is necessary to validate and refine the outputs of GAI models, especially in high-stakes applications such as healthcare, legal, and autonomous systems. Ensuring that GAI systems are designed with mechanisms for human intervention and control is vital to prevent misuse and mitigate potential risks associated with their deployment.

1.5 Current research gaps and future directions

Despite the significant advancements in GAI, there remain numerous research gaps and areas that need further exploration. Addressing these gaps will not only enhance the capabilities and applications of GAI but also ensure its ethical and responsible use. Below are some of the key research gaps and future directions in the field of GAI.

- One of the primary challenges in GAI is the reliance on large datasets, which often contain biases and may lack diversity. Current research is focusing on developing methods to enhance the quality and diversity of training data. Techniques such as data augmentation, synthetic data generation, and transfer learning are being explored to mitigate data limitations. Future research should aim to create more inclusive and representative datasets that minimize biases and ensure fairness in GAI applications. Additionally, developing techniques to identify and mitigate biases in existing datasets is crucial for improving the reliability and ethical standards of GAI systems.
- The black-box nature of many GAI models, particularly DL-based models, poses significant challenges in understanding and interpreting their outputs. Improving model interpretability is essential for gaining trust and ensuring accountability, especially in critical applications. Current research is exploring methods such as explainable AI (XAI), which aims to make AI models more transparent and understandable. Future directions should focus on developing standardized approaches for model interpretability, enabling users to comprehend the decision-making process and ensuring that GAI systems can be audited and validated effectively.
- The ethical and social implications of GAI such as bias, misinformation, and privacy concerns are areas that require continuous attention. Research is needed to develop robust frameworks for the ethical use of GAI, ensuring that these systems adhere to principles of fairness, accountability, and transparency. Future research should focus on creating guidelines and best practices for the ethical deployment of GAI technologies. This includes developing tools for bias detection and mitigation, establishing standards for data privacy, and implementing mechanisms for human oversight and intervention in GAI systems.
- The high computational requirements of training and deploying GAI models pose significant barriers, particularly for smaller organizations with limited resources. Research is needed to develop more efficient algorithms and architectures that reduce the computational and energy demands of GAI systems. Future directions should include exploring novel model compression techniques such as pruning and quantization and developing energy-efficient hardware tailored for GAI workloads. This will democratize access to GAI technologies and reduce their environmental impact.
- While GAI has made strides in various domains, there are still many areas where its potential is underexplored. Expanding the applications of GAI to underserved areas, such as low-resource healthcare settings, rural development, and disaster response, can have a significant positive impact. Future research should focus on adapting GAI technologies to meet the specific needs and constraints of these underserved areas. This includes developing lightweight and cost-effective GAI solutions that can operate in resource-constrained environments and addressing unique challenges faced by these communities.

- Most GAI models are designed for specific tasks and modalities such as text generation, image synthesis, or music composition. However, integrating multimodal and multitask learning can enhance the versatility and performance of GAI systems. Current research is exploring the development of models that can handle multiple tasks and modalities simultaneously, leveraging shared knowledge across different domains. Future directions should focus on creating unified GAI frameworks that can seamlessly integrate and generate content across various types of data such as combining text, images, and audio.

1.6   Conclusion

GAI has emerged as an innovative technology, redefining the landscape of numerous industries and applications. From its foundational role in generative models such as GANs, VAEs, and transformer-based architectures, GAI demonstrates versatility and transformative potential. This comprehensive exploration highlights both the promise and challenges of GAI, providing an understanding of its current state and future implications. The applications of GAI extend beyond traditional creative and business domains, showcasing its ability to enhance text generation through transformer-based models, enable realistic speech synthesis, and revolutionize image generation in fields such as healthcare and scientific discovery.

GAI's impact in healthcare is represented by its role in enhancing tumor detection in clinical trials, where it refines diagnostic accuracy and assists medical professionals in early intervention. In cybersecurity, GAI is instrumental in developing sophisticated threat detection mechanisms, leveraging synthetic data generation techniques to bolster system resilience. Additionally, GAI enhances data privacy by producing synthetic datasets that retain statistical fidelity while mitigating risks of exposure. The industrial sector benefits significantly from GAI's contributions to Industry 4.0 and digital transformation, enabling intelligent automation and smart manufacturing solutions. Beyond conventional applications, GAI's influence extends into space exploration, as seen in its role in astronomical data analysis and cosmic creativity.

Despite these advancements, the limitations of GAI underscore the necessity for ongoing research and development. Challenges such as data dependency, lack of interpretability, ethical concerns, adversarial vulnerabilities, and computational inefficiencies present significant obstacles. Addressing these limitations is crucial to ensure the robustness, reliability, and ethical deployment of GAI systems. Additionally, the responsible deployment of deepfake technology, safeguarding intellectual property rights, and maintaining ethical standards in GAI applications remain critical concerns.

In conclusion, GAI stands at the forefront of technological innovation, offering transformative solutions across various domains. However, the path forward necessitates collaborative efforts among researchers, policymakers, and industry stakeholders to address the inherent challenges and unlock the full potential of

GAI. By fostering a responsible and equitable development approach, GAI can continue to drive progress, enhancing both industry capabilities and societal well-being. The future of GAI holds immense promise, and with concerted efforts, it can pave the way for a more advanced, efficient, and ethical technological landscape.

References

[1] Morales-Chan, M., Amado-Salvatierra, H.R., and Hernandez-Rizzardini, R. (2024). Workshop: Educational innovation through generative artificial intelligence: Tools, opportunities, and challenges. In *Proceedings of the 2024 IEEE World Engineering Education Conference (EDUNINE)* (pp. 1–2). Piscataway, NJ: IEEE.

[2] Kumar, S., and Dhawan, S. (2020). A detailed study on generative adversarial networks. In *Proceedings of the 2020 5th International Conference on Communication and Electronics Systems (ICCES)* (pp. 641–645). Piscataway, NJ: IEEE.

[3] Mansouri, N., and Lachiri, Z. (2020). Laughter synthesis: A comparison between variational autoencoder and autoencoder. In *Proceedings of the 2020 5th International Conference on Advanced Technologies for Signal and Image Processing (ATSIP)* (pp. 1–6). Piscataway, NJ: IEEE.

[4] Fui-Hoon Nah, F., Zheng, R., Cai, J., Siau, K., and Chen, L. (2023). Generative AI and ChatGPT: Applications, challenges, and AI–human collaboration. *Journal of Information Technology Case and Application Research*, 25(3), 277–304.

[5] Lin, Z. (2024). Building ethical guidelines for generative AI in scientific research. arXiv preprint arXiv:2401.15284.

[6] Akhtar, Z.B. (2024). Unveiling the evolution of generative AI (GAI): A comprehensive and investigative analysis toward LLM models (2021–2024) and beyond. *Journal of Electrical Systems and Information Technology*, 11 (1), 22.

[7] Mohamed, A.R., Dahl, G., and Hinton, G. (2009). Deep belief networks for phone recognition. In *Proceedings of the Nips Workshop on Deep Learning for Speech Recognition and Related Applications* (Vol. 1, No. 9, p. 39).

[8] Brown, T.B., Mann, B., Ryder, N., *et al.* (2020). Language models are few-shot learners. In *Proceedings of the 34th International Conference on Neural Information Processing Systems*. Curran Associates Inc., Red Hook, NY (Article 159, pp. 1877–1901).

[9] van den Oord, A., Dieleman, S., Zen, H., *et al.* (2016). WaveNet: A generative model for raw audio. In *Proceedings of the 9th ISCA Workshop on Speech Synthesis Workshop (SSW9)* (p. 125).

[10] Wang, Y., Skerry-Ryan, R.J., Stanton, D., *et al.* (2017). Tacotron: Towards end-to-end speech synthesis. In *Proceedings of the Interspeech 2017* (pp. 4006–4010), https://doi.org/10.21437/Interspeech.2017-1452.

[11]   Kazeminia, S., Baur, C., Kuijper, A., *et al.* (2020). GANs for medical image analysis. *Artificial Intelligence in Medicine*, 109, 101938, https://doi.org/10.1016/j.artmed.2020.101938.

[12]   Choi, E., Biswal, S., Malin, B., Duke, J., Stewart, W.F., and Sun, J. (2017). Generating multi-label discrete patient records using generative adversarial networks. In *Proceedings of Machine Learning Research* (Vol. 68, pp. 286–305), https://proceedings.mlr.press/v68/choi17a.html.

[13]   Lu, Y., Liu, C., Wang, K.I.-K., Huang, H., and Xu, X. (2020). Digital twin-driven smart manufacturing: Connotation, reference model, applications and research issues. *Robotics and Computer-Integrated Manufacturing*, 61, 101837, https://doi.org/10.1016/j.rcim.2019.101837.

[14]   El Mestari S.Z., Lenzini G., and Demirci H. (2024). Preserving data privacy in machine learning systems. *Computers and Security*, 137, 103605.

[15]   Bandi A., Adapa P.V.S.R., and Kuchi Y.E.V.P.K. (2023). The power of generative AI: A review of requirements, models, input–output formats, evaluation metrics, and challenges. *Future Internet*, 15, 260.

[16]   Raman R., Kumar Nair V., Nedungadi P., *et al.* (2024). Fake news research trends, linkages to generative artificial intelligence and sustainable development goals. *Heliyon*, 10, e24727.

[17]   Bansal V., Jain A., and Kaur Walia N. (2024). Diabetic retinopathy detection through generative AI techniques: A review. *Results in Optics*, 16, 100700.

Chapter 2

Unveiling the generative power: an introduction to generative AI algorithms and their evolution

Suganya Ramamoorthy[1], Abhiram Sharma[1], Saksham Anand[1] and Vijayalakshmi Ramasamy[2]

Abstract

Artificial intelligence (AI) has become a significant transformative force for its well-established analytical prowess and remarkable ability to create new, original, life-like data. We begin by exploring the fundamental concepts of *generative models* and contrasting them with traditional *discriminative models* that dominate AI. This sets the stage for a historical journey of how AI has developed and evolved from a theoretical construct to a reality transforming lives.

Generative models, which aim to generate new data instances that resemble a given training dataset, differ fundamentally from discriminative models, which focus on distinguishing between different data instances. While discriminative models have achieved significant success in tasks such as image classification and language translation, generative models have opened new possibilities in creative domains, including art, music, and literature.

The narrative then focuses on the evolution of generative AI (GenAI) algorithms, tracing their path from early probabilistic models like variational autoencoders (VAEs) to the current dominance of deep learning. VAEs represent one of the earliest attempts to merge probabilistic graphical models with neural networks, providing a framework for learning latent variable models in a scalable manner.

This chapter further explores the diverse landscape of *GAN architecture*, building upon our foundation. We will explore popular variations like conditional GANs or CGAN, Wasserstein GANs or WGAN, and StyleGANs. This analysis will highlight the unique strengths and weaknesses of these variations while also delving into their applications across various creative tasks such as real-time image processing, synthetic literature generation, music, and audiovisual creations.

Moving beyond GANs, this chapter examines other prominent AI algorithms for data generation, including VAE, *autoregressive models*, and *generative transformer models*. By exploring their fundamental mechanisms and comparing them to

[1]School of Computer Science and Engineering, Vellore Institute of Technology - Chennai, India
[2]Department of Computer Science, Georgia Southern University, USA

GANs, we gain a nuanced understanding of their advantages and reliability for different generation tasks.

In conclusion, this chapter comprehensively analyzes key GenAI algorithms and their evolution. By acknowledging both the strengths and challenges of these tools, we aim to promote their responsible development and use. We are on the cusp of a future shaped by innovative GenAI applications, expanding the boundaries of human creativity and transforming various aspects of human experience.

Keywords: Generative artificial intelligence; deep learning; generative adversarial networks; variational autoencoders; autoregressive models; creative AI applications

2.1   Introduction

Artificial intelligence (AI) refers to the ability of a computer program or a machine to think, learn, and take actions without being explicitly programmed. It involves developing systems that can perform tasks, process and analyze large amounts of data, and identify patterns. AI is often considered highly transformative because it can not only complete tasks that typically require human intelligence but also at speeds beyond human capability. As a result, AI systems that follow predetermined patterns and rules have traditionally focused on enabling machines to learn from experience, adapt to new inputs, and perform human-like tasks. Traditional AI excels at classification, pattern recognition, and prediction tasks and typically involves discriminative (conditional) models that perform computations based on huge input data and focus on predicting a label or category given input data.

The advent of superfast processors called graphical processing units (GPUs) is specialized for parallel processing tasks and handling massive amounts of data from various sources, including academic, commercial, and public data sources, the Internet of Things, and social media. However, the world of AI has undergone a paradigm shift with the advent of generative AI (GenAI). GenAI models use neural networks and leverage different learning approaches, including unsupervised or semi-supervised learning, to identify patterns within the input data and generate new content like text, images, animation, art, and other data types without explicit instructions. They tend to learn the underlying distributions and patterns hidden within the data and leverage that knowledge to generate entirely new yet believable data points. AI can generate synthetic data to train other models when real data is scarce, sensitive, expensive, or impossible to obtain. These models can accelerate the discovery process and design materials with groundbreaking functionalities.

The potential applications of GenAI are vast and continue to evolve remarkably. This literature serves as a medium to comprehend and integrate the core algorithms driving this revolution, its evolution over time, and its potential for the future. As these models continue to develop, we can anticipate the emergence of even more transformative applications that will reshape various industries and push the boundaries of human creativity to new heights.

Before delving into the specific GenAI algorithms, it is important to understand some of their fundamental distinctions from the more established and widely used discriminative models. Discriminative models are trained on a labeled dataset where each data point has a corresponding label or category. Imagine a vast mountain of photographs, each categorized as "a cat" or "a dog." These models eventually learn to map the given input data to a specific output, thereby excelling at tasks involving classifying these images with highly impressive accuracy. Similarly, they might as well work on unlabeled data to predict price variations in the stock market based on historical data trends or recognize handwritten digits with human-like proficiency and accuracy.

However, GenAI models operate on a completely different approach. They do not require labeled data. Instead, they focus on the more ambitious goal of uncovering the hidden language of the data by analyzing large amounts of unknown data. Thus, GenAI models learn the underlying statistical distribution, which is the probability of encountering certain patterns and features within the data. This concept supports them in generating an entirely new reference data point that might closely resemble the training data regarding similar characteristics and patterns. For instance, a model trained on a dataset of human portraits could create a new face that has never existed before. Hence, there is the potential to create artificial medical scans for a rare disease, compose music in the style of a specific artist, or design a novel material with specific features, all thanks to the capabilities of generative models.

High computing requirements and associated costs are the most significant challenges of GenAI. Massive computational power is required to train large language models (generative pre-trained transformer (GPT) and bidirectional encoder representations from transformers (BERT)), which involves thousands of GPUs running for weeks, significantly raising financial and environmental costs. The inference process—where models generate outputs—can also be resource-intensive, especially when scaled for real-time applications. This cost factor makes it difficult for smaller organizations or academic institutions to experiment with or deploy such advanced models, as they lack tech giants' financial and infrastructure capabilities. As models become more complex, improving performance comes at significantly higher costs, resulting in diminishing returns. Therefore, addressing these challenges is crucial for GenAI to be more sustainable and accessible.

2.2   The evolution of GenAI algorithms

The field of AI has a rich and dynamic history, evolving through distinct phases that reflect advances in both computational theory and practical applications. Initially, AI systems were primarily rule-based, relying on manually coded instructions to perform tasks. The old systems were rigid and unable to adapt without reprogramming. Predictive AI, using machine learning, can analyze data to make predictions or decisions. The pivotal innovations that have reshaped the landscapes of traditional AI versus GenAI techniques, shown in Table 2.1, are discussed in the following subsections.

Table 2.1   Evolution of traditional AI versus GenAI techniques

Year	Traditional AI techniques	GenAI techniques
1950–1960	Symbolic AI, rule-based systems	
1980–1990	Expert systems	
1989	Backpropagation [1]	
1990s	LeNet-5 [2]	Early generative probabilistic models [3]
2006	Deep Belief Networks (DBNs) [4]	Restricted Boltzmann machines (RBMs), deep belief networks (DBNs) [4]
2012	AlexNet [5]	
2013		Variational autoencoders (VAEs) [6]
2014	DeepFace	Generative adversarial networks (GANs) [7]
2015	ResNet [8]	
2016	AlphaGo—DeepMind [9]	Wavenet, DCGANs (convolutional GANs)
2017	Transformers [10]	Progressive GAN, Wasserstein GANs (WGANs), Pix2Pix (Karras, 2017)
2018		BERT
2019		StyleGAN, BigGan [11]
2020		GPT-3
2022		DALL-E, CHATGPT [12]
2023		GPT-4

The key milestones in the evolution of GenAI algorithms are given below.

2.2.1   *Probabilistic models (1990s)*

Early GenAI models, mainly developed in the 1990s, were based on a probabilistic approach to create synthetic data points. These earlier techniques laid the foundation for the more sophisticated models we see today such as the variational auto-encoder (VAE). VAEs work by learning a compressed representation of the data, known as the latent space, which captures the essence of the data. The encoder model efficiently encodes and decodes information using this latent space to generate new data points that share characteristics with the training data. While auto-encoders represented a significant advancement in generative modeling, they had limitations. Capturing complex data distributions, especially those with multiple intricate details, proved challenging for encoders. Training these autoencoders could also be unstable, leading to inconsistencies in the generated synthetic data. Despite these limitations, encoders remain a foundational concept in generative modeling, inspiring the development of more robust and versatile techniques.

2.2.2   *Deep learning revolution (2010s)*

The early 2000s marked the start of a new era for GenAI with the introduction of deep learning architectures, a subset of machine learning that utilizes multilayered deep neural networks to simulate the complex decision-making abilities of human brains. These models have revolutionized the field by making it possible to extract complex patterns from large datasets, which represent a significant paradigm shift. Generative models have achieved remarkable performance by leveraging the capacity of deep learning to capture intricate representations. Among these models, generative adversarial networks (GANs) have emerged as leaders in the field of GenAI.

2.3   Generative adversarial networks: a significant innovation of adversarial training

GANs, the deep learning-based generative models introduced by Ian Goodfellow in 2014 [7], revolutionized the concept of GenAI. A GAN is a class of machine learning frameworks designed to generate new data that closely resembles a given dataset. This process involves two neural networks competing against each other in a game format, leading to continuous improvement. GANs are innovative approaches to training a generative model. This approach involves framing the problem as a supervised learning task with two sub-models: The *generator* model trained to create new examples, essentially serving as an artist that generates synthetic datasets mimicking the patterns and distributions of the training dataset, and the *discriminator* model that classifies examples as either real (from the domain) or fake (generated), acting as a critic meticulously analyzing each data point to differentiate real data from that created by the generator. The two models are trained simultaneously in an adversarial process until the discriminator is fooled about half the time, indicating that the generator produces believable examples. Therefore, the training process in a GAN involves a constant battle between the generator and the discriminator.

The process unfolds in the following steps:

Step 1: The generator starts by creating synthetic data points from random noise.
Step 2: The discriminator receives a real data point from the training set and a synthetic data point from the generator. It then attempts to classify each data point as real or synthetic.
Step 3: Based on the feedback from the discriminator, the generator adjusts its algorithm. It updates its parameters to improve the quality of its generated synthetic data, making it harder for the discriminator to distinguish it from the real dataset.
Step 4: This process repeats, with the generator refining its algorithm based on the discriminator's evolving ability to detect forgeries.

Through this adversarial training process, the generator and the discriminator become highly skilled. The generator learns to produce more realistic data points, while the discriminator gains the ability to distinguish between real and fake.

2.3.1 *A spectrum of GAN architectures: catering to diverse needs*

The core architecture of GAN has various adaptations designed to tackle specific challenges or cater to tasks involving new content generation. Here are a few notable examples:

- *Conditional generative adversarial networks:* These networks utilize an additional input and a random noise vector, allowing the generator to produce synthetic data based on a specific input. For instance, a conditional generative adversarial network (CGAN) trained using images of different dog breeds could be conditioned on a label like "Golden Retriever" to generate a realistic image of a Golden Retriever.

- *Wasserstein generative adversarial networks:* These networks address the "mode collapse" issue, where the generator becomes stuck in a loop, only producing a limited set of outputs. Wasserstein generative adversarial networks (WGANs) introduce a different loss function that improves training stability and reduces the likelihood of mode collapse.

2.3.2   StyleGANs

The StyleGAN model, developed by NVIDIA in 2019, is known for its ability to create high-quality images. It uses a progressive, growing approach to gradually add detail to the generated images, starting from a low resolution and increasing it over time. StyleGANs offer separate control over the content and style of the images, making them very versatile for different image manipulation tasks. These are just a few examples of GANs, and the field of architecture design for these networks is evolving rapidly. AI developers and researchers continually work on new methods to improve training and address challenges such as interpretability and bias. They aim to expand the capabilities of these networks to generate even more complex and diverse data types.

While GANs have emerged as the most prominent form of networking technology in GenAI, other notable algorithms offer an alternative approach, each with particular strengths and weaknesses. A few of these alternatives are listed below.

2.3.3   Variational autoencoders

VAEs are designed to learn a compressed representation of data in what is known as the "latent space." This is achieved using two neural networks: an encoder and a decoder. The *encoder* network takes input from the original dataset and aims to compress it into the latent space, capturing the essential features within the data. On the other hand, the *decoder* network takes a random sample from the points within the latent space. It attempts to reconstruct the original data point from its compressed representation, verifying the model's accuracy and integrity. Autoencoders have advantages such as a probabilistic interpretation of data and its application to tasks involving dimensionality reduction and anomaly detection. However, compared to GANs, VAEs can struggle to accurately capture intricate details in complex data distributions. This can lead to generated synthetic data appearing blurry or lacking fine details from the authentic data.

2.3.4   Autoregressive models

Autoregressive models generate their synthetic data sequentially, one element at a time. This approach predicts the next element in the sequence based on the previously generated synthetic elements. This method has proven effective,

Table 2.2   Comparison of GAN, VAE, and autoregressive models

Feature	GAN	VAE	Autoregressive models
Data types	Images, audio, text, code, etc.	Images, text, etc.	Text, music, etc.
Weaknesses	Potential for mode collapse, training instability.	May lack detail in complex data and can be computationally expensive.	May not be suitable for non-sequential data.
Training complexity	Generally, more complex and requires careful tuning.	Less complex than GANs.	Computationally expensive, depending on the model.

particularly for tasks involving text generation, where the model predicts the next word in a sentence based on the words that have previously been generated. Popular examples of such autoregressive models include:

- *Recurrent neural networks (RNN)* are designed to handle sequential data. They possess an internal memory state that allows them to retain information from previous elements in the sequence, which is then used to predict the next element [13].
- *Long-short-term memory networks (LSTM)* are a specific derivative type of RNN architecture designed to address the vanishing gradient problem, a common issue in RNNs that can hinder their ability to learn long-term dependencies within sequences. LSTMs have a more complex internal structure that allows them to store and access information over extended periods in the sequence.

While autoregressive models excel at tasks involving text generation with a well-defined sequential structure, they may not be as well suited for generating complex data types like images or audiovisuals where the relationship between elements is not necessarily sequential. Due to the sequential nature of generation, autoregressive models can be computationally expensive for generating particularly larger data structures.

2.3.5   GAN versus other approaches: a comparative analysis

Selecting the appropriate GenAI algorithm for a particular application depends on several important factors. These include the type of synthetic data to be generated, the desired level of realism and complexity, and the computational resources available for the generation process. Table 2.2 briefly compares GAN, VAN, and autoregressive models.

2.4   Emerging applications and future directions of GenAI

GenAI has advanced beyond its initial applications and is making significant strides in various fields. This evolution offers endless possibilities, as big companies such as Meta, OpenAI, Google, and Microsoft *heavily invest* in advancing GenAI. Some fascinating areas where GenAI is shaping the future are given below.

2.4.1   Content creation

Lately, AI is bringing a revolution in the field of content creation by revolutionizing how visual media, music, and text are produced and customized. In visual media, advancements like GANs enable the generation of realistic images and videos, significantly impacting advertising and digital media. Similarly, AI-driven models in music composition create original tracks and synthesize human-like voices, enhancing multimedia experiences. Text generation technologies, such as language models, craft engaging narratives and personalize content to suit individual preferences, from tailored news articles to interactive storytelling. This rapid production and refinement process, facilitated by AI, accelerates content creation, fosters innovative, creative collaborations, and expands interactive experiences in virtual and augmented reality.

GenAI's impact is expected to broaden further with emerging trends and applications. AI-driven content curation enhances user engagement by recommending personalized content based on sophisticated behavioral analysis. The rise of synthetic media and deepfakes presents opportunities for creative expression and challenges related to misinformation and ethical use. AI's role in procedural content generation in gaming and interactive media offers dynamic and unique experiences. Additionally, AI is improving accessibility through automated translation and adaptive content and facilitating personalized learning in education. As these technologies advance, they will continue to intersect with diverse fields, shaping the future of creative endeavors and raising important considerations about ethical and responsible use.

2.4.2   Drug discovery and materials science

GenAI models are making significant strides in drug discovery and materials science, offering innovative approaches that enhance efficiency and effectiveness in these complex fields. In drug discovery, GenAI is employed to accelerate the identification of new pharmaceuticals by generating and optimizing molecular structures. Techniques such as deep learning and reinforcement learning predict drug interactions and biological targets, identify potential side effects, and design novel compounds with desired properties. This approach speeds up drug development, reduces costs, and increases the likelihood of discovering effective disease treatments.

Similarly, GenAI models are used in materials science to design and discover new materials with specific characteristics. By leveraging generative models, researchers can predict and create materials with tailored properties for applications ranging from electronics to energy storage. AI-driven simulations and optimization algorithms can explore vast chemical spaces, identify promising material compositions, and accelerate the development of advanced materials. These advancements pave the way for innovations in high-performance materials and novel applications, potentially transforming industries such as manufacturing, renewable energy, and electronics.

Overall, GenAI is transforming drug discovery and materials science by enhancing predictive capabilities, optimizing processes, and facilitating the discovery of novel compounds and materials. This integration of AI-driven methods is expected to lead to breakthroughs in both fields, driving scientific research and technological innovation.

2.4.3 Personalized medicine and healthcare

GenAI has become a pivotal tool in personalized medicine by generating synthetic patient data, which is crucial in areas where real data is scarce or sensitive. This synthetic data mimics real patient data, allowing for the training of AI models without compromising patient privacy. Using deep learning algorithms, GenAI can create diverse patient profiles encompassing various medical conditions and demographic factors. This diversity is essential for developing robust AI-powered diagnostic tools capable of generalizing across different populations, thereby improving the accuracy and reliability of medical diagnostics.

Another significant application of GenAI is in simulating complex medical scenarios, which provides healthcare professionals with a safe and controlled environment for skill development. This is particularly valuable in specialties such as laparoscopic and endoscopic surgery, where precision and technique are critical. By simulating these minimally invasive procedures, surgeons can practice and refine their skills, including navigating the endoscope or laparoscope and handling surgical instruments. These realistic simulations help prepare practitioners for various clinical situations, including rare or complicated cases, enhancing their readiness and confidence.

GenAI's effectiveness in healthcare lies in its use of deep learning algorithms. These algorithms enable the creation of highly realistic synthetic data and simulations, which are crucial for research and training. For example, deep learning models can analyze video feeds in laparoscopic and endoscopic surgeries to provide real-time feedback and guidance, helping surgeons avoid potential complications. This technology improves the quality of surgical training and supports ongoing professional development by allowing practitioners to keep up with the latest techniques and advancements in their field.

Several critical challenges, including data privacy, access to diverse data, and the scalability of training programs, drive the need for GenAI in medicine and healthcare. Synthetic data generated by GenAI addresses privacy concerns, allowing researchers and developers to work with data free from identifiable information. Additionally, by simulating various medical scenarios, GenAI provides a scalable solution for training healthcare professionals, particularly in complex surgical fields like laparoscopy and endoscopy. These capabilities not only enhance the quality of healthcare education but also improve the accuracy and efficiency of medical procedures, ultimately leading to better patient outcomes.

2.5   Creative design and engineering

GenAI has become essential in creative design and engineering, offering innovative solutions and enhancing efficiency. In the realm of creative design, GenAI assists artists, designers, and content creators in brainstorming and exploring new ideas by generating a wide array of design variations quickly. This capability allows for experimentation with different styles, colors, and compositions, helping creatives overcome creative blocks and discover unique approaches. For example, graphic designers can leverage GenAI to produce multiple iterations of a logo, enabling them to refine and select the most effective design.

GenAI optimizes designs for specific functionalities and performance metrics, particularly in automotive engineering. One notable example is its application in redesigning automotive parts such as vehicle structural components. Companies like General Motors have collaborated with technology firms like Autodesk to use generative design to develop new vehicle parts. For instance, using GenAI, they created a new seat bracket that was 40% lighter and 20% stronger than conventional designs. This innovative bracket, designed as a unified piece, improved performance and reduced material usage and manufacturing costs. These examples illustrate how GenAI is pushing the boundaries of traditional design and engineering practices. In creative fields, it enables blending different artistic elements and styles, fostering cross-disciplinary innovation. Engineering, particularly in the automotive industry, leads to more efficient and sustainable product designs. By simulating real-world conditions and optimizing material usage, GenAI ensures that new designs are practical and ground-breaking, paving the way for advancements in creative and industrial applications.

2.6   Addressing the challenges: ethical considerations and future research directions

Despite the groundbreaking advancements, GenAI continues to face challenges that require extensive research and development:

(i)   **Bias and fairness**: GenAI models, while powerful and innovative, can inadvertently propagate biases present in the data they are trained on. These models learn patterns and relationships from existing datasets, which may contain implicit or explicit biases related to race, gender, socioeconomic status, or other factors. As a result, the outputs generated by these models can reflect and even amplify these biases, leading to unfair or discriminatory results. GenAI models, while offering significant potential for enhancing legal processes, must address inherent biases present in the datasets on which they are trained. In the legal domain, these biases can have profound implications. For example, suppose a generative model is trained on historical legal case data that reflects existing biases in judicial decisions, such as disparities based on race or gender. In that case, the model may perpetuate and even exacerbate these biases in its predictions and recommendations. This can lead to unfair legal outcomes, reinforcing systemic inequalities.

Several techniques are crucial to mitigate such biases. Bias detection and measurement involve scrutinizing legal datasets for imbalances such as overrepresentation or underrepresentation of certain groups. For instance, if a model is used to predict sentencing outcomes, it is vital to analyze whether the predictions disproportionately impact specific demographic groups. Bias mitigation techniques include preprocessing the data to address imbalances, such as balancing case records to ensure diverse representation, and implementing in-processing adjustments such as fairness-aware algorithms that modify the model's learning process to minimize biased outcomes.

An example of these techniques can be seen in efforts to reduce racial disparities in predictive policing tools. GenAI models trained on historical arrest records may reflect and perpetuate existing racial biases. By applying fairness constraints during model training and adjusting the data to ensure diverse representation, researchers and developers can work to reduce these biases. Similarly, ensuring that AI tools are trained on comprehensive and representative datasets in legal research and case analysis helps minimize the risk of biased recommendations or predictions.

Addressing bias in GenAI is essential for promoting fairness and equity in legal applications. We can work toward more just and inclusive AI systems that support fair legal practices and outcomes by implementing robust bias detection and mitigation techniques and ensuring diverse training data. This ongoing effort is crucial for maintaining the ethical integrity of AI in the legal field and ensuring that technology serves all individuals equitably.

(ii) **Interpretability and explainability**: Understanding the sequential algorithm of how generative models arrive at their outputs is essential to gaining trust and responsible deployment toward it. Research on interpretable AI models and Explainable AI (XAI) will be crucial for ensuring transparency and accountability of AI models.

(iii) **Control and security**: Malicious internet members could misuse GenAI to create deepfakes or other forms of synthetic media to generate misleading and disinformation campaigns. Developing robust security measures to detect and prevent such misuse is crucial.

(iv) **Alignment with human values**: As AI capabilities continue to unfold and evolve, it is critical to ensure that these models are developed and deployed in alignment with human values. It includes fostering open discussions about GenAI's ethics and establishing clear guidelines for its responsible development and usage.

2.7 Conclusion: a generative future beckons

GenAI has become a powerful tool for creating new synthetic data and expanding human creativity. Understanding the core algorithms and their evolution helps us grasp the potential and challenges of this growing field of GenAI. GenAI can unlock new possibilities, innovation, and a deeper understanding of our world by tackling these challenges and advancing with ethical principles. This literature provides a comprehensive overview of GenAI algorithms, explores their evolution, and highlights their potential across various domains. Through ongoing research and responsible development, we can ensure that GenAI becomes a transformative force, empowering creativity, accelerating progress, and contributing to a brighter future for humanity.

References

[1] Williams, R. J., and Zipser, D. (1989). A learning algorithm for continually running fully recurrent neural networks. *Neural Computation*, 1(2), 270–280.

[2] LeCun, Y., Boser, B., Denker, J. S., *et al.* (1989). Backpropagation applied to handwritten zip code recognition. *Neural Computation*, 1(4), 541–551.

[3] Rabiner, L. R. (1989). A tutorial on hidden Markov models and selected applications in speech recognition. *Proceedings of the IEEE*, 77(2), 257–286. DOI:10.1109/5.18626

[4] Hinton, G. E., Osindero, S., and Teh, Y. W. (2006). A fast learning algorithm for deep belief nets. *Neural Computation*, 18(7), 1527–1554.

[5] Krizhevsky, A., Sutskever, I., and Hinton, G. E. (2012). ImageNet classification with deep convolutional neural networks. *Advances in Neural Information Processing Systems (NIPS)*, 25, 1097–1105.

[6] Jordan, M. I., Ghahramani, Z., Jaakkola, T. S., and Saul, L. K. (1999). An introduction to variational methods for graphical models. *Machine Learning*, 37(2), 183–233. DOI:10.1023/A:1007665907178

[7] Goodfellow, I., Pouget-Abadie, J., Mirza, M., *et al.* (2014). Generative adversarial nets. *Advances in Neural Information Processing Systems*, 27, 2672–2680.

[8] He, K., Zhang, X., Ren, S., and Sun, J. (2016). Deep residual learning for image recognition. In *Proceedings of the IEEE Conference on Computer Vision and Pattern Recognition (CVPR)* (pp. 770–778). DOI:10.1109/CVPR.2016.90

[9] Silver, D., Huang, A., Maddison, C. J., *et al.* (2016). Mastering the game of go with deep neural networks and tree search. *Nature*, 529(7587), 484–489. DOI:10.1038/nature16961

[10] Vaswani, A., Shazeer, N., Parmar, N., *et al.* (2017). Attention is all you need. *Advances in Neural Information Processing Systems (NeurIPS)*, 30, 5998–6008, arXiv:1706.03762.

[11] Karras, T., Laine, S., and Aila, T. (2019). A style-based generator architecture for generative adversarial networks (StyleGANs). In *Proceedings of the IEEE/CVF Conference on Computer Vision and Pattern Recognition* (pp. 4401–4410).

[12] Ramesh, A., Pavlov, M., Goh, G., *et al.* (2021). Zero-shot text-to-image generation, arXiv:2102.12092.

[13] Cho, K., Van Merriënboer, B., Bahdanau, D., Bougares, F., Schwenk, H., and Bengio, Y. (2014). Learning phrase representations using RNN encoder–decoder for statistical machine translation, arXiv preprint arXiv:1406.1078.

Chapter 3

Generative transformers and text generation models

M. Karthi[1], G. Raghul[2], Deepak Sai Pendyala[3] and Jaggajit Vasishta[4]

Abstract

With its wide range of uses and constant advancement, Generative AI (GenAI) has emerged as a leading technical innovation, enthralling a variety of sectors. This chapter delves deeply into the cutting edge of GenAI, paying particular attention on generative transformers and how they are enhancing text generation models in the field of natural language processing (NLP). The chapter opens with a detailed explanation of transformer models and emphasizes their superiority over conventional deep learning models, providing a strong framework for the rest of the chapter. Transformers are able to process long-range dependencies and context modeling efficiently because they incorporate innovative mechanisms, particularly attention mechanisms, that go beyond the constraints of classic designs like recurrent neural networks (RNNs) and sequence-to-sequence (Seq2Seq) models. The chapter acknowledges the transforming power of transformer models but also addresses the inherent problems with text production, including the creation of false or misleading information, a phenomenon known as "hallucination." Tactics for reducing hallucinations are examined through a critical analysis of existing approaches and methodology. These tactics include adversarial training, knowledge grounding, and commonsense reasoning. The hierarchy of text generation models is then exhaustively investigated, including a wide range of algorithms as GloVe, Word2Vec, and FastText in addition to RNNs, long short-term memory networks, and gated recurrent units. Furthermore, the chapter addresses the frustrating difficulties that plague generative adversarial networks and variational autoencoders in the context of text production applications. An insightful analysis of pretrained language models and large language models which are specifically designed for generating texts tasks concludes the chapter. This chapter offers a comprehensive

[1]Department of Information Technology, St. Joseph's Institute of Technology, India
[2]Independent Researcher, Chennai, India
[3]Department of Computer Science and Research Assistant, North Carolina State University, USA
[4]Department of Applied Cyber Security, Queen's University, UK

overview of the revolutionary potential of the encoder-based models, decoder-based models, encoder–decoder-based models, and other core open-source models by methodically dissecting their scalability through an in-depth analysis of generative transformers and text generation models, this chapter provides a clear and comprehensive discussion of the state-of-the-art developments influencing the direction of GenAI. This chapter illuminates the way forward in the field of GenAI and NLP, covering a wide range of opportunities and potentialities through a thorough analysis of approaches, difficulties, and developments.

Keywords: Generative artificial intelligence; natural language processing; text generation models, pretrained language models; large language models

3.1   Introduction

The development of software and hardware systems with intelligence on par with or even higher than that of humans has become the primary focus of a growing body of research in artificial intelligence (AI) in recent years, returning the field's attention to its initial, lofty objectives. The original driving force for AI research was this goal, referred to as artificial general intelligence (AGI). But because of the difficulties and complexity that AGI has been shown to provide, many researchers have turned their attention to more focused, manageable issues. As such, research on AGI has occasionally come to resemble the quest for an endless motor, an undertaking that is considered unfeasible or unworkable [1]. However, current scientific understanding indicates that AGI is still theoretically viable, in contrast to the latter, which is barred by well-established physical laws. It is seen as "just an engineering problem," albeit an extraordinary difficult one, akin to the challenges faced in nanotechnology. The architectural invention of transformers [2], a type of neural networks that solely use the attention mechanism and do not require recurrences or convolutions, is fundamental to the breakthroughs in AGI. Transformers first shown to be superior in machine translation, where they produced outputs of higher quality while also allowing for more parallelization and much faster training durations. Since its introduction, the transformer architecture has broadened its applications significantly. Today, it is utilized across diverse domains, including text generation, sentiment analysis, question-answering systems, text summarization, speech recognition, and even music composition. These advancements highlight the architecture's adaptability and effectiveness in handling various complex tasks.

There are several distinct kinds of transformer-based models available today, including topologies that are encoder-only, decoder-only, and combined encoder–decoder structures. These models cover a broad variety of jobs and were created by many research institutions. We shall examine the difficulties in training generating transformers later in this chapter. Since generative artificial intelligence (GenAI) has so many uses and is developing so quickly, it is revolutionizing a number of industries. Generative transformers, which have dramatically improved text creation capabilities in natural language processing (NLP), are at the center of this change. This chapter offers a thorough analysis of these cutting-edge technologies, emphasizing their underlying principles, the difficulties they pose, and their wider ramifications.

3.1.1   Importance and objectives of this chapter

It is impossible to overstate the importance of generative transformers or their remarkable powers. It is crucial to comprehend and make use of this synergy if AI is to advance. The following main goals are the focus of this chapter.

- To provide a thorough analysis of generative transformers, emphasizing their essential elements and showing how they differ from more conventional deep learning models like sequence-to-sequence (S2S) and recurrent neural networks (RNNs).
- To examine the inherent difficulties with generative transformers, such as model complexity, hallucinations, and the availability of sufficient hardware for deployment and training.
- To provide an explanation of the text generation models' hierarchical development, following the progression from basic NLP, natural language understanding (NLU), and natural language generation (NLG) models to more sophisticated methods such as Word2Vec, RNNs, and pretrained large language models (LLMs) with support for retrieval-augmented generation. Furthermore, while generative adversarial networks (GANs) and variational autoencoders (VAEs) are mainly used for image generation, they face specific challenges in text synthesis, including difficulties with coherence, stability, and control due to the sequential nature of text data.

This chapter will examine the crucial elements of transformers that have helped bring GenAI to the forefront of technological advancement, namely in the area of text generation, a well-known and significant application of AI. We will examine why generative transformers have emerged as a key discussion point in the AI field using thorough examples and analysis.

3.1.2   Chapter structure and organization

This chapter is organized as follows:

- **Generative transformers**: The principles of generative transformers, including their training procedures, will be covered in this chapter. We will explore the ideas behind transformers' encoder and decoder methods, which allow them to outperform more conventional deep learning models like S2S and RNNs. We will also look at one of the main drawbacks of Generative Transformers namely hallucinations.
- **Hierarchy of text generation model**: The foundational models for text generation are introduced in this section, which covers the transition from Word2Vec to pretrained LLMs. We will discuss about state-of-art models

namely Word2Vec, GloVe & FastText, RNN, long short-term memory (LSTM), and gated recurrent units (GRUs). We will also elucidate about the drawbacks and problems of using GANs and VAEs, which are commonly widely applied in image synthesis, to text synthesis.

• **Pretrained large language models and large language models**: The concept of pretrained LLMs is being introduced in this section. We will discuss about encoder-only models, decoder-only models, and encoder–decoder-based models in detail. As these models contribute to the text generation scenario, we will be discussing about the model architecture improvements, and optimization of GAI models. Finally, we will be delving into the evolution of LLMs.

3.2   Generative transformers

3.2.1   Overview of generative transformers

Because of their exceptional NLP capabilities, LLMs have gained considerable interest from academia and business in recent years, making them a key focus in the AI area. LLMs are advanced deep learning frameworks initially pretrained on extensive textual datasets and subsequently fine-tuned to align closely with human preferences. The advent of the generative transformer is the conceptual breakthrough that underpins LLMs. A novel model architecture called the generative transformer completely relies on attention techniques to control global relationships between input and output vectors, doing away with recurrence [2]. This method employs self-attention, generating representations of input and output sequences independently of sequence-aligned RNNs or convolutional layers, transformed transduction models, including language translation models. Transformers are characterized by their encoder–decoder structure a hallmark of transduction models [3,4,19]. An input sequence of symbol representations $(x_1, x_2, x_3, \ldots x_n)$ is initially transformed by the encoder into a continuous representation sequence $(z = z_1, z_2, z_3, \ldots z_n)$. This encoded sequence is then utilized by the decoder, which sequentially generates the output symbols $(y_1, y_2, y_3, \ldots y_n)$ one element at a time. Notably, the model operates in an autoregressive manner, a statistical technique where past values are used to predict future values in a time series, incorporating previously generated symbols as additional inputs during text generation [5]. The architecture of the generative transformer will be examined in detail in this section, along with the mechanisms and parts that have contributed to its success and broad use in the AI field.

In the transformer model, the core structure consists of two main layers: the encoder stack and the decoder stack. The encoder stack's design is centered on two fundamental components: the multi-head self-attention mechanism and the position-wise network. Each of these is enhanced with layer normalization and residual connections to improve stability and performance. $LayerNorm(x + SubLayer(x))$ represents the encoder stack's output, where $SubLayer(x)$ is the function that the sublayer itself implements. Though the decoder stack adds a multi-head attention layer over the encoder's output, it largely resembles the encoder stack. The primary function of attention in transformers is to allow each position to attend to all positions in the preceding layer, capturing contextual relationships. Keeping the details of attention processes in consideration, Transformer architecture primarily uses two schemes: multi-head attention and scaled dot-product attention [6–9]. These strategies improve the model's capacity to produce coherent and contextually correct sequences by making it easier to handle global relationships between input and output vectors.

It is important to examine the limitations of traditional deep learning models and how the encoder–decoder stack leverages self-attention to overcome them. The motivations underlying the implementation of self-attention techniques will be clarified by this comparative examination. Conventional deep learning models, such as S2S and RNNs, have a number of drawbacks, such as inefficiencies in parallel processing and challenges in capturing long-range relationships. On the other hand, the encoder–decoder stack provides notable enhancements in these domains due to its features. We will go into more depth about these restrictions in Section 2.2 and talk about how the transformer design gets around them to provide readers a solid foundation for comprehending how important self-attention is to improving model performance.

3.2.2 Idea behind encoder and decoder that surpasses the RNN and S2S models

NLP research prior to the transformer model was mainly focused on deep learning architectures, such as S2S models, attention-based S2S models, multilayer perceptron's, convolutional neural networks (CNNs), RNNs, LSTMs, GRUs, and S2S models. Specific constraints were shown by each of these models, which made it difficult for them to work perfectly in text creation tasks. Transformer model is a great option for text production since it overcomes several of these drawbacks with its unique encoder–decoder block design. Table 3.1 presents a summary of the different deep learning models together with their limitations, highlighting the reason. Transformers have become a strong contender in the industry.

According to the discussion in [2], Table 3.2 lists the difficulty of each layer, sequence, and maximum path length. Interestingly, the recurrent layer needs $(O(n))$ sequential operations, but the self-attention layer connects all spots with a fixed number of operations carried out in parallel.

In light of these parallels, transformers have made a name for themselves in the research community thanks to their effective encoder–decoder design, which is particularly good at producing text. Self-attention, or intra-attention, has shown remarkable performance in a variety of activities, including question-answering and language modeling, in addition to text production. Transformers continue to suffer a number of difficulties in text generation and conformity to industry norms, despite their fame and notoriety. Section 2.3 will examine these matters.

Table 3.1 *Various deep learning models with their drawbacks toward text generation tasks*

Model name	Definition	References	Drawbacks of the model
Multi-layer per-ceptron (MLP)	Feedforward neural networks with many layers, including input, hidden, and output layers, are called multi-layer perceptrons, or MLPs. Most importantly, all layer's neurons are fully coupled to every layer's neuron, a pattern known as dense connectivity. MLPs are renowned for being accessible and simple to learn because of their simplicity and ease of implementation	[10,11]	MLPs interpret each input token as independent, ignoring sequence information and finding it difficult to discern semantic linkages. While MLPs can learn statistical patterns, they have difficulty capturing the semantic information within input sequences
Convolutional neural networks (CNNs)	Treating text as a one-dimensional image, CNNs, which were first created for image processing, may also be modified for text synthesis. Unlike MLPs, CNNs can accurately represent the input data since they use convolutional layers to learn features from text or images	[12,13]	By convolving the input data, CNNs may efficiently learn local characteristics (n-grams); but they have difficulty capturing long-term relationships, which are essential for text production. CNNs require substantial computational resources for training and use, as achieving high-quality results demands a large number of parameters
Recurrent neural network (RNN)	The purpose of RNNs is to analyze sequential data, such text and time series. RNNs are able to analyze sequential data and manage inputs of different durations because they keep track of a hidden state that stores the context from earlier stages	[14–16]	The vanishing gradient issue affects RNNs. While LSTM and GRU models help to some degree to alleviate this problem, they are still unable to accurately represent long-term dependencies
Variants of RNN	As sophisticated RNN models, long short-term memory (LSTM) and gated recurrent unit (GRU) networks developed. By including gating mechanisms that control the information flow throughout the sequence, these models are able to efficiently store the most crucial information	[3,17,18]	RNNs and their variations create a bottleneck for parallel processing by processing input sequences token by token. The calculation process is slowed signifi-cantly by this sequential techniqueIn general, LSTM and GRU models assume equal lengths for input and output sequences. However, in natural language generation, input and output sequences often differ in length, creating challenges for these models
Seq2Seq	Sequence-to-sequence (Seq2Seq) models are intended to manage jobs when the sequence lengths of the input and output are different. They were first created for machine translation, but they have subsequently been used for a variety of NLP applications. These models process the input sequence and produce the output sequence using an encoder and a decoder, which may be based on RNN, LSTM, or GRU architectures	[19,20]	When an input sequence is lengthy, a fixed-size context vector frequently is unable to capture all of the information in the sequence. The attention mechanism was created in order to solve this problem [21,22]. However, RNNs still struggle with long-term depen-dencies and the vanishing gradient problem

Table 3.2 Complexity analysis between self-attention layers and RNN/CNN layers stated in [2], where n is the sequence length, d is the representation dimension, k is the kernel size of the convolutions, and r is the size of the neighborhood in restricted self-attention

Layer type	Complexity per layer	Sequential operations	Maximum path length
Self-attention	$O(n^2.d)$	$O(1)$	$O(1)$
Recurrent	$O(n^2.d)$	$O(n)$	$O(n)$
Convolutional	$O(k.n.d^2)$	$O(1)$	$O(\log_k(n))$
Self-attention (restricted)	$O(r.n.d)$	$O(1)$	$O(\frac{n}{r})$

3.2.3 Challenges behind generative transformers for text generation: hallucinations

LLMs are beneficial for text production, but they have a serious risk of creating hallucinations, or sufficient evidence that deviates from user inputs or real-world facts. In LLMs, created output that is incoherent or dishonest to the supplied source material is sometimes referred to as hallucinations. This taxonomy has been reformulated by, who has introduced a more sophisticated framework for LLM applications [23,24]. They divide hallucinations into two categories: factuality hallucinations and faithfulness hallucinations. An overview of these many kinds of hallucinations, together with descriptions and illustrations for each, may be found in Table 3.3. There are several origins of hallucinations, such as pre-training procedures, data, or inference phases. Thankfully, detection methods like those listed in Table 3.1 are now often used to lessen these problems. Furthermore, benchmarks cited in have developed best-in-class techniques for model testing and evaluating the influence of models on output quality [24].

3.3 Hierarchy of text generation models

3.3.1 Introduction to text generation models

Over time, text generation models have developed significantly, moving from simple statistical techniques to intricate deep learning structures. These models are used in NLP to generate text that makes sense and is relevant to the context. NLU and NLG are the two primary domains of fundamental activities within NLP. Creating believable and accessible content in human language from a variety of input forms, including as text, graphics, tables, and knowledge bases, is the main goal of text generation, a crucial area of NLG. Text generation models have been widely used in many different fields during the last ten years. For example, they are used in machine translation to translate text across languages in dialogue systems to

Table 3.3 Different hallucination types with detection steps stated in [24], with sample inputs and model outputs

Hallucination type	Sub-hallucination type	Hallucination detection techniques	Example inputs	Model outputs	Explanation
Factuality hallucination	Factual inconsistency *Even when LLMs provide outputs with a solid factual foundation in real-world data, they may nonetheless have inconsistencies. These inconsistencies are frequent and might have a number of causes*	1. Retrieve external facts 2. Uncertainty estimation (a) LLM internal states (b) LLM behavior	Tell me about the first person to land on the Moon	**Yuri Gagarin** was the first person to land on the Moon	The LLMs answer falsely claims that Yuri Gagarin was the first person to set foot on the moon, exhibiting factual contradiction. Actually, Yuri Gagarin became the first human to travel into space, whereas Neil Armstrong was the first to step onto the Moon
	Factual fabrication *Facts generated by LLMs may contain information that cannot be cross-referenced with actual knowledge*		Tell me about the historical origins of unicorns	**Unicorns** were documented to have roamed the plains of Atlantis around 10,000 BC, where they were considered sacred creatures and were often associated with royalty	Since there is no credible, real-world evidence to corroborate the presence of unicorns in Atlantis, especially in relation to monarchy, the LLMs response is false

(Continues)

Faithfulness hallucination	Instruction inconsistency
	
	It is possible for LLMs to provide results that differ from the user's initial instructions
		1. Fact-based metrics
		  (a) N-gram based
		  (b) Entity-based
		  (c) Relation-based
		  (d) Knowledge-based
			Translate the following English question into Spanish: "What is the capital of France?"	**The capital of France is Paris**	The user gave the LLM specific instructions to translate the English query into Spanish. However, the LLM decided to respond to the question directly rather than according to this directive

	Context inconsistency
	
	The data that the user provides may not be accurately reflected in LLM outcomes
		2. Classifier-based metrics
		  (a) Entailment-based
		  (b) Weekly supervised
		
		3. Question answering-based metrics
		
		4. Uncertainty estimation
		  (a) Entropy based
		  (b) Log–probability based
		  (c) Model based
		
		5. Prompting-based metrics
			Summarize the following paragraph about the Nile: The Nile is a major north-flowing river in northeastern Africa. It is traditionally considered the longest river in the world. ***Originating in the Great Lakes region of central Africa***, it flows through several countries before emptying into the Mediterranean Sea	The Nile originates from **the mountain ranges of central Africa** and flows into the Mediterranean	The passage makes it rather evident that the Nile originates in the Great Lakes area of central Africa, contrary to the LLM's description, which falsely asserts that the Nile originates in the "mountain ranges of central Africa"

	Logical inconsistency *Internal logical conflicts, which are frequently seen in reasoning problems, can be seen in LLM results*		Solve the equation $2x + 3 = 11$ step by step	Step 1: Subtract 3 from both sides to get: $2x = 8$. Step 2: Divide both sides by 2 to get: **$x = 3$. So, the result of the equation is $x = 3$**	With x, the word is appropriately isolated in the first step, yielding $2x = 8$. Nevertheless, the next step divides 8 by 2 incorrectly, producing $x = 3$, which defies the logic from before

Bold – hallucinated output, bold italics – user instruction that contradicts the LLM hallucination.

provide replies in discussions, and in text summarization to produce concise summaries of source material [25–27]. In order to provide an end-to-end solution with the least amount of human interaction, the primary goal of text generation is to automatically learn a mapping from input to output based on data. This can be shown as follows:

$$y = f_M(x, C) \tag{3.1}$$

where, given the input data x, the fundamental model f_M (also known as the text generation model) produces the output text y, meeting the user-defined criterion C. With the help of this mapping function, the generation system may produce free text depending on the input and generalize across a variety of circumstances. Earlier methods generally relied on statistical language models (LMs) to estimate the probability of a word conditioned on an n-gram context [27,28]. Nevertheless, data sparsity was a common problem for many statistical techniques. Deep learning models were presented as a solution to this. In spite of their success, deep learning models also face several challenges which are detailed in Table 3.1. NLU, on the other hand, is concerned with understanding human language. A key component of many NLU tasks is learning vector-space representations of text, such as words and phrases. Both assessing natural language (GLUE – General Language Understanding Evaluation) and learning representations (MTL – Multi-Task Learning) are areas of active study [29].

A promising paradigm in AI is called self-supervised learning, which allows models from many modalities such as audio, image, or language to learn background information from vast amounts of unlabeled data [30,31]. This method has developed as a pretraining model substitute for supervised learning by taking use of the enormous volumes of unlabeled data that are available. Although self-supervised learning and supervised learning both require supervision, the source of this monitoring is different in self-supervised learning. While self-supervised learning creates supervision automatically from the data, supervised learning depends on human-labeled data. Below, let us examine the hierarchy of text generation models in greater detail.

3.3.2   Word2Vec

These models are designed to either predict a target word based on a given context (continuous bag of words, or CBOW) or to predict the context surrounding a target word (skip-gram model), Word2Vec is a feed-forward, fully connected artificial neural network architecture [32]. With the introduction of the CBOW and skip-gram models, transformed the idea of word embeddings [33]. While the Skip-gram model calculates the surrounding context words based on a center word, The CBOW model aims to predict a target word's probability by using the surrounding context words. The fundamental premise is that context surrounds the target symmetrically, with the distance in each direction determined by the window size. Prediction accuracy usually increases as word embedding dimensions increase. Nevertheless, one significant drawback of word embeddings is that they cannot accurately represent sentences. For example, the term "hot potato" is not considered a separate entity. A popular outcome of Word2Vec is the following analogy: "King − Man + Woman = Queen."

3.3.3   GloVe and FastText

Word2Vec's dependence on the local context of phrases is one of its limitations; as a result, while it mostly collects semantic information, it does not always do so well. GloVe (global vectors), on the other hand, tackles this by capturing vocabulary's global and local contexts when turning words into vectors [34]. Every strategy offers benefits of its own. For example, Word2Vec excels at jobs requiring analogies. Conversely, GloVe operates by the examination of word co-occurrence data. The idea behind GloVe embeddings is to use neural networks to break down a co-occurrence matrix and create dense, meaningful vectors. Generally speaking, GloVe train more quickly than Word2Vec vectors. Both Word2Vec and GloVe have limits when it comes to giving conclusive outcomes in the setting of distributed representations, notwithstanding their advantages. FastText is an additional word representation technique that builds upon the Word2Vec paradigm [35]. FastText represents each word as a sequence of character n-grams instead of treating them as single units. When attempting to capture the semantics of small or uncommon words that were maybe missed during training, this method is quite helpful. In comparison to Word2Vec, FastText has shown better results across a range of criteria. It is crucial to utilize effective word representation algorithms Given that word representation significantly influences the outcomes of deep generative models.

3.3.4   RNN, LSTM, and GRUs

For NLP issues, RNNs are an effective technique, especially when modeling sequential data. Sequence modeling tasks are greatly facilitated by RNNs' internal memory, which allows them to retain both past and present inputs. RNNs are very useful for tasks like sentiment analysis, language synthesis, and translation since the result at every given time step depends not only on the current input but also on the outputs created at prior time steps. The non-linear dynamics and high-dimensional hidden state of RNNs enable them to represent sequences. Unfortunately, RNNs are not widely used in many NLP applications because to their notoriously difficult training. As such, research in this field has been scarce over the past 20 years, despite their promise for sequential modeling. The inability to accurately simulate long-term dependencies and concerns with inflating or disappearing gradients are two of the main training challenges with RNNs.

The design of RNNs is built upon by LSTM networks, who improve it with a more complex memory mechanism. Unlike conventional RNNs, LSTM units are termed cells, and they contain memory units that determine what information to keep and discard past input's and present states. This enables LSTMs to ignore irrelevant input and selectively recall pertinent information for predicting outcomes. GRUs are a further RNN version that introduces a gating network into the LSTM architecture. In order to enable updates to the current activation and network state, this network provides signals to regulate the relationship between the present input and the prior memory. Because they simplify the gating method and parameter updates, GRUs are less complicated than LSTMs. Several deep generative models for text production have used GRUs.

Choosing the right algorithm is essential when creating deep learning models. For the purpose of producing output sequences, bidirectional recurrent neural networks (BRNNs) have been proposed. The main benefit of BRNNs is their ability to depend on both past and future sequence parts to determine the output at any given time step. BRNNs are built using two separate RNNs, one of which processes the sequence ahead and the other. Neural Turing machines (NTMs) are another important development in neural networks. Unlike LSTMs, which store memory in a hidden state, NTMs incorporate an external memory that can be interacted with via an attention mechanism, extending the capabilities of typical RNNs. Table 3.1 summarizes the capabilities of CNNs for text production and provides a thorough examination of RNNs, LSTMs, GRUs, and other deep-learning models.

3.3.5   Issues behind VAEs and GANs for text generation

Deep learning models largely require well-labeled data to perform effectively. Nonetheless, a sizable amount of data is unlabeled or unstructured, and deep learning models usually need a lot of structured data to be trained well. Unstructured data labeling takes a lot of time. Using unsupervised techniques that can train on unlabeled data is one way to overcome this obstacle. VAEs are potent deep generative models that can handle unlabeled data [36]. The components of a VAE are an encoder, which encodes data into latent variables and then decodes these variables to reconstruct the original data. Though promising, very little use of VAEs has been made in producing discrete data, like text. The condition known as KL collapse, which happens when the decoder gets excessively strong and generates output independent of the latent space representation, is a significant problem with VAEs. The posterior distribution in this case is independent of the input data, as the KL term is approaching zero. RNNs have been used recently to capture subjects and styles, shared characteristics of sentences represented as continuous variables; however, the problem of KL collapse still exists. Although methods such as word dropout and KL annealing have been proposed to alleviate KL collapse, the issue has not been entirely remedied by these approaches.

Because of its adversarial structure, GANs provide a unique deep learning strategy that departs from conventional neural network techniques. Two models that have been trained against one another make up a GAN. The discriminator assesses data samples produced by the generator to ascertain if they are authentic (derived from the training data) or fraudulent (made by the generator). The discriminator's goal is to correctly distinguish between genuine and created samples. In contrast, the generator aims to produce samples that closely resemble the real data to deceive the discriminator. This structure is similar to a game-theoretic situation in which the goal function is expressed as a minimax issue. Even with their noteworthy achievements, GANs have two major drawbacks that restrict their practical use:

- **Mode collapse**: In a multi-modal distribution, mode collapse happens when the generator converges to producing a restricted range of outputs, essentially representing just one mode. As a result, the generator creates comparable samples often in order to take use of the discriminator.
- **Vanishing gradient**: This problem occurs in adversarial training when the discriminator converges fast and becomes very successful, so that the generator has too few gradients to perform better. As a result, a situation known as a vanishing gradient occurs in which the generator is unable to learn efficiently [37].

3.3.6   Pretrained large language models for text generation

Advanced deep neural networks called pretrained language models (PLMs) are first trained on large-scale unlabeled corpora. After that, these models might be adjusted for different downstream tasks. PLMs are very promising for increasing language understanding and text creation quality since they have shown to be able to encode large amounts of linguistic knowledge within their many parameters [38,39]. Text generation PLMs may be divided into three main categories are encoder-only models, decoder-only models, and encoder–decoder models. This classification is based on the architectural architecture of the models. The specific traits and uses of each category are described in the subsections that follow. It is essential for researchers to grasp the routes for input and output vectors in order to understand the design of PLM structures for text synthesis. The PLM design formula as it is presented in [39] outlines the foundational structure of these models.

$$P_M(y|,x) = \prod_{k=1}^{N} P_M(y_k|y_{<k}, x) \tag{3.2}$$

where y_k denotes the *j*th output token, and $y_{<k}$ denotes the previous tokens $y_1, y_2, y_3, \ldots, y_{k-1}$. The foundation of existing PLMs for text creation is usually either a single Transformer or an encoder–decoder architecture based on Transformers. Single transformer decoders are used by models such as UniLM and GPT-3 to process input encoding and output decoding at the same time [40,41]. Single transformer PLMs generally fall into two categories: LMs that only use encoders and models that only use decoders. These models use different attention mask techniques. The input encoding and output decoding operations are separated in PLMs that use the transformer encoder–decoder design, also known as encoder–decoder LMs.

1. **Encoder-only models**
   LMs based on the Transformer encoder architecture are often pre-trained using the masked language modeling (MLM) task, which entails predicting masked

tokens based on bidirectional context, and are generally endowed with complete attention mechanisms. The popular BERT method is a noteworthy illustration of this strategy for language comprehension problems [42]. However, masked LMs are not commonly used for text generation tasks because their structure is incompatible with generation needs pre-training job and the needs of text production [43]. Instead, because of their potent bidirectional encoding powers, masked LMs are more frequently employed as the encoder part in text production systems. For example, Rothe *et al.* [44] showed that performance may be achieved by initializing a generation model's encoder and decoder with BERT [42].

2. **Decoder-only models**

Decoder-only LMs are highly suited for text production since they are made exclusively for language modeling, which entails word prediction based on previous words. Causal decoders and prefix decoders are the two main variations of these schemes.

- *Causal decoders:* These models make use of a lower-diagonal attention matrix (with negative infinity on the upper triangular and zero on the bottom triangular) to guarantee that each token can only focus on the tokens that come before it. Autoregressive text creation is supported by this architecture by default. The first causal LM for text creation was GPT [45]. Expanding on this, GPT-2 [46] investigated language models' potential for zero-shot generation, while GPT-3 [41] showed that, even with few prompts, scaling model parameters greatly improves performance on downstream generation tasks. With more than ten billion parameters, causal LMs like ChatGPT, GPT-4 and PaLM are now the top designs in this category [47,48].

- *Prefix decoders*: These models use a mixed attention matrix, which allows tokens in the input to attend to each other and tokens in the output to attend to both input tokens and previous output tokens. The input and output use bi-directional attention and a lower-diagonal matrix, respectively. This method was first used for conditional generating jobs by UniLM [40]. Scaled prefix decoders are used in later models, including GLM and GLM-130B, to produce bilingual LMs [49,50].

Studies have shown that, in general, decoder-only learning machines (LMs) perform better in zero-shot scenarios than alternative designs that do not use multi-task fine-tuning [51]. Models such as PanGu-α and CPM have concentrated on training large-scale autoregressive models for the Chinese language [52,53]. Additionally, Decoder-only LMs continue to see performance improvements in line with scaling laws, further enhancing their efficacy [54].

3. **Encoder–decoder models**

Encoder–decoder models employ the classic Transformer structure, combining both encoder and decoder layers for text generation tasks. Sequences containing masked segments are sent into the encoder in pre-training models such as MASS and ProphetNet and the decoder generates masked tokens in an autoregressive manner [55,56]. In contrast, T5 uses unique tokens to substitute random spans in the source text, and the decoder anticipates each substituted span in turn [57]. Using a denoising auto-encoder technique, BART trains the model to recreate the original text from damaged variants, perhaps involving token deletion or sentence permutation [58]. According to, encoder–decoder LMs are superior than decoder-only LMs when storage is not an issue since these models frequently provide faster throughput at the expense of more parameters [59]. On the other hand, prefix LMs are a good substitute when there are substantial parameter limitations. Prefix LMs and span bribery encoder–decoder models (like T5) deliver distinct advantages across different sub-tasks, with decoder-only LMs (GPT-like) usually performing worse in certain configurations, according to Comparing GPT-style decoder-only models with T5-style encoder–decoder models [59]. Nonetheless, as model sizes continue to rise, the benefits of GPT-like decoder-only LMs have been brought to light by recent developments in big LMs.

3.3.7   Model architecture improvement and model optimization

Three main ideas are proposed in to enhance fundamental architectures: decoding techniques, module adaptability, and input modalities [39]. PLMs find it difficult to simulate cross-sentence (paragraph) semantics and extract the most important information when faced with lengthy documents that contain numerous paragraphs, as is the case in many text creation jobs [60]. Structured data, such as tables, graphs, and trees, is also an essential form of input for text production. But because PLMs are usually pre-trained on natural language texts, there is a conceptual gap between structured data and PLMs [61]. Long text inputs may be handled by efficient modules, numerous input sources can be integrated by extra attention modules, and performance can be further improved by mixture-of-experts (MoE) models [62]. Because MoE allows numerous experts to learn from dozens of languages across diverse areas, it is frequently utilized in multilingual translation systems. By substituting a position-wise MoE layer with a top-2 gating network for the dense feed-forward network, GShard expanded the MoE idea to transformers [63]. By routing to a single expert, switch transformer significantly simplified this while preserving performance and lowering computation costs [64]. In PLM-based text generation models, obtaining high performance depends on using efficient optimization techniques. We take into account three primary categories of optimization techniques: property-tuning, prompt-tuning, and fine-tuning. Vanilla fine-tuning, intermediate fine-tuning, multitask fine-tuning, and parameter-efficient fine-tuning are further subcategories of fine-tuning. The majority of generative PLMs are trained with language modeling goals in mind, but they are refined with task-specific goals on text production tasks. Prompt learning reformulates subsequent duties (text generation tasks) into the language modeling challenge employed during pre-training in order to resolve the disparity between pre-training and fine-tuning [65]. There are two types of prompts for text production tasks: discrete prompts and continuous prompts.

3.3.8   *Evolution of large language models*

From GPT-1, BERT, to the most recent DeBERTa PLMs have made great strides, most notably in lowering the quantity of labeled data needed to train task-specific models [42,45,66–69]. These models follow the "pretrain then fine-tune" paradigm, in which a model is pretrained on a large dataset first, and then fine-tuned to suit certain tasks. The process of fine-tuning, which is necessary to customize pretrained models for specific NLP tasks, requires labeled data and generates a unique model instance for every job, hence raising development and deployment expenses [68]. PLMs are hence frequently seen as limited AI systems, designed for particular tasks rather than broad problem-solving. On the other hand, research efforts have been directed toward creating AGI systems whereby are built to do a variety of jobs and, like humans, can adapt to new ones by employing their prior experience. LLMs are used to differentiate these versus smaller pretrained models. Larger in terms of model size, pretraining corpus, and processing resources, LLMs are a subset of PLMs [70,71]. These are transformer-based deep learning models, which are pretrained on large amounts of textual data and then tweaked through meta-training to conform to human tastes. Meta-training guarantees that LLMs follow user objectives, encompassing clear instructions and implicit objectives like accuracy maintenance and avoiding errors, in addition to having universal language knowledge.

The two main axes of LLM evolution have been closed-source and open-source models. GPT-3 marked the start of the LLM era, and models like InstructGPT, Codex, ChatGPT, and GPT-4 from OpenAI followed [47,72,73]. While DeepMind created Gopher, Chinchilla, AlphaCode, and Sparrow, Google responded with GLaM, PaLM, PaLM2, LaMDA, and Bard [48,74–81]. Amazon, Baidu, and AI21 Labs are a few of the companies that have released models like Jurassic-1, AlexaTM, and Ernie 3.0 Titan [82–84]. Even while closed-source LLMs function quite well, their main flaw is that the weights they use are not made public, and access is sometimes limited to commercial APIs that charge depending on consumption. The scientific community has made it a priority to build open-source LLMs using publicly accessible weights in order to alleviate this issue. OPT, OPT-IML, Galactica, LLaMA, LLaMA2, and Falcon are a few notable instances [85–88]. These open-source models perform as well as, or sometimes better than, their closed-source equivalents. Galactica, for example, performs better than closed-source models such as GPT-3, Chinchilla, and PaLM. The success of these models in English has led academics to concentrate on developing bilingual and multilingual LLMs. For multilingual jobs, examples include BLOOM and BLOOMZ whereas for bilingual applications, examples are JAIS (English and Arabic), GLM (English and Chinese), and FLM-101B (English and Chinese) [89–93]. The evolution of LLMs is depicted in Figure 3.1 respectively.

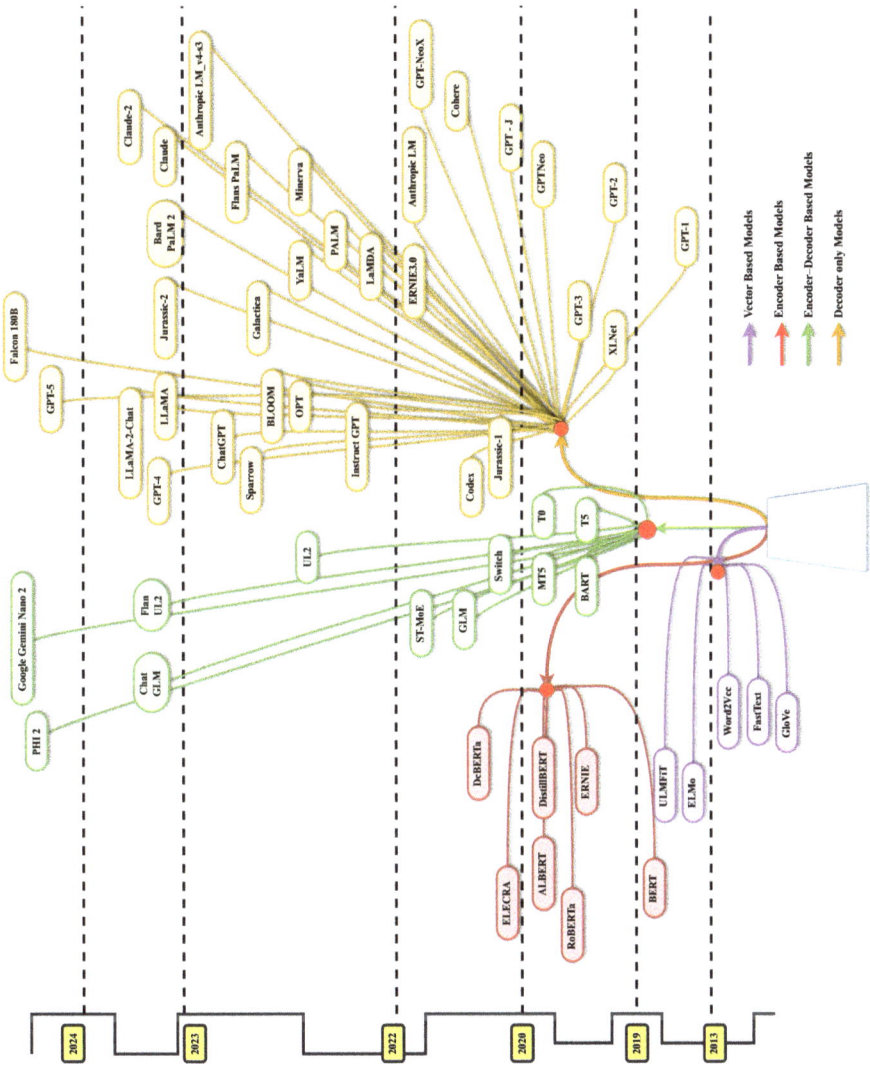

Figure 3.1 Tree-like structure of evolution of large language models for text generation

3.4 Conclusion

We have examined the developments in text generation in this chapter, emphasizing the shift from conventional RNN and S2S models to more complex structures such as transformers. Specifically, the encoder–decoder architecture has advanced significantly, outperforming RNNs and S2S models in handling sequence modeling complexity and capturing complicated relationships in text data. Notwithstanding these developments, generative transformers still have several difficulties, the most important of which is the hallucination problem. This issue, which happens when models provide information that seems convincing but is erroneous or irrelevant, highlights the need for more reliable methods to guarantee the accuracy of material that is created. Additionally, we looked at the text production model hierarchy, tracing the development of LLMs from early PLMs. The need for these models has increased due to the development of increasingly complicated designs and the growing availability of cutting-edge technology. Consequently, LLMs have shown impressive performance, even if scalability and cost concerns sometimes limit their adoption. Overall, even though a lot of progress has been done, additional studies and developments are needed to solve the problems and improve text generation models' capabilities. The text modality and hierarchical structure of generative transformers were examined in this chapter. This modality is being expanded by ongoing research to encompass a variety of forms, including audio, video, pictures, and more; these are referred to as multi-modal generative transformers. In order to guarantee that input and output vectors match the desired generating process, a more complex attention mechanism is required.

References

[1]   C. Pennachin and B. Goertzel, 'Contemporary approaches to artificial general intelligence', *Cognitive Technologies*, vol. 8, pp. 1–30, 2007, doi:10.1007/978-3-540-68677-4_1.

[2]   A. Vaswani, N. Shazeer, N. Parmar, *et al.*, 'Attention is all you need', *Advances in Neural Information Processing Systems*, vol. 2017, pp. 5999–6009, 2017, Accessed: Jul. 20, 2024 [Online]. Available: https://arxiv.org/abs/1706.03762v7

[3]   K. Cho, B. van Merriënboer, C. Gulcehre, *et al.*, 'Learning phrase representations using RNN encoder–decoder for statistical machine translation', *Proceedings of the 2014 Conference on Empirical Methods in Natural Language Processing (EMNLP 2014)*, pp. 1724–1734, 2014, doi:10.3115/v1/d14-1179.

[4]   D. Bahdanau, K. H. Cho, and Y. Bengio, 'Neural machine translation by jointly learning to align and translate', *Proceedings of the 3rd International Conference on Learning Representations, ICLR 2015 – Conference Track*, 2014, Accessed: Jul. 24, 2024. [Online]. Available: https://arxiv.org/abs/1409.0473v7

[5] A. Graves, 'Generating sequences with recurrent neural networks', 2013, Accessed: Jul. 24, 2024. [Online]. Available: https://arxiv.org/abs/1308. 0850v5

[6] J.-B. Cordonnier, A. Loukas, and M. Jaggi, 'Multi-head attention: collaborate instead of concatenate', 2020, Accessed: Jul. 23, 2024. [Online]. Available: https://arxiv.org/abs/2006.16362v2

[7] J. Mercat, T. Gilles, N. El Zoghby, G. Sandou, D. Beauvois, and G. P. Gil, 'Multi-head attention for multi-modal joint vehicle motion forecasting', *Proceedings of the IEEE International Conference on Robotics and Automation*, pp. 9638–9644, 2020, doi:10.1109/ICRA40945.2020.9197340.

[8] Q. Du, L. Zhao, J. Xu, Y. Han, and S. Zhang, 'Log-based anomaly detection with multi-head scaled dot-product attention mechanism', *Lecture Notes in Computer Science (including subseries Lecture Notes in Artificial Intelligence and Lecture Notes in Bioinformatics)*, vol. 12923, LNCS, pp. 335–347, 2021, doi:10.1007/978-3-030-86472-9_31.

[9] S. Leelaluk, T. Minematsu, Y. Taniguchi, F. Okubo, T. Yamashita, and A. Shimada, 'Scaled-dot product attention for early detection of at-risk students', *Proceedings of the 2022 IEEE International Conference on Teaching, Assessment and Learning for Engineering, TALE 2022*, pp. 316–322, 2022, doi:10.1109/TALE54877.2022.00059.

[10] H. Taud and J. F. Mas, 'Multilayer perceptron (MLP)', In *Geomatic Approaches for Modeling Land Change Scenarios*, Cham: Springer International Publishing, pp. 451–455, 2018, doi:10.1007/978-3-319-60801-3_27.

[11] M. Popescu, V. Balas, L. Perescu-Popescu, and N. Mastoraki, 'Multilayer perceptron and neural networks', *WSEAS Transactions on Circuits and Systems*, 2022, Accessed: Jul. 29, 2024. [Online]. Available: https://www.academia.edu/download/69679997/29-485.pdf

[12] N. Kalchbrenner, E. Grefenstette, and P. Blunsom, 'A convolutional neural network for modelling sentences', *Proceedings of the 52nd Annual Meeting of the Association for Computational Linguistics, ACL 2014*, vol. 1, pp. 655–665, 2014, doi: 10.3115/v1/p14-1062.

[13] Y. Zhang and B. Wallace, 'A sensitivity analysis of (and practitioners' guide to) convolutional neural networks for sentence classification', 2015, Accessed: Jul. 29, 2024. [Online]. Available: http://arxiv.org/abs/1510.03820

[14] H. Salehinejad, S. Sankar, J. Barfett, E. Colak, and S. Valaee, 'Recent advances in recurrent neural networks', 2017, Accessed: Jul. 29, 2024. [Online]. Available: http://arxiv.org/abs/1801.01078

[15] W. Yin, K. Kann, M. Yu, and H. Schütze, 'Comparative study of CNN and RNN for natural language processing', 2017, Accessed: Jul. 29, 2024. [Online]. Available: http://arxiv.org/abs/1702.01923

[16] M. Karthi, S. Jothi, and A. Chandrasekar, 'The self-adaptive dwarf mongoose optimized bidirectional network approach for enhanced recognition of overlapped English cursive characters', *Signal Image and Video Processing*, vol. 17, no. 8, pp. 4465–4473, 2023, doi:10.1007/S11760-023-02680-2/ FIGURES/6.

[17] S. Hochreiter, and J. Schmidhuber, 'Long short-term memory', *Neural Computation*, vol. 9, no. 8, pp. 1735–1780, 1997, Accessed: Jul. 29, 2024. [Online]. Available: https://ieeexplore.ieee.org/abstract/document/6795963/

[18] J. Chung, C. Gulcehre, K. Cho, and Y. Bengio, 'Empirical evaluation of gated recurrent neural networks on sequence modeling', 2014, Accessed: Jul. 29, 2024. [Online]. Available: http://arxiv.org/abs/1412.3555

[19] I. Sutskever, O. Vinyals, and Q. V. Le, 'Sequence to sequence learning with neural networks', *Advances in Neural Information Processing Systems*, 2014, Accessed: Jul. 29, 2024. [Online]. Available: https://proceedings.neurips.cc/paper/2014/hash/a14ac55a4f27472c5d894ec1c3c743d2-Abstract.html

[20] T. Young, D. Hazarika, S. Poria, and E. Cambria, 'Recent trends in deep learning based natural language processing', *Computational Intelligence Magazine*, 2018, Accessed: Jul. 29, 2024. [Online]. Available: https://ieeexplore.ieee.org/abstract/document/8416973/

[21] D. Bahdanau, K. H. Cho, and Y. Bengio, 'Neural machine translation by jointly learning to align and translate', *Proceedings of the 3rd International Conference on Learning Representations (ICLR 2015) – Conference Track*, 2015.

[22] M. T. Luong, H. Pham, and C. D. Manning, 'Effective approaches to attention-based neural machine translation', *Proceedings of the 2015 Conference on Empirical Methods in Natural Language Processing (EMNLP 2015)*, pp. 1412–1421, 2015, doi:10.18653/v1/d15-1166.

[23] Z. Ji, N. Lee, R. Frieske, *et al.*, 'Survey of hallucination in natural language generation', *ACM Computing Surveys*, vol. 55, no. 12, 2023, doi:10.1145/3571730.

[24] L. Huang, W. Yu, W. Ma, *et al.*, 'A survey on hallucination in large language models: principles, taxonomy, challenges, and open questions', 2023, Accessed: Aug. 02, 2024. [Online]. Available: https://arxiv.org/abs/2311.05232v1

[25] L. Zhou, J. Gao, D. Li, and H. Y. Shum, 'The design and implementation of XiaoIce, an empathetic social chatbot', *Computational Linguistics*, vol. 46, no. 1, pp. 53–93, 2020, doi:10.1162/COLI_A_00368.

[26] W. Samy El-Kassas, C. R. Salama, A. A. Rafea, and H. K. Mohamed, 'Automatic text summarization: a comprehensive survey', *Expert Systems with Applications*, vol. 165, p. 113679, 2021, doi:10.1016/j.eswa.2020.113679.

[27] P. F. Brown, J. Cocke, S. A. Della Pietra, *et al.*, 'A statistical approach to machine translation', *Computational Linguistics*, vol. 16, no. 2, pp. 79–85, 1990, https://aclanthology.org/J90-2002.pdf

[28] R. Brown, and R. Frederking, 'Applying statistical English language modelling to symbolic machine translation', *Proceedings of the 6th Conference on Theoretical and Methodological Issues in Machine Translation of Natural Languages*, 1995, Accessed: Aug. 01, 2024. [Online]. Available: https://aclanthology.org/1995.tmi-1.17.pdf

[29]   A. Wang, A. Singh, J. Michael, F. Hill, O. Levy, and S. R. Bowman, 'GLUE: a multi-task benchmark and analysis platform for natural language understanding', 2018, Accessed: Aug. 01, 2024. [Online]. Available: https://arxiv.org/abs/1804.07461

[30]   X. Liu, F. Zhang, Z. Hou, *et al.*, 'Self-supervised learning: generative or contrastive', *IEEE Transactions on Knowledge and Data Engineering*, vol. 35, no. 1, pp. 857–876, 2023, doi:10.1109/TKDE.2021.3090866.

[31]   J. Gui, T. Chen, J. Zhang, *et al.*, 'A survey on self-supervised learning: algorithms, applications, and future trends', *IEEE Transactions on Pattern Analysis and Machine Intelligence*, vol. 46, no. 12, pp. 9052–9071, 2024, doi:10.1109/TPAMI.2024.3415112.

[32]   X. Rong, 'word2vec parameter learning explained', 2014, Accessed: Aug. 02, 2024. [Online]. Available: http://arxiv.org/abs/1411.2738

[33]   Z. Xiong, Q. Shen, Y. Xiong, Y. Wang, and W. Li, 'New generation model of word vector representation based on CBOW or skip-gram', Accessed: Aug. 02, 2024. [Online]. Available: https://search.ebscohost.com/login.aspx?direct=true&profile=ehost&scope=site&authtype=crawler&jrnl=15462218&AN=137193557&h=2wbCbsuH3IQemQPLBifVBoMT9H200lJrzVr%2Fi4LVdPk%2FN1EsbXnWO3mnSmimPBOGMEf37i0HUxFbK5eFxKNl0A%3D%3D&crl=c

[34]   R. Brochier, A. Guille, and J. Velcin, 'Global vectors for node representations', pp. 2587–2593, 2019, doi:10.1145/3308558.3313595.

[35]   A. Joulin, E. Grave, P. Bojanowski, M. Douze, H. Jégou, and T. Mikolov, 'FastText.zip: compressing text classification models', 2016, Accessed: Aug. 02, 2024. [Online]. Available: https://arxiv.org/abs/1612.03651v1

[36]   L. Pinheiro Cinelli, M. Araújo Marins, E. A. Barros da Silva, and S. Lima Netto, 'Variational autoencoder', *Variational Methods for Machine Learning with Applications to Deep Networks*, pp. 111–149, 2021, doi:10.1007/978-3-030-70679-1_5.

[37]   S. Hochreiter, 'The vanishing gradient problem during learning recurrent neural nets and problem solutions', *International Journal of Uncertainty, Fuzziness and Knowledge-Based Systems*, vol. 6, p. 107–116, 1998. Accessed: Aug. 02, 2024. [Online]. Available: https://www.worldscientific.com/doi/abs/10.1142/s0218488598000094

[38]   L. F. R. Ribeiro, M. Schmitt, H. Schütze, and I. Gurevych, 'Investigating pretrained language models for graph-to-text generation', *Proceedings of the 3rd Workshop on NLP for Conversational AI, NLP4ConvAI 2021*, pp. 211–227, 2021, doi:10.18653/v1/2021.nlp4convai-1.20.

[39]   J. Li, T. Tang, W. X. Zhao, J. Y. Nie, and J. R. Wen, 'Pre-trained language models for text generation: a survey', *ACM Computing Surveys*, vol. 56, no. 9, 2024, doi:10.1145/3649449.

[40]   L. Dong, N. Yang, W. Wang, *et al.*, 'Unified language model pre-training for natural language understanding and generation', *Advances in Neural Information Processing Systems*, 2019, Accessed: Aug. 01, 2024. [Online]. Available: https://proceedings.neurips.cc/paper_files/paper/2019/hash/c20bb2d9a50d5ac1f713f8b34d9aac5a-Abstract.html

[41] T. B. Brown, B. Mann, N. Ryder, *et al.*, 'Language models are few-shot learners', *Advances in Neural Information Processing Systems*, 2020, Accessed: Aug. 01, 2024. [Online]. Available: https://proceedings.neurips. cc/paper/2020/hash/1457c0d6bfcb4967418bfb8ac142f64a-Abstract.html

[42] J. Devlin, M. W. Chang, K. Lee, and K. Toutanova, 'BERT: pre-training of deep bidirectional transformers for language understanding', *Proceedings of the 2019 Conference of the North American Chapter of the Association for Computational Linguistics: Human Language Technologies (NAACL HLT 2019)*, vol. 1, pp. 4171–4186, 2019.

[43] Z. Yang, Z. Dai, Y. Yang, J. Carbonell, R. Salakhutdinov, and Q. V. Le, 'Xlnet: generalized autoregressive pretraining for language understanding', *Advances in Neural Information Processing Systems*, 2019, Accessed: Aug. 01, 2024. [Online]. Available: https://proceedings.neurips.cc/paper/2019/ hash/dc6a7e655d7e5840e66733e9ee67cc69-Abstract.html

[44] S. Rothe, S. Narayan, and A. Severyn, 'Leveraging pre-trained checkpoints for sequence generation tasks', *Transactions of the Association for Computational Linguistics*, vol. 8, pp. 264–280, 2020, doi:10.1162/TACL_A_ 00313/96450.

[45] A. Radford, K. Narasimhan, T. Salimans, and I. Sutskever, 'Improving language understanding by generative pre-training', 2018, Accessed: Aug. 01, 2024. [Online]. Available: https://www.mikecaptain.com/resources/pdf/ GPT-1.pdf

[46] A. Radford, J. Wu, R. Child, D. Luan, D. Amodei, and I. Sutskever, 'Language models are unsupervised multitask learners', Accessed: Aug. 01, 2024. [Online]. Available: https://insightcivic.s3.us-east-1.amazonaws.com/language-models.pdf

[47] J. Achiam, S. Adler, S. Agarwal, *et al.*, 'GPT-4 technical report', 2023, Accessed: Aug. 01, 2024. [Online]. Available: https://arxiv.org/abs/2303. 08774v6

[48] B. Bi, C. Li, C. Wu, *et al.*, 'PALM: pre-training an autoencoding and autoregressive language model for context-conditioned generation', *Proceedings of the 2020 Conference on Empirical Methods in Natural Language Processing (EMNLP 2020)*, pp. 8681–8691, 2020, doi:10.18653/v1/2020.emnlp-main.700.

[49] Z. Du, Y. Qian, X. Liu, *et al.*, 'GLM: general language model pretraining with autoregressive blank infilling', *Proceedings of the Annual Meeting of the Association for Computational Linguistics*, vol. 1, pp. 320–335, 2022, doi: 10.18653/v1/2022.acl-long.26.

[50] A. Zeng, X. Liu, Z. Du, *et al.*, 'GLM-130B: an open bilingual pre-trained model', 2022, Accessed: Aug. 01, 2024. [Online]. Available: http://arxiv.org/ abs/2210.02414

[51] T. Wang, A. Roberts, D. Hesslow, *et al.*, 'What language model architecture and pretraining objective works best for zero-shot generalization?', *Proceedings of the International Conference on Machine Learning*, 2022, Accessed: Aug. 01, 2024. [Online]. Available: https://proceedings.mlr.press/ v162/wang22u.html

[52] W. Zeng, X. Ren, T. Su, *et al.*, 'PanGu-: large-scale autoregressive pre-trained Chinese language models with auto-parallel computation', 2021, Accessed: Aug. 01, 2024. [Online]. Available: https://arxiv.org/abs/2104.12369

[53] Z. Zhang, X. Han, H. Zhou, *et al.*, 'CPM: a large-scale generative Chinese pre-trained language model', Accessed: Aug. 01, 2024. [Online]. Available: https://www.sciencedirect.com/science/article/pii/S266665102100019X

[54] J. Kaplan, S. McCandlish, T. Henighan, *et al.*, 'Scaling laws for neural language models', 2020, Accessed: Aug. 01, 2024. [Online]. Available: http://arxiv.org/abs/2001.08361

[55] K. Song, X. Tan, T. Qin, J. Lu, and T. Y. Liu, 'MASS: masked sequence to sequence pre-training for language generation', *Proceedings of the 36th International Conference on Machine Learning, ICML 2019*, vol. 2019, pp. 10384–10394, 2019.

[56] W. Qi, Y. Yan, Y. Gong, *et al.*, 'ProphetNet: predicting future n-gram for sequence-to-sequence pre-training', *Findings of the Association for Computational Linguistics Findings of ACL: EMNLP 2020*, pp. 2401–2410, 2020, doi:10.18653/v1/2020.findings-emnlp.217.

[57] C. Raffel, N. Shazeer, A. Roberts, *et al.*, 'Exploring the limits of transfer learning with a unified text-to-text transformer', *Journal of Machine Learning Research*, vol. 21, pp. 1–67, 2020, Accessed: Aug. 01, 2024. [Online]. Available: https://www.jmlr.org/papers/v21/20-074.html

[58] M. Lewis, Y. Liu, N. Goyal, *et al.*, 'BART: denoising sequence-to-sequence pre-training for natural language generation, translation, and comprehension', *Proceedings of the Annual Meeting of the Association for Computational Linguistics*, pp. 7871–7880, 2019, doi:10.18653/v1/2020.acl-main.703.

[59] Y. Tay, M. Dehghani, V. Q. Tran, *et al.*, 'UL2: unifying language learning paradigms', 2022, Accessed: Aug. 02, 2024. [Online]. Available: https://arxiv.org/abs/2205.05131v3

[60] X. Gu, K. Yoo, and J. Ha, 'Dialogbert: discourse-aware response generation via learning to recover and rank utterances', *Proceedings of the AAAI Conference on Artificial Intelligence*, 2021, Accessed: Aug. 02, 2024. [Online]. Available: https://ojs.aaai.org/index.php/AAAI/article/view/17527

[61] S. Hasan, and O. Farri, 'Clinical natural language processing with deep learning', *Data Science for Healthcare: Methodologies and Applications*, 2019, Accessed: Aug. 02, 2024. [Online]. Available: https://link.springer.com/chapter/10.1007/978-3-030-05249-2_5

[62] A. Kazemnejad, I. Padhi, K. N. Ramamurthy, P. Das, and S. Reddy, 'The impact of positional encoding on length generalization in transformers', *Advances in Neural Information Processing Systems*, 2024, Accessed: Aug. 02, 2024. [Online]. Available: https://proceedings.neurips.cc/paper_files/paper/2023/hash/4e85362c02172c0c6567ce593122d31c-Abstract-Conference.html

[63] D. Lepikhin, H. Lee, Y. Xu, *et al.*, 'GShard: scaling giant models with conditional computation and automatic sharding', 2020, Accessed: Aug. 02, 2024. [Online]. Available: http://arxiv.org/abs/2006.16668

[64]   W. Fedus, B. Zoph, and N. Shazeer, 'Switch transformers: scaling to trillion parameter models with simple and efficient sparsity', *Journal of Machine Learning Research*, vol. 23, pp. 1–39, 2022, Accessed: Aug. 02, 2024. [Online]. Available: https://www.jmlr.org/papers/v23/21-0998.html

[65]   P. Liu, W. Yuan, J. Fu, *et al.*, 'Pre-train, prompt, and predict: a systematic survey of prompting methods in natural language processing', *ACM Computing Surveys*, vol. 55, no. 195, 2023, doi:10.1145/3560815.

[66]   P. He, J. Gao, and W. Chen, 'DeBERTaV3: improving DeBERTa using ELECTRA-style pre-training with gradient-disentangled embedding sharing', 2021, Accessed: Aug. 02, 2024. [Online]. Available: http://arxiv.org/abs/2111.09543

[67]   P. He, X. Liu, J. Gao, and W. Chen, 'DeBERTa: decoding-enhanced BERT with disentangled attention', *Proceedings of the 9th International Conference on Learning Representations (ICLR 2021)*, 2021.

[68]   K. S. Kalyan, A. Rajasekharan, and S. Sangeetha, 'AMMUS: a survey of transformer-based pretrained models in natural language processing', 2021, Accessed: Aug. 01, 2024. [Online]. Available: https://arxiv.org/abs/2108.05542v2

[69]   K. Kalyan, A. Rajasekharan, and S. Sangeetha, 'AMMU: a survey of transformer-based biomedical pretrained language models', *Journal of Biomedical Informatics*, vol. 386, p. 103982, 2022, Accessed: Aug. 02, 2024. [Online]. Available: https://www.sciencedirect.com/science/article/pii/S153 2046421003117

[70]   S. Bubeck, V. Chandrasekaran, R. Eldan, *et al.*, 'Sparks of artificial general intelligence: early experiments with GPT-4', 2023, Accessed: Aug. 02, 2024. [Online]. Available: http://arxiv.org/abs/2303.12712

[71]   B. Goertzel, 'Artificial general intelligence: concept, state of the art, and future prospects', *Journal of Artificial General Intelligence*, vol. 5, no. 1, pp. 2013–2015, 2014, doi:10.2478/jagi-2014-0001.

[72]   L. Ouyang, J. Wu, X. Jiang, *et al.*, 'Training language models to follow instructions with human feedback', *Advances in Neural Information Processing Systems*, 2022, Accessed: Aug. 02, 2024. [Online]. Available: https://proceedings.neurips. cc/paper_files/paper/2022/hash/b1efde53be364a73914f58805a001731-Abstract-Conference.html

[73]   M. Chen, J. Tworek, H. Jun, *et al.*, 'Evaluating large language models trained on code', 2021, Accessed: Aug. 02, 2024. [Online]. Available: http://arxiv. org/abs/2107.03374

[74]   J. W. Rae, S. Borgeaud, T. Cai, *et al.*, 'Scaling language models: methods, analysis and insights from training gopher', 2021, Accessed: Aug. 02, 2024. [Online]. Available: http://arxiv.org/abs/2112.11446

[75]   J. Hoffmann, S. Borgeaud, A. Mensch, *et al.*, 'Training compute-optimal large language models', *Proceedings of the Advances in Neural Information Processing Systems*, vol. 35, 2022.

[76]   Y. Li, D. Choi, J. Chung, *et al.*, 'Competition-level code generation with AlphaCode', *Science (1979)*, vol. 378, no. 6624, pp. 1092–1097, 2022, doi:10.1126/SCIENCE.ABQ1158.

[77] A. Glaese, N. McAleese, M. Trębacz, *et al.*, 'Improving alignment of dialogue agents via targeted human judgements', 2022, Accessed: Aug. 02, 2024. [Online]. Available: http://arxiv.org/abs/2209.14375

[78] N. Du, Y. Huang, A. M. Dai, *et al.*, 'GLaM: efficient scaling of language models with mixture-of-experts', *International Conference on Machine Learning, 2022*, vol. 24, pp. 1–113, 2023, Accessed: Aug. 02, 2024. [Online]. Available: https://proceedings.mlr.press/v162/du22c.html

[79] A. Chowdhery, S. Narang, J. Devlin, *et al.*, 'PaLM: scaling language modeling with pathways', *Journal of Machine Learning Research*, vol. 24, pp. 1–113, 2023, Accessed: Aug. 02, 2024. [Online]. Available: https://www.jmlr.org/papers/v24/22-1144.html

[80] R. Anil, A. M. Dai, O. Firat, *et al.*, 'PaLM 2 technical report', 2023, Accessed: Aug. 02, 2024. [Online]. Available: http://arxiv.org/abs/2305.10403

[81] R. Thoppilan, D. D. Freitas, J. Hall, *et al.*, 'LaMDA: language models for dialog applications', 2022, Accessed: Aug. 02, 2024. [Online]. Available: http://arxiv.org/abs/2201.08239

[82] O. Lieber, O. Sharir, B. Lenz, and Y. Shoham, 'Jurassic-1: technical details and evaluation', *White Paper. AI21 Labs*, Accessed: Aug. 02, 2024. [Online]. Available: https://sharir.org/papers/jurassic_white_paper.pdf

[83] S. Soltan, S. Ananthakrishnan, J. FitzGerald, *et al.*, 'AlexaTM 20B: few-shot learning using a large-scale multilingual Seq2Seq model', 2022, Accessed: Aug. 02, 2024. [Online]. Available: http://arxiv.org/abs/2208.01448

[84] S. Wang, Y. Sun, Y. Xiang, *et al.*, 'ERNIE 3.0 Titan: exploring larger-scale knowledge enhanced pre-training for language understanding and generation', 2021, Accessed: Aug. 02, 2024. [Online]. Available: http://arxiv.org/abs/2112.12731

[85] S. Zhang, S. Roller, N. Goyal, *et al.*, 'OPT: open pre-trained transformer language models', 2022, Accessed: Aug. 02, 2024. [Online]. Available: http://arxiv.org/abs/2205.01068

[86] R. Taylor, M. Kardas, G. Cucurull, *et al.*, 'Galactica: a large language model for science', 2022, Accessed: Aug. 02, 2024. [Online]. Available: http://arxiv.org/abs/2211.09085

[87] H. Touvron, T. Lavril, G. Izacard, *et al.*, 'LLaMA: open and efficient foundation language models', 2023, Accessed: Aug. 02, 2024. [Online]. Available: http://arxiv.org/abs/2302.13971

[88] H. Touvron, L. Martin, K. Stone, *et al.*, 'Llama 2: open foundation and fine-tuned chat models', 2023, Accessed: Aug. 02, 2024. [Online]. Available: http://arxiv.org/abs/2307.09288

[89] T. L. Scao, A. Fan, C. Akiki, *et al.*, 'BLOOM: a 176B-parameter open-access multilingual language model', 2022, Accessed: Aug. 02, 2024. [Online]. Available: http://arxiv.org/abs/2211.05100

[90] N. Muennighoff, T. Wang, L. Sutawika, *et al.*, 'Crosslingual generalization through multitask finetuning', *Proceedings of the Annual Meeting of the*

Association for Computational Linguistics, vol. 1, pp. 15991–16111, 2023, doi:10.18653/v1/2023.acl-long.891.

[91] N. Sengupta, S. K. Sahu, B. Jia, *et al.*, 'Jais and Jais-Chat: Arabic-Centric Foundation and instruction-tuned open generative large language models', 2023, Accessed: Aug. 02, 2024. [Online]. Available: http://arxiv.org/abs/2308.16149

[92] A. Zeng, X. Liu, Z. Du, *et al.*, 'GLM-130B: an open bilingual pre-trained model', 2022, Accessed: Aug. 02, 2024. [Online]. Available: http://arxiv.org/abs/2210.02414

[93] X. Li, Y. Yao, X. Jiang, *et al.*, 'FLM-101B: an open LLM and how to train it with $100K budget', 2023, Accessed: Aug. 02, 2024. [Online]. Available: http://arxiv.org/abs/2309.03852

Chapter 4

Generative models for human-like speech synthesis: evolution, trends and the road ahead

Anushiya Rachel Gladston[1] and Sushanta Kumar Pani[2]

Abstract

Text-to-speech (TTS) synthesis is expected to produce intelligible and human-like speech corresponding to a given text and is useful in a wide range of applications that enhance interactions between people and with machines. Generative models have transformed the landscape of TTS, enabling the production of natural and human-like speech. This chapter explores the evolution of TTS technologies, from rule-based approaches to modern neural architectures like Tacotron2. While commercially available TTS systems produce neutral speech, it would be desirable to produce expressive speech to further improve the naturalness of synthetic speech. Therefore, the chapter describes methods to accomplish this. Further, deep generative models are notoriously data-hungry and so measures to handle data scarcity in a low-resource scenario are also discussed. Finally, the metrics that are commonly used to assess the performance of a TTS system are enumerated and the challenges and possible avenues for future research are presented.

Keywords: Text-to-speech; speech synthesis; generative models for speech

4.1 Introduction

Speech is the primary mode of communication among human beings and hence people are more inclined to communicate with machines through speech as well. A machine's ability to speak is facilitated by a text-to-speech (TTS) system, which converts any given text in a language to intelligible and natural or human-like speech. Apart from enabling a more natural mode of communication with machines, TTS systems are also instrumental in aiding people with disabilities. They are used in screen readers, which enable visually challenged (as well as semi-literate and elderly) individuals to navigate through smart phones and computers with ease and also to read content on these devices. TTS systems are also immensely useful in aiding

[1]Department of Computer Science and Engineering, Shiv Nadar University, Chennai, India
[2]Department of Computer Science and Engineering, Michigan State University, USA

people with dysarthria, aphasia and other speaking disorders that affect these people's ability to communicate effectively with others. This could be accomplished through a sign language-to-speech translation or the conversion of less intelligible speech into one that is more understandable by others.

Speech synthesis essentially attempts to mimic the process by which speech is produced by humans. Speech is produced when air from the lungs enters the vocal tract through the vocal cords. The air is modulated in the vocal tract based on the position of the articulators to produce different sounds. These sounds may either be voiced or unvoiced. In order to produce voiced sounds air from the lungs is pushed through the vocal cords, which causes them to open and close at regular intervals. This results in the excitation of the vocal tract with quasi-periodic pulses of air. However, to produce unvoiced sounds, a constriction is formed somewhere along the vocal tract and air is forced through it. This process of speech production is commonly modelled using a train of impulses (for voiced sounds) or random noise (for unvoiced sounds) as the source of excitation, and an all-pass filter, whose coefficients differ based on the nature of the sound to be produced, to mimic the function of the vocal tract [1]. In TTS synthesis, the given text must be converted into a sequence of sound units and based on the characteristics of these sounds, an appropriate excitation source and filter coefficients must be derived.

In this regard, a TTS system conventionally consists of two main components, namely a text analysis module and a waveform synthesis module [2], as shown in Figure 4.1. The text analysis module primarily helps resolve ambiguities in the text, such as abbreviations and acronyms, homographs, and interpreting numbers and punctuations, and extracts phonetic and prosodic information from the text. The waveform synthesis module then synthesises speech based on extracted information. The first of these modules requires a knowledge of the language for which the TTS system is to be trained, making it language-dependent. The second module, however, is language-independent and TTS systems generally differ in terms of the algorithms used in this module. The algorithms have evolved from being rule-based to model-based and modern-day TTS systems employ generative models for impressive results. While conventional TTS systems were able to produce intelligible speech, they were lacking in naturalness. The use of generative models, however, brought about a breakthrough in producing speech that is almost indistinguishable from a human.

This chapter initially takes the reader through the evolution of TTS systems, leading ultimately to the use of generative models. It then gives an account of the popular TTS architectures that are in use today. While TTS systems that are now available produce highly intelligible and almost human-like speech, there is still a

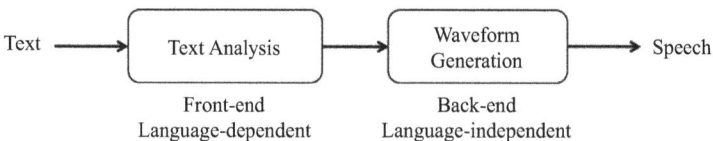

Figure 4.1   Components of a text-to-speech synthesis system

challenge in incorporating appropriate prosody and portraying emotion. The efforts taken in this direction are described in the chapter next. Generative TTS models generally require a huge amount of training data and even more so when prosody modelling is involved. However, for certain languages and for certain applications, it might be difficult to obtain enough data and hence the chapter also discusses methods that could be adopted in such scenarios. The chapter finally deals with evaluation metrics that are adopted to assess TTS systems and closes with an account of the challenges that are yet to be addressed and possible avenues for future research.

4.2   Evolution of TTS systems: the journey towards generative models

One of the first attempts at speech synthesis was carried out by Homer Dudley in the 1930s, when he developed the Voder at Bell Labs. The Voder, short for Voice Operating Demonstrator, involved a skilled human operator manually choosing one of 14 keys to generate appropriate buzzer-like sounds to produce voiced sounds and hiss-like sounds to produce unvoiced sounds, and pressing a pedal to adjust the pitch period [3]. This gradually evolved into automated systems which were initially rule-based and ultimately model-based. Some of the prominent TTS synthesis methods that were developed over the years are described in the following sections.

4.2.1   Rule-based TTS systems

Rule-based methods are essentially an extension of the Voder, where a skilled human operator is replaced by a set of rules. These rules dictate the characteristics that a speech signal corresponding to each sound unit ought to possess, such as the type of source (periodic for voiced and noisy for unvoiced sounds) to be used, the corresponding formant frequencies, the formant bandwidths and amplitudes, the duration of the sound unit, amplitude and pitch contour. This method is generally referred to as formant synthesis and is adopted in TTS systems such as the Klatt synthesiser [4] and DECTalk [5]. Further, the rules formulated may also govern the dimensions of the vocal tract and positions and movements of the articulators, to simulate the physical movements of the speech organs. This method is referred to as articulatory synthesis [6,7].

These rule-based methods are advantageous since they do not need a large training dataset and hence may be useful in a low-resource setting. These methods also provide a high level of control over the phonetic and prosodic features. However, the speech produced by these methods, though intelligible, is very robotic and it is quite impossible to mimic a specific speaker's identity [2]. This led to the development of waveform concatenation approaches.

4.2.2   Waveform concatenation systems

These systems, as the name suggests, involve the concatenation of pre-recorded speech signals based on the text that is to be synthesised. A popular method is unit selection synthesis (USS) [8], shown in Figure 4.2. This requires a large dataset containing text and the corresponding speech signals. The speech signals are

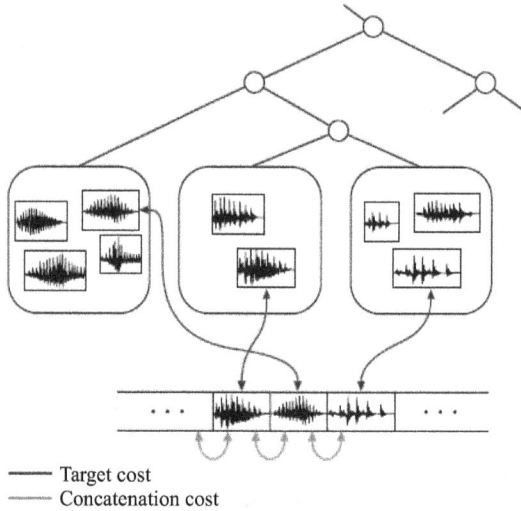

Figure 4.2   Unit selection synthesis [2]

generally broken down into words or sub-word units (such as phonemes, diphones, syllables), and a classification and regression tree is used to cluster these units. Given a text, this system first breaks it down into the appropriate sound units and the signal/waveform corresponding to each unit is selected from the dataset such that two cost functions, namely the target cost and the concatenation cost, are minimised. The target cost is a measure of how well each of the potential units in the dataset would match the target unit, while the concatenation cost is a measure of how well a selected unit would join smoothly with the adjacent units.

This system is capable of producing highly intelligible and human-like speech. However, this depends on the size of the unit used and the amount of data available. When larger units such as words, are used, there are fewer concatenation points and hence less perceived discontinuities in the synthesised speech, resulting in better quality. Larger units, though, require more data to cover the desired vocabulary. In order to develop an unrestricted vocabulary system, all possible units would have to be recorded in many different contexts, and this would be almost impossible to do with larger units. With smaller units such as phonemes, all possible units can be covered in a smaller amount of data. However, these result in a larger number of concatenation points and hence more discontinuities. Therefore, a USS system is better suited for limited-vocabulary applications. Further, the quality of synthetic speech would depend on the accuracy with which the speech signals are segmented while training the system. Inaccurate segmentation would mean that the segment corresponding to one sound might contain a part of the adjacent sounds as well, thereby affecting intelligibility. Further, since this method requires that the recorded waveforms be available at all times, the system would occupy a larger footprint, in the order of gigabytes. In order to overcome the shortcomings of the waveform concatenation approaches, a statistical parametric approach was then proposed.

4.2.3   *Statistical parametric TTS system*

A statistical parametric TTS system basically extracts parameters from speech signals and stores statistics of these instead of the speech signals as such. Hidden Markov models (HMMs), which are one of the first generative models, are popularly used here. The HMM-based speech synthesis system (HTS–H Triple S) [9] involves training an HMM for each speech unit, usually a context-dependent phoneme. These models are trained on spectral and excitation features derived from speech signals, which are the Mel generalised cepstral coefficients and the log fundamental frequency, respectively, and their first and second derivatives. Since the training data would not be able to cover all possible contexts that each phoneme may occur in, decision tree-based clustering is also performed to handle any unseen contexts that may occur in the future. During the testing phase, given a text, it is initially converted into a sequence of context-dependent phonemes. HMMs corresponding to these phonemes are then concatenated to form a sentence HMM. The spectral and excitation features are then predicted from the sentence HMM and used in a Mel log spectral approximation (MLSA) filter to synthesise a speech signal. This process is portrayed in Figure 4.3.

HTS is capable of producing highly intelligible speech and it also requires a much smaller footprint (in the order of a few megabytes) and less training data, compared to a USS system. It also provides a great deal of flexibility in transforming speech/speaker characteristics by transforming HMM parameters

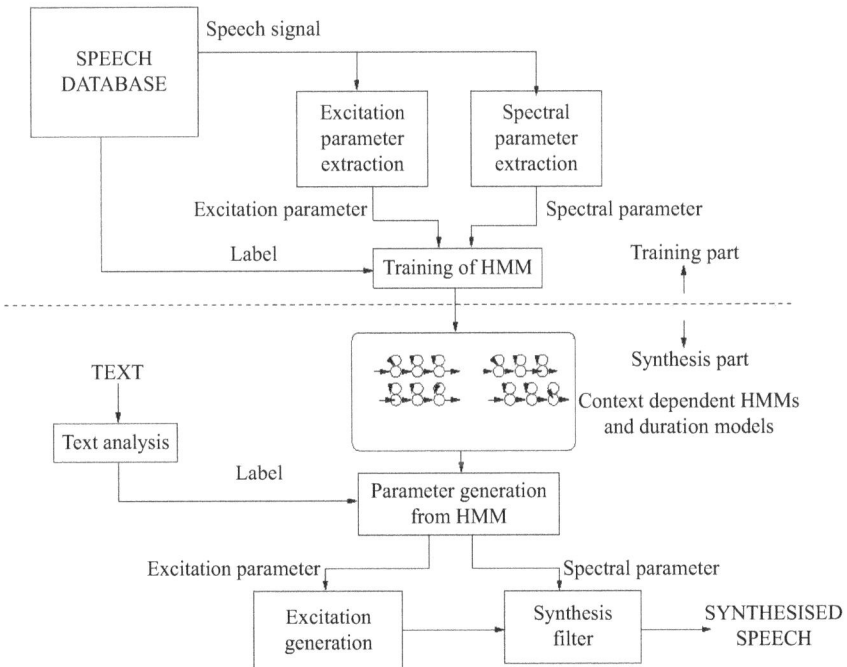

Figure 4.3   HMM-based speech synthesis [16]

appropriately. However, while the synthesised speech does not sound robotic as in the case of a rule-based system, it does lack naturalness and is easily distinguishable from human speech. The limited naturalness can in part be attributed to the vocoding technique, that is the use of the MLSA filter. In this regard, the MLSA filter was then replaced by vocoders such as STRAIGHT [10] and WORLD [11] for a marked improvement in quality. Another factor that could affect the naturalness of synthetic speech is the over-smoothing effect caused by two types of averaging that take place in HTS, one that is inherent to HMMs and another owing to the tree-based clustering that is performed [12]. This resulted in the quest for a different model [13–15], ultimately leading to the use of deep neural networks (DNNs).

4.2.4   Neural TTS systems

Early neural TTS systems retained some modules of the HTS, while replacing others with DNNs. Initially, these systems made use of DNN for acoustic modelling alone [17–20], while the text analysis and speech waveform generation modules were similar to those employed in HTS. Next, the text analysis module, which extracts linguistic features from the text, was replaced by a neural model [21]. Later, the speech waveform generation module was also replaced by neural models such as WaveNet [22], sample recurrent neural network (RNN) [23], WaveGlow [24] and an RNN-based LPCNet [25]. While early methods made use of separate modules for text analysis, acoustic modelling and speech waveform generation, more recently efforts are directed towards end-to-end TTS systems. The end-to-end systems are preferable since they are expected to be more robust, while eliminating the need for laborious feature engineering and allowing rich conditioning of attributes such as speaker, language and sentiment. The following section describes some of the popular deep learning architectures developed for TTS synthesis in detail.

4.3   Popular deep learning architectures

Present-day TTS architectures attempt to go for an end-to-end approach. However, popular architectures generally are not fully end-to-end, but rather have an optional text analysis module for grapheme-to-phoneme conversion, a network to map text or a sequence of phonemes to a spectrogram and possibly other features and finally a vocoder (Griffin–Lim or GAN-based like HiFi-GAN, Mel GAN, etc.) to convert the spectrogram/features into speech, as shown in Figure 4.4. Three of the widely used architectures are as follows:

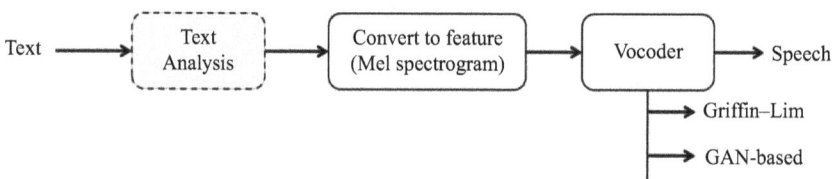

Figure 4.4   General block diagram of current deep learning methods

4.3.1   Tacotron/Tacotron2

Tacotron [26] is a groundbreaking encoder–decoder model, devised by Google, that introduced an almost end-to-end approach to TTS synthesis. It maps the input text directly to a linear spectrogram, which is then converted into speech using an external vocoder. Tacotron's encoder converts a given input text (sequence of characters) into a series of feature embeddings, capturing linguistic and contextual information. The embeddings are passed through a pre-net, which is a set of non-linear transformations, and the resultant vectors are passed through a CBHG module (consisting of 1D convolutional layers, highway networks and bidirectional gated recurrent units (GRUs)) to obtain the final encoder representations. These encoder representations are then passed on to an attention-based decoder, consisting of GRUs with vertical residual connections, which is responsible for producing spectrograms. The attention mechanism in the decoder aligns the encoder vectors with corresponding time frames in the output spectrogram, ensuring smooth and accurate synthesis. The spectrogram is finally fed into a vocoder (originally, Griffin–Lim) to produce the corresponding speech signal. An overview of Tacotron's architecture is presented in Figure 4.5.

A refinement over this architecture resulted in Tacotron2 [27]. Here, Mel spectrograms are used instead of linear spectrograms and the convolutional layers and bidirectional long short-term memory (LSTM) replace the complex CBHG module and GRUs, as shown in Figure 4.6. The convolutional layers effectively capture local patterns, such as phoneme-level features, while the LSTM layers model long-term dependencies, such as sentence structure and context. This combination allows Tacotron2 to understand and process complex linguistic inputs more effectively. Additionally, the encoder includes positional encodings to help the model retain the sequential nature of text data. These encodings ensure that the temporal relationships between words are preserved, enabling the system to produce speech with appropriate timing and rhythm. The decoder architecture is

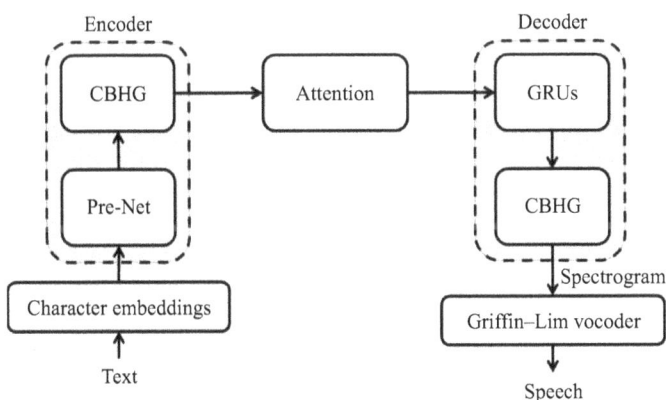

Figure 4.5   Simplified block diagram of Tacotron

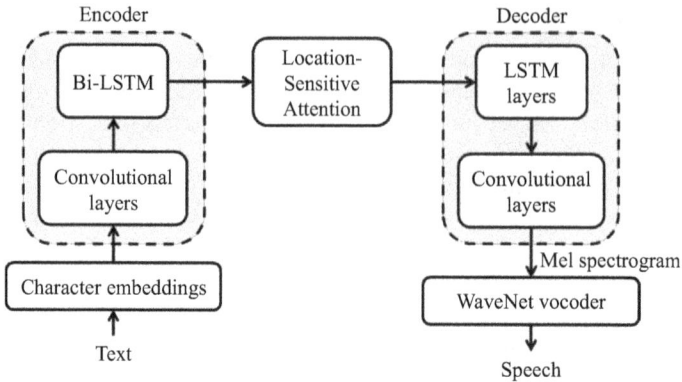

Figure 4.6   Simplified block diagram of Tacotron2

equally innovative. It employs a location-sensitive attention mechanism, which improves the alignment between text inputs and audio outputs. Unlike standard attention mechanisms, location-sensitive attention takes into account previous alignment positions, reducing errors like skipped or repeated words. This mechanism proved particularly useful for synthesising long and complex sentences, where maintaining accurate alignment is challenging. Further, a neural vocoder, namely WaveNet, is used instead of the Griffin–Lim algorithm.

Despite its strengths, Tacotron2 faced challenges, particularly in real-time deployment scenarios. The autoregressive decoding process could still lead to issues such as skipped or repeated words, especially for long or complex sentences. Additionally, the high computational cost of the WaveNet vocoder limited its scalability and applicability for real-time systems. These limitations prompted the development of alternative approaches such as non-autoregressive models like FastSpeech and improved vocoders like HiFi-GAN.

4.3.2   FastSpeech/FastSpeech2

FastSpeech [28] was proposed by Microsoft with the intention of reducing the inference time, as evident from the name. It is a non-autoregressive model and hence is capable of generating Mel spectrograms in parallel and does not depend on previous elements. It consists of a set of feedforward transformer blocks, as shown in Figure 4.7, each containing a self-attention layer and 1D convolutional layers. It also consists of a length regulator to handle the difference in the number of phonemes and the number of frames in the Mel spectrogram, which can also be used to control the speech rate, partly aiding in manipulating prosody. This length regulator relies on a duration predictor, consisting of 1D convolutional layers, and it predicts the length of the Mel spectrograms to be generated for each phoneme. While training the duration predictor, phoneme durations are required, and these are generally estimated from an autoregressive encoder–decoder teacher model.

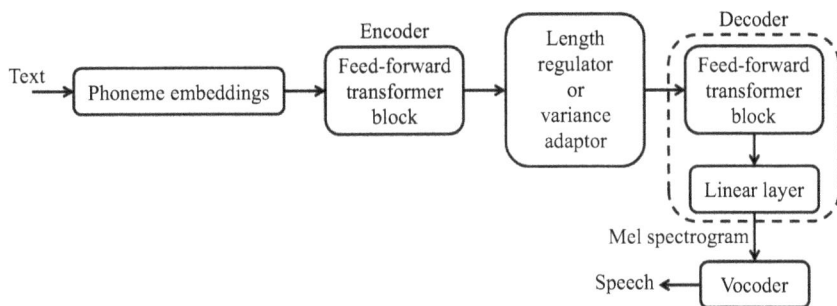

Figure 4.7   Simplified block diagram of FastSpeech/FastSpeech2

FastSpeech is able to achieve better inferencing speed than autoregressive models like Tacotron, while producing speech of similar quality. However, it has a complicated pipeline which relies on phoneme durations derived from a teacher model that might not be very accurate. This brought about FastSpeech2 [29], which attempts to simplify the training pipeline and thereby increase the training speed. It also attempts to produce synthetic speech of better quality. The FastSpeech2 architecture is different from FastSpeech in that it does not rely on a teacher model to obtain the phoneme durations, but rather obtains it using an independent forced alignment tool. The duration predictor is now a part of a variance adaptor module (instead of the length regulator as in FastSpeech), which also predicts the pitch and the energy. These added features help improve the naturalness of synthetic speech. While FastSpeech and FastSpeech2 are not fully end-to-end models, FastSpeech2s is. This architecture is similar to FastSpeech2, except for the decoder, which is designed to generate a speech signal directly from the output of the variance adaptor. Another fully end-to-end architecture is the variational inference with adversarial learning, briefly described below.

4.3.3   Variational inference with adversarial learning TTS (VITS)

VITS [30] uses a conditional variational autoencoder. It consists of two encoders, namely a posterior and a prior encoder, where the former consists of dilated convolutional layers and the latter consists of a transformer, which is used to encode the text. These are followed by a decoder and a discriminator, which are fundamentally HiFi-GAN's generator and discriminator, respectively. Finally, the architecture also has a stochastic duration predictor, consists of convolution layers and predicts phoneme durations. Of these, the posterior encoder and the discriminator are not required at the time of inferencing. The end-to-end learning in VITS eliminates the need for separate vocoders. It delivers both high-quality and efficient synthesis, making it a promising choice for commercial applications. However, it would need a larger amount of training data compared to Tacotron and FastSpeech.

4.4   Prosody modelling for expressive speech synthesis

Present-day commercial TTS systems are capable of producing speech that is highly intelligible and also quite natural. However, the synthetic speech often lacks appropriate prosody and does not convey emotion. However, TTS systems when employed to engage in conversation with a user or to create audio books or in speech-to-speech translation systems must be capable of producing expressive speech. Expressive speech could mean full-blown emotions or a certain style of speaking, such as news-reading or storytelling. One way of obtaining expressive synthetic speech is to train the TTS system with expressive/emotional speech with appropriate labels representing the speaking style. However, this would require a huge amount of labelled training data in each speaking style, which is difficult to obtain. Therefore, unsupervised techniques are preferred and these generally extract prosodic information/speaking style from a reference speech signal [31]. Following are some approaches to prosody modelling for expressive speech synthesis.

4.4.1   Using a reference encoder

This method involves the use of an encoder to derive prosody embeddings from a speech signal [32,33]. Here, the spectrogram, Mel frequency cepstral coefficients or prosodic features are extracted from a reference speech signal, and these are fed into the encoder, which provides an embedding vector. This is used TTS model along with the text embedding to synthesise speech with a preferred speaking style. The reference encoder could also be a variational auto-encoder [34], which maps the reference speech signal to a low-dimensional latent space. Further, auto-regressive models result in issues such as repetitions, skipping and accumulation of error. Therefore, diffusion models [35], which are capable of handling complex distributions, have now gained popularity.

4.4.2   Using global style tokens

Global style tokens (GSTs) [36] are an extension of the prosody embedding derived from a reference encoder. The prosody embedding is usually passed through an attention unit which measures the amount of similarity between this embedding and a set of style tokens. These tokens are initially generated randomly and then learnt while training the model. Each style is basically the weighted sum of the style tokens. Certain TTS systems employ multiple style token layers [37] and certain others go for a supervised [38] or semi-supervised [39] approach to deriving the GSTs as well. Further, to eliminate the need for a reference speech signal, GSTs may also be estimated from text [40].

4.4.3   Post-processing neutral synthetic speech

Another approach to deriving expressive speech is by modifying the neutral speech produced by a TTS system. This can be accomplished by means of signal processing algorithms such as the time-domain pitch synchronous overlap and add method, as well as generative models that are used for voice conversion.

4.5   TTS systems in a low-resource setting

Deep learning methods are notorious for needing an exorbitant amount of training data (tens or hundreds of hours) for producing impressive results. While this requirement can be met for languages that are globally spoken like English, there are several other languages in the world that are not data rich. Further, even in the case of widely spoken languages, there are certain applications such as prosody modelling or developing systems for people with speaking disorders, where sufficient speech data is hard to find. Therefore, a lot of research has recently gone into identifying ways to address data scarcity. Following are some methods that may be adopted in a low-resource setting [41]:

(i)   Considering data from multiple speakers and multiple languages
(ii) Training a model on a different language(s) and using transfer learning to finetune the model to a desired language
(iii) Artificially synthesising additional data
(iv) Using automatic speech recognition (ASR) or other methods to handle an untranscribed speech dataset

4.5.1   Multispeaker/multilingual TTS systems

Conventionally, a TTS system is trained on data from a single speaker and for a single language. However, recording tens of hours of data from one speaker might be difficult, especially when developing applications for people with speaking disorders. In such cases, a few minutes/hours of data can be recorded from multiple speakers. A multispeaker TTS system typically involves the use of speaker embeddings, along with the speech signal or spectrogram or any other feature extracted from speech, while training the TTS system. When synthesising speech corresponding to a given text, the embedding corresponding to a certain speaker may be given as an additional input to obtain speech in a desired speaker's voice.

For certain languages, it might be difficult to obtain sufficient data even when there are multiple speakers involved. In such cases, the TTS system may be trained on multiple languages, preferably those that have a similar set of phonemes and phonotactics as the desired language.

4.5.2   Few-shot and zero-shot TTS systems

When there is insufficient data from a speaker to train a model, transfer learning may be used to finetune a model trained on another speaker(s)'s data with little data from a preferred speaker. This can be extended across languages as well. A multilingual model may be trained on data from a set of languages (including or excluding the desired language) and this may be finetuned with a few minutes of data from the desired low-resource language [42–44]. In this regard, organisations like Microsoft and Google have attempted to develop a universal TTS model that is trained in several languages (and speakers) and can be adapted to any desired speaker's voice with just a few seconds of speech data in their voice, and to a new language with as low as 5–6 minutes of data in that language [45,46]. These methods are examples of few-shot learning, where a few seconds/minutes of data from a desired language/speaker can be used to adapt or finetune an existing model. Attempts have also been made at zero-shot learning [47,48], which does not require the model to be finetuned but instead uses a reference speech signal to extract the desired characteristics to produce them in the desired speech signal. However, this method is mainly useful to capture a desired speaker's identity and prosody.

4.5.3   Data augmentation

Another approach to handle data scarcity is to artificially synthesise speech data to augment the available data. This usually involves uniformly increasing or decreasing the pitch period or speech rate of the available speech data [49]. Voice conversion could also be used here, where given speech data from one speaker, the same can be replicated in other speakers' voices, thereby resulting in additional data [50].

4.5.4   Handling untranscribed speech data

In some cases, while sufficient speech data might be available, these might not be transcribed. In such cases, if an ASR system is available, it may be used to derive the text corresponding to the available speech data. However, for several low-resource languages, an ASR system might not be readily available. In fact, certain languages do not have a written form. Under such circumstances, linguistic/acoustic units may be derived, and these may be used instead of text. The TTS system will now be trained on (linguistic/acoustic units, speech) pairs instead of (text, speech) pairs [51,52].

4.6   Evaluation metrics

As evident through the discussions throughout the chapter, the performance of a TTS system is reflected in the quality of synthetic speech, characterised in terms of intelligibility and naturalness, and wherever applicable, speaker similarity. The quality of speech can be assessed by subjective or objective measures, and these are described below.

4.6.1   Subjective metrics

Subjective metrics for evaluation of synthetic speech generally involve the conduction of a listening test, where the participants (ideally native speakers of the language being tested) are required to rate the synthetic speech played to them. The following metrics may be derived from the listening tests:

- *Mean opinion score (MOS):* This involves playing synthetic speech signals to several listeners and obtaining scores on a scale of 1–5, where a score of 5 implies that the synthetic speech is highly intelligible and natural, and a score of 1 implies that the speech is barely intelligible and very unnatural. The scores obtained are averaged to get the MOS.

- *Degradation mean opinion score (DMOS):* The DMOS is quite similar to the MOS, except that along with the synthetic speech signal, the corresponding recorded speech signal is also played to the listeners. The listeners are now required to provide a score on a scale of 1–5, which is representative of the amount of degradation that is evident in the synthetic speech compared to the recorded speech. Here, a score of 5 means that the synthetic speech sounds exactly like the recorded speech and a score 1 means that the two speech signals are barely similar.
- *Word error rate (WER):* The WER can be used to measure the intelligibility of synthetic speech. Here, the listeners would be required to listen to the synthetic speech and jot down the sentence as perceived by them. The percentage of incorrectly identified words can be calculated to obtain the WER.
- *ABX test:* While the MOS and DMOS could also potentially be used to assess the extent to which the synthetic speech signal bears the identity of the desired speaker, the ABX test, which is generally intended to test voice conversion systems, may also be used. This test involves playing the synthetic speech signal (X), along with speech uttered by the desired speaker (A or B) and another speaker (B or A). The listeners are expected to identify if X sounds similar to A or B in terms of speaker identity, and the percentage of utterances that contain the desired speaker's identity is calculated.

4.6.2   Objective metrics

While subjective metrics are best suited to assess the quality of synthetic speech, it is often difficult and expensive to find a sufficient number of participants to carry out the listening tests. In such cases, objective metrics, which basically compare features extracted from synthetic and the corresponding recorded speech, may be used. A few of these are as follows:

- *Mel cepstral distortion (MCD):* The MCD is a measure of the spectral similarity and is computed as the average difference between the Mel frequency cepstral coefficients extracted from the synthesised speech and the corresponding recorded speech.
- *Log-F0 root mean squared error:* As the name suggests, this metric is a measure of the difference between the frame-wise log fundamental frequency (F0) of the synthetic speech and the corresponding recorded speech.
- *Conditional Fréchet speech distance:* This metric involves deriving speech embeddings from the synthetic and recorded speech signals and computing the conditional Fréchet distance between them.
- *Pseudo MOS:* This involves training models to predict the MOS for any given speech signal.
- *WER:* While the previous section described WER as being computed through a listening test, it can also be derived by feeding the synthetic speech to an ASR system, thereby overcoming the need for human participation.
- *Speaker embedding cosine similarity:* This metric is a measure of speaker similarity and is computed as the cosine similarity between speaker embeddings derived from synthetic speech and a reference speech signal from the same speaker.

4.7   Challenges and future directions

TTS synthesis plays a vital role in several applications that involve communicating with machines as well as other people. As evident from the discussions in this chapter, generative models have been instrumental in facilitating the production of natural and almost human-like speech. However, despite the various efforts taken towards improving the expressiveness of synthetic speech, there is still room for improvement, especially in the case of low-resource languages. Yet another aspect that could be addressed is the inference time. While FastSpeech2 has been successful in this regard, the inference time must be reduced further especially when the TTS system is to be employed in handheld/edge devices with less computing power. It would be beneficial to design an architecture that reduces the training time as well, since current architectures typically require a few days to train even with a reasonable amount of computing power. Architecture requiring fewer parameters to be trained and a smaller footprint size are also highly desired.

There is also a need for efficient methods to automatically evaluate TTS systems, especially in terms of how expressive they are. Ideally, a MOS obtained from people is the best way to assess the quality. However, it is often very difficult to obtain sufficient participants, who are native speakers of the language the TTS system is trained for. Therefore, steps may be taken towards an objective measure that very closely emulates the MOS. Finally, as TTS systems become equipped to produce speech that is increasingly difficult to distinguish from that of a human, there are growing security and ethical concerns. Therefore, the advancements in TTS technology must also be complemented by advances in efficient anti-spoofing techniques.

4.8   Conclusion

Generative models have significantly transformed the landscape of TTS systems, facilitating enhanced communications between humans and machines. By leveraging deep learning, TTS systems have achieved significant improvements in prosody, expressiveness and scalability. Key advancements include encoder–decoder architectures and innovations in prosody modelling and handling data scarcity. Future directions primarily include further improving the expressiveness of synthetic speech, reducing the training and inferencing times and identifying efficient ways to evaluate synthetic speech.

References

[1]   L.R. Rabiner, and R.W. Schafer, *Digital Processing of Speech Signals*, Prentice-Hall, Englewood Cliffs, NJ, 1978.
[2]   J. Benesty, M.M. Sondhi, and Y. Huang, *Springer Handbook of Speech Processing*, Springer, Berlin, 2007.

[3]   H. Dudley, "The carrier nature of speech", *The Bell System Technical Journal*, Vol. 19, No. 4, pp. 495–651, 1940.

[4]   D.H. Klatt, "The klattalk text-to-speech conversion system", in *Proceedings of the International Conference on Acoustics, Speech and Signal Processing (ICASSP)*, 1982, pp. 1589–1592.

[5]   D.H. Klatt, "DecTalk 'user's manual," *Digital Equipment Corporation Report*, 1990.

[6]   P. Rubin, G. Ramsay, and M. Tiede, "The history of articulatory synthesis at Haskins laboratories", in *Proceedings of the ISCA Auditory-Visual Speech Processing*, 2005, pp. 117–118.

[7]   J.E. Lloyd, I. Stavness, and S. Fels, "ArtiSynth: A fast interactive biomechanical modeling toolkit combining multibody and finite element simulation", in Y. Payan (ed.), *Soft Tissue Biomechanical Modeling for Computer Assisted Surgery*, Studies in Mechanobiology, Tissue Engineering and Biomaterials, Vol. 11, Springer, Berlin, pp. 355–394, 2012.

[8]   A.J. Hunt, and A.W. Black, "Unit selection in a concatenative speech synthesis using a large speech database", in *Proceedings of the IEEE International Conference on Acoustics, Speech and Signal Processing (ICASSP)*, 1996, pp. 373–376.

[9]   H. Zen, K. Tokuda, and A.W. Black, "Statistical parametric speech synthesis", *Speech Communication*, Vol. 51, No. 11, pp. 1039–1064, 2009.

[10] H. Zen, T. Toda, M. Nakamura, and K. Tokuda, "Details of Nitech HMM-based speech synthesis system for the Blizzard Challenge 2005," *IEICE Transactions on Information and Systems*, Vol. E90-D, No. 1, pp. 325–333, 2007.

[11] M. Morise, F. Yokomori, and K. Ozawa, "WORLD: A vocoder-based high-quality speech synthesis system for real-time applications", *IEICE Transactions on Information and Systems*, Vol. E99-D, No. 7, pp. 1877–1884, 2016.

[12] O. Watts, G.E. Henter, T. Merritt, Z. Wu, and S. King, "From HMMs to DNNs: Where do the improvements come from?", in *Proceedings of the International Conference on Acoustics, Speech, and Signal Processing (ICASSP)*, 2016, pp. 5505–5509.

[13] M. Shannon, H. Zen, and W. Byrne, "Autoregressive models for statistical parametric speech synthesis," *IEEE Transactions on Audio, Speech, and Language Processing*, Vol. 21, No. 3, pp. 587–597, 2013.

[14] Z.H. Ling, L. Deng, and D. Yu, "Modeling spectral envelopes using restricted Boltzmann machines for statistical parametric speech synthesis", in *Proceedings of the International Conference on Acoustics, Speech and Signal Processing (ICASSP)*, 2013, pp. 7825–7829.

[15] Z.H. Ling, L. Deng, and D. Yu, "Modeling spectral envelopes using restricted Boltzmann machines and deep belief networks for statistical parametric speech synthesis", *IEEE Transactions on Audio, Speech, and Language Processing*, Vol. 21, No. 10, pp. 2129–2139, 2013.

[16] R. Boothalingam, V.S. Solomi, A.R. Gladston, *et al.*, "Development and evaluation of unit selection and HMM-based speech synthesis for Tamil", in

Proceedings of the IEEE National Conference on Communication (NCC), 2013, pp. 1–5.

[17]   H. Zen, A. Senior, and M. Schuster, "Statistical parametric speech synthesis using deep neural networks", in *Proceedings of the International Conference on Acoustics, Speech and Signal Processing*, 2013, pp. 7962–7966.

[18]   H. Zen, and A. Senior, "Deep mixture density networks for acoustic modeling in statistical parametric speech synthesis", in *Proceedings of the International Conference on Acoustics, Speech and Signal Processing*, 2014, pp. 3844–3848.

[19]   T. Kaneko, H. Kameoka, N. Hojo, Y. Ijima, K. Hiramatsu, and K. Kashino, "Generative adversarial network-based postfilter for statistical parametric speech synthesis", in *Proceedings of the International Conference on Acoustics, Speech and Signal Processing (ICASSP)*, 2017, pp. 4910–4914.

[20]   Y. Fan, Y. Qian, F.-L. Xie, and F.K. Soong, "TTS synthesis with bidirectional LSTM based recurrent neural networks", in *Proceedings of Interspeech*, 2014, pp. 1964–1968.

[21]   J. Ni, Y. Shiga, and H. Kawai, "Global syllable vectors for building TTS frontend with deep learning", in *Proceedings of Interspeech, 2017*, pp. 769–773.

[22]   A. van den Oord, S. Dieleman, H. Zen, *et al.*, "WaveNet: A generative model for raw audio", arXiv:1609.03499, 2016.

[23]   S. Mehri, K. Kumar, I. Gulrajani, *et al.*, "SampleRNN: An unconditional end-to-end neural audio generation model", arXiv:1612.07837, 2017.

[24]   R. Prenger, R. Valle, and B. Catanzaro, "WaveGlow: A flow-based generative network for speech synthesis", in *Proceedings of the International Conference on Acoustics, Speech, and Signal Processing (ICASSP)*, 2019, pp. 3617–3621.

[25]   J.-M. Valin, and J. Skoglund, "LPCNet: Improving neural speech synthesis through linear prediction", in *Proceedings of the International Conference on Acoustics, Speech, and Signal Processing (ICASSP)*, 2019, pp. 5891–5895.

[26]   Y. Wang, R.J. Skerry-Ryan, D. Stanton, *et al.*, "Tacotron: Towards end-to-end speech synthesis", in *Proceedings of Interspeech*, 2017, pp. 4006–4010.

[27]   J. Shen, R. Pang, R.J. Weiss, *et al.*, "Natural TTS synthesis by conditioning WaveNet on Mel spectrogram predictions", in *Proceedings of the International Conference on Acoustics, Speech, and Signal Processing*, 2018, pp. 4779–4783.

[28]   Y. Ren, Y. Ruan, X. Tan, *et al.*, "FastSpeech: Fast, robust and controllable text to speech", in *NeurIPS*, 2019, pp. 3165–3174.

[29]   Y. Ren, C. Hu, X. Tan, *et al.*, "FastSpeech 2: Fast and high-quality end-to-end text to speech", arXiv:2006.04558, 2020.

[30]   J. Kim, J. Kong, and J. Son, "Conditional variational autoencoder with adversarial learning for end-to-end text-to-speech", in *Proceedings of the Machine Learning Research*, 2021.

[31]   H. Barakat, O. Turk, and C. Demiroglu, "Deep learning-based expressive speech synthesis: A systematic review of approaches, challenges, and resources", *EURASIP Journal on Audio, Speech, and Music Processing*, Vol. 11, pp. 1–34, 2024.

[32]   R. Skerry-Ryan, E. Battenberg, Y. Xiao, *et al.*, "Towards end-to-end prosody transfer for expressive speech synthesis with Tacotron", in *Proceedings of the International Conference on Machine Learning Research (PMLR)*, 2018, pp. 4693–4702.

[33]   Y. Gao, W. Zheng, Z. Yang, T. Kohler, C. Fuegen, and Q. He, "Interactive text-to-speech system via joint style analysis", in *Proceedings of Interspeech*, 2020, pp. 4447–4451.

[34]   Y.J. Zhang, S. Pan, L. He, and Z.H. Ling, "Learning latent representations for style control and transfer in end-to-end speech synthesis", in *Proceedings of the International Conference on Acoustics, Speech and Signal Processing (ICASSP)*, pp. 6945–6949.

[35]   H.-S. Oh, S.-H. Lee, and S.-W. Lee, "DiffProsody: Diffusion-based latent prosody generation for expressive speech synthesis with prosody conditional adversarial training", *IEEE Transactions on Audio, Speech, and Language Processing*, Vol. 32, pp. 2654–2666, 2024.

[36]   Y. Wang, D. Stanton, Y. Zhang, *et al.*, "Style tokens: Unsupervised style modeling, control and transfer in end-to-end speech synthesis", in *Proceedings of the International Conference on Machine Learning Research (PMLR)*, 2018, pp. 5180–5189.

[37]   X. An, Y. Wang, S. Yang, Z. Ma, and L. Xie, "Learning hierarchical representations for expressive speaking style in end-to-end speech synthesis", in *IEEE Automatic Speech Recognition and Understanding Workshop (ASRU)*, 2019, pp. 184–191.

[38]   S. Lei, Y. Zhou, L. Chen, Z. Wu, S. Kang, and H. Meng, "Towards expressive speaking style modelling with hierarchical context information for mandarin speech synthesis", in *Proceedings of the International Conference on Acoustics, Speech and Signal Processing (ICASSP)*, 2022, pp. 7922–7926.

[39]   P. Wu, Z. Ling, L. Liu, Y. Jiang, H. Wu, and L. Dai, "End-to-end emotional speech synthesis using style tokens and semi-supervised training", in *Proceedings of the Asia-Pacific Signal and Information Processing Association Annual Summit and Conference (APSIPA ASC)*, 2019, pp. 623–627.

[40]   R. Li, Z. Wu, Y. Huang, J. Jia, H. Meng, and L. Cai, "Emphatic speech generation with conditioned input layer and bidirectional LSTMs for expressive speech synthesis", in *Proceedings of the International Conference on Acoustics, Speech and Signal Processing (ICASSP)*, 2018, pp. 5129–5133.

[41]   A.R. Gladston, and K.V. Pradeep, "Exploring solutions for text-to-speech synthesis of low-resource languages", in *Proceedings of the 4th International Conference on Signal Processing and Communication*, 2023, pp. 168–172.

[42]   W. Zhang, H. Yang, X. Bu, and L. Wang, "Deep learning for Mandarin-Tibetan cross-lingual speech synthesis", *IEEE Access*, Vol. 7, pp. 167884–167894, 2019.

[43]   K. Azizah, M. Adriani, and W. Jatmiko, "Hierarchical transfer learning for multilingual, multi-speaker, and style transfer DNN-based TTS on low-resource languages", *IEEE Access*, Vol. 8, pp. 179798–179812, 2020.

[44]   A. Prakash, and H.A. Murthy, "Exploring the role of language families for building Indic speech synthesisers", *IEEE Transactions on Audio, Speech, and Language Processing*, Vol. 31, pp. 734–747, 2023.

[45]   J. Yang, and L. He, "Towards universal text-to-speech", in *Proceedings of Interspeech*, 2022, pp. 3171–3175.

[46]   I. Demirsahin, M. Jansche, and A. Gutkin, "A unified phonological representation of south Asian languages for multilingual text-to-speech", in *Proceedings of the 6th International Workshop on Spoken Language Technologies for Under-Resourced Languages*, 2018, pp. 80–84.

[47]   E. Casanova, J. Weber, C.D. Shulby, A.C. Junior, E. Golge, and M.A. Ponti, "YourTTS: Towards zero-shot multi-speaker TTS and zero-shot voice conversion for everyone", in *Proceedings of the International Conference on Machine Learning (PMLR)*, 2022, pp. 2709–2720.

[48]   Ed. Casanova, K. Davis, E. Gölge, *et al.*, "XTTS: A massively multilingual zero-shot text-to-speech model", in *Proceedings of Interspeech*, 2024, pp. 4978–4982.

[49]   Z. Byambadorj, R. Nishimura, A. Ayush, K. Ohta, and N. Kitaoka, "Text-to-speech system for low-resource language using cross-lingual transfer learning and data augmentation", *EURASIP Journal on Audio, Speech, and Music*, Vol. 42, pp. 1–20, 2021.

[50]   G. Huybrechts, T. Merritt, G. Comini, B. Perz, R. Shah, and J. Lorenzo-Trueba, "Low-resource expressive text-to-speech using data augmentation", in *Proceedings of the IEEE International Conference on Acoustics, Speech and Signal Processing (ICASSP)*, 2021, pp. 6593–6597.

[51]   H. Zhang, and Y. Lin, "Unsupervised learning for sequence-to-sequence text-to-speech for low-resource languages", in *Proceedings of Interspeech*, 2020, pp. 3161–3165.

[52]   D.S. Karthik Pandia, and H.A. Murthy, "Zero resource speech synthesis using transcripts derived from perceptual acoustic units", in *Proceedings of Interspeech*, 2019, pp. 1113–1117.

Chapter 5

Generative AI in image synthesis: review and recent advancements

*Vijayarajan Rajangam[1], Sangeetha Nagarajan[2] and
Alex Noel Joseph Raj[3]*

Abstract

The current decade has witnessed a rapid evolution of image-based applications
due to the advent of fast computing infrastructure. The computer vision algorithms
using deep learning models have opened new avenues for image processing
and analysis. One of the important reasons for the deep learning or artificial
intelligence-based solution is the availability of huge image datasets for model
training. However, the complexity behind generating a huge dataset is one of the
bottlenecks to explore the new avenues of image-based solutions in various applications. The researchers have come up with other options for encountering the
shortage of image datasets with artificially generated images according to the
requirements. The fast-growing research in image processing applications has
offered many image synthesis models that can generate images from different
inputs. This chapter presents the deep learning models particularly generative
adversarial network for image synthesis for various image-based applications.

Keywords: Image synthesis; GAN; generator; discriminator; variational auto
encoders; conditional GAN

5.1 Image synthesis

Synthetic image generation can be accomplished by the models that generate artificial images from the inputs in the form of text, labels, sketch, graph, layout, other
images, audio/speech, etc. Certain image synthesis models are employed to generate high-resolution images from the low-resolution inputs. In medical applications, image synthesis models are used to generate one modality image from other

[1]Centre for Healthcare Advancement, Innovation and Research, School of Electronics Engineering,
Vellore Institute of Technology Chennai, India
[2]School of Computer Science and Engineering, Vellore Institute of Technology Chennai, India
[3]Cyber AI Hub, ECIT, Queens University, UK

modality images. The major categories of image synthesis based on the input sources are listed out as

   (i)   Image-to-image synthesis
   (ii)   Text-to-image synthesis
  (iii)   Sketch-to-image synthesis
  (iv)   Audio-to-image synthesis
   (v)   Video-to-image synthesis
  (vi)   3D modelling from 2D images
 (vii)   Data-to-image synthesis
(viii)   Multimodal image synthesis

5.1.1   Need for image synthesis

The applications of image synthesis are widespread and the need for image synthesis in various fields is listed out below

- The necessity of a greater number of multimodal medical images and annotations for model training requires image synthesis models which often guarantee robustness and precision
- Generation of images that cannot be captured by the imaging systems – e.g. images of adverse weather conditions
- Challenging arts, exploration of different styles and mastering art without professional training
- Creating realistic environments and images for the gaming world
- Virtual experiments, visualisation of scientific data and synthetic images without exposing to radiation, cost and time.
- Creating prototypes, computer-aided design, 3D printing and 3D modelling of products
- Quality control by creating artificial defects and customisation
- Conducting training and simulation in autonomous vehicles, military, remote sensing, medical procedures, space missions and energy generation
- Restoration and reconstruction of damaged or missing structures in archaeological images and artworks
- Synthesising interactive learning tools, 3D models and simulations for education and professional learning

The scarcity of datasets in medical image research due to various obstacles hampers the progress of applications of AI. The dataset shift existing in medical images is categorised into population shift, acquisition shift, annotation shift, manifestation shift and prevalence shift [1]. The reasons for the population shift are due to the biases in sex, ethnic identity and age. The variability in the scanners, technician expertise and other adjustable parameters are the cause of acquisition shift. The third one is due to the subjective annotation strategies, experience and tools. The disease prevalence among different populations is subjective and the sampling of data leads to prevalence shift of data. The awareness about various diseases, the availability of infrastructure, government policies and the mindset of the population resulting in manifestation shift. The above-mentioned requirements necessitate the evolution of image synthesis.

5.1.2 Categories of image synthesis

Image synthesis has evolved over the years from conventional image processing techniques to GANs and diffusion methods. The computing capabilities of the recent image synthesis models find their applications in various fields. The classification is presented in Table 5.1.

Table 5.1 Classification of image synthesis

S.No.	Type	Synthesised output	Methodology
1	Procedural image synthesis – employs specific algorithms and rules for image generation	Textures, patterns and landscapes	Noise-based methods, fractal geometry
2	Neural network-based synthesis – employs neural networks/GANs	Synthetic images	GAN, variational autoencoders and diffusion models
3	Physical simulation-based synthesis – employs physical phenomena	Synthetic images	Ray tracing, fluid dynamics simulation and photon mapping
4	Style transfer/image-to-image synthesis – performs style or attribute transfer from one image to another image	Synthetic images	Neural style transfer, Pix2Pix models and cycle GAN
5	Parametric image synthesis – employs parameterised models with control over the attributes of the images	Synthetic images	Parameter and morphable-based models
6	Hybrid image synthesis – combination different image synthesis models	Synthetic images	Neural networks with procedural methods, GAN with attention models
7	3D image synthesis – generates 3D rendering and visualisations	3D images	Voxel-based methods, mesh models and neural radiance fields
8	Text-to-image synthesis (T2I) – synthesise images from text descriptions, captions, dialogue, etc.	Synthetic images	Transformers and stable diffusion models
9	Medical image synthesis – generates other modality images from one modality and augmented images for training DL models	Synthetic images	GANs
10	Augmented reality and mixed reality synthesis – integrates real images with artificially generated images	Images and videos	Overlaying methods, image synthesis with spatial mapping

5.1.3   Applications of image synthesis

The widespread applications of image synthesis are listed below:

1. Medical image generation – one modality images from other modality images, high-resolution images from low-resolution images, generation of same modality images for image augmentation
2. Text-to-image generation – context-based image generation using labels and text
3. Agriculture – prediction of soil organic contents with respect to other related inputs
4. Art generation and architectural visualisation
5. Computer-aided design, 3D printing and 3D modelling
6. Super resolution, photo editing and photo inpainting
7. Education
8. Human-machine interface
9. Biotechnology
10. Security
11. Visual effects in entertainment, animation and gaming

5.1.4   Image synthesis models

The proposed image synthesis models for various applications are presented in Table 5.2. These models are the backbones for the other models proposed for various applications.

Table 5.2   Various existing models for image synthesis

Type of image synthesis	Existing models
Text-to-image synthesis	• Stable diffusion models • Transformer-based text encoder • Autoregressive models • GANs • Variational autoencoders
Image-to-image synthesis	• GANs – cycleGAN, StyleGANs • Diffusion-based models • Image-to-image translation models • CNN-based models • Pix2Pix
Speech-to-image synthesis	• Contrastive language-image pretraining • GANs • Diffusion models • Audio encoders • Transformers
3D image synthesis	• Neural radiance fields • GANs combined with 3D modelling • DreamFusion using diffusion models

5.2 Generative adversarial neural networks

Generative adversarial network (GAN) [2] proposed this model comprising a generator (G) and discriminator (D). The role of generator is to generate photo-realistic images thus fooling the discriminator, whereas the discriminator tries to discriminate between the generated and real images. GAN employs a minimax two-player game that always tries to minimise the gap between generated and original images, whereas the discriminator performs maximisation of the correctness of the classification probability between the real and generated images. The major blocks of classic GAN are presented in Figure 5.1.

5.2.1 Speech-to-image synthesis

This is a process of generating visual components that convey the semantics of speech input. The success of the model relies on how far the generated visual representation maps the speech content. The complexity of the speech-to-image synthesis line on how far the GAN model perceives the speech elements to generate synthetic images. Effective future extraction like spectrograms, waveform encoding, Mel frequency cepstral coefficients will map audio features into realistic image synthesis.

5.2.2 Text-to-image synthesis

The evolution of GAN models to generate high-resolution multiobject images and suitable performance evaluation strategies has attracted more researchers towards text and image (T2I) synthesis [3]. The T2I models act as a bridge between human ability to read textual content and visualising the same in pictorial forms. The T2I is inspired by the cognitive process of visualising any content that is currently read text descriptions, recalled from the memory and heard from the external audio resources. The models should be able to generate photorealistic representation from the text. The models need to ensure the semantic consistency with the text description [4].

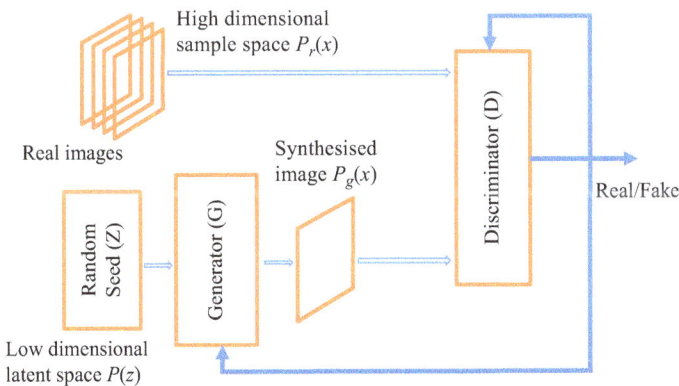

Figure 5.1   Generative adversarial network

T2I image synthesis models generate image representation from the meaning of the text description, labels of object classes, keywords and the key attributes describing the context of the objects to be generated [4]. T2I GANs also synthesise images from single caption, multiple captions, caption-dialogue, caption-layout, caption-semantic masks, scene-graphs, multiple captions and multiple caption-mouth traces [3]. The inputs are given to the models as functions or networks and deterministic mappings. There are different methods to generate images by encoding the text description into text embeddings.

Challenges in T2I are as follows [3]:

1. Generating complex images with multiple objects from the limited text description
2. Limitations of large language models to understand the context of the words in the language: different meaning for the same word according to the context
3. Generation of images with high spatial resolution
4. Performance analysis of image synthesis models with respect to human perceptions which is subjective for text descriptions.

5.2.3   Image-to-image synthesis

This is a processing of mapping the attributes of a source image in one domain to an output image in another domain. GANs synthesise images from sketches, greyscale input images, segmentation maps. Segmentation maps or edge maps are generated as colourful images using image-to-image synthesis GANs.

5.2.4   Controllable image synthesis

Controllable image synthesis (CIS) allows the user to take control over the attributes of image generated, editing one object without disturbing other objects and so on [5]. This could be achieved by providing appropriate input conditions or modifying latent representations. The specific control over the attributes will tend to generate an image which is different from the previously synthesised image. The control over the generated image deals with orientation and position of the objects, the background, object itself and even overall layout.

CIS can be further classified into (i) conditional CIS (CO-CIS), (ii) GAN space-based CIS (GS-CIS) and (iii) causally CIS (CA-CIS). The first category GAN models are based on specific set of conditions, labels, text descriptions, masks, etc. GS-CIS models generate images or attributes of images based on latent representations with semantically meaningful directions. This helps to control the attributes of the sections of the images. CA-CIS models generate images using a set of probability distributions by exposing the cause-and-effect relationship that exists between image entities and actions.

5.2.5   Evolution of GANs

The evolution of GANs started with the classic GAN and numerous deviations are proposed thereon for various image synthesis applications. This section briefs about

Table 5.3 Evolution of GANs

Year	Models
2014	Classic GAN [2], Conditional GAN (CO-GAN)
2015	Deep convolutional GAN
2016	3DGAN, StackGAN, VGAN, InfoGAN
2017	ProGAN (progressive growing GAN), Pix2Pix, CycleGAN, super-resolution GAN (SRGAN), unsupervised image-to-image translation (UNIT)
2018	StyleGAN, enhanced SRGAN (ESRGAN), StarGAN, attention GAN (AttnGAN), MocoGAN, GANimation, Evolutionary GAN (eGAN)
2019	HoloGAN, BigGAN, BigBiGAN, GANPaint, SinGAN, GauGAN
2020	StyleGAN2, neural radiance fields GAN (NeRF-GAN), StarGAN2
2021	StyleGAN3, GANformer, FastGAN
2022	Diffusion GAN, global information utilisation GANs (GIU-GANs)
2023	Re-GAN, graph transformer GAN (GTGAN), stylised projected GAN
2024	ArtGAN, FaceGAN, Quantum GAN, Generalised GANs (G-GANs), probability mass function GAN (PMF-GAN)
2025	R3GAN

the major image synthesis and evolution of GAN from 2014. The evolution of major path-breaking GANs is presented in Table 5.3.

5.3 Review on GAN-based image synthesis models

The last decade has seen quite a few GAN models proposed for image synthesis. This section reviews a few for different applications. C4synth model [6] performs T2I using multiple captions ensuring consistency of generated images with similar sentences. This is accomplished using cross-caption cycle consistency by iterating sequentially over multiple captions. Another method, RiFeGAN, uses a knowledge base, comprising of real images with captions for caption matching and compatible items recovery. An ultrasound image generator is enriched by the multiple features extracted from the captions.

A dialogue-based control is employed in VQA-GAN in which the image generator is controlled by locally related texts derived from the questions–answers (QA) [7]. The QAs are taken from VQA2.0 which is built from COCO dataset. The three components of VQA-GAN are a QA encoder that generates local–global representations using QA pairs, a GAN controlled by the above QA encoder-generated images in two-level process and a VQA model to evaluate VQA loss.

Hinz *et al.* [8] and 2020 proposed a layout-based GAN in which an object pathway is incorporated into both generator and discriminator. This pathway explicitly represents the appearance and location of the objects. The background of the generated image is constructed by a global pathway ensuring that the background fits with the overall layout and image description. The meaningful generator of objects in the appropriate locations is carried out by local pathway. Additional pathways are added in OP-GAN and bounding box matching loss is also evaluated. OC-GAN uses a scene graph similarity module to address the merged objects problem.

The modelling of drylands and paddy fields for soil matter prediction is a challenge due to varying image spectra in remote sensing. The multitemporal image synthesis combined with the modelling of multispectral image data does not yield the expected prediction of soil matter. The authors proposed separate methods for modelling and image synthesis [9].

5.3.1   GANs for medical image synthesis

The limitations of datasets for specific clinical pathologies are an impediment for deep learning-based image analysis and classification employed in radiology and oncology [10]. The evolution of GANs has helped the researchers to use synthetic images but often face challenges. The heterogeneity nature of tumorous region within and between patients, small size, complexity of cancerous tissues, difficulty and cost of annotation of cancerous region in large scale, data imbalance between cancerous and healthy patients and ethical issues for handling the patient population who are in the advanced stage of cancer.

BreathVisionNet [11] generates expiratory CT images from inspiratory CT to avoid radiation exposure and expenditure. By assessing air trapping in the respiration tract, expiratory CT can help to correctly detect chronic obstructive pulmonary disease (COPD). The proposed model is the combination of convolutional neural network (CNN) and transformer to detect irregular phenotypic distribution among COPD patients. This model can learn long-range and global context information by providing global information into the encoder. The edge information combined with multiview data is used to enhance the generated CT images. The generated expiratory CT and inspiratory CT images are used to estimate the phenotypes of COPD using parametric response mapping.

Yu *et al.* [12] proposed a 3D CO-GAN for generating FLAIR MRI images from T1-weighted brain images. The details of the FLAIR images are better depicted using a local adaptive fusion method. T1-weighted brain images exhibit sharp contrast changes between the tissues of white matter and grey matter, whereas the lesion tissues are highlighted by fluid attenuation inversion recovery. The generation of FLAIR images from the widely referred T1-weighted imaging would help to reduce the cost of multimodality imaging for brain tumour localisation and size evaluation. The discontinuity experienced between coronal and sagittal direction in 2D GAN could be overcome by a 3D CO-GAN that includes both global non-linear and local linear mapping from T1-weighted images to FLAIR images.

The 3D CO-GAN uses U-Net architecture as its backbone with seven down and up convolutional blocks in the generator module followed by a discriminator with five convolutional blocks and sigmoid activation function. The combination weights are estimated from the generated FLAIR images and real image for polishing the local and global details present in the synthesised FLAIR images.

Sequential GAN [13] with semi-supervised learning is used to generate images to two medical imaging modalities. A joint probability distribution of two modalities is learnt using supervised learning, whereas the marginal distribution of each modality is learnt from the unpaired images. This model ensures spatial correlation between synthetic images of two modalities using supervised learning, meanwhile, highly realistic images are generated using unsupervised learning.

The lack of medical ultrasound image is alleviated by GAN-based image synthesis [14]. Breast ultrasound images were synthesised by DCGAN [15], where noise is used as input. BGGAN was proposed to train a model for anomaly detection. The four GANs proposed for US image synthesis gave emphasis to pixel information of the US images without considering semantic details present in the images. The GANs were able to generate US images but with unrealistic features and structures. Attentional GAN guided by semantic information was proposed to generate US images in which semantic information, background structure and lesion information are given as priori input information. Background texture enhancement is carried out to synthesise even more realistic clinical images.

PathopixGAN [16] is used for data augmentation in the histopathology segmentation architecture. This model is a supervised DL method that uses real and synthesised images with masks for segmentation. The pathopixGAN has control over the histological regions by first training the GAN using real images with masks. After learning the distribution of important details, a Fast GAN-based data augmentation workflow is employed to generate augmented images with masks. This GAN-based segmentation workflow is tested on the following datasets: Prostate carcinoma glands, micro/macrovesicular steatosis of liver and breast cancer tubules.

5.3.2 GAN applications in cancer imaging

GAN models are not only used for image synthesis but also play various roles in image segmentation pipeline [10]. The other contributions of GAN are (i) adversarial training for scrutinising the outputs of segmentation models, (ii) enforcing the segmentation model to adapt the domain's latent representation, (iii) discriminator as classifier, (iv) inpainting of lesions and (v) detection of anomalies and outliers.

5.3.3 Variational autoencoders

Variational autoencoders (VAE) [4] maps inputs into a latent space using a probabilistic model and generates new data using a decoder from the sampled latent space. VAE formulates a foreground latent variable and a background latent variable using two autoencoders. It uses two decoders to reconstruct a combined image from the foreground and background maps using visibility map. The shape and position of the foreground are evaluated using the visibility mask. DRAW [17] is a model that used deep recurrent neural network comprising VAE and an attention module using image patches.

5.4   Performance analysis of GANs

Performance analysis of the GANs is very important to get high-resolution and realistic synthetic images [5]. The widely used performance measures for GAN models are inception score (IS) and Fréchet inception distance (FID) [18]. These measures are evaluated between the extracted features of original and synthetic images. To extract high-level feature space, InceptionNet which is trained on ImageNet dataset is used.

5.4.1   *Fréchet inception distance*

FID or Wasserstein-2 distance between the Gaussian distribution of features extracted from the real and synthetic images [18]. The features are from the high-level feature space that are extracted using pre-trained deep learning models. The lower the FID score, the better the similarity between original and synthetic images. The similarity is referred to as in the form of information and Gaussian distribution.

$$FID = \left\| \mu_r - \mu_g \right\|^2 + Tr\left(\mathrm{cov}_r + \mathrm{cov}_g - 2\left(\mathrm{cov}_r \times \mathrm{cov}_g \right)^{\frac{1}{2}} \right) \tag{5.1}$$

$\mu_r,\ \mu_g$ – mean of real and generated images
$\mathrm{cov}_r,\ \mathrm{cov}_g$ – covariance of real and generated images
$Tr(.)$ – trace of a matrix

5.4.2   *Inception score*

IS is evaluated considering the entropy of individual and entire set of images [19]. The Kullback–Leibler (KL) divergence measures how far the predicted image distribution, *P(Y/X)*, deviates from the overall probability distribution, *P(Y)*, of all generated images, *N*. The *IS* evaluated as the exponential of *KL* divergence between *P(Y/X)* and *P(Y)*

$$IS = \exp\left(\frac{1}{N} \sum_N KL\left(P\left(\frac{Y}{X} \right) \| P(Y) \right) \right) \tag{5.2}$$

5.4.3   *Structural similarity index*

Structural similarity index (SSIM) measures the similarity between the real and generated images [19]. It correlates with human visual perception using luminance, contrast and correlation factors.

$$SSIM(r,\ g) = \left(\frac{2\mu_r\mu_g + C_1}{\mu_r^2 + \mu_g^2 + C_1} \right) \left(\frac{2\sigma_r\sigma_g + C_2}{\sigma_r^2 + \sigma_g^2 + C_2} \right) \left(\frac{\sigma_{rg} + C_3}{\sigma_r\sigma_g + C_3} \right) \tag{5.3}$$

$\mu_r,\ \mu_g$ are the mean of real and generated images
$\sigma_r,\ \sigma_g$ are the variance of real and generated images
σ_{rg} is the covariance between real and generated images

Table 5.4   Performance metrics for image synthesis

Type	Performance metrics
Text-to-image synthesis	Contrastive language image pretraining (CLIP) score, FID, IS, R-precision, diversity score
Image-to-image synthesis	Mean squared error, peak signal to noise ratio, SSIM, FID, perceptual loss, kernel inception distance (KID), intra-class diversity, mode score, accuracy, intersection over union
Audio-to-image synthesis	FID, KID, SSIM, learned perceptual image patch similarity (LPIPS), CLIP similarity, audio-to-visual feature cosine similarity, semantic accuracy, cross-modal mutual information, mode score, intra-class diversity
Controllable image synthesis	FID, IS, KID, LPIPS, mutual information, conditional entropy, accuracy, mode coverage, intra-class diversity, semantic consistency

The loss functions in CO-CIS are categorised into pixel-level loss, perception-level loss and attribute consistency loss [5]. Pixel level loss function evaluates the difference between the input and output images to ensure pixel-level details like colour differences and edge information. This loss includes L1 loss, L2 loss and smooth-II loss [20]. Perception loss is evaluated as a difference between generated images and real images using pretrained CNN models. The third loss function is used to find the attributes' consistency between source and synthetic images. The widely used performance metrics for different types of image synthesis using GANs are presented in Table 5.4. The few metrics are subjective and hence application specific performance metric evaluation is still a challenge in image synthesis.

5.5   Future directions

The evolution of fast computing infrastructure has opened many pathways to image synthesis and hence the future paradigms of fast computing systems will open more avenues for image-based applications. The progress of image synthesis would be in the following directions:

- High resolution and more realistic image generation for all the applications
- Scalability and generalisation of image synthesis models
- Multimodal image synthesis in healthcare
- More user interaction and control over the attributes of generated images
- Generative models other than GANs like diffusion models, neural radiance fields for different applications
- Generation of different dimensions using disentangled latent spaces for better human perception
- 3D modelling of complicated visualisation for education and entertainment
- Robust, responsible and ethical models for image synthesis

References

[1] Castro, D.C., Walker, I., and Glocker, B., Causality matters in medical imaging. *Nature Communications*, 11(1), 2020, 1–10.

[2] Goodfellow, I., Pouget-Abadie, J., Mirza, M., *et al.*, Generative adversarial nets. In *Advances in Neural Information Processing Systems*, 2014, pp. 2672–2680.

[3] Frolov, S., Hinz, T., Raue, F., Hees, J., and Dengel, A., Adversarial text-to-image synthesis: a review. *Neural Networks*, 144, 2021, 187–209, https://doi.org/10.1016/j.neunet.2021.07.019.

[4] Baraheem, S.S., Le, T.N., and Nguyen, T.V., Image synthesis: a review of methods, datasets, evaluation metrics, and future outlook. *Artificial Intelligence Review*, 56, 2023, 10813–10865, https://doi.org/10.1007/s10462-023-10434-2.

[5] Huang, S., Li, Q., Liao, J. *et al.*, Controllable image synthesis methods, applications and challenges: a comprehensive survey. *Artificial Intelligence Review*, 57, 2024, 336, https://doi.org/10.1007/s10462-024-10987-w.

[6] Joseph, K.J., Pal, A., Rajanala, S., and Balasubramanian, V.N., C4Synth: cross-caption cycle-consistent text-to-image synthesis. In *IEEE Winter Conference on Applications of Computer Vision*, 2018, pp. 358–366.

[7] Wang, R., Heimann, A.F., Tannast, M., and Zheng, G., CycleSGAN: a cycle-consistent and semantics-preserving generative adversarial network for unpaired MR-to-CT image synthesis. *Computerized Medical Imaging and Graphics*, 117, 2024, 102431, https://doi.org/10.1016/j.compmedimag.2024.102431.

[8] Hinz, T., Heinrich, S., and Wermter, S., Generating multiple objects at spatially distinct locations. In *International Conference on Learning Representations*, 2019, https://doi.org/10.48550/arXiv.1901.00686.

[9] Ma, H., Wang, C., Liu, J., *et al.*, Separate prediction of soil organic matter in drylands and paddy fields based on optimal image synthesis method in the Sanjiang Plain, Northeast China. *Geoderma*, 447, 2024, 116929, https://doi.org/10.1016/j.geoderma.2024. 116929.

[10] Osuala, R., Kushibar, K., Garrucho, L., *et al.*, Data synthesis and adversarial networks: a review and meta-analysis in cancer imaging, *Medical Image Analysis*, 84, 2023, 102704.

[11] Zhang, T., Pang, H., Wu, Y., *et al.*, BreathVisionNet: a pulmonary-function-guided CNN-transformer hybrid model for expiratory CT image synthesis. *Computer Methods and Programs in Biomedicine*, 259, 2025, 108516, https://doi.org/10.1016/j.cmpb.2024. 108516.

[12] Yu, B., Zhou, L., Wang, L., Fripp, J., and Bourgeat, P., 3D cGAN based cross-modality MR image synthesis for brain tumor segmentation. In *IEEE 15th International Symposium on Biomedical Imaging (ISBI 2018)*, Washington, DC, USA, 2018, pp. 626–630, https://doi.org/10.1109/ISBI.2018.8363653.

[13] Yang, X., Lin, Y., Wang, Z., Li, X., and Cheng, K.-T., Bi-modality medical image synthesis using semi-supervised sequential generative adversarial networks. *IEEE Journal of Biomedical and Health Informatics*, 24(3), 2020, 855–865, https://doi.org/10.1109/JBHI.2019.2922986.

[14] Shi, S., Li, H., Zhang, Y., and Wang, X., Semantic information-guided attentional GAN-based ultrasound image synthesis method. *Biomedical Signal Processing and Control*, 102, 2025, 107273, https://doi.org/10.1016/j.bspc.2024.107273.

[15] Fujioka, T., Mori, M., Kubota, K., *et al.*, Breast ultrasound image synthesis using deep convolutional generative adversarial networks. *Diagnostics*, 9, 2019, 176.

[16] Gregor, K., Danihelka, I., Graves, A., Rezende, D.J., and Wierstra, D., DRAW: a recurrent neural network for image generation. In *Proceedings of the 32nd International Conference on Machine Learning*, Lille, France, 2015, JMLR: W&CP, Volume 37.

[17] Borji, A., Pros and cons of GAN evaluation measures: new developments. *Computer Vision and Image Understanding*, 215, 2022, 103329, https://doi.org/10.1016/j.cviu.2021.103329.

[18] Jehanzaib, M., Almalioglu, Y., Bengisu Ozyoruk, K., *et al.*, A robust image segmentation and synthesis pipeline for histopathology. *Medical Image Analysis*, 99, 2025, 103344, https://doi.org/10.1016/j.media.2024.103344.

[19] Lopes D.J.V., Monti G.F., Burgreen G.W., *et al.*, Creating high-resolution microscopic cross-section images of hardwood species using generative adversarial networks. *Frontiers in Plant Science*, 12, 2021, 760139, https://doi.org/10.3389/fpls.2021.760139.

[20] Dorta G., Vicente S., Campbell N.D., and Simpson I.J., The GAN that warped: semantic attribute editing with unpaired data. In *Proceedings of the IEEE/CVF Conference on Computer Vision and Pattern Recognition*, 2020, pp. 5356–5365.

Chapter 6

Harnessing generative AI for enhanced brain tumor detection in clinical trials

MV Sujan Kumar[1], Ganesh Khekare[1], Shashi Kant Gupta[2] and Sharnil Pandya[3]

Abstract

Artificial intelligence (AI) in integrating its method of generative models in the healthcare sector has proven beneficial in enhancing diagnostic efficiency and, subsequently, patient experience. The major limitation relevant to the proposed approaches for detecting brain tumor problems is that various and sufficient datasets for brain tumor detection are rare. This research seeks to overcome this parameter by applying and enhancing the application of generative AI in medical imaging, particularly generative adversarial networks (GANs) in data augmentation in the diagnosis of brain tumors. It also uses GANs for data augmentation, specifically generating synthetic magnetic resonance imaging (MRI) images to enhance brain tumor detection. Our study introduces a hybrid model that combines GANs for realistic image generation with a pre-trained ResNet50 architecture for feature extraction and classification. By employing GANs, new, diverse MRI samples are generated, significantly expanding the available dataset. The augmented dataset is used to train the hybrid model, resulting in high accuracy and AUC-ROC score, demonstrating a substantial improvement over the traditional method. Key metrics such as precision and recall also indicate the model's enhanced ability to distinguish between tumor and non-tumor images. This approach highlights the potential of GAN-based data augmentation to improve generalization in medical imaging, addressing the scarcity of large, varied datasets. The findings contribute to advancing AI-driven diagnostic tools in healthcare, with the potential to enhance early diagnosis and treatment outcomes for brain tumor patients. However, ethical concerns related to data privacy, bias, and the responsible deployment of AI in clinical practice remain important challenges that must be addressed in future work.

Keywords: Brain tumor; convolutional neural network (CNN); data augmentation; generative AI; image processing; magnetic resonance imaging (MRI)

[1]School of Computer Science and Engineering, Vellore Institute of Technology Vellore, India
[2]Computer Science and Engineering, Eudoxia Research University, USA
[3]Faculty of Technology, Linnaeus University, Sweden

6.1   Introduction

Brain tumors are among the most complex and life-threatening conditions, characterized by abnormal cell growth within the brain or surrounding tissues. They can be classified as benign (non-cancerous) or malignant (cancerous), with the latter posing a more severe threat to a patient's health. The incidence of brain tumors varies worldwide, but according to recent estimates, about 308,000 new cases of primary brain and central nervous system tumors are diagnosed annually, with higher mortality rates associated with malignant tumors. The survival rate for patients with malignant brain tumors remains low, with a 5-year survival rate of around 36% around the world, highlighting the critical need for early and accurate diagnosis. The causes of brain tumors are still largely unknown, although genetic predispositions and environmental factors such as exposure to radiation have been linked to increased risk [1]. Brain tumors can lead to severe neurological effects, including headaches, seizures, cognitive impairments, and personality changes, depending on the tumor's size, location, and growth rate [2]. Timely diagnosis is crucial in managing the disease and improving patient outcomes, as early detection often allows for more effective treatment options such as surgery, radiation therapy, and chemotherapy [3].

Traditionally, brain tumors are diagnosed through imaging techniques such as magnetic resonance imaging (MRI) and computed tomography (CT) scans, which provide detailed views of brain structures [4]. However, the manual analysis of these medical images is time-consuming and requires highly skilled radiologists. It is prone to human error, especially in complex cases where small or irregular tumors may be overlooked. The variability in interpretation between radiologists further complicates the process, making it difficult to ensure consistent and reliable diagnosis [5]. As a result, manual analysis alone is insufficient for handling the growing demand for faster and more accurate diagnostic methods in modern healthcare. The need for automation in medical imaging has become increasingly apparent in recent years [6]. Automated systems can assist radiologists in identifying brain tumors more accurately and efficiently, reducing the burden on healthcare professionals and potentially improving patient outcomes. Machine learning and deep learning (DL) methods have shown great promise in medical image analysis [7]. These techniques leverage large datasets to learn intricate patterns within images, enabling the detection of abnormalities such as brain tumors with greater precision than traditional methods. Among these approaches, convolutional neural networks (CNNs) have been widely used for tasks such as image classification and segmentation [8], proving effective in recognizing complex structures within medical images.

However, one of the key challenges in developing reliable AI models for brain tumor detection is the scarcity of large, diverse, and well-annotated datasets [9]. This is where generative adversarial networks (GANs) play a crucial role. GANs are a class of DL models that generate synthetic data by learning the distribution of real datasets. In the context of medical imaging, GANs can be used to create realistic synthetic images, effectively augmenting small datasets and improving model generalization. By introducing variability and new data points, GANs help address the issue of overfitting and enhance the model's ability to detect tumors in unseen data. The proposed system leverages GANs for data augmentation, creating synthetic MRI images to address the dataset limitations in brain tumor detection. By integrating GANs with a pre-trained ResNet50 model for feature extraction and classification, this hybrid approach aims to improve the accuracy, precision, and reliability of automated brain tumor detection systems. This research addresses the critical gap in existing diagnostic tools by offering a scalable, automated solution that enhances early diagnosis and treatment outcomes for brain tumor patients.

6.2   Literature review

Brain tumors, caused by abnormal cell growth inside the brain or surrounding tissues, require early detection for effective treatment. Traditional diagnostic practices involving MRI or CT scans rely heavily on manual interpretation by radiologists, which can be labor-intensive and prone to variability in results. These challenges, coupled with the need for quicker and more accurate diagnosis, have driven the development of automated detection systems based on machine learning and DL [10]. Over the years, CNNs have emerged as a leading approach for medical image analysis, particularly for brain tumor detection and segmentation [11].

Early studies on CNNs demonstrated their potential to recognize tumors from medical images by leveraging pattern recognition capabilities. Various architectures such as VGG-16, ResNet-50, and Inception V3 have been used, often in conjunction with transfer learning to improve accuracy. Transfer learning allows pre-trained models on large datasets to be fine-tuned for specific tasks like tumor detection, saving both time and computational resources [12]. This approach has been particularly effective in addressing the need for more efficient diagnostic systems. Some studies have reported significant improvements by combining CNNs with temporal models like long short-term memory networks to handle sequential data [13].

However, while these techniques show promising results, a critical challenge in medical imaging remains: insufficient and imbalanced datasets. Limited access to diverse, well-annotated brain tumor images makes it difficult to train robust models that generalize well to unseen data. This is where GANs play an essential role [14]. GANs, a class of generative models, help by generating synthetic data that mimics the real distribution of medical images. They consist of two components: a generator, which creates fake images, and a discriminator, which distinguishes between real and synthetic images. Through this adversarial training, GANs can produce highly realistic MRI images, augmenting datasets and improving the performance of DL models [15].

Several studies have integrated GANs into brain tumor detection pipelines. For instance, Khekare *et al.* [16] employed GANs to generate synthetic MRI data, enhancing the generalization of a tumor detection model. Similarly, Kerai and

Khekare [17] used GAN-augmented datasets to improve the precision of tumor classification systems. Such augmented datasets mitigate overfitting, a common issue in DL models when trained on small datasets, by providing diverse training examples. Hybrid models that combine GANs with CNNs, such as U-Net and ResNet, have also achieved state-of-the-art (SOTA) segmentation results. These hybrid approaches capitalize on the strengths of both GANs (data generation) and CNNs (feature extraction).

Incorporating generative models has not been without challenges. Training GANs can be computationally intensive, requiring extensive resources and time. Furthermore, GANs are prone to instability during training, resulting in mode collapse, where the generator produces limited variations in output. This issue can limit the diversity of synthetic images, making it difficult to capture all potential tumor variations. To overcome these challenges, researchers have explored optimization techniques to improve model stability and training efficiency. For example, Bayesian optimization has been proposed to fine-tune hyperparameters, including learning rates, batch sizes, and optimizer settings, yielding better performance compared to traditional methods like random search or genetic algorithms.

The application of YOLOv7, a real-time object detection model, demonstrates the importance of hyperparameter optimization in brain tumor detection. YOLOv7 uses Bayesian optimization to efficiently search the hyperparameter space, achieving superior performance compared to Genetic Algorithm and random search. The study highlights that Bayesian optimization is approximately 1.5 times faster than random search and four times faster than GA, making it ideal for scenarios with limited computational resources. Moreover, this optimization process helps the YOLOv7 model achieve better precision and recall, which are critical metrics in medical imaging for reducing false negatives.

Generative AI also plays a critical role in reducing bias and ensuring that AI models generalize well across different patient populations. The GAN-based approach introduces synthetic variability, helping to overcome the scarcity of specific tumor types in real datasets. Recent research proposed a two-stage model that combines CycleGAN with diffusion models, enabling the transformation of healthy MRI images into diseased states [18]. This helps simulate various tumor conditions and provides more balanced datasets for training DL models. Although promising, such advanced models require significant computational power, which can limit their use in real-world clinical settings.

Despite these advances, certain challenges remain in the deployment of AI-driven diagnostic tools in healthcare. Ethical considerations such as patient privacy, data security, and algorithmic transparency need to be addressed to ensure trust and adoption by medical practitioners Interpretability of AI models is also crucial, as clinicians need to understand how the models arrive at specific predictions to incorporate them into their workflows confidently. Future research should focus on developing explainable AI techniques to bridge the gap between AI models and clinical practice. Furthermore, regulatory approval will play a pivotal role in the widespread adoption of these technologies, ensuring they meet the necessary standards for safety and reliability (Table 6.1).

Table 6.1 Techniques utilized by earlier researchers in the detection of brain tumors

Approach used	Strengths	Limitations
Two-stage generative model (TSGM) Variance exploding joint diffusion (VE-JP) model [18]	The model eliminates the need for annotated training data, reducing reliance on costly, time-consuming manual Labels. Effective in generating paired images from unpaired data, handling the transformation from healthy to diseased states. By learning joint distributions, it more precisely detects abnormalities and addresses uncertainty in image reconstructions	The combined cycle GAN and diffusion model increase computational complexity, requiring significant resources and training time and can suffer from instability and mode collapse during training, leading to poor reconstructions Despite improvements from regularization and diffusion models, the diseased-to-healthy image translation remains challenging
adGAN (adversarial generative adversarial network) [19]	By progressively refining the fake pool during training, adGAN simulates abnormal data effectively, ensuring that the generated samples represent the boundary area of the normal distribution. It also avoids the reconstruction process typical of other GAN-based models, making it faster and more efficient for anomaly detection	The performance of adGAN can be sensitive to hyperparameter settings, especially the weight assigned to concentration loss. Although adGAN performs well, its performance on more complex real-world datasets (like BraTS) shows some decline, indicating room for improvement in handling highly variable data
VAE, GAN, GradCAM [20]	The study is the most extensive comparison of UPD methods in medical imaging, covering diverse datasets and approaches. It also demonstrates that domain-specific pre-training can improve performance, especially for certain feature-modeling methods	Image-reconstruction methods are sensitive to the intensity differences between normal and abnormal regions, affecting their localization performance for low-contrast anomalies
GANs, U-Net CNN, ResNetV2 CNN, Xception CNN [21]	Provides a comprehensive solution for brain tumor detection, segmentation, and classification	Combining multiple DL models can increase computational complexity and resource requirements
VGG16 [22]	Utilizing VGG16's pre-trained weights shortens training time and improves accuracy by leveraging prior knowledge of image features. Additional CNN	By freezing the VGG16 layers, the model may not fully adapt to domain-specific features unique to medical imaging, potentially restricting further

(Continues)

Table 6.1 (*Continued*)

Approach used	Strengths	Limitations
	layers allow the model to capture more complex features specific to brain tumors that are not present in the original ImageNet training data	performance improvements. The performance gap between training and validation accuracy suggests a risk of overfitting, especially if the model is highly specialized to the training data
PNN [12]	Automatic utilization of ROIs within tumor areas. Learning vector quantization helps in model training. Simulation results showed 100% accuracy with modified PNN when the spread value is 1	Computational time and accuracy of image processing algorithms were less compared to the neural network approach
SVM, logistic regression, CNN [23]	Provides a detailed methodology for data preparation, model training, and evaluation	The accuracy or F1 score for detecting other tumor types (e.g., glioma, meningioma) is not mentioned
YOLOv7 [24]	Bayesian optimization was the most efficient method, being 1.5 times faster than random search and four times faster than genetic algorithm	Random search lacks learning from previous iterations. Genetic algorithm risks getting trapped in local optima. Bayesian optimization struggles with highly non-linear spaces and discrete parameter handling
WU-Net++ [25]	The weighted pooling function in each convolution layer increases the effectiveness of basic feature extraction. It reduces the size of an attribute map required for segmentation, improving the model's performance	The model has many trainable parameters (14,387,041), which can make it computationally expensive to train and deploy
CNN, U-Net [26]	Some methods work well for complete tumor regions	DL models require high computing power and large memory

6.3   Methodology

6.3.1   Data acquisition and pre-processing

The dataset in this study consisted of brain MRI images, divided into two folders: comprising two sets of brains with tumors, and those of normal individuals, respectively. The pictures were availed and resized to a unified size of 256×256 pixels for the sake of processing efficiency. Figure 6.1 shows the brain tumor images of both classes.

6.3.2   Data augmentation

To supplement the limited data the authors used data augmentation to increase the size of the dataset and hence improve the generalization ability of the system. These include horizontal flipping of the images and the vertical flipping of the images and flipping of images both horizontally and vertically. The augmented dataset consisted of 1,000 images for each class (normal and tumor). Figure 6.2 shows augmented pictures of both the normal and tumor class.

6.3.3   Data preparation

The augmented images were combined, and corresponding labels were assigned (0 for normal and 1 for tumor). The complete dataset is bifurcated as 70% for training and 30% for testing.

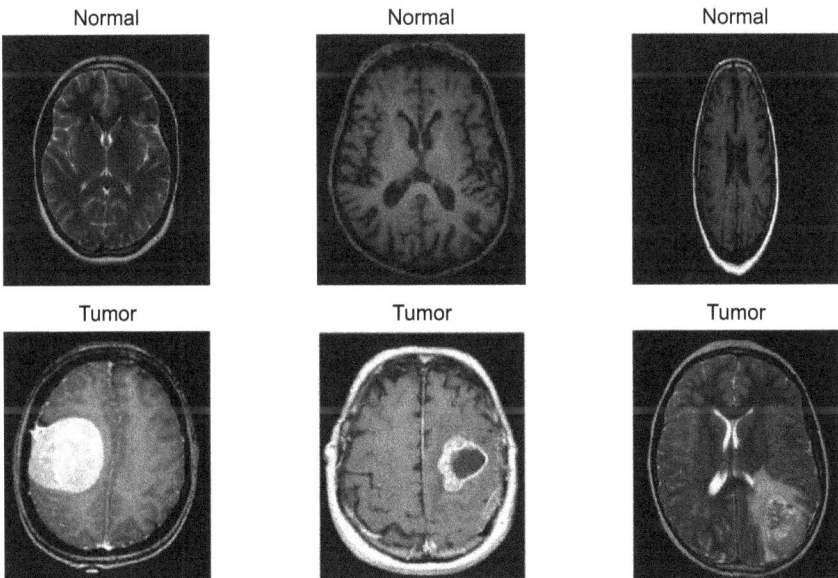

Figure 6.1   Brain tumor images of both the classes

Augmented Normal   Augmented Normal   Augmented Normal

Augmented Tumor   Augmented Tumor   Augmented Tumor

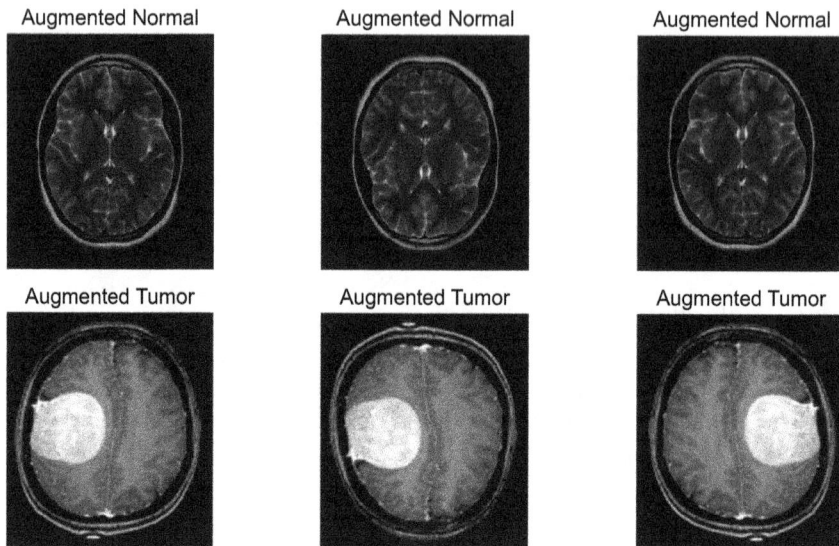

Figure 6.2   Augmented images of both the normal and tumor class

6.3.4   Model architecture

The model was based on a GAN and a pre-trained ResNet50 so constructed. The architecture of GAN employed a creator and a discriminator, implemented using CNNs. The discriminator was a classifier that revealed whether the input pictures were genuine or fake, while the generator drew realistic pictures that could trick the discriminator. Feature extraction was accomplished using a ResNet50 system pre-trained on the ImageNet dataset as the attribute extractor. Its input was flattened and followed a dense layer with a dropout layer, and then the last dense level with a sigmoid activation formula for binary classification.

6.3.5   Model training

The combined model, consisting of the GAN and the ResNet50 feature extractor, was trained on the augmented dataset. During training, the ResNet50 layers were frozen, and only the GAN and the additional dense layers were updated. During the training process, we froze the weights of the ResNet50 layers to preserve the pre-trained features while allowing the GAN components and additional dense layers to be updated. This transfer learning approach enabled us to leverage general image features while fine-tuning the model for our specific brain tumor detection task.

The model was trained for 10 epochs with a batch size of 32, using the binary cross-entropy loss function and the Adam optimizer. The accuracy of the model was evaluated on the held-out testing set. This methodology leveraged the strengths of both GANs and pre-trained models to accurately classify brain tumors. The data augmentation methods helped enhance the volume and complexity of the training data, potentially improving the system's performance and generalization capability.

When using the concept of AI for medical diagnosis, we ensured that we considered the ethical issues surrounding its application at each stage of development. To address the limits of generalizing data collected online, we took steps to more effectively protect our subjects' identities and to reduce possible prejudicial dangers in our proposed model. More work will be done in the future to verify the model against the traditional techniques and assess the generalization capability of the model to other medical imaging modalities.

6.4　Architecture diagram

The architecture diagram is shown in Figure 6.3. The architecture reflects the training process of a hybrid system that is eventually applied to classifying brain

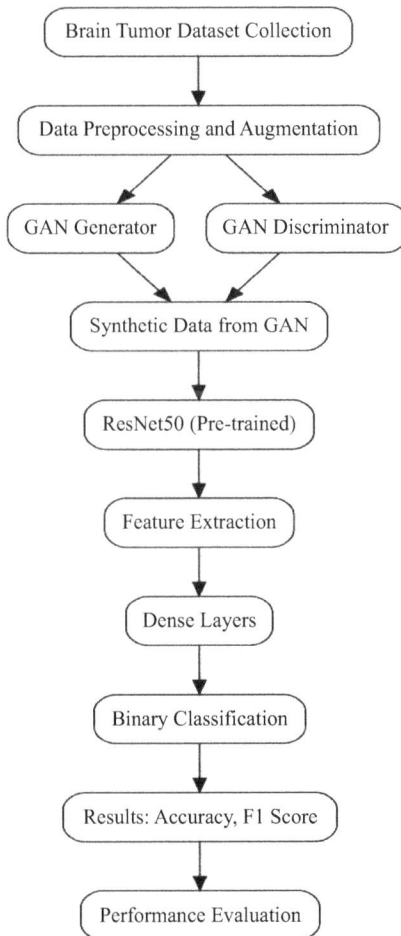

Figure 6.3　The proposed brain tumor detection framework

tumor data sets through binary classification. It consists of a preliminary stage during which the brain tumor dataset is collected, followed by pre-processing and enhancement that increases the dataset quality. The GAN technique is exploited to create numerous data, and as an output, the system performance is improved. Image attributes are then extracted using a ResNet50 neural network which has been trained prior. These features are whole hounded through dense layers, and the model gives a pitch whether an image contains a brain tumor or not. The evaluations are carried out through metrics of precision and F1 score which makes the system fast, precise, and efficient in the detection of brain tumors.

6.5   Dataset specifications

The dataset used for this study comprises MRI images sourced from Kaggle, specifically the "Brain MRI Images for Brain Tumor Detection" dataset. It contains a total of 253 images, with 155 labeled as positive cases (images showing the presence of a tumor) and 98 as negative cases (images without a tumor). This results in a class distribution of 61.3% positive and 38.7% negative examples. The images, available in JPG format, are used for binary classification to identify the presence or absence of tumors. The dataset's balanced representation of both cases allows for a comprehensive analysis of the study's focus.

There are certain important pieces of information missing from the dataset including the demography of the patients, the nature of the tumor, either the classification or the type, and the parameters through which the images were acquired. Some of these restrictions were considered while designing the generative AI strategy, and proper measures were taken to overcome these drawbacks and achieve the best result from using this model. The environment was prepared for the chapter with the help of Google Collab using T4 GPU as well and Google Drive was used to upload and download datasets consisting of images. This setup is greatly helpful for easily training ML models and taking advantage of Collab's GPU for computation (Table 6.2).

Table 6.2   Dataset specifications

Characteristic	Details
Dataset source	Kaggle
Total images	253
Positive cases (yes)	155
Negative cases (no)	98
Image format	JPG
Classification type	Binary (tumor/no tumor)

6.6   Results and discussion

We incorporated GANs as a key component to address the challenge of limited dataset availability. The GAN was designed with a generator and discriminator, both implemented using CNNs. The generator was trained to produce synthetic brain MRI images, and the discriminator was taught to differentiate between real and generated images. Using this adversarial process, the researchers were able to synthesize realistic images which, in this case, looked like genuine MRI scans. We also used these synthetic images to increase our dataset which was used in training the hybrid GAN+ResNet50 model. The incorporation of the data augmentation technique through GAN contributed to the better performance of the model on synthesized images of brain tumors.

6.6.1   Qualitative results—synthetic image generation

Using GAN, we generated synthetic brain MRI images for both tumor and non-tumor classes. These images were visually inspected for realism and compared with the original images in the dataset. The generated images closely mimicked the distribution and characteristics of the real MRI scans, particularly in terms of texture and tumor appearance. Figures 6.4 and 6.5 show examples of synthetic brain tumor and non-tumor MRI images generated by the GAN model.

6.6.2   Quantitative results—model performance

The combined model, integrating GAN with a pre-trained ResNet50, was evaluated on both the training and testing datasets. By using the GAN-generated synthetic images alongside the real images, we significantly enhanced the model's ability to

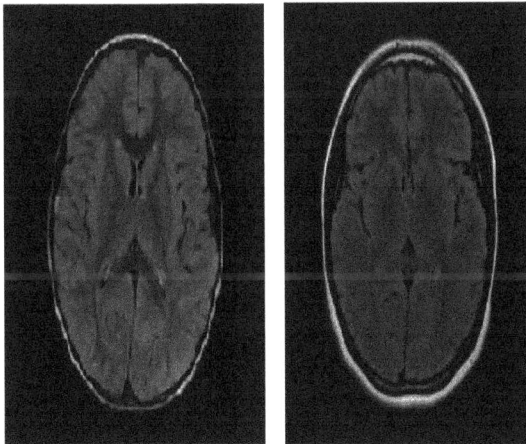

Figure 6.4   Normal synthetic

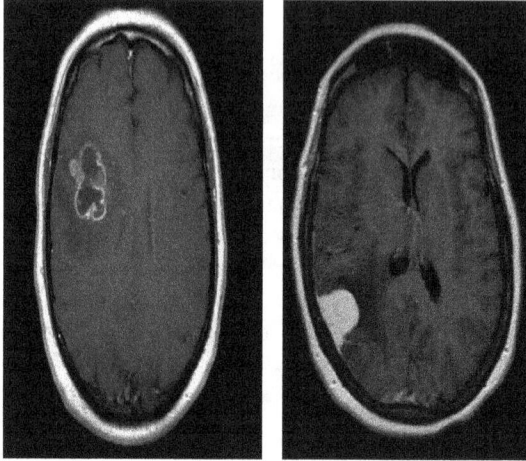

Figure 6.5   Tumor synthetic

classify brain MRI scans as either tumor or non-tumor. The model achieved an accuracy of 98.87% on the training dataset, and a 92.43% accuracy on the validation set, demonstrating superior performance in comparison to standalone CNN models. Key performance metrics such as precision, recall, F1-score, and area under the receiver operating characteristic curve (AUC-ROC) were computed to evaluate the classification results:

6.6.2.1   Accuracy

Accuracy is calculated by splitting the quantity of correctly predicted samples by the number of samples within the data set. The formula used to determine accuracy is as follows:

$$\text{Accuracy} = \left(\frac{TN + TP}{TP + TN + FP + FN} \right) \times 100\% \qquad (6.1)$$

where

TP is true positive;
TN is true negative;
FN is false negative;
FP is false positive.

6.6.2.2   Area under the curve

AUC is the total area lying under the curve. In sum, the model's ability to distinguish positive and negative classes is being evaluated by the AUC. The larger the AUC value the more successful the model.

6.6.2.3 Recall

Recall is one of the most important indicators that may be used to assess the results of an ML algorithm. It is calculated from the following equation:

$$\text{Recall} = \frac{TP}{TP + FN} \tag{6.2}$$

whereas

TP is true positive;
FN is false negative.

Figure 6.6 shows the confusion matrix of the proposed model (GAN +ResNetT50). Figure 6.7 shows the receiver operating characteristics (ROC) curve for the proposed model (GAN+ResNetT50). The hybrid model combining a GAN and a pre-trained ResNet50 architecture demonstrated exceptional capability in discriminating between brain MRI images with and without tumors. The Area Under the ROC Curve score achieved by the model was an impressive 0.96 on the training dataset. An AUC-ROC score close to 1 indicates an excellent ability to distinguish between the two classes, with minimal false positives and false negatives.

This high AUC-ROC value suggests that the proposed GAN-based data augmentation approach, coupled with the powerful feature extraction capabilities of the ResNet50 model, has significantly enhanced the model's performance in brain tumor detection. The incorporation of synthetic data generated by the GAN has

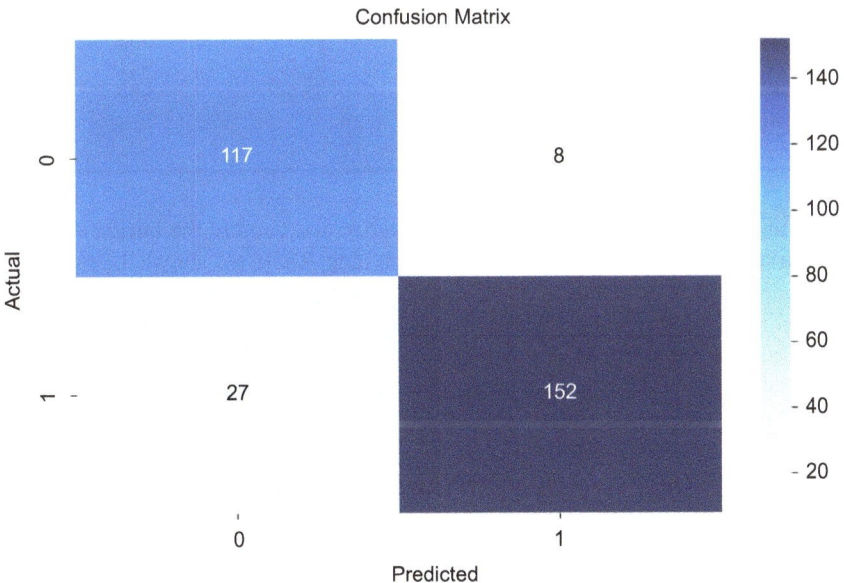

Figure 6.6   Confusion matrix of the proposed model (GAN+ResNetT50)

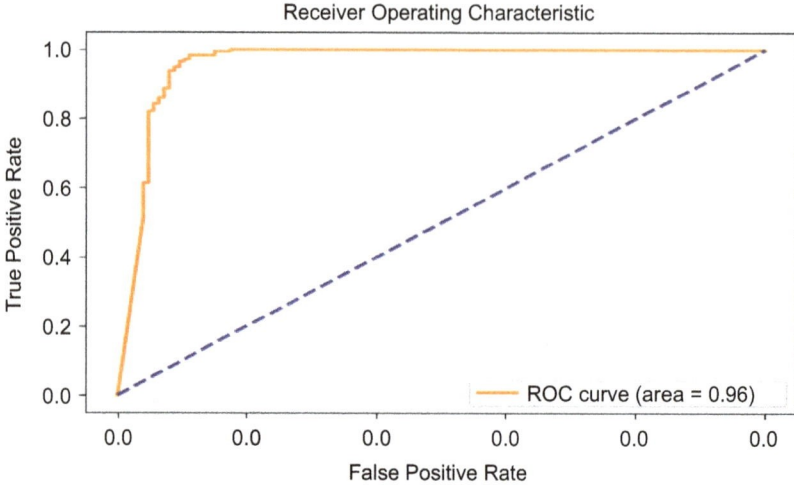

Figure 6.7   Receiver operating characteristics (ROC) curve proposed model (GAN+ResNetT50)

Table 6.3   Evaluation metrics of models on test data

Model	Precision (in %)	Recall (in %)	F1 score (in %)	Accuracy (in %)
Google Net	60.29	70.39	64.95	55.26
VGG16	72.41	93.85	81.75	75.33
DenseNet	58.8	100	74.1	58.8
Custom CNN	90.0	95.5	92.6	91.0
Proposed model (GAN+Re-sNetT50)	93.74	92.14	92.93	98.87

likely improved the model's ability to generalize and capture the intricate patterns and variations present in brain tumor imaging data. Table 6.3 shows the evaluation metrics of models on test data. Table 6.4 shows the performance evaluation of brain tumor detection techniques. The incorporation of synthetic data helped improve both the sensitivity (recall) and precision of the model. This indicates that the GAN model was instrumental in generating diverse training samples that contributed to better generalization.

6.6.3   Performance comparison with SOTA models

The proposed GAN+ResNet50 model is compared with several SOTA models, including Google Net, VGG16, and DenseNet121.

The results clearly show the superiority of our proposed model, which leverages GANs for data augmentation and a pre-trained ResNet50 for feature extraction.

Table 6.4 Performance evaluation of brain tumor detection techniques

Reference	Model	Dataset	Performance
[18]	CNN	The dataset consists of 3264 MR images, which include 926 pictures of glioma tumors, 937 pictures of meningioma tumors, 500 pictures without any tumors, and 901 pictures of pituitary tumors	Accuracy: CNN (proposed model): 93.3% ResNet-50: 81.1% VGG16: 71.6% Inception V3: 80%
[19]	Base model VGG16 With the addition of CNN layers	A publicly available Kaggle brain tumor dataset containing MRI scans of meningioma, pituitary, glioma, and healthy brain images. The image collection comprised 7,023 samples in total. The majority, 5,712 images, were allocated to the training set. For testing purposes, 1,263 images were set aside. The remaining 48 images formed a small validation subset	Accuracy of 96.52% F1 scores for each class: glioma (0.95), meningioma (0.93), no tumor (1.00), pituitary (0.98)
[20]	CNN	A publicly available Kaggle brain tumor dataset containing MRI scans of meningioma, pituitary, glioma, and healthy brain images. The dataset had 7,023 images, with 5,712 used for training, 1,263 for testing, and 48 for validation	Validation accuracy: 0.9782 Evaluation accuracy: 0.9715760636329651
[21]	GANs	A publicly available Kaggle brain tumor dataset containing MRI scans of meningioma, pituitary, glioma, and healthy brain images. The dataset had 7,023 images, with 5,712 used for training, 1,263 for testing, and 48 for validation	Validation accuracy: 95.3%
[22]	Hybrid CNN-LSTM model	The data used in this research is MRI brain tumor data obtained from Kaggle, a publicly available database. The data consists of 253 pictures, with 98 images in the "no tumor" folder and 155 pictures in the "tumor" folder	Accuracy—99.1% F1 score—99.0%
[12]	Canny edge detection algorithm, PNN	The research involved the use of MRI to acquire a set of brain scans. The dataset was composed of 64 grayscale formatted	Accuracy—100%

(Continues)

Table 6.4 (Continued)

Reference	Model	Dataset	Performance
		images with each image having a dimension of 220 × 220 pixels. To verify the effectiveness of their approach, the researchers split the dataset into two equal groups. For the testing data, they selected the scans of 18 randomly selected patients. The remaining 46 images were used for the training of the system	
[23]	SVM, CNN, logistic regression	A publicly available Kaggle brain tumor dataset containing MRI scans of meningioma, pituitary, glioma, and healthy brain images. The dataset had 7,023 images, with 5,712 used for training, 1,263 for testing, and 48 for validation	Validation Accuracy—85.34%, training Accuracy—94.64%
[24]	YOLOv7 object detection algorithm	BraTS2020 dataset from the MICCAI benchmark challenge, containing 369 3D MRI images with four patterns (T1, T2, T1CE, and FLAIR)	F1 score: 0.888
[25]	WU-Net++	BraTS 2018 dataset for brain tumor segmentation (210 high-grade glioma patients) ATLAS V2.1 dataset for intracranial hemorrhage classification TCIA and BTCV datasets for multi-organ segmentation from abdominal CT scans	Brain tumor segmentation (BraTS 2018): Whole tumor: F1 score = 0.94 Core tumor: F1 score = 0.88 Enhancing tumor: F1 score = 0.95 Intracranial hemorrhage classification (ATLAS V2.1): Accuracy = 0.9949, F1 score = 0.9041
[26]	CNN, U-Net	BraTS (2012–2020 challenges) Harvard RIDER ISLES (2015–2017)	Not explicitly mentioned

6.7 Conclusion

This study demonstrates the effectiveness of GANs in addressing the challenge of limited brain tumor imaging datasets. By augmenting MRI data with synthetically generated images, we developed a hybrid model that integrates GANs for data generation and ResNet50 for feature extraction and classification. The model demonstrated a notable improvement in brain tumor detection accuracy and AUC-ROC score. These results confirm that GAN-based data augmentation can significantly enhance the generalization and performance of diagnostic models by generating diverse, realistic imaging data However, several challenges remain, especially in clinical adoption. Ethical considerations such as data privacy, informed consent, and bias must be addressed before widespread implementation in healthcare settings. Additionally, ensuring model interpretability and trustworthiness is essential for gaining clinical acceptance. Future research should aim to validate this approach across different medical imaging modalities, refine the interpretability of AI models, and engage with regulatory bodies to establish safe and responsible frameworks for AI deployment in clinical environments.

References

[1] Khalighi S, Reddy K, and Midya A. Artificial intelligence in neuro-oncology: Advances and challenges in brain tumor diagnosis, prognosis, and precision treatment. *npj Precision Oncology*, vol. 8, p. 80, 2024, https://doi.org/10.1038/s41698-024-00575-0.

[2] Lagogiannis I, Meissen F, Kaissis G, and Rueckert D. Unsupervised pathology detection: A deep dive into the state of the art. *IEEE Transactions on Medical Imaging*, vol. 43, no. 1, pp. 241–252, 2024, https://doi.org/10.1109/TMI.2023.3298093.

[3] Hossain T, Shishir FS, Ashraf M, Al Nasim MA, and Muhammad Shah F. Brain tumor detection using convolutional neural network. *1st International Conference on Advances in Science, Engineering and Robotics Technology (ICASERT)*, Dhaka, Bangladesh, 2019, pp. 1–6, https://doi.org/10.1109/ICASERT.2019.8934561.

[4] Soundarya C, Kalaiselvi A, and Surya J. Brain tumor detection using image processing. *8th International Conference on Advanced Computing and Communication Systems (ICACCS)*, Coimbatore, India, 2022, pp. 582–587, https://doi.org/10.1109/ICACCS54159.2022.9785298.

[5] Khekare G, and Verma P. Prophetic probe of accidents in Indian smart cities using machine learning. In: Bhateja V, Satapathy SC, Travieso-González CM, and Aradhya VNM (eds), *Data Engineering and Intelligent Computing*. Advances in Intelligent Systems and Computing, vol. 1407, 2021, Springer, Singapore, https://doi.org/10.1007/978-981-16-0171-2_18

[6] Anaya-Isaza A, Mera-Jiménez L, Verdugo-Alejo L, and Sarasti L. Optimizing MRI-based brain tumor classification and detection using AI: A

comparative analysis of neural networks, transfer learning, data augmentation, and the cross-transformer network. *European Journal of Radiology Open*, vol. 10, p. 100484, 2023, https://doi.org/10.1016/j.ejro.2023.100484. PMID: 36950474; PMCID: PMC10027502.

[7]   Alsubai S, Khan HU, Alqahtani A, Sha M, Abbas S, and Mohammad UG. Ensemble deep learning for brain tumor detection. *Frontiers in Computational Neuroscience*, vol. 16, p. 1005617, 2022, https://doi.org/10.3389/fncom.2022.1005617. PMID: 36118133; PMCID: PMC9480978.

[8]   Shen H, Chen J, Wang R, and Zhang J. Counterfeit anomaly using generative adversarial network for anomaly detection. *IEEE Access*, vol. 8, pp. 133051–133062, 2020, https://doi.org/10.1109/ACCESS.2020.3010612.

[9]   Abdusalomov AB, Mukhiddinov M, Whangbo TK. Brain tumor detection based on deep learning approaches and magnetic resonance imaging. *Cancers (Basel)*, vol. 15, no.16, p. 4172, 2023, https://doi.org/10.3390/cancers15164172.

[10]   Das S, Dubey R, Jena B, Tsai L-W, and Saxena, S. WU-Net++: A novel enhanced Weighted U-Net++ model for brain tumor detection and segmentation from multi-parametric magnetic resonance scans. *Multimedia Tools and Applications*, vol. 10, pp. 1–24, 2024, https://doi.org/10.1007/s11042-024-18336-3.

[11]   ZainEldin H, Gamel SA, El-Kenawy EM, *et al.* Brain tumor detection and classification using deep learning and sine-cosine fitness grey wolf optimization. *Bioengineering (Basel)*, vol. 10, no. 1, p. 18, 2022, https://doi.org/10.3390/bioengineering10010018.

[12]   Hossain S, Chakrabarty A, Gadekallu TR, Alazab M, and Piran MJ. Vision transformers, ensemble model, and transfer learning leveraging explainable AI for brain tumor detection and classification. *IEEE Journal of Biomedical and Health Informatics*, vol. 28, no. 3, pp. 1261–1272, 2024, https://doi.org/10.1109/JBHI.2023.3266614.

[13]   Mathur S, and Jaiswal A. Demystifying the role of artificial intelligence in neurodegenerative diseases. In: Gaur L, Abraham A, and Ajith R (eds), *AI and Neuro-Degenerative Diseases*. Studies in Computational Intelligence, vol. 1131, 2024, Springer, Cham, https://doi.org/10.1007/978-3-031-53148-4_1

[14]   Asif S, Zhao M, Li, Y *et al.* AI-based approaches for the diagnosis of Mpox: Challenges and future prospects. *Archives of Computational Methods in Engineering*, vol. 31, pp. 3585–3617, 2024, https://doi.org/10.1007/s11831-024-10091-w

[15]   Chen, X, Xie, H, Tao, X *et al.* Artificial intelligence and multimodal data fusion for smart healthcare: topic modeling and bibliometrics. *Artificial Intelligence Review*, vol. 57, p. 91, 2024, https://doi.org/10.1007/s10462-024-10712-7

[16]   Khekare G, Masudi C, Chukka YK, and Koyyada DP. Text normalization and summarization using advanced natural language processing. *International Conference on Integrated Circuits and Communication Systems (ICICACS)*,

Raichur, India, 2024, pp. 1–6, https://doi.org/10.1109/ICICACS60521.2024.
10498983.

[17]   Kerai S, and Khekare G. Contextual embedding generation of underwater
       images using deep learning techniques. *IAES International Journal of Arti-
       ficial Intelligence (IJ-AI)*, vol. 13, no. 3, pp. 3111–3118, 2024, http://doi.org/
       10.11591/ijai.v13.i3.pp3111-3118.

[18]   Wang T-W, Shiao Y-C, Hong J-S, *et al.* Artificial intelligence detection and
       segmentation models: A systematic review and meta-analysis of brain tumors
       in magnetic resonance imaging, *Mayo Clinic Proceedings: Digital Health*,
       vol. 2, no. 1, pp. 75–91, 2024, https://doi.org/10.1016/j.mcpdig.2024.01.002.

[19]   Karthik A, Shiek Aalam S, Sivakumar M, *et al.* Improving brain tumor
       treatment with better imaging and real-time therapy using quantum dots,
       Biomedical Signal Processing and Control, vol. 95, Part B, p. 106286, 2024,
       https://doi.org/10.1016/j.bspc.2024.106286.

[20]   Khekare G, Patel Y, Nishit P, Engineer D, and Badal P. Detection of brain
       tumor using data science: A survey. *International Journal of Engineering
       Applied Sciences and Technology*, vol. 6, no. 9, pp. 176–179, 2022.

[21]   Esmaeilzadeh P. Challenges and strategies for wide-scale artificial intelli-
       gence (AI) deployment in healthcare practices: A perspective for healthcare
       organizations. *Artificial Intelligence in Medicine*, vol. 151, p. 102861, 2024,
       https://doi.org/10.1016/j.artmed.2024.102861.

[22]   Nasarian E, Alizadehsani R, Acharya UR, and Tsui K-L. Designing
       interpretable ML system to enhance trust in healthcare: A systematic review
       to proposed responsible clinician-AI-collaboration framework. *Information
       Fusion*, vol. 108, p. 102412, 2024, https://doi.org/10.1016/j.inffus.2024.
       102412.

[23]   Xu M, Guo L, and Wu H-C. Novel robust automatic brain-tumor detection
       and segmentation using magnetic resonance imaging. *IEEE Sensors Journal*,
       vol. 24, no. 7, pp. 10957–10964, 2024, https://doi.org/10.1109/JSEN.2024.
       3367123.

[24]   Ting H, and Liu M. Multimodal transformer of incomplete MRI data for
       brain tumor segmentation. *IEEE Journal of Biomedical and Health Infor-
       matics*, vol. 28, no. 1, pp. 89–99, 2024, https://doi.org/10.1109/JBHI.2023.
       3286689.

[25]   Wang W, Cui Z-X, Cheng G, *et al.* A two-stage generative model with
       CycleGAN and joint diffusion for MRI-based brain tumor detection. *IEEE
       Journal of Biomedical and Health Informatics*, vol. 28, no. 6, pp. 3534–3544,
       2024, https://doi.org/10.1109/JBHI.2024.3373018.

[26]   Mahmud MI, Mamun M, and Abdelgawad A. A deep analysis of brain tumor
       detection from MR images using deep learning networks. *Algorithms*, vol.
       16, p. 176, 2023.

Chapter 7

A systematic review of GAN-based models in data synthesis for privacy protection

M. Srimathi[1], B. Rajesh Kanna[1] and Ulrich Furbach[2]

Abstract

In today's digital era, ensuring the privacy and security of data is crucial as large volumes of data are generated and shared. Data privacy, also known as information privacy, involves the proper storage, access, retention, immutability, and security of sensitive data. This includes the appropriate handling of personally identifiable information such as names, addresses, social security numbers, and credit card numbers. Among various data privacy methods, generative adversarial networks (GANs) are one of the recent and advanced approaches for generating realistic synthetic data. GANs enhance data privacy by creating synthetic data that maintains the characteristics of the original data while masking sensitive information, allowing for secure data sharing and analysis. This work systematically reviews existing data synthesis models, focusing on GAN models used for data privacy, compares these methods and models, and discusses their advantages and disadvantages.

Keywords: Data privacy; generative adversarial networks; data synthesis; generative models

7.1 Introduction

Automatic synthesis of data refers to the generation of new data instances using machine learning techniques without the need for manual data collection or labeling [1]. This method is beneficial for tasks such as data augmentation, anomaly detection, and domain translation, where additional data samples can enhance model performance and enable new applications. It is particularly beneficial when facing limited or imbalanced data. It facilitates the development of deep learning techniques, such as transfer learning with deep neural networks [2], and researchers can develop novel datasets to enhance model accuracy and resilience. The

[1]Computer Science (Artificial Intelligence & Machine Learning), Rajiv Gandhi National Institute of Youth Development, India
[2]Department of Computer Science, University of Koblenz, Germany

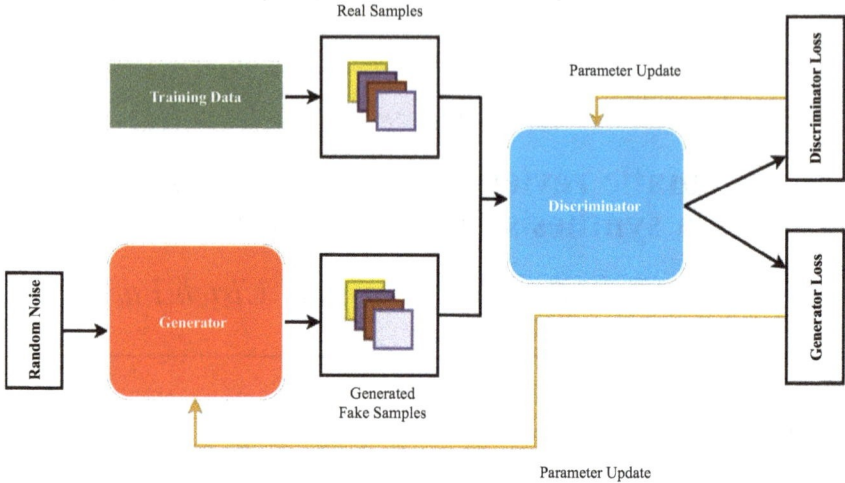

Figure 7.1   An architectural representation of GAN

utilization of automatic data synthesis spans various practical domains like cyberse-curity systems, smart cities, healthcare, e-commerce, and agriculture [3], aiming to boost the intelligence and functionalities of real-world applications. Furthermore, within the realm of consumer credit risk prediction, machine learning methodologies have been leveraged to build nonlinear nonparametric models, significantly elevating classification accuracies, and resulting in cost efficiencies and improved risk prog-nostication amid financial downturns [4].

Generative adversarial networks (GANs) are particularly effective in the automatic synthesis of data due to their ability to produce realistic and diverse samples. In a GAN framework, two neural networks—a generator and a dis-criminator—engage in an adversarial training process. The generator creates syn-thetic data that mimics real data, while the discriminator learns to distinguish between real and generated data. This interaction results in synthetic data that accurately reflects the underlying data distribution, as depicted in the architectural representation of GANs in Figure 7.1 [5].

One of the principal advantages of GANs lies in their capacity to enhance data privacy protection. By producing realistic synthetic data, GANs can effec-tively substitute sensitive information in various applications, such as training machine learning algorithms or conducting empirical research. This capability diminishes the reliance on actual private data, thereby mitigating the risk of disclosing sensitive information, including personally identifiable information (PII). In contrast to conventional methodologies, which may either eliminate or obfuscate data but consequently compromise data integrity, GANs generate artificial data that retains essential patterns from the original dataset. This char-acteristic renders them particularly valuable for institutions that must adhere to rigorous privacy regulations, such as the General Data Protection Regulation and the Health Insurance Portability and Accountability Act. For instance, consider a healthcare institution that is required to share patient data for research purposes. Rather than disseminating actual data, which could contravene privacy legislation, it can employ GANs to produce synthetic patient data that preserves the same statistical characteristics without compromising individual anonymity. This approach not only safeguards privacy but also enables researchers to pursue their investigations without legal apprehensions. Additionally, GANs prove instrumental in addressing challenges related to biased or imbalanced datasets. For example, if a corporation possesses a disproportionate number of exemplars across various customer demographics, GANs can generate supplementary synthetic instances to equilibrate the dataset. This intervention contributes to enhancing the equity of machine learning models. GANs are currently being utilized in privacy-preserving applications, such as establishing secure communication pathways via steganography [6], protecting public data dissemination within wireless sensor networks [7], fortifying supervised learning models with privacy-centric mechanisms [8], and defending against membership inference attacks, wherein adversaries attempt to ascertain whether a specific data point was incorporated into a model's training dataset [9]. They are also employed in federated learning contexts, where data remains decentralized and secure across multiple devices, utilizing privacy-preserving image distribution methodologies [10]. By providing adaptable and secure mechanisms for data management, GANs are forging new pathways for enhanced privacy practices across diverse industries, while simultaneously fostering greater collaboration among researchers and developers.

In this study, we conducted a systematic review of GANs for data generation, focusing on their application in safeguarding data privacy across six main areas: image data synthesis, video data synthesis, textual data synthesis, speech data synthesis, spatiotemporal data synthesis, and graph data synthesis, depending on the type of data being generated. Figure 7.2 illustrates the effective use of various GANs across these different domains.

Section 7.2 focuses on image data synthesis, exploring three main applications: face images, medical images, and street-view images, and discussing the associated privacy concerns and protection models. Section 7.3 addresses video data synthesis, with a particular emphasis on video event detection. Section 7.4 examines textual data synthesis, covering textual data, natural language processing (NLP), public records, and medical records. Section 7.5 is dedicated to speech data synthesis, discussing remote health monitoring and voice assistants. Section 7.6 explores spatio-temporal data synthesis, particularly in the context of location-based services (LBSs). Section 7.7 investigates graph data synthesis, focusing on graph sharing and embedding. Each section includes a detailed discussion of the privacy models relevant to the respective applications. Section 7.8 will address the limitations of current privacy models and techniques. Finally, Section 7.9 will provide the conclusion and suggest directions for future research in data privacy.

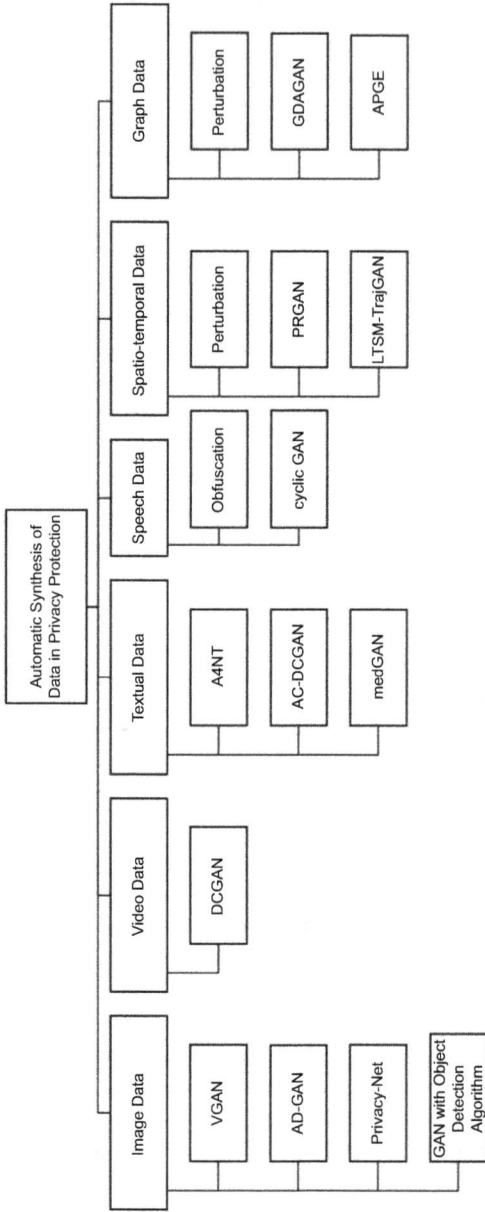

Figure 7.2 Categorization of GAN-based data synthesis models for privacy protection

7.2 Image data synthesis

In image data synthesis, the protection is applied to prevent any sensitive visual data that can be used or viewed without authorization from its owner. This also includes protecting photos that show PII or identifiable information, like license plates, facial features, and so forth in efforts to limit identity theft or privacy infringement. There are other ways to preserve privacy for image data as well—some of the most straightforward include encryption (to protect against leaks in storage and/or communication), certain types of anonymizations, such as face-masking or blurring identifiable features (e.g., by setting them recorded pixels values use an encrypted key) on images. Other processes around synthetic data generation techniques have been used where GANs can produce realistic-looking non-identifiable images that can serve analytical insight and ML training purposes without revealing personal details inputted into machine-learning models. Image data privacy is a crucial issue in the contemporary digital realm, primarily due to the presence of sensitive data within images, including facial characteristics, medical information, and location details. The emergence of GANs has provided a robust solution to tackle these privacy concerns by facilitating the creation of synthetic images that can obscure or de-identify sensitive information while upholding data utility. Several GAN-based strategies have been devised for diverse applications such as image steganography, image anonymization, and image encoding, extending beyond conventional image categories like facial, medical, or street-view images.

GANs have been applied in various real-world scenarios, particularly in the realm of image data privacy, such as safeguarding sensitive medical information like chest X-ray data for the diagnosis of COVID-19 pneumonia. Innovative frameworks like compressive privacy GAN (CPGAN) [11], federated differentially private GAN (FedDPGAN) [12], and FedGP [13] have been introduced by researchers to tackle privacy issues by utilizing GANs to produce synthetic data while ensuring privacy preservation through methods such as differential privacy and federated learning. Moreover, advancements in privacy protection strategies encompass the utilization of Hensel's Lemma for reducing dimensionality and the application of differential privacy on compacted datasets, thereby establishing robust privacy measures without compromising accuracy [14]. Furthermore, adversarial reconstruction learning frameworks have been devised to counter-model inversion attacks, thereby enhancing privacy protection while upholding utility performance in tasks like predicting face attributes [15]. Ongoing research endeavors in this domain persist in exploring novel methodologies and applications to fortify data privacy further.

7.2.1 VGAN

The privacy-preserving representation-learning variational generative adversarial network (PPRL-VGAN) offers various potential applications, such as expression morphing and image completion. Chen *et al.* developed a framework that merges the advantages of variational autoencoders (VAEs) and GANs to produce an identity-agnostic representation of facial images, as illustrated in the architectural framework of the VAE in Figure 7.3 [16]. This representation aims to be

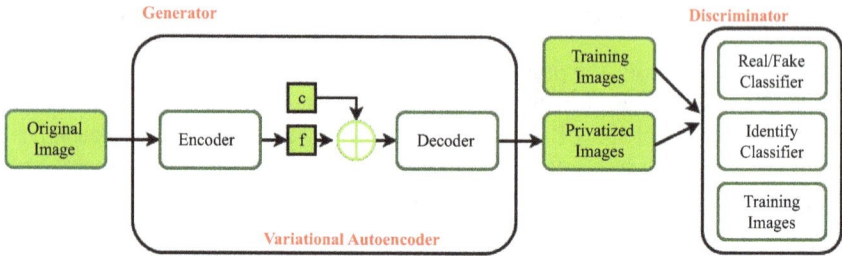

Figure 7.3   Architectural framework of VGAN

discriminative for facial expression recognition and enable the generation of expression-conserving images. The model is applicable in contexts where user privacy is crucial, like in human–machine interactions analyzing facial expressions without compromising personal identity.

The datasets utilized for validation consist of the Facial Expression Recognition Group (FERG) dataset, comprising 55,769 annotated images of cartoon characters portraying various facial expressions, and the Multimedia Understanding Group (MUG) dataset, composed of realistic video sequences featuring 86 individuals demonstrating seven fundamental expressions. The methodology entails a novel architecture that integrates a VAE with a GAN. The VAE encoder maps input images to a latent representation, while the GAN's generator produces images based on this representation. The discriminator is trained to differentiate between real and synthetic images, as well as to identify identities and expressions.

The model utilizes a customized artificial neural network (ANN) with 3 hidden layers, each comprising 256 nodes, demonstrating superior performance in identification and expression recognition accuracy. Performance outcomes reveal that while identification accuracy may decline, expression recognition accuracy improves considerably, indicating the effective separation of identity and expression information in the learned representations. The PPRL-VGAN framework introduces a promising approach to facial expression recognition that emphasizes user privacy while upholding high performance in facial expression recognition and synthesis.

7.2.2   AD-GAN

The model delineated by Cao *et al.* referred to as 3D-aided duet generative adversarial networks (AD-GAN), exhibits substantial potential applications in domains such as virtual reality, video games, and facial recognition frameworks [17]. By facilitating the amalgamation of multi-view facial images from a singular input, it can enrich user interactions in virtual settings and enhance the precision of identity validation systems. The findings of the study illustrate that AD-GAN not only generates lifelike images but also effectively conserves identity details, attaining cutting-edge outcomes in facial recognition assignments on openly accessible datasets.

Adversarial disentanglement GANs (AD-GANs) represent a significant advancement in the field of generative modeling, offering enhanced control and flexibility in generating data with distinct, manipulable features. AD-GANs are particularly effective in applications that demand precise control over various aspects of the generated content such as image synthesis, face generation, data augmentation, style transfer, semantic manipulation, and medical imaging. Their ability to disentangle different latent factors within the data allows for more nuanced and independent manipulation of features, thereby addressing limitations seen in traditional GANs.

The AD-GAN method centers around its dual-GAN framework, which incorporates two specialized GAN networks working synergistically. The first GAN, Generator 1 (G1), is responsible for generating high-resolution images from a specific viewpoint, such as the frontal view. G1 is trained using 3D facial models, which provide detailed geometric and textural information. This detailed training enables G1 to produce realistic, high-quality frontal face images by accurately capturing intricate facial features and textures. The second GAN, Generator 2 (G2), focuses on producing images from alternative viewpoints, such as profiles or 3/4 views. G2 ensures that the images from these other perspectives maintain coherence with those generated by G1. This coherence is critical for preserving a consistent appearance of the face across various angles. G2 is supported by Discriminator 2 (D2), which evaluates the realism and consistency of these images, ensuring they align well with the frontal images created by G1. A crucial aspect of this method is the multi-view consistency loss, which penalizes discrepancies between images generated from different perspectives. This loss function ensures that the synthesized images maintain the same underlying facial structure and texture, contributing to the overall coherence of the multi-view synthesis. The combined use of adversarial, reconstruction, and consistency losses guides the GANs in producing high-quality, realistic, and coherent multi-view face images. By balancing these various loss functions, the AD-GAN method leverages the strengths of 3D models and GANs to address the challenges of facial image synthesis effectively.

To achieve effective disentanglement within AD-GAN layers, several key techniques are employed. Latent space regularization is one such technique, which imposes constraints on the latent space to encourage the separation of different factors of variation. This can involve variational regularization, which ensures distinct aspects of the data are captured by different latent variables, or orthogonality constraints, which promote independence among latent factors. Factorized latent variables are another technique, where the latent space is designed to explicitly represent separate aspects of the data. This is achieved by creating distinct latent vectors for different features or by applying specialized encoding methods that separate these factors. Additionally, auxiliary networks are often integrated into the GAN architecture to enforce disentanglement. These networks provide additional supervision or guidance, helping both the generator and discriminator focus on producing and evaluating data with well-separated features. Together, these techniques facilitate a controlled and flexible generation process, allowing for independent manipulation of various aspects of the generated data.

The applications of AD-GANs are extensive and impactful. In controlled image generation, AD-GANs allow for precise manipulation of features such as background and foreground, enabling users to adjust different attributes independently. In face synthesis, AD-GANs enable detailed control over facial attributes like identity, expression, and pose, making them invaluable for creating lifelike avatars and performing face editing. For data augmentation, AD-GANs generate diverse, attribute-specific samples that enhance the robustness and generalization of machine learning models. AD-GANs disentangle style and content in style transfer, ensuring accurate stylistic modifications while preserving the underlying content. They also facilitate semantic image manipulation, allowing for changes to specific semantic attributes while maintaining overall image coherence, and assist in medical imaging by producing synthetic images with controlled variations, which supports research and diagnostics.

7.2.3   Privacy-Net

Kim *et al.* proposed a model that possesses noteworthy potential applications within the realm of medical image analysis, especially in situations where safeguarding patient confidentiality is crucial [18]. Through the utilization of an adversarial methodology for identity-obscured segmentation of medical images, the model adeptly conserves patient anonymity while facilitating precise image analysis. Privacy-Net represents a pioneering approach to developing a semantic medical image segmentation system that maintains patient privacy. It is particularly challenging to obfuscate identities while ensuring the accuracy of pixel-level segmentation tasks. Privacy-Net introduces a client-server framework designed to facilitate multi-centric medical image analysis without compromising patient privacy. The system consists of three primary components, encoder network is responsible for transforming raw medical images into an encoded form that obfuscates patient-specific features while retaining essential information for the analysis. The Discriminator Network is to discern whether two encoded images originate from the same patient. It provides feedback to the encoder to improve its ability to remove identity-specific features.

This network, typically a segmentation convolutional neural network (CNN), analyzes the encoded images to perform the target task (e.g., segmentation of brain MRI). The encoder network converts raw medical images into encoded representations on the client side. The encoding process obfuscates identity-specific details, ensuring that the server receives images without direct patient identifiers. This process preserves the crucial semantic information needed for accurate medical analysis. On the server side, encoded images are sent to the server where the medical image analysis network processes them. For instance, in the context of brain MRI segmentation, the analysis network performs pixel-level segmentation on the encoded images. The results are then communicated back to the client.

Privacy-Net employs an adversarial learning approach, inspired by GANs, but with distinct adaptations. The encoder's goal is to obfuscate the identity while preserving task-relevant information. The discriminator's task is to identify whether two encoded images are from the same patient. This adversarial setup helps the encoder to refine its ability to mask identities effectively. The segmentation network operates on encoded images to perform medical image analysis, ensuring that the information necessary for segmentation is preserved despite identity obfuscation. The model integrates two CNNs (encoder and segmentation network) with a Siamese CNN for the discriminator. This combination allows for effective identity obfuscation and high-quality task-specific performance. An important finding is that the encoder trained on one dataset can be used to encode images from other datasets effectively. This cross-dataset usability enhances the practical application of Privacy-Net in various medical imaging contexts. Privacy-Net addresses critical privacy concerns while ensuring that medical imaging tasks such as segmentation remain accurate and effective. The model holds significant potential for applications in various commercial sectors, such as change detection and object localization in street-view images. Through the effective elimination and inpainting of moving objects, the framework enhances the usability of street-view imagery, all the while guaranteeing privacy.

7.2.4   GAN with object detection algorithm

Uittenbogaard *et al.* established a framework that acts as an alternative to conventional blurring techniques for safeguarding privacy in street-view images. The framework employs an innovative moving object segmentation algorithm in conjunction with a multi-view inpainting GAN to identify, eliminate, and paint moving objects like pedestrians and vehicles in street-view imagery [19]. This method produces a more authentic output image where the moving object is no longer visible, thereby preserving privacy without compromising image quality. The model has a wide range of applications, including enhancing street-view services to address privacy issues and enhancing image quality for commercial purposes. The evaluation datasets consist of a set of 1,000 images that were evaluated based on performance metrics such as peak signal-to-noise ratio and L1 loss.

Uittenbogaard's research seeks to address critical challenges in object detection by leveraging GANs. The primary objective is to enhance object detection performance by generating synthetic data that augments limited real-world datasets and improves model robustness. By using GANs to create realistic synthetic images and annotations, Uittenbogaard aims to overcome data scarcity issues and bolster model accuracy. Additionally, the work focuses on integrating adversarial training techniques to make detection models more resilient to variations and perturbations in the input data. The methodology involves several key components. GANs are utilized to generate high-quality synthetic images and their corresponding annotations, providing an enriched dataset for training object detection models. This synthetic data generation is achieved through advanced GAN architectures, such as Deep Convolutional Generative Adversarial Network (DCGAN) or Style-based Generative Adversarial Network (StyleGAN). The generated images, which

Table 7.1   Comparison of GAN-based mechanisms for image data privacy protection

Model	Application	Input	Output	Data utility	Data privacy
VGAN	Expression recognition	Facial images	Synthetic face images	Expression analysis	The focus is on preserving the privacy of the individual's identity
AD-GAN	3D face image generation	Facial images	3D synthetic face images	3D face synthesis	
DCGAN	Medical imaging	Medical scans	Synthetic medical images	Image segmentation	
DCGAN	Street image synthesis	Street images	Inpainted street images	Street image synthesis	The focus is not to disclose private or sensitive information about individuals or locations

include realistic variations of objects and backgrounds, are combined with real-world data to create a more comprehensive training set. Object detection models, including You Only Look Once (YOLO) and Faster R-CNN, are then trained or fine-tuned using this augmented dataset. Furthermore, Uittenbogaard incorporates adversarial training by using GAN-generated adversarial examples to enhance the models' robustness and ensure their reliability across diverse conditions. Uittenbogaard's work makes several significant contributions to the field of object detection. First, it addresses the challenge of limited annotated data by demonstrating the effectiveness of synthetic data generated by GANs in improving model performance. Second, the integration of synthetic images and adversarial examples leads to notable improvements in detection accuracy and robustness. The approach also highlights the successful application of adversarial training techniques to enhance model resilience, making detection systems more reliable in the presence of variations and adversarial perturbations. Each of the GAN-based models presented offers distinct approaches to balancing data utility with privacy protection in various applications. A detailed comparison of these models, including their input data, output results, and privacy focus, is provided in Table 7.1.

7.3   Video data synthesis

Privacy of video data pertains to a guarantee that confidential and reliable information will not be leaked, sold, or tampered with the cornerstone purpose of which alone serves in quality end-user videos. This consists of protecting PII or privacy-sensitive visual data, such as the faces and actions/locations of individuals in videos who may face potential risks due to their visibility. Examples of video data privacy

protection techniques include: face blurring or voice modification for anonymization, encryption to protect the information in the storage and transfer process, and
applying various effective methods that enable us to analyze content without
exposure. Thus, by implementing these measures enterprises can continue to
facilitate significant video data consumption under legal and sensitive- ethics-based
evaluation tools while ensuring an individual's privacy rights are maintained.
Through the utilization of GANs, scholars have investigated innovative methodologies such as generative adversarial privacy and DataLens [20,21] to produce
synthetic datasets with assurances of differential privacy. These endeavors facilitate the development of models using sensitive video data while upholding privacy
standards. These advancements not only tackle the hurdles associated with data
sharing and privacy protection but also open avenues for practical implementations
in video data privacy. For instance, the creation of privacy-preserving synthetic
video datasets for training machine learning models without compromising confidential details is now achievable. The integration of GANs in the domain of video
data privacy underscores the adaptability and promise of generative models in
preserving privacy while supporting data-centric applications in diverse sectors
[21–23].

7.3.1   DCGAN

The innovative model proposed by Ren *et al.* demonstrates substantial potential for
application across various domains, encompassing security surveillance, safeguarding personal privacy in intelligent devices, and automated analysis of video
footage in public areas [24]. This signifies a noteworthy progression in techniques
for safeguarding privacy in video analysis. This research tackles the crucial
requirement of upholding individual privacy in video datasets utilized for action
detection through the introduction of an innovative approach to anonymize faces
without compromising the efficacy of action detection systems. The fundamental
concept revolves around the development of a model capable of concealing facial
identities in video frames while maintaining the essential features necessary for
precise action recognition. The methodology leverages a GAN to accomplish this
dual aim. The generator network is formulated to generate anonymized renditions
of faces that preserve crucial action-related attributes, while the discriminator
network verifies that the anonymized faces are authentic and indistinguishable from
genuine faces to an external observer. Furthermore, a specialized action detection
network is incorporated into the framework to ensure that the anonymized faces
continue to facilitate accurate detection and categorization of actions. A critical
advancement in this methodology is the incorporation of an adversarial loss in
conjunction with a task-specific loss for action detection. This dual-loss mechanism
steers the generator towards producing faces that not only safeguard privacy but
also sustain the usefulness of the video data for action detection assignments. The
training procedure entails the management of these losses to guarantee that the
generated faces are both anonymized and effective for action recognition. Through
the anonymization of faces, this technique facilitates the utilization of video

datasets for action detection without jeopardizing the exposure of individuals' identities. This equilibrium between privacy and functionality paves the way for novel opportunities in leveraging video data for research and commercial purposes while upholding privacy regulations and ethical standards.

7.4   Textual data synthesis

Textual data privacy, on the other hand, pertains to the protection of the confidentiality and integrity of textual information to prevent unauthorized access, misuse, or sharing of sensitive data. This encompasses the safeguarding of documents, emails, messages, and other text formats containing PII, financial information, or confidential messages. Techniques for maintaining textual data privacy include data anonymization to eliminate or obscure identifiable information, encryption for securing data in storage and transmission, and access controls to limit the individuals who can access or modify the information. Moreover, differential privacy approaches can be utilized to analyze aggregated textual data without disclosing individual details. By incorporating these methods, organizations can adhere to data privacy regulations and ethical standards, ensuring the protection of individual privacy rights while still leveraging the valuable insights provided by textual data for diverse applications. GANs serve as a mechanism for upholding the confidentiality of textual data through the generation of synthetic data that replicates the original content while safeguarding sensitive information. GANs such as SecureNetGAN and PowerGAN utilize a generator to fabricate data that resembles attacks or power records, alongside a discriminator that differentiates between authentic and synthetic data, thereby ensuring data privacy [7,25]. Furthermore, GANs are pivotal in the production of artificial text by instructing a generator to craft text examples and a discriminator to differentiate between authentic and artificial text, thus enhancing the consistency and caliber of the produced text [26]. Furthermore, in the realm of tabular information, GANs are utilized to generate artificial data that strikes a harmonious blend between usefulness and confidentiality, as demonstrated by the creation of DP-TLDM, a Differentially Private Tabular Latent Diffusion Model. This model enhances the resemblance of data, utility for subsequent tasks, and data discriminability while also preserving privacy [27,28]. Through the utilization of GANs, organizations can safeguard the privacy of textual data by generating authentic synthetic data.

7.4.1   A4NT

Shetty *et al.* introduce a sophisticated approach that is utilized to anonymize author attributes in text, emphasizing the essential requirement to safeguard authors' identities while upholding the effectiveness of neural machine translation (NMT) [29]. The A4NT framework is specifically crafted to eliminate identifiable author attributes from text, such as writing style or distinct linguistic patterns, which have the potential to unveil the author's identity. The methodology incorporates a new adversarial training mechanism comprising a generator and a discriminator. The primary goal of the generator is to generate translations that aim to eradicate author-specific characteristics, while the discriminator's role is to identify these traits within the translated text. This adversarial procedure guarantees that the generator is trained to produce translations that effectively conceal the author's identity while maintaining coherence and precision.

A pivotal advancement in A4NT is the incorporation of attribute classifiers that steer the anonymization procedure. These classifiers are trained to identify particular author attributes, like the writing style and their input aids the generator in concentrating on altering these elements of the text. The training process involves a blend of multiple loss functions to strike a balance between anonymity and translation quality. Figure 7.4 shows the GAN framework for Training this network. The adversarial loss motivates the generator to generate text that is indistinguishable from the anonymized text by the discriminator, thus heightening privacy. Moreover, a translation loss ensures that the semantic content and fluency of the text are conserved, upholding the overall quality of the NMT output. Additionally, A4NT employs a reconstruction loss to maintain the original meaning of the text while modifying the author-specific traits. This loss function guarantees that the anonymization process does not diminish the informativeness or readability of the translated text. By harmonizing these diverse loss functions, A4NT attains a high level of privacy without compromising the quality of the NMT output. The implications of A4NT are far-reaching and substantial, particularly in sectors necessitating stringent privacy protocols, such as legal documents, academic literature, and confidential communications. Through the anonymization of author attributes, A4NT facilitates the secure exchange and examination of text data without jeopardizing individual identities. This equilibrium between privacy and functionality introduces novel prospects for leveraging text data in academic and commercial contexts while conforming to privacy statutes and ethical guidelines. The A4NT approach signifies a notable progression at the intersection of privacy

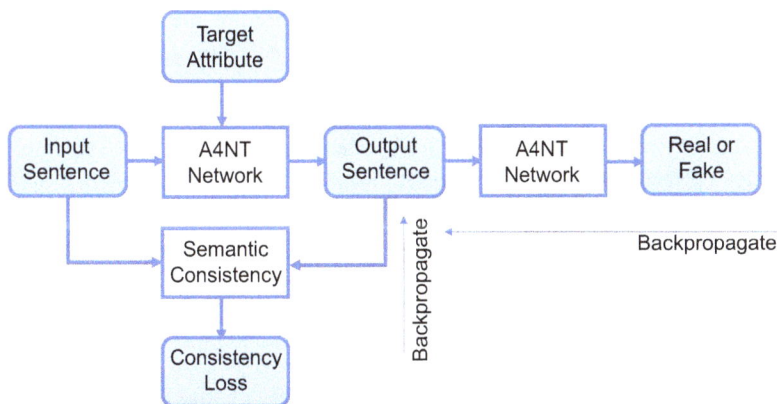

Figure 7.4   GAN framework to train A4NT network

preservation and NLP, presenting a robust resolution for safeguarding author anonymity within NMT systems.

The evaluation strategies focus on two main aspects: privacy efficacy, assessing the A4NT network's ability to mislead attribute classifiers, and semantic resemblance, quantifying the preservation of the original input's meaning post-transformation. The findings based on empirical evidence reveal that the system attains an F1 score of 0.88 for age-group categorization at the document level, whereas gender identification presents obstacles, showing a decline in F1 score from 0.93 during training to 0.75 in validation. The findings indicate that the A4NT network can be adjusted to function at different levels of privacy efficacy and semantic similarity, providing users with versatility.

7.4.2 AC-DCGAN

Park *et al.* introduce a novel approach referred to as table-GAN, which employs GANs to create artificial tables that preserve statistical resemblance to original datasets while upholding privacy [30] and delves into the utilization of GANs for data synthesis, addressing the growing need for top-notch synthetic data across various sectors. This research explores how GANs can be leveraged to create realistic and representative synthetic datasets, which find applications in data augmentation, privacy-preserving data analysis, and scenario simulation. At the core of this methodology lies a traditional GAN structure consisting of a generator and a discriminator. The generator's role is to generate synthetic data samples that emulate the real data distribution, while the discriminator assesses the data's authenticity by distinguishing between real and synthetic samples. By engaging in iterative adversarial training, the generator enhances its capacity to produce data that closely resembles real data, posing a challenge for the discriminator to differentiate between the two.

A pivotal aspect of this strategy involves the meticulous design of loss functions that steer the training process. The adversarial loss serves as the primary driver compelling the generator to produce lifelike data by gauging the disparity between the real and synthetic data distributions, prompting the generator to narrow this gap. Furthermore, to ensure that the synthetic data upholds the essential statistical properties of real data, the method integrates a feature-matching loss. This loss function compares intermediate features extracted from real and synthetic data by the discriminator, ensuring that the synthetic data encapsulates crucial characteristics of real data beyond superficial similarities. It also introduces a reconstruction loss, which proves particularly beneficial in upholding specific data attributes or constraints during the synthesis phase. This loss function is vital when generating data that must adhere to specified rules or distributions, penalizing deviations from these predefined criteria. The potential applications of this GAN-based data synthesis technique are far-reaching. In data augmentation, the synthetic data produced using this method can enrich machine learning models by supplying extra training samples, thus enhancing their resilience and generalization capabilities. For privacy-preserving data analysis, synthetic datasets can substitute sensitive real data, enabling analysis without compromising individual privacy. Moreover, in scenario simulation, the capacity to create authentic synthetic data facilitates the testing and validation of algorithms and systems within a controlled setting. By intricately balancing diverse loss functions and ensuring that the synthetic data retains crucial properties of real data, this approach furnishes a versatile and potent tool for crafting high-caliber synthetic datasets that can be applied across a broad spectrum of domains.

7.4.3 medGAN

Choi *et al.* introduce a methodology known as medGAN, which is designed to create authentic synthetic electronic health records (EHRs) while tackling the privacy issues linked to actual patient data and also This strategy aims to fulfill the requirement for authentic synthetic healthcare data that is suitable for research, training, and validation of machine learning models, all while upholding patient confidentiality. By utilizing a blend of GANs and autoencoders, the model generates high-dimensional discrete variables such as binary and count features from genuine patient records [31]. This strategy is particularly notable due to its capacity to produce diverse EHR data without confinement to particular illnesses, thus enabling its application in a variety of healthcare scenarios.

The methodology utilizes a specialized GAN framework designed to manage the intricacies of multi-label discrete patient records. Within this framework, the generator network is responsible for crafting synthetic patient records, while the discriminator network assesses their genuineness by distinguishing between authentic and synthetic records. Through an adversarial training procedure, the generator's capacity to generate records resembling real data in terms of distribution and attributes is progressively enhanced. An essential aspect of this methodology is the integration of multi-label classification into the GAN structure. Patient records consist of multiple labels denoting various medical conditions, treatments, and outcomes, all of which need to be accurately portrayed in the synthetic data. The generator is trained not only to create authentic records but also to guarantee that the generated records maintain accurate associations among these labels.

The adversarial loss compels the generator to produce lifelike patient records by penalizing variations between real and synthetic data distributions. Additionally, to ensure the fidelity of synthetic records, a feature matching loss is introduced, comparing the statistical attributes of intermediate features derived from real and synthetic records. This comparison guarantees that the synthetic data captures crucial characteristics of real patient data beyond superficial resemblances. Furthermore, a multi-label classification loss is implemented to enforce precise associations among medical conditions and treatments in the synthetic records. This particular loss function penalizes the generator for generating records with inaccurate label associations, consequently enhancing the precision and dependability of the synthetic data. In healthcare research, these synthetic records can facilitate the development and validation of novel machine-learning models without compromising sensitive patient data. Synthetic data also serves as a valuable resource for training healthcare

Table 7.2   Comparison of GAN-based mechanisms for textual data privacy protection

Model	Application	Input	Output	Data utility	Data privacy
A4NT	Text generation	Text data	Synthetic text	Text generation	The focus is on preserving the
AC-DCGAN	Public record sharing	Public records	Synthetic records	Record generation	privacy of the individual's
medGAN	Medical data sharing	EHR data	Synthetic EHR records	Record generation	identity

professionals in a safe learning environment. Moreover, synthetic patient records allow for extensive scenario testing and system validation in healthcare information technology, ensuring reliable performance without infringing upon patient confidentiality. The utilization of GANs for the creation of multi-label discrete patient records signifies a notable progression in the domain of synthetic data generation for healthcare applications. By meticulously balancing diverse loss functions and ensuring that synthetic data retains essential properties and accurate label associations, this approach furnishes a potent mechanism for generating top-tier synthetic healthcare data that is relevant across various domains.

The assessment datasets used, encompassing three distinct EHR datasets, enable a thorough evaluation of the model's efficacy. medGAN has proven its ability to create synthetic records that exhibit performance akin to real data, with empirical assessments indicating minimal risks of identity and attribute exposure. In essence, it makes a substantial contribution to the domain of synthetic data generation in healthcare by furnishing a sturdy framework for generating authentic patient records while addressing privacy concerns The approaches to preserving privacy in textual data vary across different GAN-based models, each demonstrating unique strengths in balancing utility and confidentiality. A comparison of these models, including their input types, generated outputs, and privacy considerations, can be found in Table 7.2.

7.5   Speech data synthesis

Speech data privacy focuses on safeguarding sensitive audio information to prevent unauthorized access, misuse, or sharing. This encompasses the safeguarding of recordings of conversations, voice commands, or other audio data that may contain PII or sensitive content. Measures to ensure privacy for speech data include the utilization of encryption to secure audio files both during storage and transmission, anonymization techniques to eliminate or conceal identifiable voices, and the implementation of stringent access controls to restrict who can access or analyze the recordings. Moreover, advanced privacy-preserving algorithms can evaluate speech data without revealing sensitive details, thereby ensuring compliance with data privacy regulations and ethical standards, and safeguarding individuals' privacy rights while facilitating the utilization of speech data for diverse applications. Diverse research endeavors put forth novel methodologies to tackle this issue. For instance, a GAN-based model is devised to conceal particular sensitive details within speech data, ensuring the retention of the intended message [32]. These progressions underscore the importance of GANs in fortifying speech data privacy through strategies such as signal manipulation, confidentiality maintenance, knowledge condensation, and gradient restriction, ultimately establishing an equilibrium between safeguarding individuals' identities and sustaining the data's usability for subsequent applications.

7.5.1   Obfuscation

The concept of remote health monitoring has emerged as a viable strategy for continuous assessment and tracking of individuals' health status with minimal exertion. This objective can be partially realized through the utilization of passive audio recording technology, which has the potential to compromise individuals' confidentiality. Vatanparvar *et al.* confront the issue of background noise in speech data, a crucial factor in passive health monitoring setups. The efficacy of such systems heavily depends on the clarity and quality of speech recordings for precise health parameter monitoring. Nonetheless, noise interference can considerably undermine the dependability of these recordings [33].

To address this challenge, Vatanparvar *et al.* present a novel methodology for enhancing the resilience of speech obfuscation methods in passive health monitoring systems. The study focuses on the issue of effectively capturing and examining speech signals in noisy surroundings by employing generative models to characterize and adjust to different levels of background noise. The proposed technique utilizes a generative model framework to amplify speech obfuscation, which entails creating clear, noise-free representations of speech from recordings contaminated with background noise. The fundamental component of the method is a generative model, like a GAN or VAE, that is trained to generate high-quality, noise-resistant speech profiles based on noisy input data. Within this framework, the generator network creates de-noised speech signals, while the discriminator network (in the case of GANs) or the reconstruction loss (in the case of VAEs) assesses the quality and precision of the generated speech in comparison to clean references. An important feature of this methodology is the integration of audio profiling, which involves developing personalized models that adapt to unique speech characteristics and noise patterns. This individualized approach enhances the generative model's capacity to precisely process and obscure speech in varied and dynamic noise environments. The training procedure combines multiple loss functions to attain optimal performance. The primary loss function is the adversarial loss, which steers the generator towards producing realistic and clean speech by penalizing inconsistencies between the generated and genuine clean speech. Furthermore, a reconstruction loss ensures that the generated speech preserves faithfulness to the original speech content, while a noise adaptation loss aids the model in adapting to changing noise conditions. This approach's use cases are notably pertinent in passive health monitoring systems, where precise and non-intrusive speech analysis is crucial. By boosting the durability of speech obfuscation in noisy surroundings, this technique bolsters the dependability of health monitoring systems reliant on speech data for identifying and monitoring health conditions. Additionally, it holds promise for applications in domains like voice-activated systems, communication aids, and environmental noise adjustment in various contexts. Through the utilization of audio profiling and the integration of diverse loss functions, this strategy offers a robust solution for enhancing the precision and resilience of speech analysis in demanding acoustic settings.

7.5.2   Cyclic GAN

Aloufi *et al.* examine the escalating apprehension regarding privacy in voice-activated interactions, particularly within the Internet of Things frameworks. They advocate a privacy-conserving framework that purifies voice input before transmission to cloud services, to uphold speech utility while safeguarding sensitive data like emotional states [34]. They explore the crucial matter of privacy in speech analysis for voice assistants through the introduction of a new framework aimed at examining speech while safeguarding sensitive emotional data. The primary focus of this method is on upholding user privacy while facilitating efficient voice-based interactions and features. The Emotionless framework is structured on the concept of anonymizing and concealing emotional aspects within speech data. The block diagram of the privacy-preserving framework for this speech analysis is shown in Figure 7.5. The fundamental approach entails the utilization of a generative model to convert speech recordings into representations that maintain linguistic content while obscuring emotional features. This process of transformation is executed through an adversarial framework, where a generator network produces emotion-

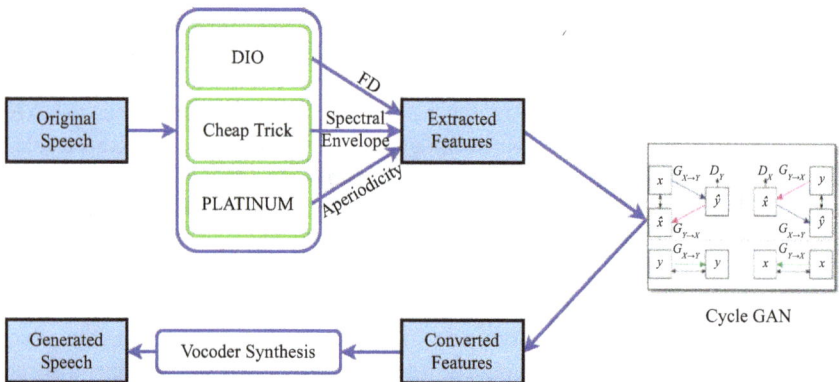

Figure 7.5   Block diagram of the privacy-preserving framework for speech analysis

neutral speech representations, and a discriminator network verifies the realism and retention of essential linguistic details for precise speech analysis. The main dataset employed for assessment is the RAVDESS dataset, which encompasses recordings of emotional speech.

An essential aspect of this strategy is the incorporation of emotion obfuscation methods within the GAN structure. The generator is educated to generate speech representations that diminish the presence of emotional signals, while the discriminator is responsible for ensuring that these representations do not compromise the overall quality and usefulness of the speech data. The framework employs various loss functions to strike a balance between privacy and performance. The adversarial loss compels the generator to create emotionless yet authentic speech, while a reconstruction loss guarantees the preservation of the linguistic content. Furthermore, an emotion classification loss is implemented to penalize the generator if the output can still be confidently categorized into specific emotional classes, thereby enhancing the efficacy of the obfuscation process. The potential use of the Emotionless framework is substantial within the realm of voice assistants and similar voice-oriented technologies. By safeguarding emotional privacy, this approach bolsters user confidence and adherence to privacy protocols, while also facilitating effective voice interactions. Its relevance is particularly noteworthy in scenarios where emotional data may be delicate or subject to regulatory constraints, such as in personal assistants, customer service chatbots, and tools for mental health monitoring. This model is especially pertinent in scenarios where user privacy is of utmost importance, such as in personal aides, mental health supervision, and targeted marketing, where interpreting user emotions can enhance service provision without jeopardizing privacy. The findings of the study reveal that the suggested approach can notably diminish the detection of sensitive emotional states by roughly 96% while having minimal impact on the precision of speech recognition and speaker identification methodologies, which is critical for preserving user experience in voice-operated systems.

The approach involves the utilization of a CycleGAN architecture, a variant of GAN, comprising two generators and two discriminators to convert sensitive data in speech into non-sensitive information without sacrificing usefulness for specific assignments. The model's performance is gauged based on its capability to conceal genuine emotions while upholding a low word error rate of 35% for speech recognition and a marginal decline of about 0.12% in speaker recognition accuracy. This equilibrium between privacy and functionality is crucial for the efficient integration of voice analysis systems in practical settings, guaranteeing that user information remains private while still furnishing valuable insights for service providers. It marks a notable progression in the realm of privacy-safeguarding speech analysis, underscoring the significance of safeguarding user data in an increasingly interconnected environment. GAN-based mechanisms for speech data privacy protection address distinct challenges depending on the input and desired output. A side-by-side comparison of these models, highlighting their applications and privacy preservation strategies, is shown in Table 7.3.

Table 7.3   Comparison of GAN-based mechanisms for speech data privacy protection

Model	Application	Input	Output	Data utility	Data privacy
Obfuscation	Health monitoring	Audio data	Synthetic audio	Audio generation	Prioritizes privacy of background sounds
Cyclic GAN	Voice assistance	Voice signal	Synthetic video	Voice generation	Emphasizes protecting emotional privacy

7.6   Spatio-temporal data synthesis

Spatial-temporal data privacy is concerned with safeguarding data that integrates spatial (location-based) and temporal (time-based) information to safeguard against the exposure or misuse of sensitive details of individuals' movements and activities. This category of data often comprises location tracking records, sensor data, and time-stamped logs, which can unveil patterns and routines. Privacy strategies for spatial-temporal data encompass anonymization techniques to obscure specific locations or times, aggregation methods that summarize data without disclosing individual specifics, and encryption to protect data throughout storage and transmission. The implementation of these strategies aids in preventing unauthorized access and misuse, thereby protecting individuals' privacy while still enabling the examination of spatial-temporal patterns for various applications. GANs, such as TS-TrajGAN and P-GAN, are employed for the generation of synthetic trajectory data while upholding privacy [35,36]. These models utilize GAN architectures to create realistic trajectory sequences, ensuring both data utility and privacy protection. Additionally, GANs like LSTM-GANs are utilized in safeguarding passenger privacy within privacy-preserving taxi-demand systems by generating synthetic trajectories [37]. Furthermore, approaches such as privacy-preserving GANs have been developed to generate artificial medical records with a high quality of generation while reducing the risk of data leakage, especially in crucial industries like healthcare [38].

7.6.1   Perturbation

Yin and Yang investigate the application of GANs to improve privacy in mobility data, addressing the escalating issue of privacy violations in LBSs that frequently expose sensitive user data [39]. Yin and Yang present a novel technique for safeguarding privacy in mobility data by utilizing GANs. The method aims to tackle the increasing apprehension regarding the confidentiality of location and movement data, which is being gathered and examined for diverse purposes such as smart city governance and personalized amenities. The strategy put forward utilizes GANs to create artificial mobility data that upholds the statistical attributes of the authentic data while concealing individual identities. The GAN framework comprises a generator and a discriminator, where the generator's role is to produce synthetic mobility data mirroring the density distribution of the original data, while the discriminator assesses the authenticity of the generated data in comparison to the real data. Using adversarial training, the generator is trained to generate data that closely imitates the real data in terms of statistical features but does not disclose specific individual details.

An essential aspect of this technique is its emphasis on safeguarding density distribution privacy. In contrast to directly anonymizing individual data points, the GAN model is focused on conserving the overall statistical distribution of the mobility data while obscuring individual trajectories. This methodology is devised to ensure that the artificial data preserves valuable patterns and trends for analysis while safeguarding individual privacy. The primary objective of the adversarial loss in this technique is to drive the generator to produce data that cannot be distinguished from authentic mobility data by the discriminator. A distribution loss is integrated to guarantee that the synthetic data aligns with the statistical distribution of the real data, thereby preserving crucial patterns and trends. Moreover, a privacy loss function is introduced to penalize any disclosure of individual-specific details in the synthetic data, thereby reinforcing privacy protection. The use cases of this privacy-preservation method based on GANs hold significance across various sectors involving mobility data. In smart urban environments, the capacity to scrutinize mobility trends without compromising individual privacy facilitates improved urban development and traffic control. In the realm of transportation and logistics, artificial data can be utilized to enhance route optimization and operational efficiency while safeguarding confidential information. Furthermore, this approach proves valuable in any context where mobility data is amassed and assessed, necessitating a harmonious blend of data usefulness and privacy protection.

7.6.2   PRGAN

Rezaei *et al.* presented a privacy-preserving framework that enhances an adversary's uncertainty regarding sensitive labels while upholding privacy assurances based on Pufferfish privacy, a variant of differential privacy (DP) [40]. The framework is devised to manage correlations and prior knowledge in data, diverging from previous methods assuming uncorrelated data attributes. By framing the issue as an optimization assignment, it strives to diminish the performance decrement of one classifier when utilizing perturbed data and heighten uncertainty in predicted values of another classifier, all within the constraints between the two classifiers. To accomplish this, GAN are employed to generate customized perturbations for each data point, involving two neural networks competing to produce authentic synthetic data records.

The methodology proposed utilizes a GAN framework to produce data that conceal sensitive attributes while preserving essential aspects of the data. Consisting of a generator and a discriminator network, the system operates by producing artificial data that conceals private characteristics, while the discriminator evaluates the legitimacy and confidentiality of the generated data. The datasets utilized in the research comprise MNIST, PubFig, WiFi, and OccuTherm, each incorporating distinct model architectures for neural networks Dy and Dz. The efficacy of the proposed privacy-preserving framework in concealing identity-revealing attributes from depth images is demonstrated, illustrating minimal performance decrement when applied to various demographic groups. The utilization strategies involve distorting images with the noise generator and categorizing them in a privacy-preserving manner with the target classifier, underscoring the model's practical utility in safeguarding sensitive data while upholding classification precision. An integral aspect of this methodology lies in the formulation of loss functions that direct the training process of the GANs. The primary adversarial loss function incentivizes the generator to develop data that closely resembles real data, thereby ensuring that the synthetic data retains realistic properties while safeguarding sensitive information. Additionally, to enhance the protection of sensitive attributes, a privacy loss function is integrated into the methodology, imposing penalties on the generator for any inadvertent disclosure of sensitive attributes in the synthetic data. This loss function plays a crucial role in maintaining the confidentiality of sensitive information, thereby bolstering privacy safeguards. Furthermore, the methodology incorporates a utility loss function to strike a balance between privacy preservation and data utility, ensuring that the generated data remains valuable for analytical and modeling purposes by preserving essential data features and relationships. Through a careful calibration of privacy and utility losses, the methodology attains an optimal equilibrium between safeguarding sensitive attributes and upholding the overall data quality.

The potential uses of this methodology encompass a broad range of fields such as healthcare, finance, and social sciences, where datasets frequently incorporate sensitive attributes. In these domains, the GAN-based approach offers a means to share and analyze data without compromising individual privacy, particularly beneficial in scenarios necessitating data sharing among researchers or organizations while adhering to privacy regulations and safeguarding sensitive information.

7.6.3   LSTM-TrajGAN

Rao *et al.* introduce an innovative methodology that integrates long short-term memory (LSTM) networks with GANs to produce synthetic trajectory data that safeguards privacy [41]. This approach holds particular significance within the realm of LBSs, given the escalating privacy apprehensions surrounding individual trajectory data. The key applications of this approach encompass the sharing and publication of trajectory data, where it can function as a safeguarding mechanism to prevent the inadvertent disclosure of sensitive information while enabling meaningful data analysis. The LSTM-TrajGAN framework combines LSTM networks with GANs to effectively model and obscure trajectory data. The LSTM network captures the sequential dependencies and structures present in the trajectory data, whereas the GAN element generates artificial trajectories that maintain the statistical characteristics of the original data while concealing individual trajectory information.

Within this framework, the GAN's generator network produces synthetic trajectories that strive to replicate the temporal structures and distribution of the actual data, as discerned by the LSTM model. The discriminator network assesses the authenticity and confidentiality of the generated trajectories, distinguishing between authentic and artificial data. The process of adversarial training enhances the generator's capacity to create realistic yet privacy-preserving trajectories. Figure 7.6 shows the workflow of the LSTM-TrajGAN model. The primary adversarial loss incentivizes the generator to generate synthetic trajectories that are indistinguishable from authentic data by the discriminator. Furthermore, a reconstruction loss is implemented to ensure that the synthetic trajectories retain crucial temporal structures and attributes of the original data. To reinforce privacy protection, a privacy loss function is introduced, penalizing the generator if the synthetic data discloses sensitive details about individual trajectories. This particular loss function aids in upholding individual privacy while upholding the general quality of the synthetic data. The potential application of the LSTM-TrajGAN methodology holds significant importance in domains dealing with trajectory data, such as urban planning, transportation, and LBSs. By presenting a means to safeguard delicate trajectory details, this methodology facilitates the utilization of trajectory data for examination and modeling without compromising individual privacy. It proves particularly beneficial in scenarios where trajectory data is exchanged or examined across diverse organizations or research entities. The focal point of the research pertains to trajectory privacy preservation, a pivotal domain within the spheres of data science and artificial intelligence, notably within the context of geographic information systems. Spatio-temporal data presents unique privacy challenges, and different GAN-based models tackle these through varied techniques. A comparative overview of these models, focusing on their input types, outputs, and privacy preservation methods, is provided in Table 7.4.

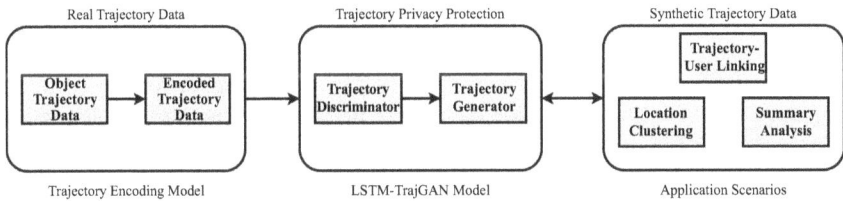

Figure 7.6   Workflow of LSTM-TrajGAN model

Table 7.4   Comparison of GAN-based mechanisms for spatio-temporal data privacy protection

Model	Application	Input	Output	Data utility	Data privacy
Perturbation	Data distribution	Mobile data	Synthetic mobile data	Mobile data generation	Safeguards sensitive information
PRGAN	Data distribution	Mobile data	Synthetic mobile data	Voice data generation	Ensures sensitive information protection
LSTM-TrajGAN	Location services	Trajectory data	Synthetic trajectories	Trajectory generation	Prioritizes identity privacy

7.7   Graph data synthesis

Graph data privacy focuses on protecting information represented in graph structures, where nodes and edges capture relationships and interactions between entities. This type of data is often used in social networks, organizational frameworks, and recommendation systems. Maintaining privacy in graph data involves methods such as anonymizing node identifiers, perturbing graph structures to prevent the inference of sensitive relationships, and using secure multi-party computation to analyze data without revealing private connections. Privacy-preserving algorithms can also create synthetic graphs that retain structural patterns while preserving individual privacy. These methods help maintain confidentiality and integrity in graph data while enabling valuable analysis and insights. Various GAN-based strategies, including WDP-GAN and RDP-GAN, have been developed to address privacy issues inherent in graph data. These methods use approaches such as feature learning frameworks, Rényi differential privacy, and entropic regularization to generate authentic samples while protecting sensitive data in graphs with varying weights. By integrating stochastic noise mechanisms and adaptive gradient perturbation algorithms, GANs can effectively obscure graph data, ensuring privacy protection without compromising the usefulness of the generated graphs. [42–44].

7.7.1   *Perturbation*

Perturbation is a vital technique in graph-based GANs, especially when applied to the task of graph data anonymization. Perturbation involves making controlled modifications to the graph structure or node attributes to obscure sensitive information while attempting to retain the overall utility of the data. This section details the mechanisms and considerations for implementing perturbation in graph-based GANs, particularly within the context of the GDAGAN framework [45]. In the context of GDAGAN, perturbation can be applied to both the graph structure and node attributes. The primary goal is to create a balance between privacy protection and data utility. Structural perturbation modifies the connections between nodes in the graph. This can include operations such as adding or removing edges, swapping node pairs, or altering node degrees. For instance, randomly adding or removing edges can help in making the true connections between nodes, thus preventing re-identification attacks. This method, however, must be used judiciously to avoid significantly distorting the graph's overall structure. Swapping pairs of nodes or their labels can obscure the identity of specific nodes without drastically changing the graph's structural properties. In weighted graphs, the weights of edges can be slightly altered to introduce ambiguity about the strength or nature of relationships between nodes. Node attributes often contain sensitive information that needs protection. Attribute perturbation can involve introducing random noise into numerical attributes to obscure the exact values while maintaining the overall distribution. Replacing specific attribute values with more general categories reduces the precision of the information without losing its broader meaning. Additionally, attributes of different nodes can be exchanged to obscure direct associations between nodes and their attributes. The GDAGAN framework leverages perturbation to enhance the privacy of generated graph data. The training phase of GDAGAN involves both the generator and the discriminator networks. Perturbation can be applied to the real graph data before feeding it to the discriminator. This helps in training the discriminator to distinguish between real but perturbed data and synthetic data generated by the generator. By learning to handle perturbed data, the discriminator becomes more robust, and the generator, in turn, produces more resilient synthetic graphs. Once the GAN is trained, perturbation mechanisms can be directly incorporated into the generator's processes. The generator not only attempts to mimic the real graph's structure and attributes but also integrates perturbation techniques to ensure that the generated graph data has built-in privacy protections. For instance, while generating edges and node attributes, the generator can apply noise or generalization techniques to create anonymized yet realistic graph data.

The key challenge in perturbation is balancing privacy with data utility. Excessive perturbation can lead to significant loss of information, rendering the anonymized data useless for practical applications. In GDAGAN, this balance is achieved by dynamically adjusting the level of perturbation based on the sensitivity of the data and the requirements of the application. For example, more perturbation might be applied to highly sensitive attributes or densely connected subgraphs. Utility preservation metrics help in fine-tuning the perturbation processes to ensure that essential structural properties and attribute distributions are maintained.

7.7.2 Graph data anonymization with GDAGAN

Graph data represents relationships between entities, including social networks, bioinformatics, and recommendation systems. However, sharing graph data raises privacy concerns due to potential re-identification attacks. Fang *et al.* [46] introduce a novel approach to anonymizing graph data, ensuring privacy while maintaining data utility. Traditional anonymization techniques, such as k-anonymity, l-diversity, and t-closeness, focus primarily on tabular data and often fail to adequately protect graph data. Graph anonymization presents unique challenges due to the complex structure and relationships inherent in graphs. GANs provide a promising avenue for developing effective graph anonymization methods. GDAGAN adapts the GAN framework to graph data by incorporating graph-specific operations. The architecture comprises a Graph Generator, which generates synthetic graph data that mimics the structure and properties of the original graph, and a graph discriminator, which differentiates between real and synthetic graphs, guiding the generator to produce realistic graph structures. The anonymization process involves several steps. Preprocessing extracts structural features and node attributes from the original graph. Training involves the GAN using the original graph data, where the generator learns to create synthetic graphs, while the discriminator helps refine the generator's outputs. Generation uses the trained generator to produce anonymized graph data, and postprocessing ensures the generated graph meets privacy and utility requirements. The

GDAGAN framework's training phase involves both the generator and the discriminator networks. Perturbation can be applied to the real graph data before feeding it to the discriminator. This helps in training the discriminator to distinguish between real but perturbed data and synthetic data generated by the generator. By learning to handle perturbed data, the discriminator becomes more robust, and the generator, in turn, produces more resilient synthetic graphs. Once the GAN is trained, perturbation mechanisms can be directly incorporated into the generator's processes. The generator not only attempts to mimic the real graph's structure and attributes but also integrates perturbation techniques to ensure that the generated graph data has built-in privacy protections. For instance, while generating edges and node attributes, the generator can apply noise or generalization techniques to create anonymized yet realistic graph data.

The graph feature learning model in [47] leverages a GAN-based approach to incorporate Laplace noise during the graph reconstruction process, resulting in an anonymized graph. Despite the added noise, the reconstructed graph retains its usefulness for link prediction, thanks to GAN's strong feature learning abilities. By embedding Laplace noise, the model also provides protection against community detection and de-anonymization attacks.

7.7.3   APGE

Li *et al.* introduce a new methodology for graph embedding that prioritizes user privacy preservation while upholding data utility. The approach put forth integrates privacy-disentangling and privacy-pruning mechanisms, collaborating within an end-to-end pipeline to bolster defense against inference attacks [48]. Adversarial perturbation graph embedding (APGE) is a method used within graph-based GANs to enhance the anonymization process by embedding adversarial perturbations into the graph data. APGE is inspired by the concept of adversarial learning, where perturbations are deliberately introduced to the data to make it more resilient to attacks. In the context of graph-based GANs, APGE involves embedding these perturbations directly into the graph data during the generation process. The motivation behind APGE is to create a robust anonymization method that can withstand various re-identification attacks while preserving the essential properties of the graph.

APGE operates by introducing perturbations in both the structural aspects of the graph and the node attributes. Structural perturbations involve modifications to the connections between nodes, such as adding or removing edges and altering node degrees. These changes help obscure the original graph's structure, making it difficult for attackers to identify specific nodes or relationships. APGE systematically applies these perturbations to ensure that the generated graph data does not reveal sensitive information. Attribute perturbations involve altering the attributes of nodes within the graph. This can include adding noise to numerical attributes, generalizing categorical attributes, or swapping attributes between nodes. By embedding these perturbations into the graph data, APGE ensures that sensitive attributes are protected while maintaining the overall distribution and correlations of the attributes. The system architecture features an expansion layer that amplifies

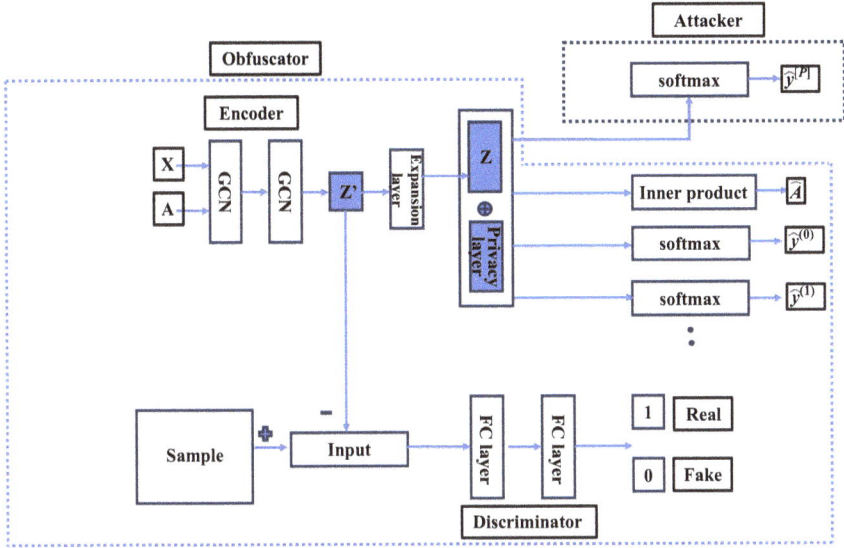

Figure 7.7   Adversarial privacy graph embedding

embedding performance, facilitating enhanced utility retention and reduced risks of disclosing sensitive attributes as shown in Figure 7.7.

Within the GDAGAN framework, APGE significantly enhances both the privacy and robustness of anonymized graph data. During training, APGE applies adversarial perturbations to the real graph data before it enters the discriminator. This forces the discriminator to differentiate between genuine yet perturbed data and synthetic data generated by the generator. Consequently, the generator learns to produce graph data that is realistic while also being resistant to re-identification attempts. In the generation phase, the trained generator incorporates APGE techniques to embed privacy-preserving perturbations into the synthetic graph data. This ensures that the generated data comes with built-in privacy safeguards, making it safer for distribution and sharing. APGE strikes a balance between privacy and utility by preserving key structural features and attribute distributions while concealing sensitive information.

The challenge with APGE, as with other perturbation methods, is to balance privacy protection with data utility. Excessive perturbations can degrade the quality of the graph data, making it less useful for analytical tasks. Conversely, insufficient perturbations may leave the data vulnerable to attacks. APGE addresses this balance by dynamically adjusting the level of perturbation based on the sensitivity of the data and the requirements of the application. This adaptive approach ensures that highly sensitive attributes or densely connected subgraphs receive more perturbation, while less sensitive parts of the graph are minimally altered. To further refine this balance, APGE incorporates utility preservation metrics that measure the impact of perturbations on data utility. These metrics guide the perturbation

Table 7.5   Comparison of GAN-based mechanisms for graph data privacy protection

Model	Application	Input	Output	Data utility	Data privacy
Perturbation	Graph distribution	Graph data	Anonymized graph	Graph generation	Protects community structures
GDAGAN	Graph distribution	Graph data	Anonymized graph	Graph generation	Defends against identity attacks
APGE	Graph embedding	Graph data	Graph representations	Representation generation	Shields sensitive attributes

process, ensuring that the generated graph data retains its usefulness for various analytical and research purposes. Additionally, APGE employs iterative refinement, where the utility of the perturbed data is continuously evaluated, and the perturbation strategies are adjusted to optimize both privacy and utility outcomes. Graph data privacy protection involves distinct methodologies, and various GAN-based models employ unique strategies to address these challenges. Table 7.5 presents a comparative analysis of these models, outlining their applications, data inputs, outputs, and privacy protection techniques.

7.8   Limitations

This comparative analysis of different GAN models and alternative privacy-preserving techniques highlights their respective limitations and advantages. Each model undergoes assessment grounded on its efficacy in upholding privacy, the computational obstacles it encounters, and its suitability for a variety of assignments such as image manipulation, medical image partitioning, movement identification, and path creation. The objective is to provide perspectives on how these models address privacy issues and data usability, delivering a comprehensive portrayal of their strengths and limitations. Table 7.6 shows the limitations and advantages of each GAN model. This holds significance for scholars and professionals in the realms of artificial intelligence, machine learning, and data confidentiality seeking to opt for suitable models for their distinct applications while weighing the compromises between privacy and usability.

   To mitigate the constraints associated with GAN-based models, particularly in intricate domains such as healthcare and intelligent urban environments, it is imperative to investigate specific methodologies and remedies customized for these sectors. In the realm of healthcare, for example, models such as VGAN and medGAN encounter considerable challenges related to privacy, including the potential for exposure of sensitive information or the identification of outliers within synthetic datasets. Strategies such as differential privacy, homomorphic encryption, and federated learning represent feasible solutions for safeguarding

Table 7.6 Limitations and advantages of the GAN models

Models	Limitations	Advantages
VGAN	Privacy attacks are possible with access to the encoder network and latent representation. Additionally, there is a computational burden associated with reversible privacy methods using encryption	VGAN learns an identity-invariant representation for face images, making it useful for facial expression recognition and identity-altered face image synthesis. It can synthesize new face images with or without an input image and has versatile applications in image-processing tasks such as expression morphing and image completion
AD-GAN	Imbalanced training data affects results, and genuine data scarcity hampers face frontalization performance. Accurate alignment is also crucial for model preprocessing	AD-GAN decomposes the synthesis problem into well-constrained subtasks, including a face normalizer and face editor, for precise yaw angle rotation of face images. It employs a UV correspondence field for pixel-wise dense facial texture maps, enhancing the generation of photo-realistic local details and accelerating convergence
DCGAN	Anonymization methods cannot prevent identity recovery from image content. Federated learning lacks centralized cloud-based model use for predictions, and homomorphic encryption slows neural networks and incurs communication overhead	DCGAN allows for highly accurate segmentation results while removing privacy-specific features from medical images. An encoder trained on a specific dataset can be used for segmenting other datasets without the need for retraining
DCGAN In Street Images	There are detection challenges with class-agnostic moving object segmentation. Inpainting artifacts may be visible, which can reveal privacy-sensitive information in rare cases	DCGAN ensures complete privacy protection by removing and inpainting moving objects in street-view imagery. It mitigates blurring artifacts and removes occluded regions, which is beneficial for commercial applications
DCGAN	Baselines can harm action detection while improving anonymization, and existing methods lack optimality, which may hurt recognition performance	DCGAN leverages existing large-scale labeled face datasets for learning identity information. It can be trained on action detection datasets without identity annotations
A4NT	Meteor scores indicate a significant semantic loss in the anonymization process. Gender classification is challenging with an F1 score drop	A4NT offers a better trade-off between privacy effectiveness and semantic similarity. It is end-to-end trainable and applicable to different author attributes and datasets without changing the framework

(Continues)

Table 7.6 (*Continued*)

Models	Limitations	Advantages
AC-DCGAN	Privacy methods can leak data when background knowledge is available, and existing methods impact data utility	It creates synthetic tables with no one-to-one relationship between real and synthetic records, preventing re-identification attacks. It balances privacy level, model compatibility, with performance similar to models trained using original data
medGAN	Limited work has been done on synthetic data generation in the healthcare domain. There are privacy concerns due to personal identifiers in EHR data, and there is an attribute disclosure risk in synthetic patient records. Additionally, few outliers in synthetic data have been identified by medical experts	medGAN efficiently avoids mode collapse through minibatch averaging. It demonstrates limited privacy risk in identity and attribute disclosure, making it suitable for generating synthetic patient records
Cyclic GAN	The privacy-preserving framework minimally affects emotion recognition accuracy	Cyclic GAN effectively hides real emotion with a significant drop in emotion recognition accuracy of 96%. It preserves privacy in speech analysis while maintaining speech quality
Perturbation	The utility-preservation ability does not improve when training times exceed 130 for the MoMo dataset and 170 for the SFC dataset, indicating a plateau in performance. The method's utility loss is sensitive to the noise level parameter, which can affect the practical usage of the generated dataset, especially when the utility loss is high	Perturbation outperforms differential privacy approaches in both data utility and attack error. It achieves high privacy-preserving ability while maintaining high utility through training steps
PRGAN	Prior work relies on acceptable/unacceptable data, limiting generalizability. Some methods create private encodings for specific neural network architectures	PRGAN effectively hides sensitive attributes while ensuring high performance in target applications for property inference and training purposes. It can perform privacy-preserving tasks, such as hiding subjects' identities, with minimal performance drops after learning about different groups
LSTM-TrajGAN	The deep learning model requires extensive computation and training processes. It generates trajectories of the same length, limiting global-scale applicability. The model focuses on city-scale trajectories, which may not suit global-scale data	LSTM-TrajGAN better prevents user re-identification, enhancing privacy protection. It preserves essential spatial, temporal, and thematic characteristics of real trajectory data, maintaining utility for spatial and temporal analyses

patient information within telemedicine frameworks and medical research endeavors. These methodologies facilitate decentralized data exchange without jeopardizing patient confidentiality, thereby allowing institutions to collaborate effectively on clinical research and diagnostic efforts. For instance, federated learning frameworks implemented in medical facilities enable the exchange of insights derived from facial expression recognition algorithms without necessitating access to unprocessed patient information.

In the context of smart cities, models like DCGAN and LSTM-TrajGAN encounter obstacles pertaining to scalability, computational demands, and privacy when processing extensive datasets, such as street imagery or public transportation trajectories. Strategies to address these issues encompass the application of advanced inpainting algorithms and motion detection technologies to safeguard privacy in street-view imagery while preserving the integrity of image quality. Furthermore, hierarchical modeling and distributed computing architectures can be employed to enhance scalability, thereby facilitating city-wide applications of trajectory analysis without overwhelming computational infrastructures. For example, metropolitan areas such as Tokyo and Singapore have implemented such strategies within their surveillance and urban development systems, wherein data from video feeds and transit patterns are anonymized and utilized for traffic management, ensuring that personal identifiers are adequately protected. Empirical instances elucidate how these challenges are being effectively addressed. Within surveillance frameworks, the implementation of models that identify and eliminate identifiable objects or faces from video recordings aids in preserving privacy while still generating valuable insights for urban planning. In a similar vein, institutions such as the Mayo Clinic have embraced synthetic data generation techniques utilizing models like medGAN, thereby ensuring the confidentiality of patient information during expansive research initiatives. These instances exemplify how focused strategies can tackle the distinctive challenges posed by data privacy issues in healthcare and smart cities, presenting a framework that scholars can apply to analogous scenarios within their respective disciplines. By capitalizing on these methodologies, both domains can achieve a harmonious equilibrium between data utility and privacy preservation, thus ensuring that the benefits of GAN models are comprehensively harnessed in practical, real-world applications.

7.9   Conclusion

GANs have emerged as a powerful tool for safeguarding data privacy. By synthesizing highly realistic artificial data, GANs effectively protect sensitive information while preserving data utility. This study has demonstrated the versatility of GANs across various data modalities, including images, videos, text, speech, graphs, and spatiotemporal data. While challenges remain, such as generating high-quality synthetic data for complex domains and developing robust evaluation metrics, the potential of GANs in privacy preservation is undeniable. The generative models discussed exhibit a range of strengths and weaknesses in balancing privacy protection and data utility. VGAN and AD-GAN are particularly adept at learning identity-invariant representations and decomposing tasks for precise facial synthesis, respectively, but both are vulnerable to privacy attacks if their encoder networks are compromised. DCGAN excels in anonymizing medical images while maintaining segmentation accuracy, yet struggles with identity recovery and computational efficiency in federated learning. Similarly, A4NT offers a trade-off between privacy effectiveness and semantic similarity but suffers from semantic loss during anonymization. In contrast, AC-DCGAN generates synthetic data with no direct links to real records, thus mitigating re-identification risks, while medGAN addresses privacy concerns in healthcare but has identified outliers in synthetic datasets. Perturbation models outperform differential privacy approaches in utility but face sensitivity to noise levels. LSTM-TrajGAN enhances privacy protection in trajectory data but is limited by its computational demands and fixed-length outputs. APGE integrates mechanisms for privacy protection against inference attacks while maintaining accuracy in link prediction. While these models demonstrate innovative approaches to preserving privacy, they each contend with unique challenges that impact their effectiveness and applicability across different domains. To fully realize this potential, future research should focus on developing advanced GAN architectures, combining GANs with other privacy-enhancing techniques, establishing rigorous evaluation methodologies, and addressing ethical considerations. By prioritizing these areas, the field can contribute to a future where data-driven innovations coexist harmoniously with robust privacy safeguards.

References

[1]   L. Exibard. (2021). Automatic synthesis of systems with data. *Formal Languages and Automata Theory* [cs.FL]. Aix Marseille Université (AMU); Université libre de Bruxelles (ULB). English.

[2]   C. Yang, H. Zhao, L. Bruzzone *et al.* (2020). Lunar impact crater identification and age estimation with Chang'E data by deep and transfer learning. *Nature Communications*, 11, 6358, https://doi.org/10.1038/S41467-020-20215-Y.

[3]   Iqbal H. Sarker. (2021). Machine learning: Algorithms, real-world applications and research directions, *SN Computer Science*, 2(3), 160, https://doi.org/10.1007/S42979-021-00592-X.

[4]   A. E. Khandani, A. J. Kim, and A. W. Lo. (2010). Consumer credit-risk models via machine-learning algorithms. *Journal of Banking and Finance*, 34(11), 2767–2787, https://doi.org/10.1016/J.JBANKFIN.2010.06.001.

[5]   I. Goodfellow, J. Pouget-Abadie, M. Mirza, *et al.* (2014). Generative adversarial nets. *Advances in Neural Information Processing Systems*. Curran Associates, Inc., Newry, pp. 2672–2680.

[6]   T. Tikhe, P. Thorat, and V. Rodge. (2024). GAN-based steganography: Enhancing data concealment. *International Journal of Advanced Research in Science, Communication, and Technology*, 93(1), 46–52, https://doi.org/10.48175/ijarsct-18546.

[7]   S. Kalyanaraman, S. Ponnusamy, S. Saju, R. Vijay, and R. Karthikeyan. (2024). GAN-based privacy protection for public data sharing in wireless sensor networks. In S. Ponnusamy, J. Antari, P. Bhaladhare, A. Potgantwar, and S. Kalyanaraman (eds.), *Advances in Information Security, Privacy, and Ethics Book Series*, (pp. 259–273). Hershey, PA: IGI Global, https://doi.org/10.4018/979-8-3693-3597-0.ch018.

[8]   Z. Jiang, W. Ni, and Y. Zhang. (2024). PATE-TripleGAN: Privacy-preserving image synthesis with Gaussian differential privacy. arXiv preprint, https://doi.org/10.48550/arxiv.2404.12730.

[9]   M. Shateri, F. Messina, F. Labeau, and P. Piantanida. (2024). Preserving privacy in GANs against membership inference attack. *IEEE Transactions on Information Forensics and Security*, 19, 215–228, https://doi.org/10.1109/tifs.2023.3342654.

[10]   Y. Ma, Y. Yao, and X. Xu. (2024). PPIDSG: A privacy-preserving image distribution sharing scheme with GAN in federated learning. In *Proceedings of the AAAI Conference on Artificial Intelligence*, 38(13), 14272–14280, https://doi.org/10.1609/aaai.v38i13.29339.

[11]   B-W. Tseng, and P-Y. Wu. (2020). Compressive privacy generative adversarial network. *IEEE Transactions on Information Forensics and Security*, 15, 1231–1243, https://doi.org/10.1109/TIFS.2020.2968188.

[12]   L. Zhang, B. Shen, A. Barnawi, S. Xi, N. Kumar, and Y. Wu. (2021). FedDPGAN: Federated differentially private generative adversarial networks framework for the detection of COVID-19 pneumonia. *Information Systems Frontiers*, 23(6), 1341–1354, https://doi.org/10.1007/S10796-021-10144-6.

[13]   A. Triastcyn, and B. Faltings. (2020). Federated generative privacy. *IEEE Intelligent Systems*, 35(4), 50–57, https://doi.org/10.1109/MIS.2020.2993966.

[14]   A. E. Ouadrhiri, and A. Abdelhadi. (2022). Differential privacy for deep and federated learning: A survey. *IEEE Access*, 10, 22359–22380, https://doi.org/10.1109/access.2022.3151670.

[15]   T. Xiao, Y-H. Tsai, K. Sohn, M. Chandraker, and M-H. Yang. (2020). Adversarial learning of privacy-preserving and task-oriented representations. In *Proceedings of the AAAI Conference on Artificial Intelligence*, 34(7), 12434–12441, https://doi.org/10.1609/AAAI.V34I07.6930.

[16]   J. Chen, J. Konrad, and P. Ishwar. (2018). VGAN-based image representation learning for privacy-preserving facial expression recognition. In *Proceedings of the IEEE CVPR Workshops*. IEEE, Piscataway, NJ, pp. 1570–1579.

[17]   J. Cao, Y. Hu, B. Yu, R. He, and Z. Sun. (2019). 3D aided duet GANs for multi-view face image synthesis. *IEEE Transactions on Information Forensics and Security* 14, 8 (2019), 2028–2042.

[18]   B. N. Kim, J. Dolz, P-M. Jodoin, and C. Desrosiers. (2021). Privacy-Net: An adversarial approach for identity-obfuscated segmentation of medical images. *IEEE Transactions on Medical Imaging*, 40(7), 1737–1749, https://doi.org/10.1109/TMI.2021.3065727.

[19]   R. Uittenbogaard, C. Sebastian, J. Vijverberg, B. Boom, D. M. Gavrila, and P. H. N. de With. (2019). Privacy protection in street-view panoramas using

depth and multi-view imagery. In *Proceedings of the IEEE Conference on Computer Vision and Pattern Recognition.* IEEE, Piscataway, NJ, pp. 10581–10590.

[20] C. Huang, P. Kairouz, X. Chen, L. Sankar, and R. Rajagopal. (2017). Context-aware generative adversarial privacy. *Entropy*, 19(12), 656, https://doi.org/10.3390/E19120656.

[21] A. Triastcyn, and B. Faltings. (2018). Generating differentially private datasets using GANs. https://openreview.net/forum?id=rJv4XWZA-.

[22] Z. Cai, Z. Xiong, H. Xu, P. Wang, W. Li, and Y. Pan. (2021). Generative adversarial networks: A survey toward private and secure applications. *ACM Computing Surveys*, 54(6), 128, https://doi.org/10.1145/3459992.

[23] Z. Lin, A. Jain, C. Wang, G. Fanti, and V. Sekar. (2020). Using GANs for sharing networked time series data: Challenges, initial promise, and open questions. In *Proceedings of the ACM Internet Measurement Conference (IMC '20)*, New York, NY, USA, pp. 464–483, https://doi.org/10.1145/3419394.3423643.

[24] Z. Ren, Y. J. Lee, and M. S. Ryoo. (2018). Learning to anonymize faces for privacy preserving action detection. In *Proceedings of the European Conference on Computer Vision.* Springer, Berlin, pp. 620–636.

[25] Z. Wang, Z. Liu, C. Fu, A. Wen, M. Zhang, and W. Zhang. (2023). Privacy-preserving multiparty power data sharing based on generative adversarial network, *Eighth International Conference on Energy System, Electricity, and Power (ESEP 2023)*, 13159A9, https://doi.org/10.1117/12.3024222.

[26] N. Sahal, R. Krishnamoorthy, and N. Singh. (2024). Generating synthetic text using generative adversarial networks. In *Proceedings of the International Conference on Communication and Wireless Communication (ICOCWC)*, https://doi.org/10.1109/ICOCWC60930.2024.10470722.

[27] C. Zhu, J. Tang, H. Brouwer, J. F. Pérez, M. van Dijk, and L. Y. Chen. (2024). Quantifying and mitigating privacy risks for tabular generative models. arXiv Preprint, https://arxiv.org/abs/2403.07842.

[28] M. F. Yousuf, and M. S. Mahmud. (2024). Generating synthetic time-series data on edge devices using generative adversarial networks. In *International Conference on Computing, Networking and Communications (ICNC)*, Big Island, HI, USA, pp. 441–445, https://ieeexplore.ieee.org/document/10556140.

[29] R. Shetty, B. Schiele, and M. Fritz. (2018). A4NT: author attribute anonymity by adversarial training of neural machine translation. In *27th USENIX Security Symposium.* USENIX Security. pp. 1633–1650.

[30] N. Park, M. Mohammadi, K. Gorde, S. Jajodia, H. Park, and Y. Kim. (2018). Data synthesis based on generative adversarial networks. In *Proceedings of the VLDB Endowment* 11, 10, 1071–1083.

[31] E. Choi, S. Biswal, B. Malin, J. Duke, W. F. Stewart, and J. Sun. (2017). Generating multi-label discrete patient records using generative adversarial networks. In *Machine Learning for Healthcare Conference.* PMLR, pp. 286–305.

[32] D. Ericsson, A. Östberg, E. Listo Zec, J. Martinsson, and O. Mogren. (2020). Adversarial representation learning for private speech generation. arXiv Preprint, https://arxiv.org/abs/2006.09114.

[33] K. Vatanparvar, V. Nathan, E. Nemati, M. M. Rahman, and J. Kuang. (2020). Adapting to noise in speech obfuscation by audio profiling using generative models for passive health monitoring. In *2020 42nd Annual International Conference of the IEEE Engineering in Medicine & Biology Society*. IEEE, Piscataway, NJ, 5700–5704.

[34] R. Aloufi, H. Haddadi, and D. Boyle. (2019). Privacy preserving speech analysis using emotion filtering at the edge. In *Proceedings of the 17th Conference on Embedded Networked Sensor Systems (SenSys '19)*. ACM, New York, NY, USA, 426–427, https://doi.org/10.1145/3356250.3361947.

[35] K. Zhao, and N. Wang. (2024). Generating spatiotemporal trajectories with GANs and conditional GANs. In B. Luo, L. Cheng, Z. G. Wu, H. Li, C. Li (eds.), *Neural Information Processing. ICONIP 2023. Communications in Computer and Information Science* (pp. 407–421). Singapore: Springer, https://doi.org/10.1007/978-981-99-8126-7_32.

[36] Y. Qu, S. Yu, W. Zhou, and Y. Tian. (2020). GAN-driven personalized spatial-temporal private data sharing in cyber-physical social systems. *IEEE Transactions on Network Science and Engineering*, 7(4), 2576–2586, https://doi.org/10.1109/TNSE.2020.3001061.

[37] Ren O., Haruki Y., Hamada R., and Hirozumi Y. (2022). Sharing without caring: Privacy protection of users' spatio-temporal data without compromise on utility. In *Proceedings of the 30th International Conference on Advances in Geographic Information Systems (SIGSPATIAL '22)*. Association for Computing Machinery, New York, USA, pp. 1–2, https://doi.org/10.1145/3557915.3565534.

[38] N. Ashrafi, V. Schmitt, R. Spang, S. Möller, and J.-N. Voigt-Antons. (2023). Protect and extend – Using GANs for synthetic data generation of time-series medical records. In *15th International Conference on Quality of Multimedia Experience (QoMEX)*, Ghent, Belgium, pp. 171–176, https://doi.org/10.1109/QoMEX58391.2023.10178496.

[39] D. Yin, and Q. Yang. (2018). GANs based density distribution privacy-preservation on mobility data. *Security and Communication Networks*, 2018, 9203076, https://doi.org/10.1155/2018/9203076.

[40] A. Rezaei, C. Xiao, J. Gao, and B. Li. (2018). Protecting sensitive attributes via generative adversarial networks. arXiv Preprint, https://arxiv.org/abs/1812.10193.

[41] J. Rao, S. Gao, Y. Kang, and Q. Huang. (2021). LSTM-TrajGAN: A deep learning approach to trajectory privacy protection. In *11th International Conference on Geographic Information Science, GIScience*, Vol. 177. Schloss Dagstuhl—Leibniz-Zentrum für Informatik, pp 12:1–12:17.

[42] A. Li, J. Fang, Q. Jiang, B. Zhou, and Y. Jia. (2020). A graph data privacy-preserving method based on generative adversarial networks. In *Web Information Systems Engineering – WISE 2020*. Lecture Notes in Computer

Science, pp. 227–239. Cham: Springer, https://doi.org/10.1007/978-3-030-62008-0_16.

[43]   L. Hou, W. Ni, S. Zhang, N. Fu, and D. Zhang. (2023). WDP-GAN: Weighted graph generation with GAN under differential privacy. *IEEE Transactions on Network and Service Management*, 20(4), 5155–5165, https://doi.org/10.1109/tnsm.2023.3280916.

[44]   C. Ma, J. Li, M. Ding, *et al.* (2023). RDP-GAN: A Rényi-differential privacy based generative adversarial network. *IEEE Transactions on Dependable and Secure Computing*, 20(6), 4838–4852, https://doi.org/10.1109/tdsc.2022.3233580.

[45]   J. Li, H. Zhang, Z. Han, Y. Rong, H. Cheng, and J. Huang. (2020). Adversarial attack on community detection by hiding individuals. In *Proceedings of The Web Conference 2020*. ACM, New York, pp. 917–927.

[46]   J. Fang, A. Li, and Q. Jiang. (2019). GDAGAN: An anonymization method for graph data publishing using generative adversarial network. In *2019 6th International Conference on Information Science and Control Engineering*. IEEE, Piscataway, NJ, pp. 309–313.

[47]   A. Li, J. Fang, Q. Jiang, B. Zhou, and Y. Jia. (2020). A graph data privacy-preserving method based on generative adversarial networks. In *International Conference on Web Information Systems Engineering*. Springer, Berlin, pp. 227–239.

[48]   K. Li, G. Luo, Y. Ye, W. Li, S. Ji, and Z. Cai. (2021). Adversarial privacy-preserving graph embedding against inference attack. *IEEE Internet of Things Journal*, 8(8), 6904–6915, https://doi.org/10.1109/JIOT.2020.3036583.

Chapter 8

Impact of generative AI on Industry 4.0 and digital transformation

Shanthababu Pandian[1] and Shanthakumar Pandian[2]

Abstract

Industry 4.0 revolution is redefining the manufacturing sector by integrating advanced digital technologies such as IoT, big data analytics, cloud computing (Azure, AWS, and GCP), and AI, helping us to create highly intelligent, efficient, reactive, and proactive solutions across the industry. In recent years, generative AI has been a critical component of digital transformation in recent years, playing a comprehensive role in enhancing data-driven decision-making, optimizing operations, accessing performance, and promoting innovative solutions. Generative AI capabilities enable the following key factors: data-driven transformation, smart manufacturing, predictive, prescriptive and preventive (3Ps) maintenance, improving operational efficiency, and reducing costs. Furthermore, it drives product and process innovation, customization, and personalization, thereby shortening the time to market. As a transformative force, generative AI is also reshaping the workforce, supporting remote work models, facilitating skill development, and creating new job roles in AI management and data analysis. This chapter explores the profound impact of generative AI on Industry 4.0 in detail. It demonstrates how it aligns with and enhances the principles of this industrial revolution, ultimately leading to a more sustainable and competitive manufacturing landscape.

Keywords: Industry 4.0; data; data analytics; generative AI; smart manufacturing; data-driven decision-making; 3Ps; predictive maintenance; IoT (Internet of Things); big data analytics; cloud computing; supply chain management and logistics

8.1 Introduction

Industry 4.0, also known as the Fourth Industrial Revolution, is a transformative concept revolutionizing the manufacturing industry. It is characterized by

[1]Director Data and AI, Rolan Software and Consultancy Services, London, UK
[2]Design and Engineering Consultant, S-Square dot AI Engineering and Technologies, Chennai, India

integrating digital technologies into manufacturing and industrial processes, leveraging advancements such as the Internet of Things (IoT), big data analytics, cloud computing, and excellent automation systems [1]. This integration creates intelligent factories that are more integrated, efficient, flexible, and responsive. Central to this transformation is the use of **artificial intelligence** (AI), which helps to enhance complex decision-making, optimizes operations, streamlines the supply chain, enables new business models, and improves sustainability. The future of manufacturing is here, and it is an exciting time to be a part of this revolution [6,7].

Moreover, implementing AI into the manufacturing processes industry will open the way for developing new business models and enhance prioritized digital transformation, customization, personalization, and sustainability across every manufacturing industry. AI-driven solutions allow industries to produce high-quality goods more efficiently while minimizing waste and sustaining resources effectively, contributing to a more sustainable manufacturing ecosystem. This ability to create and customize products tailored to individual customer preferences also sets the stage for increased competitiveness and a stable global market.

In **Industry 4.0**, AI connect, especially generative AI technology, is playing a transformative role in integrating digital technologies into manufacturing at different levels, and the scope is limitless. Undoubtedly, generative AI enhances product design by automatically generating innovative models and optimizing them for production. AI-driven robotics in industries improves automation, enabling machines to adapt and increase productivity on manufacturing lines. Ultimately, AI offers a massive space for real-time simulations of physical processes through digital twins, helping optimize operations and reduce downtime in the manufacturing domain. Indeed, this will help enhance the overall performance of the operations [5,7].

AI-powered predictive maintenance analyzes sensor data with the help of Industrial Internet of Things (IIoT) to anticipate machine performance, efficiency, and failures and minimize disruptions. It also supports mass customization by allowing manufacturers to produce personalized products at scale efficiently to enhance their business. Supply chains benefit from AI's simulation capabilities, which improve logistics, inventory management, and demand forecasting, covering all the stages of supply chain management (SCM).

AI-based quality control ensures defect detection early, maintaining product consistency. Additionally, AI optimizes energy consumption and reduces waste, making processes more sustainable by predictive modeling for various stages in the manufacturing industry. Collaborative robots (cobots) powered by AI safely work alongside humans, improving factory efficiency and reducing the risk level for workers in production lanes.

Generative AI accelerates rapid prototyping, shortening product development cycles. AI-enhanced cybersecurity safeguards interconnected industrial systems from cyber threats.

8.2   Discussion

8.2.1   Impact of generative AI on Industry 4.0

Let us discuss how the impact of generative AI on Industry 4.0 and digital transformation is profound and multifaceted:

- **Data-driven transformation**: As we all know, data is often called the **new oil** because of its vital role in driving innovation and transforming industries, and it can be used for multiple purposes in the industry for various beneficiaries, including data analytics, data science, and machine learning. Generative AI's data-driven nature aligns perfectly with the principles of Industry 4.0, where data from IoT sensors, machines, and process equipment are continuously analyzed to understand performance and operations to drive improvements across the industry. Evidently, it enhances this by not only analyzing but also generating new data-driven solutions, which help in many ways. Generative AI's adaptability to the needs of Industry 4.0 is particularly reassuring [4,5]. It is capable of analyzing vast amounts of data, generating insights, predictions, and classification, and helping industries make informed decisions using data-driven solutions alongside manufacturing industries; this could optimize supply chains, predict maintenance needs, improve quality control processes and many more aspects, demonstrating its compatibility with the evolving landscape of manufacturing and digital transformation.
- **Smart manufacturing**: Since we have the facilities to connect the IoT and AI in the field, we can build smart manufacturing effectively. Especially, generative AI has significantly enhanced the capabilities of intelligent manufacturing processes because its nature supports any data format and aligns with the strategy plans well ahead. Integrating highly sophisticated AI algorithms with IoT and IIoT devices that are well connected with factory equipment and implementing autonomous monitoring and capturing real-time operations data and adjustments have led to unparalleled efficiency and precision, reducing waste and optimizing resource use from various factors such as effort, cost and time [2–4].
- **Predictive, prescriptive, and preventive (3Ps) maintenance**: Generative AI supports 3Ps with extensive applications in any manufacturing industry. Advanced machine learning models help us analyze sensor data to predict equipment failures before they happen and control them from the control room instead of someone monitoring and recording the equipment's performance. This proactive approach essentially minimizes downtime and maintenance costs, ensures smoother operations, and extends the lifespan of machinery on the manufacturing floor [1,5].
- **Improving operational efficiency**: Generative AI helps us optimize complex operations and processes, such as manufacturing design, workflows, and logistics, leading to substantial improvements in efficiency and reductions in cost, effort, etc. This is not a straightforward method; instead, it simulates various scenarios, and AI can identify the most efficient routes, schedules, or resource allocations and ensure that the goals are achieved.

- **Automation of innovative tasks**: Most of the manufacturing industries are working as traditionally requiring human creativity, such as content creation, marketing campaigns, and even some aspects of product design, which can now be partially or fully automated using Innovative ways with the help of generative AI. This approach allows entire businesses to scale up innovative processes and focus on higher-level strategic activities using available data and generated data (Figure 8.1) [6,7].
- **Product and process innovation (PnP innovation)**: Not only for marketing purposes, but generative AI can also rapidly generate new product designs, optimizing for various parameters such as cost, material usage, and performance in an effective manner, with appropriate inputs. This accelerates the design process and leads to the creation of innovative tools and products that may not have been devised through traditional and manual methods these many years ago [2,3,5].
- **Customization and personalization**: Customization and personalization are always priorities in any manufacturing industry to attract customers and enhance their satisfaction. With generative AI, this has been enhanced by sophisticated methods of analyzing multidimensional models. So, more companies can offer highly personalized products and services by tailoring them based on customer needs and demands, considering customer preferences as the first thought in their minds. This activity is essential in fashion design, automotive, and modern consumer electronics, where customization is becoming a key differentiator.

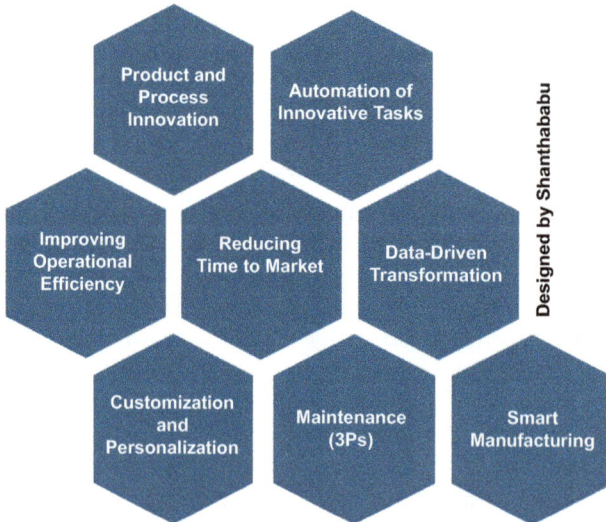

Figure 8.1   Impact of generative AI on Industry 4.0

- **Reducing time to market**: This parameter is crucial in any industry with rapidly changing consumer interest, demand, and short product life cycles. By accelerating design and development processes with the help of generative AI reduces the time it takes to bring new products to market since it ultimately supports improving operational efficiency by adopting automation of innovative tasks for identifying products and processes in creative ways and customization and personalization methods, helping us to reduce time to market and reach the customers on time.

So far, we have discussed the various parameters influencing the industry along with generative AI and IoT.

8.2.2 *Exploring the impact of generative AI on Industry 4.0*

Let us explore this in detail with specific areas

- **Predictive maintenance**: Predictive maintenance is a standout application in any manufacturing industry. Advanced machine learning models help us analyze sensor data to predict equipment failures before they happen and control them from the control room instead of someone monitoring and recording the equipment's performance. This proactive approach essentially minimizes downtime and maintenance costs, ensures smoother operations, and extends the lifespan of machinery on the manufacturing floor.
- **Impact**: Smart manufacturing: Generative AI enables the creation of advanced automation systems that can design, monitor, and optimize production processes in real-time using cloud technology and current Gen AI and AIML. This leads to higher efficiency, reduced waste, and improved quality control.

  Examples:
- AI-powered robots or cobots on assembly lines to enhance precision and speed
- AI-driven maintenance scheduling systems in factories that predict and prevent equipment failures (Figure 8.2).
- **Enhancing data-driven decision-making**: There is evidence that generative AI is a powerful tool for strengthening data-driven decision-making across various industries. This is achieved by enabling advanced data analysis, scenario simulation, personalized insights, and real-time decision-making; in other words, it empowers organizations to make more informed, efficient, and objective decisions to benefit their business sustainability for their customers and credibility for the stakeholders. As businesses navigate an increasingly complex and data-rich environment, integrating generative AI into decision-making processes will be crucial for maintaining a competitive edge and driving innovation.

Advanced analytics, such as generative AI, excels at processing and analyzing large datasets to uncover patterns and insights that inform strategic decisions in critical situations. This capability is crucial for businesses leveraging big data to gain a competitive advantage [1].

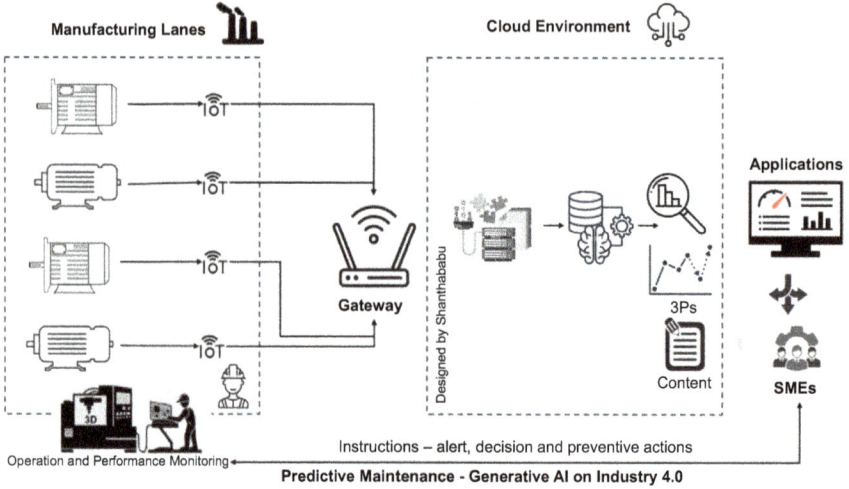

Figure 8.2   Predictive maintenance using generative AI in Industry 4.0

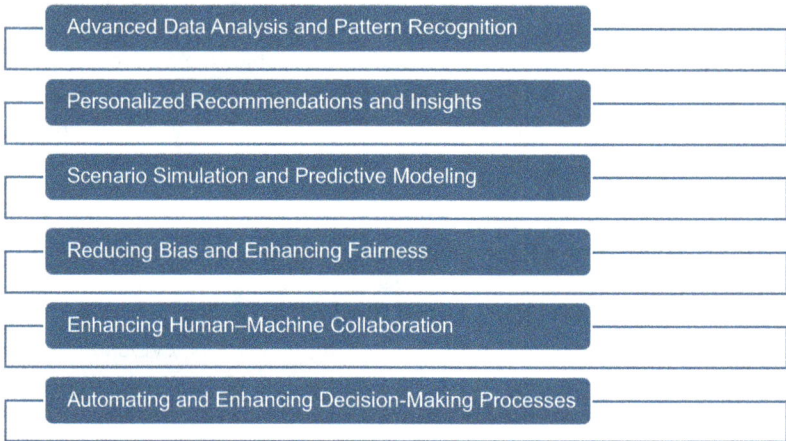

Figure 8.3   Data-driven decision-making using generative AI

Figure 8.3 represents where generative AI (Gen AI) comes into play, revolutionizing how organizations approach data-driven decision-making.

Certainly, real-time decision-making is highly supported since AI systems provide real-time analytics and timely decisions, specifically from an industry perspective. This is invaluable in fast-paced environments, such as from an order management decision perspective. These systems enhance decision accuracy and speed, leading to better outcomes (Figure 8.4).

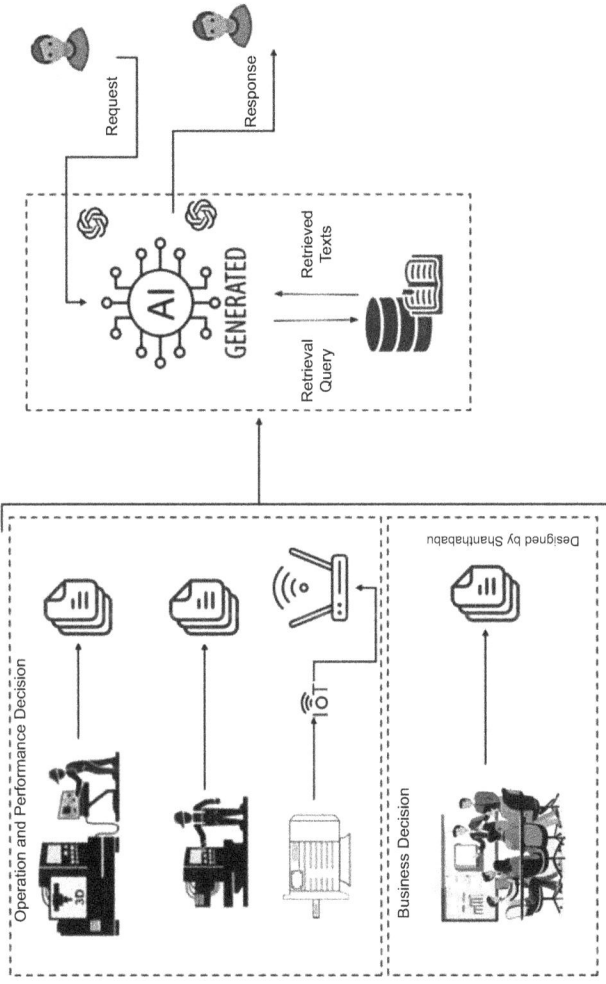

Figure 8.4 Enhancing data-driven decision-making: using generative AI in Industry 4.0

Impact: Generative AI can analyze vast amounts of data to uncover hidden patterns, trends, and insights, aiding in better decision-making processes across various organizational levels.

Real-time decision support: AI systems can provide real-time recommendations and insights, enabling us to make informed decisions quickly.

Examples:

- Retail companies use AI to analyze customer data and optimize inventory management.
- Financial services utilize AI for risk assessment and fraud detection.

- **Optimizing supply chain and logistics**: Generative AI, with its ability to generate new solutions, designs, and insights from existing data, plays a pivotal role in this transformation. Optimizing the supply chain and logistics is becoming increasingly complex and well-interconnected parts. Integrating digital technologies like the IoT and big data analytics is regularly transforming how businesses manage and optimize their supply chains regularly. Here are the classic areas and situations where and how generative AI is optimizing supply chain and logistics in Industry 4.0 (Figure 8.5). The items below are essential in supply chain management and logistics (SCM & L); we will explore them as follows:

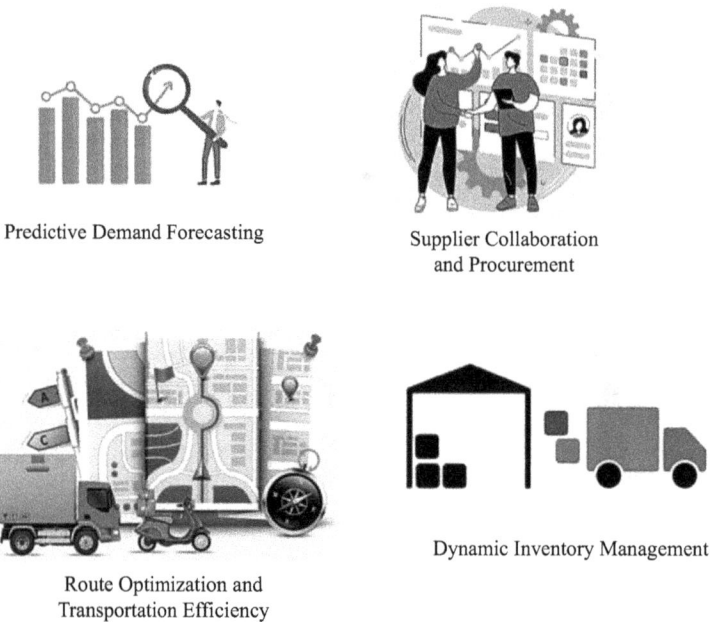

Predictive Demand Forecasting

Supplier Collaboration
and Procurement

Route Optimization and
Transportation Efficiency

Dynamic Inventory Management

Designed by Shanthababu

Figure 8.5   Optimizing supply chain and logistics: using generative AI in Industry 4.0 [8]

o   Predictive demand forecasting
o   Dynamic inventory management
o   Supply chain resilience and risk management
o   Sustainability and environmental impact
o   Continuous improvement and innovation (CII)

Demand forecasting is always a highly challenging part of any manufacturing industry. AI models can predict demand trends with high precision, enabling businesses to optimize inventory levels and reduce both stockouts and excess inventory. This leads to better cash flow management and customer satisfaction.

Logistics optimization is highly preferred. Generative AI optimizes logistics by analyzing traffic patterns, weather conditions, and delivery constraints to suggest the most efficient routes. This reduces transportation costs and improves delivery reliability.

Let us discuss a few of them here.

- **Predictive demand forecasting**: It generates highly accurate demand predictions that help organizations predict customer needs and accommodate their supply chains accordingly. Generative AI capabilities can be used to enhance demand forecasting by analyzing historical data, market demand, trends, and external factors like weather or economic indicators influencing the supply chain. This can improve demand forecasting; businesses can reduce excess inventory, minimize stockouts, and optimize production schedules.

    Generative AI, with its advanced data processing techniques and insight recognition capabilities, significantly enhances predictive demand forecasting, making it more accurate, dynamic, and responsive to real-time changes.

    Predictive demand forecasting using generative AI is a transformative approach that improves demand planning accuracy, responsiveness, and efficiency in Industry 4.0. It leverages big data, real-time input, scenario-based modeling, and continuous learning. AI-driven demand forecasts enable companies to respond proactively to market changes, optimize their supply chains, and improve overall business performance. Generative AI in demand forecasting processes will be essential for staying competitive in a rapidly evolving market (Figure 8.6).

Figure 8.6   Predictive demand forecasting: using generative AI in Industry 4.0

- o   Leveraging big data for accurate forecasting
- o   Dynamic and real-time forecasting
- o   Scenario-based forecasting

- **Leveraging big data for accurate forecasting**: Generative AI can analyze enormous amounts of historical and real-time data from multiple sources. By handling and correlating this data, AI models can identify underlying patterns and trends influencing demand. The comprehensive analysis enables more accurate demand predictions, allowing companies to anticipate market needs better.
- **Dynamic and real-time forecasting**: Generative AI enables dynamic forecasting, continuously updating demand predictions based on real-time data inputs with the help of IoT and cloud technologies. This allows companies to respond immediately to unexpected events, such as unanticipated changes in customer demand, supply chain disruptions, or competitor actions. For instance, if a new product launch generates higher-than-expected demand, AI can quickly adjust forecasts to ensure sufficient inventory levels and production capacity, preventing stockouts and lost sales prospects.
- **Scenario-based forecasting**: Of course, the generative AI can simulate manifold demand scenarios based on different expectations and variables such as changes in market conditions, pricing strategies, promotional activities, customer demand, and seasonal changes. These scenario-based forecasts provide organizations with a range of possible, reliable outcomes and enabling them to plan for various eventualities. For example, AI can model the potential impact of a price reduction on demand for a particular product, helping organizations decide whether to proceed with the pricing or product strategy. This approach reduces the risk of overrun or underproduction situations and ensures that resources are allocated efficiently.
- **Dynamic inventory management**: Conventional inventory management trusts static rules and models, as we know them well, which can lead to ineffectiveness, and we could realize during the system failure to sustain. Generative AI introduces dynamic inventory management by continuously analyzing data from various sources such as real-time data from sensors, sales, and supply chain operations.

It generates optimal inventory levels for each product, location, and time, digesting the data and appropriate inputs to help the organization maintain the right amount of stock. This reduces time, effort, and cost, minimizes waste, and ensures timely product availability at customer locations.

Impact: Demand forecasting: AI can accurately predict future demand trends, enabling better inventory management and reducing stockouts or overstock situations. Logistics and Route Optimization: AI algorithms can optimize logistics and delivery routes, reducing transportation costs and improving delivery times.

Figure 8.7   Supply Chain Resilience and Risk Management (SCR & RM): using generative AI in Industry 4.0

Examples:

- Retail giants like Amazon use AI for inventory management and demand forecasting.
- Logistics companies employ AI to optimize delivery routes and schedules.
- **Supply chain resilience and risk management (SCR & RM)**: Generative AI offers potentially transformative capabilities for enhancing "Supply Chain Resilience" and "Risk Management" in Industry 4.0. This is achieved by leveraging AI's predictive analytics, real-time monitoring system, dynamic simulation, and optimization in operation capabilities [3]. This advanced technology adoption in SCM is essential for maintaining effectiveness and confirming long-term success stories in a progressively volatile global market. This is a slightly more critical topic, so I will go deeper.

Generative AI is a powerful tool offering innovative solutions that enhance the resilience and effectiveness of SCM as mentioned below (Figure 8.7).

- **Real-time monitoring and response**: Generative AI systems can continuously monitor supply chain activities in real time, providing alerts and recommendations as soon as any deviations are detected. For instance, if a shipment is delayed due to unforeseen circumstances, AI can immediately notify supply chain managers and suggest alternate routes. At the same time, it can communicate the potential delay and prevent unnecessary noises from the system. This real-time responsiveness ensures that issues are addressed promptly, reducing the risk of delays and disruptions [4].
- **Supply chain optimization**: Generative AI can optimize SCM configurations by analyzing and restructuring networks to enhance maximum resilience. This involves evaluating supplier confidence level, consistency, transportation effectiveness, and inventory management best practices. AI-powered optimization can suggest alternative suppliers and best logistics routes to prevent the business

workflow that may be more resilient to specific risks, such as natural disasters or political instability in and out of the board. Organization can build a more robust and adaptable network by continuously improving the supply chain based on real-time data and predictive analytics.

- **Enhanced supplier collaboration**: Generative AI can extract insights and decision-making capabilities and facilitate better collaboration with suppliers by providing insights into their operational performance, risk acquaintances, and dependability. By sharing AI-driven risk assessment reports and insights with suppliers, companies can work together to address liabilities and enhance their overall supply chain platform strength [4]. This collaborative approach ensures a tight bond between manufacturers and suppliers and aligns their risk management strategies, leading to more substantial and resilient alliances.

- **Dynamic risk mitigation strategies**: Generative AI can adjust risk mitigation strategies and plans based on advancing environmental scenarios. For example, suppose a particular supplier's risk profile increases due to financial uncertainty and other political and geopolitical factors. In that case, AI can undoubtedly recommend shifting critical orders to alternative suppliers based on the demands or strategically increasing inventory buffers with appropriate actions and approaches. This dynamic approach allows companies to remain aligned with agile and reactive to changing risk environments, ensuring continuous supply chain resilience without any roadblocks.

- **Sustainability and environmental impact**: Generative AI is a highly effective transformative force in enhancing sustainability and environmental impact assessment within Industry 4.0. It helps by optimizing resource utilization and improving effectiveness, reducing waste, lowering carbon footprints, and supporting green supply chain practices; AI empowers companies to achieve their sustainability goals using strategy plans in place, tracking the goals and guiding the organization at a super significant level. As industries evolve toward green practices, generative AI will be crucial in driving innovation and ensuring that environmental initiatives and responsibilities remain at the forefront of manufacturing and SCM (Figure 8.8).
  o   Lifecycle assessment (LCA)
  o   Carbon footprint reduction
  o   Waste minimization and circular economy
  o   Sustainable SCM

Designed by Shanthababu

Figure 8.8   Sustainability and environmental impact: using generative AI in Industry 4.0 [9]

- **Lifecycle assessment**: A LCA is a critical tool for evaluating a product's environmental impact from inception to disposal of materials [6,7]. Without question, generative AI can enhance LCA by processing large datasets from the entire product lifecycle of any product manufacturing industry, including raw material extraction, manufacturing process, transportation method, usage of material and wastage, and end-of-life disposal material. Absolutely, AI can definitely identify the stages where the environmental impact is most significant and suggest improvements by analyzing the data and extracting insights with the help of sustainable materials or designing for recyclability components. This broad analysis enables manufacturing industries to create products with a lower environmental footprint.
- **Carbon footprint reduction**: Generative AI can assist in calculating and reducing the carbon footprint of manufacturing operations very similar to LCA by analyzing energy consumption, inventory, transportation, logistics, and supply chain activities. AI can identify the primary sources of carbon emissions, percentages and root causes and recommend strategies to mitigate them effectively. These AI-powered insights help manufacturing industries align their operations with global guidelines and sustainability goals such as reducing carbon emissions in line with the Paris Agreement [7].
- **Waste minimization and circular economy**: Waste reduction is a crucial aspect of sustainability, and without further questions, generative AI offers powerful tools for minimizing waste throughout the production process. AI can optimize manufacturing processes to reduce scrap and by-products, identify opportunities for reusing materials, and support the implementation of circular economic principles in tremendous ways. By enabling closed-loop production systems, where waste materials are repurposed into new innovative products, AI helps companies move toward a more sustainable and circular economy. This approach reduces environmental impact and opens new innovative streams from recycled materials and revenue [6,7].
- **Sustainable supply chain management**: Generative AI can assess the environmental impact of supply chain activities by analyzing data collected across the industry and capturing factors such as transportation emissions, waste materials, and the ecological routine of logistics networks. AI can evaluate and identify patterns and insights in suppliers' sustainability credentials and recommend those with lower ecological footprints, enabling manufacturing industries to build more sustainable supply chains. Furthermore, AI can optimize logistics routes to reduce transportation emissions and suggest using more environmentally friendly modes of transport, such as electric vehicles or rail, for a green environment perspective [5,7].
- **Continuous improvement and innovation**: In the rapidly evolving landscape of Industry 4.0 and generative AI, CII are highly required and essential for maintaining competitiveness and acclimatizing to changing market demands and customer needs in the global market. Generative AI has emerged as a powerful tool to enable all these processes and offer advanced capabilities that drive ongoing enhancements in manufacturing efficiency, product design and

development, and operational strategies regarding employees, resources, and costs incurred. By leveraging the substantial potential of generative AI, organizations can adopt a culture of CII that is integral to their success in the Industry 4.0 era.

o   Fostering a culture of innovation
o   Predictive innovation
o   Innovation in product design
o   Innovation in sustainability Practices
o   Accelerating innovative R&D processes

- **Transforming workforce**: Always-skilled augmentation is vital in any industry; AI tools augment human capabilities by automating routine tasks and providing advanced analytical support. This allows employees to focus on higher-value activities, fostering a more skilled and efficient workforce. Due to this Gen AI, new roles and opportunities are in place to enhance the entire model. Integrating AI into the industry has created new roles, such as AI specialists, data scientists, and AI ethics officers [4]. These positions are crucial for managing and guiding AI-driven transformations within organizations.

  Gen AI is emerging as a transformative force, as we understand well, especially in the landscape of Industry 4.0, where automation, IoT, and data analytics are revolutionizing industrial processes. It provides immense benefits, including transforming the workforce. Gen AI's ability to create, optimize, and innovate extends beyond machines and processes, directly impacting workers' roles, skills, and the overall workplace environment. Here is how generative AI is transforming the workforce in Industry 4.0:

  o   Driving innovation and creativity
  o   Supporting remote and hybrid work models
  o   Facilitating skill development and reskilling
  o   Improving workplace safety
  o   Personalizing employee experiences
  o   Enabling collaboration between humans and AI

  Let us explore a few of them.
- **Driving innovation and creativity**: Generative AI empowers employees to innovate by providing new tools and technologies that expand their creative possibilities and unlock their potential skills to enhance their work. In industries like design, sales, marketing, and content creation, AI can generate new concepts, designs, and ideas that serve as a foundation for human creativity. Let us say that in product development, AI can generate prototypes or suggest design improvements, allowing designers to explore a broader range of possibilities and accelerate the innovation process that the industry can implement with less cost, effort, and time.
- **Supporting remote and hybrid work models**: Generative AI further supports the shift toward remote and hybrid work models, accelerated by the COVID-19

pandemic. Many AI-driven tools can facilitate remote collaboration, virtual training, and real-time communication, ensuring that teams remain connected and productive regardless of physical location [4,5]. For example, AI can generate virtual simulations or digital twins of physical assets, allowing remote workers to interact with and manage them on-site. This indirectly reduces the cost of operations and facilitation for the organization, and at the same time, employees also benefit more concerning personal and official aspects (Figure 8.9).

- **Facilitating skill development and reskilling**: The rise of AI in Industry 4.0 necessitates new skills and capabilities among the workforce. Generative AI can play a role in training and reskilling employees in many ways by generating personalized learning paths, simulating real-world scenarios, and providing interactive training modules. AI-driven platforms can create customized training programs that adapt to each worker's pace and learning style, ensuring they acquire the skills needed for new roles in an AI-enhanced environment, no question about it.

Impact: AI tools can augment human capabilities by automating repetitive tasks and providing advanced analytical tools, enabling employees to focus on higher-value activities.

New job roles: Integrating AI into industries will undoubtedly create new job roles that require expertise in AI management, data analysis, and other advanced technical skills.

Examples:

- Manufacturing sectors where workers use AI tools for quality inspection and process optimization.

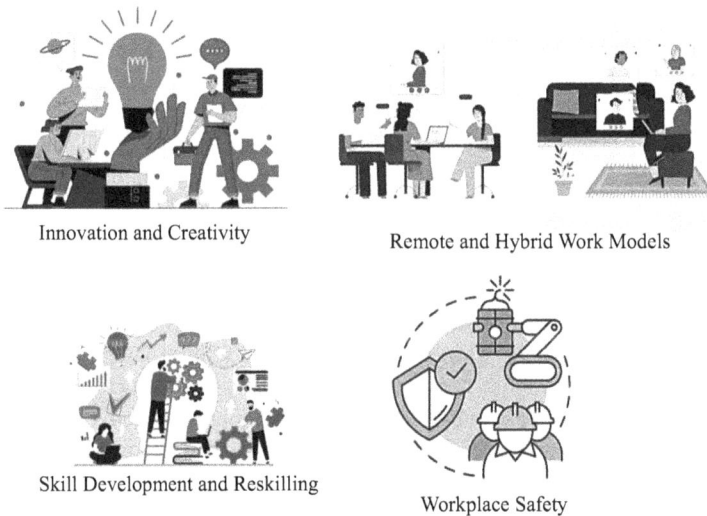

Innovation and Creativity

Remote and Hybrid Work Models

Skill Development and Reskilling

Workplace Safety

Figure 8.9   Transforming the workforce: using generative AI in Industry 4.0 [10]

- IT companies hire AI specialists and data scientists to manage AI-driven projects.

With the same passion, we can discuss more aspects as given in the list below.

- Improved quality control
- Enhancing quality control
- Personalizing customer experiences
- Accelerating product design and development

8.2.3   Challenges and limitations

So far, we have discussed that generative AI in Industry 4.0 offers significant and high potential for innovation-based automation and optimization throughout its life cycle but also presents several limitations and challenges. These include technical infrastructure issues, integration with legacy systems, and ensuring data quality and security; additionally, concerns about AI explainability in the solutions, product trustworthiness, compliance, and sustainability are vital barriers that industries must address to fully realize the potential of generative AI in this new industrial revolution.

Here are the key challenges and limitations:

- **Data-connected challenges**
  - **Data quality and availability**: As we know, large volumes of high-quality data are necessary for building generative AI solutions. However, industrial environments often produce noisy, incomplete, and lack of data standardization and unstructured data, affecting AI models' accuracy and reliability and leading to AI products' reliability.
  - **Data privacy and security**: Data security and privacy compliance are significant challenges when dealing with sensitive operational information in AI product development and deployment. Aligning with data protection laws like General Data Protection Regulation and California Consumer Privacy Act becomes complex when generative AI processes industrial data.
  - **Data silos**: Generative AI applications require integrated data from multiple sources, and breaking down these silos (data is fragmented and stored in isolated systems) is a technical and organizational challenge [2,3,5].

- **Technical challenges**
  - **Computational resources**: High computation resources are mandatory for processing data and building and deploying generative AI models, which rely on vast volumes of data (big data) and utilize robust algorithms such as deep learning, neural networks, and natural language processing. It should be the high-performance computing infrastructure environment that includes GPUs and sophisticated distributed systems. This environmental setup can be a substantial barrier for industries not already equipped with such technology to implement, as well as the cost factors.
  - **Integration with legacy systems**: Many industries have been built and in production for many years, and they have considerable orders to produce

and deliver on time as committed. Of course, all these industries rely on legacy systems and partially or entirely outdated equipment that may not be compatible with modern big data and AI tools and technologies. Integrating generative AI into these legacy systems and environments requires retrofitting or replacing existing production unit infrastructure in the manufacturing industry, which can be expensive and time-consuming. So, the management is not ready to invest in these kinds of integration and will continue with the traditional operations methodology [2,5].

o   **Energy consumption**: In industries aiming for sustainability and energy efficiency, balancing AI's benefits with its environmental impact is a growing concern. The complex, industrial AI-based application testing and training move before production can be energy-intensive while leading the AI systems contribute to the AI system's carbon footprint.

- **Model explainability and trust**
  o   **Lack of explainability**: AI Explainability is another major industry challenge across all industries. In AI, this lack of explainability is termed "black boxes." It is not easy to interpret how AI systems make decisions from the given data and use algorithms. In industrial settings where safety, reliability, and compliance are crucial, as discussed in the earlier challenges, the inability factor reduces trust in the technology and tools we offer [4].
  o   **Risk of erroneous outputs**: Generative AI can produce unexpected or erroneous outputs for various reasons, which can lead to health and safety-critical and high-stakes environments that could result in system failures, defective products, or worker safety. We must ensure that AI-generated outputs are robust and reliable, which is a significant challenge.

- **Workforce and skills gap**
  o   **Talent shortage**: While developing, implementing and maintaining generative AI-based solutions to support Industry 4.0 demands by gaining interdisciplinary skills that combine knowledge of **manufacturing processes, AI, data science, and big data**. There is a shortage of professionals with expertise in AI and industrial systems, so organizations may struggle to implement and manage generative AI technologies without this expertise.
  o   **Change management**: Existing workers in the industry may be concerned about job displacement, especially in traditionally manual labor and into the field many years without any background knowledge in AI system even at a high level and even though they are not ready to adopt AI in industrial settings requires to upskill or organizations reskill employees, which can be met with resistance.

- **Cost and resource allocation**
  o   **High implementation costs**: AI systems require high computational power, new software products, and licensing costs, and industries must invest considerable expenses in data collection, storage, and ongoing maintenance processes. These upfront costs may be unaffordable for small and medium-sized enterprises (SMEs).

     ○   **Time-intensive model training**: AI system building is highly time-consuming since it involves various stages, right from defining the problem statement, data collection, model development, training, and deploying generative AI systems can be time-consuming. In some situations, the training process may need to be repeated frequently as new data becomes available, further complicating the implementation process until satisfactory results from the system and monitoring the system are always at an acceptable level [6,7].

• **Security risks and ethical concerns**
     ○   **Cybersecurity threats**: Cybersecurity is becoming vital in the manufacturing industry since its industrial operations are increasingly connected to the Internet via IIoT devices and other distributed systems, which might lead to cyberattacks. Protecting AI models and the data they rely on from malicious attacks is the principal task for AI and cybersecurity architects in designing such a system, especially those dealing with critical processes that could become targets for cybercriminals.
     ○   **Adversarial attacks**: As mentioned earlier, industrial operations increasingly connect to the internet via IIoT, which is susceptible to adversarial attacks, where subtle changes to the critical input data disturb the precision and reliability of outputs and misleading outcomes from the AI systems, such as manufacturing defects or production delays it could take it to the severe consequences in the manufacturing operations and flow.

8.3 Conclusion

Generative AI drives Industry 4.0 and digital transformation, enabling organizations to enhance efficiency, innovate, and stay competitive. By leveraging AI's capabilities, industries can significantly improve automation, decision-making, customer experience, and overall operational excellence. We explored the impact of generative AI on Industry 4.0 from predictive maintenance, enhancing data-driven decision-making, optimizing supply chain and logistics and transforming workforce with classic examples and their implications with neat diagrams. As AI technology continues to evolve, its impact on various sectors is expected to grow, further transforming how businesses operate and deliver value.

References

[1]   Rüßmann, M., Lorenz, M., Gerbert, P. *et al.* (2015). Industry 4.0: The future of productivity and growth in manufacturing industries. https://www.bcg.com/publications/2015/engineered_products_project_business_industry_4_future_productivity_growth_manufacturing_industries.

[2]   Accialini, N. (2021). *Industry 4.0: User Guide.* https://www.amazon.com/ Industry-User-Guide-Nicola-Accialini/dp/B08Z2JNQWZ.

[3]   Galazova, S. S. (2021). Financing of public–private partnership projects based on "smart technologies". In: Popkova, E. G. and Sergi, B. S. (eds.), *"Smart Technologies" for Society, State and Economy. ISC 2020*, pp. 1696–1703. Cham: Springer, https://doi.org/10.1007/978-3-030-59126-7_185.

[4]   Singh, G., Bhardwaj, G., Singh, S V., and Chaudhary, N. (2022). Artificial intelligence led Industry 4.0 application for sustainable development. In *2nd International Conference on Innovative Practices in Technology and Management.* https://www.proceedings.com/content/063/063395webtoc.pdf.

[5]   Peres, R. S., Jia, X., Lee, J., Sun, K., Colombo, A. W., and Barata, J. (2020). Industrial artificial intelligence in Industry 4.0—Systematic review, challenges and outlook, *IEEE Access*, vol. 8, pp. 220121–220139. https://ieeexplore.ieee.org/stamp/stamp.jsp?arnumber=9285283.

[6]   Nagy, S. G. and Stukovszky, T. (2023). *Smart Business and Digital Transformation: An Industry 4.0 Perspective*. New York, NY: Routledge.

[7]   Ortiz, J. H. (2020). *Industry 4.0: Current Status and Future Trends*. London: IntechOpen.

[8]   https://theenterpriseworld.com/trucking-workflow-optimization/, https://www.slim stock.com/blog/demand-forecasting/, https://techvint.com/about-us/ and https://hdavid16.github.io/InventoryManagement.jl/dev/

[9]   https://unifiedportal-mem.epfindia.gov.in/memberinterface/ and https://first energygum.com/pages/sustainability

[10]   https://www.sleekitech.com/Digital-Marketing-Services, https://envoy.com/ workplace-management/what-is-a-hybrid-meeting   and   https://www.alamy. com/improved-work-safety-blue-gradient-concept-icon-image454394321.html

Chapter 9

Navigating the ethics and legality of deepfake technology: advancements, implications and responsible deployment

Swathi Ganesan[1], Sangita Pokhrel[1] and Nalinda Somasiri[1]

Abstract

This research explores the world of deepfake technology, particularly how generative adversarial networks can be used to create realistic synthetic images of celebrities. By using the CelebA dataset with a deep convolutional generative adversarial network (DCGAN) model, the research aims to produce high-quality deepfake images that look convincing. The objectives include producing convincing deepfake visuals, examining their practical uses in art and science, ensuring adherence to legal and ethical standards and increasing public awareness of responsible deepfake practices. Thorough testing is conducted to evaluate how well these deepfakes perform and how realistic they appear, while also considering the ethical issues and risks of misuse. The findings show that DCGANs are effective at replicating facial features and emotions, suggesting future possibilities for deepfake technology while considering the need for strong ethical guidelines and regulations.

Keywords: Generative adversarial network; deep convolutional network; DCGANs; healthcare; deepfake images

9.1 Introduction to deepfake technology

Deepfakes are AI-generated media that uses deep learning to create highly realistic but fake images or videos. By leveraging powerful learning and artificial intelligence techniques like autoencoders and generative adversarial networks (GANs), deepfakes swap faces and voices in real time, making it appear as though people are saying or doing things they never actually did. This evolvement has brought many applications in real time such as media, artistic and educational system. GAN has recently revolutionised the field of image synthesis and manipulation. It generates

[1]Department of Computer Science and Data Science, York St John University, UK

artificial intelligence algorithms to generate highly realistic images but entirely formed visual content. This technique has significantly blurred the lines between reality and fiction, raising concerns about misinformation, privacy breaches and ethical implications. As research and technology continue to develop, limitations become imperative to understand the social impact and strategies for responsible development and deployment.

This research focuses on the utilisation of GANs, specifically deep convolutional generative adversarial network (DCGAN) for generating synthesis images. For this study, CelebA dataset have been used, which has been distinguished for the diversity in its images. The technical intricacies in generating deep fake involve a critical analysis of the ethical considerations, the privacy of content and ethical dilemmas posed by synthetic images in various sectors. There is an increasing strike between technological innovation and ethical responsibility, expressing the needs and upholding ethical standards and social well-being, which is addressed in this research.

9.1.1   Understanding deepfake technology

With the advancement of technology, artificial intelligence, machine learning and deep learning play a significant role and are in high demand due to their diverse techniques and tools [1]. Derived from the terms 'Deep Learning (DL)' and 'Fake', 'Deepfake' refers to particular photo-realistic video or image materials produced using DL's assistance [2]. This name was given because of an anonymous user in 2017, the one who used deep learning techniques to make photo-realistic fake films by substituting someone else's face to replace the face of the original subject in pornographic videos. Two neural networks which are generative network and discriminative network with a face swap technique were used to create those fake videos and images. Using an encoder and a decoder, the generative network generates artificial visuals. The legitimacy of the freshly created images is determined by the discriminative network. GANs are the result of combining these two networks [1].

9.1.2   Technology advancements in GAN-based deepfake image synthesis

GANs have a remarkable performance in a variety of applications and quickly gaining popularity in computer vision and natural language processing. GANs can use for the field of image processing such as image synthesis, image generation, image semantic editing, image-to-image translation, image super resolution, image inpainting and cartoon generation. Among those applications GANs have demonstrated outstanding results in that field of image synthesis [3,4]. Since 2014, one of the most well-liked study fields has been GAN, which produces superior synthetic images than earlier generative models. A generator and a discriminator are the two neural networks that make up a GAN. The generator aims to generate realistic samples that trick the discriminator, while the discriminator seeks to discern between produced and genuine samples [4].

9.2   Ethical implications of deepfake technology

Deepfake technology continues to evolve with its potential misuse possessing a significant ethical challenge. This section delves into ethical considerations of deepfake generation and its application mainly focusing on critical issues such as misinformation, privacy violation, social implications and the dual-use dilemma of this technology. The explosive growth of this technology in recent years has raised many questions on ethical ramifications including its impact on social trust. The discussion underscores the importance of an ethical framework to ensure responsible development and deployment of deepfake solutions. We aim to illuminate the complex moral decisions that arise with the creation and application of deepfake technology.

9.2.1   Misinformation

Making fake videos, images and voices can lead to spread misinformation to the world. Making fake videos using someone else's faces, anyone can send message to the world with wrong information. This is a critical issue than what we are thinking. Public figures, politicians and celebrities are deepfake's primary victims. It propagates a misleading narrative about world leaders. Deepfake technology has been employed multiple times and may pose a threat to world peace. By showing false images of maps, it can be used to deceive military forces, which could seriously harm anyone [5].

9.2.2   Consent and privacy

When considering about privacy, if there is no any subject's permission, deepfake technology can produce anything such as a funny, sexual or political video featuring someone saying anything. The details of the technologies involved in deepfakes are what make them revolutionary, as virtually anyone with a computer can create fake films that looks like real media. This can be harm for someone's privacy [6].

9.2.3   Psychological and societal impact

On social media, misinformation travels fast and has the potential to affect millions of users. Currently, YouTube is the second most popular source of news for Internet users after Facebook. Video has become more and more popular, which emphasises the need for tools to verify the veracity of media and news material. New technologies have made it possible to manipulate video in a convincing way. It is getting harder to know who to believe due to the ease with which false information may be obtained and disseminated via social media platforms. This has negative effects on making educated decisions, among other things. Therefore, this may cause an impact for social trust as well [6].

9.2.4   Current trends and challenges in deepfake research

Although we have negativity side of deepfake technology, there are so many positive sides as well. Deepfake technology can apply for many fields like education, entertainment, online social media, healthcare, fashion, marketing and more other fields. Hence considering about current trends, it has been applied to produce virtual assistants or digital avatars to enhance video conference quality. For example, the creators of Caporusso (2020) use deepfake algorithms to extract a precise model of a person and create fresh content that is intended for benign reasons. In place of an actual or virtual presence, they produce an interactive Digital Twin of a subject. With the help of easy-to-use tools, users will be able to make their own digital replicas for a variety of purposes, including interactive storytelling, memorials, simulations and re-enactments. Additionally, deepfake technology has been used in TV show and film production to mimic the look of deceased celebrities or use face visual effects to honour them at memorial performances. It has also become more and more common in entertainment-focused smartphone applications, especially when it comes to making viral films for social media sites [7]. Deepfakes have also been used for medical image analysis to assist in patient diagnosis. When it comes to pattern matching and feature extraction from photos, deep learning models excel. They are therefore used to forecast abnormalities in X-rays, identify distinct forms of disease in magnetic resonance imaging (MRI) and detect different types of cancer present in computed tomography (CT) scans. Large amounts of data are required for deep learning algorithms to accurately complete these jobs. However, researchers were unable to access the available medical photos because of privacy concerns when processing medical data. In order to meet this issue, GAN models were added to the medical picture application, producing artificial medical images that, while not real, nevertheless manage to look as authentic as possible. This will assist in growing the dataset to the necessary quantities. Also in the medical sector, they use deepfake technology to generate deepfake chest X-rays, generating 3D lung nodules in different scales, use deepfake ECG and more [8].

While we use deepfake technology to the current working area, we may have to face few challenges as well. The main thing would be education and the awareness. Most of the people do not know what deepfake is and what can do from that. Mostly the negative side of deepfake occurs because of that. Most of the people trust what they see without going deep into the thing that they saw like fake images, fake videos and fake news. Once it comes to the positive side of the deepfake technology, the same issue occurs because of the lack of knowledge of people and the awareness to the people about deepfake technology. Another challenge is creating reliable techniques for identifying deepfakes. When someone misuse this technology, we need a technique to identify that whether it is real or a fake. Deepfake technology has major issues with consent and privacy. Large face datasets are frequently used to create deepfakes, which raises concerns with permission and data privacy. Research is required to create moral standards and legislative frameworks that safeguard people's rights in the deepfake era. To address the challenges of deepfake technology, everyone should gather and need to develop strategies to manage well this technology.

9.3   Research design and implementation

This section outlines the experimental approach, design and framework employed to generate and evaluate deepfake images using DCGAN. It details the data pre-processing steps, architecture and training procedures, emphasising the systematic approach taken to ensure the quality and reliability of the generated images.

9.3.1   Data collection and preprocessing

The dataset for this research has been taken from the MMLAB research lab at the Chinese University of Hong Kong which is made available in open research repository. This dataset is excellent for testing and training face detection models, especially those that identify facial features like brown hair, smiles and spectacles wearers. Rich annotations and a multitude of photos support the various persons, vast stance variations and backdrop clutter in the images. There are 202,599 number of face images of various celebrities and 10,177 unique identities without the names of the identities. This data is widely used by researchers in the field of computer vision for facial recognition, attribute prediction and image synthesis. The diversity in the dataset makes it ideal for training GANs, especially DCGAN. The diverse dataset helps to learn wide range of facial expressions and create synthetic images, crucial for understanding the potential limitations of deepfake technology.

The dataset is loaded and a series of transformations is applied to the dataset – resizing of the images to 64×64 pixels, centre cropped to ensure the faces in the images are centrally located, converting the images into tensors and normalised the pixel value to the range $[-1,1]$. Data loader is efficiently used to load the data for training into batches with 'batch_size' of 128. The 'weights_init' function has been used to initialise the weights in the convolution layer with values drawn from normal distribution with mean 0 and standard deviation 0.02. Also the weights of the batch normalisation layer have been initialised with mean 1, standard deviation 0.02 and set the biases to constant value 0. Weight initialisation is vital in GANs for image synthesis, as it improves the model performance by influencing the learning process. By setting the appropriate initial values, GAN training becomes more stable, efficient and capable of producing high-quality synthetic images.

9.3.2   Deep convolutional generative adversarial network (DCGAN) architecture

A GAN consists of two neural networks, i.e. a generator network, G and a discriminator network, D as shown in Figure 9.1. The generator network is random input as noise (n) and tries to generate the fake images $G(n)$. These fake-generated images closely resemble the real images from a dataset (x). In the meantime, the discriminator network tries to distinguish between the real images and fake images generated by the generator.

The discriminator compares both the real images and the fake images, finding the similarity in the visual and quality of the fake ones. When the discriminator

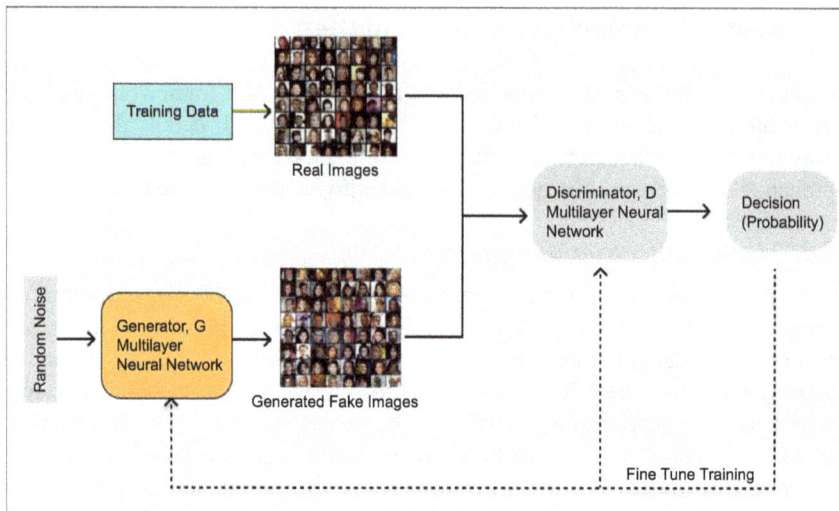

Figure 9.1   Generative adversarial network architecture

recognises that an image is real, it produces a probability value of 1 and 0 when it recognises an image as fake. The discriminator aims to improve its accuracy in correctly classifying real and fake images, whereas the generator aims to fool the discriminator, by reducing its accuracy. Basically, the two networks are engaged in a competitive game, where the discriminator attempts to correctly classify the images it receives, and the generator aims to make its fake images identical to real ones. So, the discriminator is trained to maximise the probability of correctly identifying real and fake images, while the generator is trained to minimise the probability that the discriminator correctly identifies its generated images as fake, i.e. to minimise $1 - D(G(n))$. This interpretation is represented mathematically as follows [9]:

$$V(D, G) = \min_G \max_D E_{x \sim pdata(x)}[\log D(x)] + E_{x \sim p_n(n)}[\log(1 - D(G(n)))]$$

$$(9.1)$$

where

$p_{data}(x)$ represents the data distribution of real images,

$p_n(n)$ denotes the noise distribution.

After the necessary training is completed, the generator becomes proficient in producing natural and realistic fake images from noise inputs, while the discriminator enhances its capability to differentiate between deepfake images and real ones. The next section discusses various types of GANs employed for generating deepfake images.

9.3.2.1   Generator architecture

The generator is responsible for creating fake images from random noise. It uses a series of transposed convolutional layers to upsample the input noise vector to the size of the desired image as follows.

- Input (random noise): Random noise vector with dimensions $1 \times 1 \times 100$ is the input.
- ConvolutionTranspose1: The transposed convolution layer upsamples the noise to a feature map of size $4 \times 4 \times 512$ using 512 filters of size 4×4.
- BatchNorm1: Batch normalisation is applied to stabilise and speed up the training.
- ReLU1: A ReLU activation function is applied to introduce non-linearity.
- ConvolutionTranspose2: This layer further upsamples the feature map to $8 \times 8 \times 256$ using 256 filters of size 4×4.
- BatchNorm4: Batch normalisation is applied.
- ReLU4: ReLU activation function is applied.
- ConvolutionTranspose5: The final transposed convolution layer upsamples the feature map to the desired image size of $64 \times 64 \times 3$ using three filters of size 4×4.
- Tanh: A Tanh activation function is used to ensure the pixel values of the generated image are in the range $[-1,1]$.

Table 9.1 outlines the layers in the generator network, starting with the input noise vector of size (100). The network consists of multiple transpose convolutional layers with corresponding batch normalisation and ReLU activation layers. These layers progressively upsample the input to produce an image of size (64, 64, 3), representing the height, width and number of colour channels (RGB), respectively. The final layer uses the Tanh activation function to normalise the output pixel values between -1 and 1, which is a standard practice for GANs.

Table 9.1   Generator network – architecture parameters

Input layers	Number and size of filters	Output dimension (height, width and channel)
Input (Random Noise)	–	(1, 1, 100)
ConvolutionTranspose1	512 filters with size 4×4	(4, 4, 512)
BatchNorm1	–	(4, 4, 512)
ReLU1	–	(4, 4, 512)
ConvolutionTranspose2	256 filters with size 4×4	(8, 8, 256)
BatchNorm2	–	(8, 8, 256)
ReLU2	–	(8, 8, 256)
ConvolutionTranspose3	128 filters with size 4×4	(16, 16, 128)
BatchNorm3	–	(16, 16, 128)
ReLU3	–	(16, 16, 128)
ConvolutionTranspose4	64 filters with size 4×4	(32, 32, 64)
BatchNorm4	–	(32, 32, 64)
ReLU4	–	(32, 32, 64)
ConvolutionTranspose5	3 filters with size 4×4	(64, 64, 3)
Tanh	–	(64, 64, 3)

9.3.2.2 Discriminator architecture

The discriminator is responsible for identifying the real images and fake images. A series of convolutional layers is used to down sample the input image to a single scalar output, thereby identifying if the given input image is real or fake as follows:

- Input (Image): The size of the input image is $64 \times 64 \times 3$.
- Convolution1: The convolution layer downsamples the image to a size of $32 \times 32 \times 64$ using 64 filters of size 4×4.
- LeakyReLU1: A LeakyReLU activation function is used to introduce non-linearity.
- Convolution2: The feature map is further downsampled to $16 \times 16 \times 128$ using 128 filters of size 4×4.
- LeakyReLU2: LeakyReLU activation function is applied for non-linearity.
- Convolution3: The feature map is downsized to $8 \times 8 \times 256$ using 256 filters of size 4×4.
- Convolution4: The feature map is downsized to $4 \times 4 \times 512$ using 512 filters of size 4×4.
- Similarly, batch normalisation and leaky regularisation activation function is used to introduce non-linearity in the series of convolution layer.
- Convolution5: The final convolution layer downsamples the feature map to a single scalar output of size $1 \times 1 \times 1$ using 1 filter of size 4×4.
- Sigmoid: A Sigmoid activation function is applied to produce an output value between 0 and 1, indicating the probability that the input image is real.

Table 9.2 provides a detailed view of the discriminator network layers. It begins with the discriminator consisting of a series of convolutional layers that progressively downsample the input image of size (64, 64, 3), accompanied by

Table 9.2   Discriminator network – architecture parameters

Input layers	Number and size of filters	Output dimension (height, width and channel)
Input (image)	–	(64, 64, 3)
Convolution1	64 filters with size 4×4	(32, 32, 64)
LeakyReLU1	–	(32, 32, 64)
Convolution 2	128 filters with size 4×4	(16, 16, 128)
BatchNorm2	–	(16, 16, 128)
LeakyReLU2	–	(16, 16, 128)
Convolution 3	256 filters with size 4×4	(8, 8, 256)
BatchNorm3	–	(8, 8, 256)
LeakyReLU3	–	(8, 8, 256)
Convolution 4	512 filters with size 4×4	(4, 4, 512)
BatchNorm4	–	(4, 4, 512)
LeakyReLU4	–	(4, 4, 512)
Convolution 5	1 filter with size 4×4	(1, 1, 1)
Sigmoid	–	(1, 1, 1)

BatchNorm and LeakyReLU activation functions to ensure stable training and to prevent the vanishing gradient problem. The final convolutional layer reduces the image to a single scalar output. Sigmoid function at the final layer gives the probability, indicating whether the input image is real or fake.

The generator upsample random noise into realistic images, while the discriminator downsample to differentiate between real and fake images. This comprehensive breakdown ensures a transparent understanding of the model, which is crucial for reproducing high-quality deepfake images.

9.3.3 Training and evaluation procedures

The binary cross entropy loss function and the Adam optimiser are used in the training process to improve the performance of both the networks, generator and discriminator. By minimising the discriminator's ability to distinguish real from fake images and maximising the generator's ability to produce realistic images, the training process is achieved.

9.3.3.1 Training loop

Initialisation of weights: The weights of both networks are initialised with a mean of 0 and a standard deviation of 0.02 using a normal distribution. This helps in stabilising the training process.

9.3.3.2 Training steps

Discriminator update

- Real images: A batch of real images is passed through the discriminator to compute the loss (binary cross-entropy loss) between the discriminator's output and the label indicating real images (1).
- Fake images: The generator creates a batch of fake images from random noise. The fake images are sent to the discriminator, and the loss is computed between the discriminator's output and the label indicating fake images as (0).
- Loss calculation: The total loss for the discriminator is the sum of the losses for real and fake images.
- Backpropagation: The gradients are calculated, and the discriminator's weights are updated using the Adam optimiser.

Generator update

- Fake images: A new batch of fake images is generated and passed through the discriminator.
- Loss calculation: The loss is computed between the discriminator's output and the label indicating real images (1), as the generator aims to fool the discriminator into classifying fake images as real.
- Backpropagation: The gradients are calculated, and the generator's weights are updated using the Adam optimiser.

Iterations and epochs: The training loop iterates over the dataset for five epochs. For every batch in each epoch, the above steps are repeated. During training, the generator and discriminator losses are tracked and stored for analysis.

9.3.3.3   Evaluation

A fixed set of noise vectors is used to generate images at different training stages. These images are saved and used to assess the progress and quality of the generator over time. The losses for both the generator and discriminator are plotted to visualise their convergence and to monitor the stability of the training process.

9.3.4   Ethical framework for deepfake generation

A comprehensive ethical framework to guide deepfake research is essential. This framework ensures responsible use and development of deepfake technologies, focusing on several critical aspects:

9.3.4.1   Data privacy

All images used for training were sourced from publicly available datasets, specifically the CelebA dataset, which contains celebrity images that are in the public domain. This approach ensured that no private or sensitive data was used, thereby avoiding any interference on personal privacy.

9.3.4.2   Informed consent

In situations where images could potentially identify individuals, informed consent is mandatory. Although the CelebA dataset is composed of images of public figures, the framework emphasises the importance of consent in any research involving identifiable personal data. If future work involves datasets with non-public figures, strict protocols to obtain explicit permission from individuals will be obtained, ensuring that their rights and autonomy are respected.

9.3.4.3   Usage guidelines

The following guidelines to be implemented to prevent the misuse of generated deepfake images;

- Prohibiting the use of generated images in deceptive contexts such as creating false information or misleading media.
- Banning the application of deepfake images for malicious purposes, including defamation, harassment or any form of harm to individuals.
- Restricting the dissemination of generated content to platforms and communities that adhere to ethical standards and practices.

By following these principles, the research mitigate the risks associated with deepfake technology and enhances its use for positive and legitimate purposes such as artistic expression, entertainment and educational applications.

9.3.4.4   Transparency and accountability

Transparency is vital for trust and accountability in any research, especially for the data field. Therefore, all aspects of research relating to deepfakes, including data collection, preprocessing to model training and evaluation, must be documented. This transparency allows for scrutiny and replication of the work, which is essential for scientific integrity. Also, the researchers and institution where the research is conducted are accountable for the societal implications of the research. This includes actively participating in discussions about the ethical use of deepfake technology and collaborating with stakeholders to develop robust frameworks that address potential abuses.

Ethical framework is designed to address the complex ethical considerations surrounding deepfake technology. By prioritising data privacy, obtaining informed consent, developing strict usage guidelines and maintaining transparency and accountability, the research aims to contribute positively to the field of deepfake research while minimising the risks associated with its misuse. This ethical approach not only safeguards individual rights but also enhances the credibility and integrity of our work.

9.4   Performance analysis of deepfake generators

The performance and outcomes of DCGAN model are analysed in this section. The model's effectiveness is presented mainly on the training loss trends, visual comparison of real and fake images and its quantitative assessments. The analysis also highlights the challenges and limitations, thereby providing future improvements.

9.4.1   Performance evaluation of DCGAN in deepfake generation

The training loss curves for both the generator and discriminator are plotted to evaluate the training process as in Figure 9.2. Consistent convergence and low loss values indicate successful training.

Also, generated images are visually compared to real images at various training stages to assess the visual quality and realism. Figure 9.3 compares the real images with the generated images for five epochs.

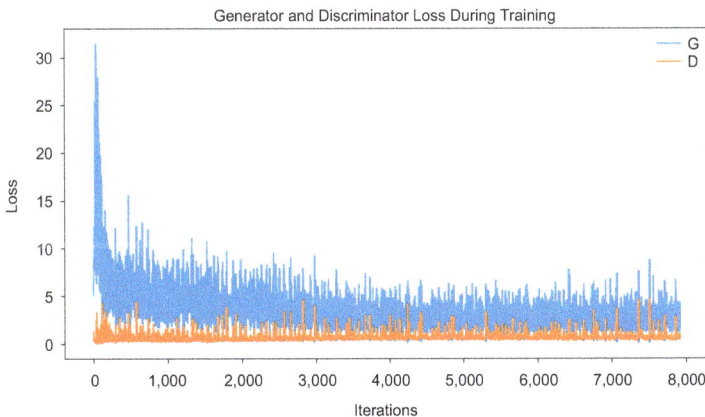

Figure 9.2   Generator and discriminator training loss

Real Images

Fake Images

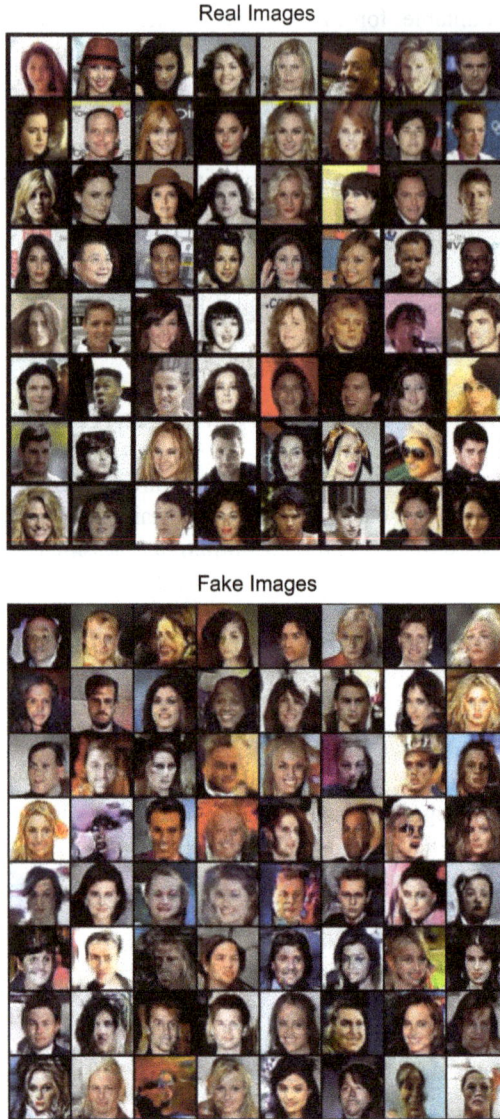

Figure 9.3   Comparison of real and fake images from DCGAN training process for five epochs

The real images, shown on the left, are directly sourced from the dataset and exhibit high-quality facial details. The generated images on the right are produced by the DCGAN after training for five epochs. Despite improvements over training iterations, the generated images still show some artefacts and inconsistencies such as blurriness or distortions. This visual comparison highlights the model's progress in synthesising realistic faces and the ongoing challenges in achieving high fidelity.

9.4.2   Visual quality and realism assessment

High quality and practicality in generated images are dominant in the domain of deepfakes to achieve convincing results.

9.4.2.1   Human perception comparison

Human perception performs a critical standard for calculating and evaluating the quality and realism of deepfake images. To make this effective, researchers often conduct perceptual studies involving human assessors. These studies typically involve presenting subjects with pairs of authentic and deepfake images, soliciting feedback on perceived differences and overall believability. By leveraging human judgement, researchers gain insights into the perceptual nuances that distinguish real from manipulated content.

9.4.2.2   Objective metrics

With subjective evaluations, empirical evaluation metrics play a vital role in quantifying the quality of deepfake images. Some common evaluation metrics are structural similarity index, peak signal-to-noise ratio and mean squared error. These metrics provide quantitative measures of resemblance between the real images and generated images, thereby offering valuable insights into the reliability of deepfake-generated outputs. However, these metrics may not always align with human perception, necessitating a detailed and comprehensive evaluation technique that combines both subjective and objective assessments.

9.4.2.3   Benchmark datasets

By standardised evaluation frameworks, the use of standard datasets plays an important role in the state-of-art in the deepfake generation. Some of the datasets such as CelebA-HQ, FFHQ and VoxCeleb are more commonly used for the research and evaluation of deepfake-generated images. These datasets feature diverse facial expressions, poses and lighting conditions, enabling researchers to evaluate the robustness of deepfake algorithms across various scenarios. By benchmarking against standard datasets, researchers can track progress, identify limitations and drive innovation in the field of deepfake analysis.

9.4.2.4   Challenges and future directions

Though there are significant progress and advancements made in assessing the quality and realism of deepfake-generated images, still there are several challenges to be addressed. One of the challenges is the extension of more advanced evaluation methodologies that might align with human perceptual decisions. Also, the emergence of deepfake detection systems stresses the need for adversarial evaluation strategies that predict the detection techniques. Addressing these challenges will require interdisciplinary collaboration and ongoing research efforts aimed at advancing the ethical and responsible use of deepfake technology.

9.4.3   Comparison with existing deepfake techniques

This section aims to provide insights into the effectiveness and limitations of DCGAN compared to several other techniques in generating visually convincing content, as illustrated in Table 9.3.

In conclusion, the comparative analysis reveals the diverse landscape of deepfake generation techniques, each offering unique advantages and challenges. While DCGAN excels in capturing spatial dependencies and maintaining training stability, it may encounter issues such as mode collapse and data requirements. Other methods like variational autoencoders (VAE), CycleGAN and StyleGAN offer alternative approaches with distinct strengths and weaknesses. Eventually, the choice of technique highly depends on the application requirements and considerations such as image quality, computational resources and interpretability. As deepfake technology continues to evolve as an ongoing research, ethical considerations are vital to ensure a responsible framework and transparent use of these powerful methodologies.

Table 9.3   Comparison with existing deepfake techniques

Technique	Description	Strengths	Weakness	References
DCGAN	Utilises a GAN framework with deep convolutional networks to generate realistic images	Captures spatial dependencies effectively, Stable training process	May suffer from mode collapse, Requires large amounts of data for training	[10,11]
Variational autoencoder (VAE)	Learns a probabilistic distribution of data in latent space, allowing for generation of new samples	Offers explicit probabilistic interpretation, Capable of generating diverse outputs	Prone to generating blurry images, Limited capacity for high-resolution image synthesis	[12,13]
CycleGAN	Employs cycle-consistency loss to learn mappings among two domains without paired data	Enables unpaired image-to-image translation, Robust to domain shifts	May produce artefacts in translated images, Requires careful hyperparameter tuning	[14,15]
StyleGAN	Introduces style-based generator architecture for more fine-grained control over image synthesis	Produces high-resolution, diverse images, Allows for disentangled manipulation of latent space	Computationally intensive, Limited interpretability of latent space representations	[16,17]
DeepFaceLab	Integrates multiple deep learning techniques for face swapping, including GANs and facial landmark detection	User-friendly interface, Supports high-quality face swapping	Requires significant computational resources, Ethical concerns regarding misuse of technology	[18,19]

9.5 Implication and future directions in deepfake research

This section delves into the broader implications of the findings, bridging the results to the wider context of deepfake technology. It explores the potential applications and challenges of advancements in the field of entertainment, media and healthcare. Further, ethical considerations, societal impacts and future research directions are discussed to ensure the integration of this technology into the real-world scenario in a responsible manner.

9.5.1 Implications of deepfake technology in entertainment and media

Deepfake technology is opening up new horizons in the entertainment and media industries. Imagine watching a film where historical figures are brought to life with uncanny realism, or enjoying a movie where an ageing actor seamlessly portrays a younger version of themselves without extensive makeup or digital effects. This technology not only enhances storytelling but also reduces production costs and time, making high-quality content more accessible. Personalised content is another exciting frontier that deep fakes can create tailored messages from celebrities or dynamic advertisements that speak directly to individual viewers, making interactions more engaging and meaningful. Some of the case studies highlighted the positive impacts of deepfakes in creative fields. For instance, the documentary 'Welcome to Chechnya' [20] used deepfakes to protect the identities of activists while conveying their stories authentically and safely. In the film industry, movies like 'The Irishman' have utilised deepfakes to convincingly show actors of different ages, demonstrating the potential of this technology to transform visual storytelling. Similarly, companies are using deepfakes for personalised marketing, creating video content that resonates more deeply with target audiences by catering to their preferences and interests.

9.5.2 Addressing ethical concerns and misuse potential

Despite the exciting possibilities, deepfake technology also poses significant ethical challenges. To address these concerns, developing advanced detection tools is essential. These tools can help identify deepfakes and prevent the spread of harmful or misleading content. Additionally, employing digital watermarks and blockchain-based systems can ensure the authenticity of videos, helping to trace their origin and confirm their legitimacy. These measures can protect against the misuse of deepfakes while maintaining trust in digital media. Policy recommendations and best practices are also crucial in mitigating the risks associated with deepfakes. Governments and organisations should work together to establish clear guidelines and regulations for the ethical use of this technology. Public awareness campaigns can educate people about the potential dangers and how to identify fake content. By fostering collaboration between technologists, policymakers and the public, we can harness the benefits of deepfake technology while minimising its potential for harm.

9.5.3   *Future directions and research opportunities*

There are still many areas in deepfake technology that require further exploration. Current research often focuses on the detection and prevention of malicious deepfakes, but more work is needed to improve the quality and ethical use of positive applications. For instance, developing more sophisticated algorithms that can create even more realistic and convincing deepfakes without crossing ethical boundaries is an important goal. Additionally, research into the social and psychological impacts of deepfakes can provide valuable insights into how this technology affects public perception and trust. Future studies should also look into the potential for integrating deepfake technology with other emerging technologies like virtual reality and augmented reality. This integration could create entirely new forms of interactive and immersive media experiences. Additionally, there is a need for ongoing dialogue and collaboration between researchers, industry leaders and policymakers to ensure that advancements in deepfake technology are aligned with ethical standards and societal needs. By addressing these gaps and seizing these opportunities, we can continue to innovate responsibly in this rapidly evolving field.

9.6   Conclusion

This chapter explores the development and evaluation of deepfake technology using DCGAN. The methodological approach highlights the use of a fixed set of noise vectors for generating images at different training stages and the monitoring of generator and discriminator losses to assess training progress. The chapter emphasises the importance of an ethical framework in deepfake research, focusing on data privacy, informed consent, usage guidelines and transparency to mitigate risks and enhance the responsible use of deepfake technology. The results section evaluates the performance of DCGAN, showcasing both the progress in generating realistic images and the challenges encountered such as artefacts and inconsistencies. Various evaluation techniques, including human perception comparisons and objective metrics, are employed to assess visual quality and realism. The chapter also compares DCGAN with other deepfake generation techniques like VAE, CycleGAN, StyleGAN and DeepFaceLab, highlighting each method's strengths and weaknesses. In the discussion, the chapter addresses the potential of deepfake technology in entertainment and media, noting its ability to enhance storytelling, reduce production costs and create personalised content. However, it also underscores the ethical concerns associated with deepfake misuse and emphasises the need for advanced detection tools, policy recommendations and public awareness. Future research directions include improving algorithm quality, exploring the social impacts of deepfakes and integrating deepfake technology with emerging technologies like virtual and augmented reality.

This chapter makes several key contributions to deepfake research, emphasising a balanced approach to leveraging the technology while addressing its ethical implications. Firstly, it offers a detailed evaluation of DCGAN, shedding light on its effectiveness in generating realistic synthetic images and identifying areas for improvement. Secondly, it introduces a comprehensive ethical framework that covers data privacy, informed consent and responsible usage guidelines, providing a model for conducting deepfake research in a manner that respects individual rights. Additionally, the chapter conducts a comparative analysis of various deepfake techniques, including VAE, CycleGAN, StyleGAN and DeepFaceLab, highlighting their respective strengths and weaknesses to guide researchers in selecting the most suitable method. Furthermore, it addresses the ethical challenges associated with deepfake technology, proposing advanced detection tools, digital watermarks and policy recommendations to mitigate risks and ensure responsible use. Overall, these contributions aim to advance the field of deepfake technology while fostering a culture of ethical responsibility and innovation.

9.6.1   Recommendations for ethical deepfake development

As we continue to advance deepfake technology, it is essential to establish guidelines that ensure its ethical use. Future research should aim to create algorithms that not only make deepfakes more realistic but also include safeguards to prevent their misuse. Prioritising the development of detection methods that can quickly and accurately identify deepfakes is key to mitigating the risks of malicious applications. From a policy perspective, governments and regulatory bodies need to work together to create clear and enforceable rules around the use of deepfake technology. These rules should cover important issues like consent, privacy and the prevention of misinformation. Ensuring transparency in the creation and distribution of deepfakes, such as requiring labels on AI-generated content, can help maintain public trust. Additionally, ethical considerations should be a part of the development process, ensuring that creators are aware of the social impacts and legal implications of their work. Promoting dialogue between technologists, ethicists, policymakers and the public is crucial for navigating the complexities of deepfake technology. Educational initiatives can help raise awareness about the capabilities and risks of deepfakes, empowering people to critically evaluate the media they encounter. By fostering a culture of responsibility and accountability, we can leverage the transformative potential of deepfake technology while protecting against its misuse.

References

[1]   M. S. Rana, M. N. Nobi, B. Murali, and A. H. Sung, "Deepfake detection: a systematic literature review," *IEEE Access*, vol. 10, pp. 25494–25513, 2022.

[2]   S. Ramachandran, A. V. Nadimpalli, and A. Rattani, "An experimental evaluation on deepfake detection using deep face recognition," *2021 International Carnahan Conference on Security Technology (ICCST)*, 2021, pp. 1–6, https://doi.org/10.1109/ICCST49569.2021.9717407.

[3]   L. Wang, W. Yang, W. Chen, F. Bi, and F. R. Yu, "A state-of-the-art review on image synthesis with generative adversarial networks," *IEEE Access*, vol. 8, pp. 63514–63537, 2020.

[4]   H. Huang, P. S. Yu, and C. Wang, "An introduction to image synthesis with generative adversarial nets," arXiv preprint, arXiv:1803.04469, 2018.

[5]   B. U. Mahmud, and A. Sharmin, "Deep insights of deepfake technology: a review," arXiv preprint, arXiv:2105.00192, 2021.

[6]   M. Westerlund, "The emergence of deepfake technology: a review," *Technology Innovation Management Review*, vol. 9, no. 11, pp. 1–14, 2019.

[7]   A. F. Gambin, A. Yazidi, A. Vasilakos, H. Haugerud, and Y. Djenouri, "Deepfakes: current and future trends," *Artificial Intelligence Review*, vol. 57, p. 64, 2024.

[8]   D. Lakshmi, and D. J. Hemanth, An overview of deepfake methods in medical image processing for health care applications. In *Design Studies and Intelligence Engineering*. IOS Press Ebooks, pp. 304–311, 2024. https://ebooks.iospress.nl/doi/10.3233/FAIA231448.

[9]   K. Remya Revi, K. R. Vidya, and M. Wilscy, "Detection of deepfake images created using generative adversarial networks: a review," *Second International Conference on Networks and Advances in Computational Technologies*, 2021 (pp. 25–35), https://doi.org/10.1007/978-3-030-49500-8_3.

[10] A. Radford, L. Metz, and S. Chintala, "Unsupervised representation learning with deep convolutional generative adversarial networks," arXiv preprint arXiv:1511.06434, 2015.

[11] I. J. Goodfellow, J. P. Abadie, M. Mirza, *et al.*, "Generative adversarial nets," In *Advances in Neural Information Processing Systems*, 2014 (pp. 2672–2680).

[12] D. P. Kingma, and M. Welling, "Auto-encoding variational bayes," arXiv preprint arXiv:1312.6114, 2013.

[13] D. J. Rezende, S. Mohamed, and D. Wierstra, "Stochastic backpropagation and approximate inference in deep generative models", In *International Conference on Machine Learning*, PMLR, 2014 (pp. 1278–1286).

[14] J. Y. Zhu, T. Park, P. Isola, and A. A. Efros, "Unpaired image-to-image translation using cycle-consistent adversarial networks," In *Proceedings of the IEEE International Conference on Computer Vision*, 2017 (pp. 2223–2232).

[15] P. Isola, J.-Y. Zhu, T. Zhou, and A. A. Efros, "Image-to-image translation with conditional adversarial networks," In *Proceedings of the IEEE Conference on Computer Vision and Pattern Recognition*, 2017 (pp. 1125–1134).

[16] T. Karras, S. Laine, and T. Aila, "A style-based generator architecture for generative adversarial networks," In *Proceedings of the IEEE Conference on Computer Vision and Pattern Recognition*, 2019 (pp. 4401–4410).

[17] T. Karras, S. Laine, M. Aittala, J. Hellsten, J. Lehtinen, and T. Aila, "Analyzing and improving the image quality of StyleGAN," In *Proceedings of the IEEE Conference on Computer Vision and Pattern Recognition Workshops*, 2020 (pp. 8110–8119).

[18] P. Esser, E. Sutter, and P. Rilinger, "FaceOff: automatic face swapping and editing in videos," arXiv preprint arXiv:1806.02007, 2018.

[19] A. Petrov, "DeepFaceLab: a simple, flexible and extensible face swapping framework," 2020. https://github.com/iperov/DeepFaceLab.

[20] J. Rothkopf, "Deepfake technology enters the documentary world," *The New York Times*, July 2020. https://www.nytimes.com/2020/07/01/movies/deepfakes-documentary-welcome-to-chechnya.html.

Chapter 10

Cosmic creativity: exploring generative AI in astronomy

Yogesh Chandra[1], Manjuleshwar Panda[2], Mukesh Kumar Pandey[3] and Shailesh Upreti[4]

Abstract

The convergence of generative artificial intelligence (GAI) with astronomy underscores the revolutionary potential of artificial intelligence (AI) in propelling the field of astronomical research forward. By addressing key challenges in the field, such as the vast scale of astronomical data, the complexity of simulating astrophysical processes, and the need for improved predictive models, this work demonstrates how GAI techniques offer innovative approaches. GAI is changing how astronomers tackle challenging cosmic issues by producing synthetic astronomical data and modeling complicated astrophysical events. With the use of AI-driven algorithms, scientists are able to make discoveries more quickly, spot hidden patterns in large datasets, and enhance the accuracy of models for phenomena like galaxy formation and astronomical events. Additionally, with an emphasis on the significance of responsible AI deployment, this chapter critically analyzes the ethical issues surrounding the use of AI in scientific research. By harnessing the potential of GAI, astronomers can overcome significant barriers in data analysis and simulation, opening the door to more accurate, effective, and morally responsible cosmic exploration. "Cosmic creativity" thus addresses the practical and theoretical implications of integrating GAI into astronomy, focusing on both its potential and its challenges.

Keywords: Cosmic creativity; generative AI; astronomy; data-driven discovery; ethical implications; interdisciplinary dialogue; future frontiers

[1]Department of Physics, Government P.G. College, Bazpur, India
[2]Independent Researcher, South West Delhi, India
[3]Department of Physics, National Taiwan University, Taiwan
[4]C4V LLC, Vestal, NY, USA

10.1   Introduction to generative AI in astronomy

Advances in artificial intelligence (AI) have made it possible to locate Earth-like planets in faraway galaxies in a matter of hours, a task that would have taken years for human astronomers. AI is radically changing the way we see, analyze, and interpret celestial occurrences, which is transforming the field of astronomy. By following AI's development from simple algorithms to complex generative models, the significant influence it has had on astronomy is explained. The application of generative artificial intelligence (GAI) is teaching astronomers new insights about the mysteries of space.

As a subset of deep learning (DL), generative AI, shown in Figure 10.1, is a discipline of AI that focuses on building models that can create new material based on data that already exists. The goal of these models is to produce information that is identical to that which could be produced by people. Popular GAI models that employ deep neural networks (DNNs) to produce realistic content like text, graphics, and even music are called generative adversarial networks (GANs).

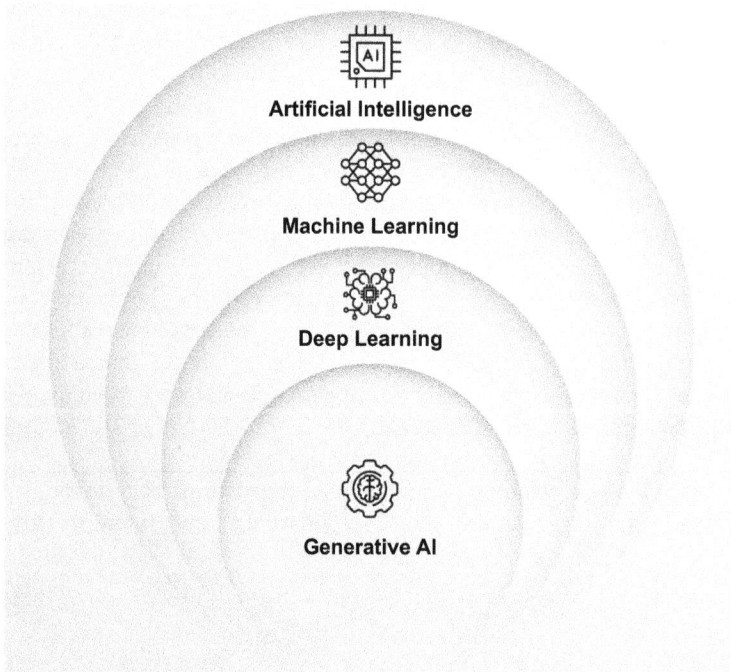

Figure 10.1   An umbrella of AI including ML, DL, and GAI. Image credit: Medium, retrieved from [https://blog.ivan.digital/a-deep-dive-into-deep-learning-94fa6ea06421].

10.1.1 The inception of artificial intelligence in astronomical studies

AI has introduced a transformative era in astronomical research. The quest for cosmic insight has been characterized by notable phases of innovation and discovery. The involvement of AI in astronomy can be traced back to the latter half of the 20th century, coinciding with the advent of the Digital Revolution. During the 1980s, initial collaborations between AI initiatives and astronomical studies established a foundation for a partnership that has since redefined our understanding of the Universe. Since that time, AI has progressed consistently, utilizing DL, neural networks, and machine learning (ML) techniques to investigate the cosmos. As we approach a new era in astronomical exploration, AI functions as both a tool and a guide, aiding in the quest to unravel the mysteries of the Universe.

Beginning with basic ML models capable of identifying exoplanets, AI has progressed to more sophisticated algorithms specifically designed for star classification. Traditionally, large-scale astronomical data analysis was a slow and painstaking manual process. However, the integration of AI has expedited this procedure, enhancing both precision and efficiency, which has enabled astronomers to achieve groundbreaking discoveries at an unprecedented pace [1]. As AI continues to evolve, its impact on astronomical research deepens. It has transcended simple object recognition and star classification, becoming an essential tool in unraveling some of the Universe's greatest mysteries. By processing vast amounts of data and detecting subtle patterns, AI provides astronomers with unparalleled depth and accuracy in their investigations of the cosmos. Insights generated by AI are fundamentally reshaping our understanding of the Universe's past, present, and future, from mapping the intricate structures of galaxies to predicting the dynamics of cosmic phenomena. As astronomy stands on the brink of a new era, the intersection of AI and astronomical research holds the potential to unveil more astonishing secrets of the Universe. Within the rapidly advancing field of AI, several methodologies emerge, represented by the terms AI, ML, DL, and GAI. While DL employs DNNs for intricate pattern recognition and ML leverages data to uncover patterns, GAI focuses on creating new content; AI remains the overarching concept. Understanding these nuanced distinctions is crucial for comprehending their respective functions and applications across various sectors.

Even while no area of AI can promise perfect precision, various technologies frequently interact to improve results in their respective fields. It is crucial to remember that while all applications of GAI are included in the category of AI, not all applications of AI are included in the category of GAI. The same holds true for ML and DL. The development of AI, ML, DL, and GAI, as illustrated in Figure 10.2, will surely influence the future of intelligent systems and propel hitherto unheard-of innovation in the field of AI as technology advances. In this constantly expanding industry, there are countless options, and as long as advancement is actively sought after, new opportunities will keep coming up.

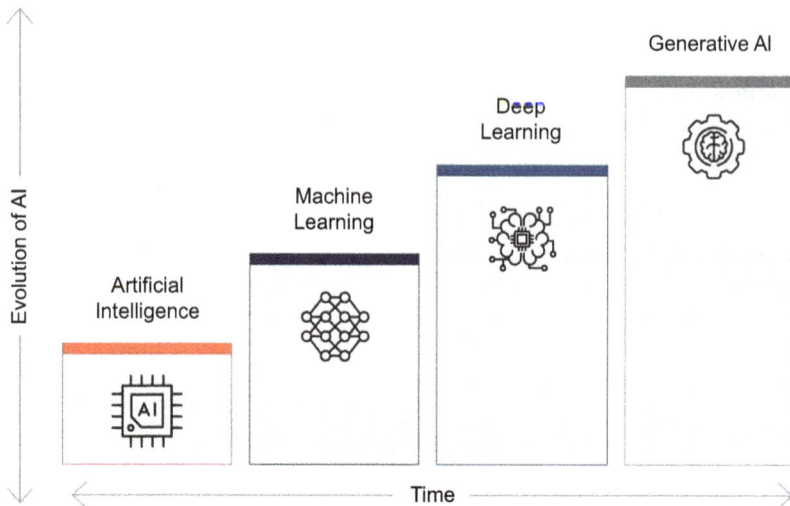

Figure 10.2   Comparative development of AI, ML, DL, and Generative AI. Image Credit: Synoptek, retrieved from [https://synoptek.com/insights/it-blogs/data-insights/ai-ml-dl-and-generative-ai-face-off-a-comparative-analysis/].

10.1.2   Connecting the dots: data to discovery

The volume of data generated by the cosmos is immense, far surpassing the capacity of human experts to process manually. AI addresses this challenge by linking data to discovery and transforming unstructured information into valuable insights. ML algorithms can sift through terabytes of data, identifying patterns and anomalies that may remain unnoticed by human analysts. This capability to process and analyze large datasets has facilitated significant advancements, including the mapping of cosmic structures and the identification of new celestial bodies. Moreover, AI not only accelerates discovery but also enhances the precision and reliability of astronomical research [2]. When it comes to trying to figure out how the cosmos works, the amount of data generated by celestial phenomena is remarkable. However, the potential for discovery extends beyond mere numerical representation. Through the application of AI, we can transform this vast data into meaningful insights, unveiling mysteries and uncovering previously unknown facts. AI serves as an invaluable tool, accelerating astronomical discovery and broadening our horizons of knowledge with each pattern it identifies and each anomaly it detects.

10.1.3   Unlocking creative potential: the significance of generative AI in astronomy

The application of GAI in Astronomy has seen significant advancements. Unlike traditional AI, which primarily focuses on analyzing existing data, GAI produces new, synthetic data that can effectively represent complex astrophysical phenomena. This capability proves particularly valuable in scenarios where observational data is sparse or nonexistent. GAI provides astronomers with unprecedented resources to explore and understand the cosmos, generating realistic models of processes such as star formation and galaxy evolution. The innovative potential of GAI enables scientists to test hypotheses, predict future astronomical events, and gain deeper insights into the fundamental workings of the Universe [3]. Let A stand for astronomy, *GAI* for generative AI, *CP* for creative potential, and CP_A represent astronomy's creative potential. Then, using proportional formalism, we can proportionately express their relationship as follows:

$$CP_A \propto (GAI) \tag{10.1}$$

This illustration highlights the direct correlation between the use of GAI and the expansion of Astronomy's creative potential. As GAI is used more and more in the area, it immediately adds to the expansion of astronomy's creative potential (CP_A), according to the proportionate relationship shown in (10.1). This is so that complex astrophysical phenomena can be represented by synthetic datasets and simulations, which GAI makes possible. When there is little or no observational data available, as is sometimes the case with uncommon or distant celestial occurrences, such capabilities become extremely significant. By using GAI, astronomers can model cosmic phenomena with improved level of detail, anticipate consequences, and investigate hypothetical situations. Thus, when GAI is used more widely, the range of innovative research prospects increases as well, enabling the development of new theories and the quest for hitherto unreachable findings. Therefore, the integration of GAI directly contributes to the advancement of astronomy's creative potential (CP_A) by introducing new methods and insights that push the limits of astronomical research.

10.2   Synthetic data generation for astrophysical simulations

The creation of synthetic data for astrophysical simulations has become a crucial method, especially in regions where direct observation is scarce. Beyond the limitations of conventional data collecting, scientists can develop precise and comprehensive models of celestial phenomena by utilizing GAI. This novel method makes it possible to simulate entire Universes, explore speculative situations, and make extremely accurate predictions about cosmic phenomena. By transforming abstract data into concrete insights, synthetic data generation is revolutionizing our understanding of the Universe and paving the way for new astronomical research horizons.

10.2.1   *Inventing the Universe: artificial intelligence as a novel approach*

The observational data that is used in traditional investigations of celestial events is frequently limited and challenging to collect. High-fidelity simulations that faithfully represent the complexity of the Universe can be produced thanks to AI, especially when it comes to generative models. AI-generated synthetic data that circumvents the shortcomings of observational data, giving scientists a more complete picture of cosmic occurrences. Through the exploration of situations that are not observable directly, these simulations enable scientists to make previously unheard-of discoveries and insights [4]. To examine this, let us look at some basic observational examples such as the discovery of exoplanets:

- **Conventional observational data methodology**: In conventional astronomy, researchers view far-off stars with telescopes. Researchers search for minute dips in a star's brightness when they think the star may host an exoplanet, or planet outside our solar system. When a planet passes in front of the star from our perspective, obstructing part of its light, the star experiences these dips, also called transits. Nevertheless, the detection of tiny planets or planets orbiting stars with changing brightness might be difficult using this method, which takes a long time and requires accurate observations.
- **Artificial intelligent approach**: Let's now incorporate AI into this procedure. AI is far quicker and more accurate than humans at analyzing large volumes of observational data. Here's how to do it:
  1. **Data collection**: Thousands of Stars' light curves, or graphs of brightness over time, are gathered by telescopes.
  2. **AI training**: Known examples of light curves demonstrating transits—the phenomenon in which an exoplanet passes in front of a star—and those that do not are used by scientists to train AI programs.
  3. **Pattern recognition**: The AI gains the ability to identify the minute patterns in the light curves that point to the existence of exoplanets.

AI generates synthetic datasets by spotting patterns that enable the modeling of different situations, improving our knowledge of exoplanet features and helping astronomers predict possible future discoveries. This method not only speeds up the process of discovery but also increases our understanding of the cosmos. This is demonstrated practically in the examination of 10,000 star light curves. In the past, astronomers would manually review such data for months or even years. However, this process is greatly accelerated by AI. All 10,000 light curves are processed quickly by AI algorithms in a matter of hours, which then detect potential transit signals and focus on 100 stars for additional research. Of them, ten new exoplanets are correctly identified by AI—finds that human observation would have overlooked. This illustrates how astronomical research is being revolutionized by AI-driven tools that offer more sophisticated capabilities than traditional data processing methods. Let us compare the two methods in terms of speed, accuracy, scalability, and overall efficiency as mentioned in Table 10.1 to better understand the impact of AI in this industry.

The comparison shows that AI-powered approaches are superior to traditional approaches in almost every way. Astronomers can now more quickly and precisely analyze massive datasets thanks to AI, revealing insights that would have taken years to find using traditional methods. This change heralds the beginning of a new era in cosmology study, one in which new discoveries are mostly driven by AI.

Table 10.1   Comparison of AI-driven versus conventional data processing method

Aspect	Traditional methods	AI-driven methods
Speed	Time-consuming; it takes months or even years to effectively process big datasets	Rapid; capable of processing hundreds of data points within just a few hours
Accuracy	Limited in its ability to identify subtle patterns and prone to human error	Powerful pattern recognition skills that make it more accurate
Scalability	Limited to manual or semi-automated processes	It can process massive volumes at once and is remarkably scalable
Data handling	Difficulties with big datasets, such thousands of light curves	Effectively organizes and examines huge datasets
Exoplanet discovery	Relies on observational data and may miss faint signals	More efficiently and effectively detects faint and complicated signals
Human involvement	Requires significant manual effort from astronomers	AI does most of the processing, but initial training is necessary
Potential for insight	Limited to actual observations, resulting in a slow discovery process	Able to model and forecast new situations, which can speed up discoveries

10.2.2   Emulation of stars: producing accurate stellar models

The development of precise stellar models and star simulations is one of the main uses of AI in astronomy. Understanding the energy transfer and nuclear fusion processes that take place inside stars is crucial for comprehending the lifetime of stars, from formation to demise. These processes can be replicated by GAI systems. Astronomers can test hypotheses and learn more about star dynamics without the constraints of observational data by using synthetic data. These AI-generated models are extremely accurate, which improves our capacity to forecast stellar behavior and expands our understanding of the principles underlying stellar evolution [5]. AI is able to anticipate significant features like mass and age based on temperature and brightness by analyzing observational data to discover the correlations between various stellar attributes. This is how AI creates precise star models:

The connection can be described as shown in the following equation:

$$y = f(x) \tag{10.2}$$

where

- x stands for the input data (e.g., temperature T and luminosity L).
- The output data, such as mass M and age A, are represented by y.
- The AI model that converts the input to the output is called $f(x)$.

As an example, A star's temperature (T) and brightness (L) are the input data. Mass (M) and Age (A) of the star are the output data. We forecast $(M,A) = f(L,T)$

using AI. Consider a scenario where a star has: 10 units of luminosity (L), and atmosphere (T) = 5,000 K. Then, $M = 2M_{\odot}$, $A = 5$ billion years is what the AI model would anticipate. This indicates the Star's Age of 5 billion years and its mass of 2 solar masses. Astronomers can better comprehend Stars and make new discoveries by using AI, which can swiftly and correctly predict stellar attributes through training on big datasets.

10.2.3   Surmounting data limitations: the efficacy of synthetic methods

Due to the immensity of space and the limitations of existing observational tools, astrophysics study is sometimes hindered by insufficient datasets. An effective way to address this problem is through synthetic data Production. The shortcomings of limited observational data can be addressed by researchers by using AI to create synthetic datasets. Building ML models, testing new ideas, and investigating different hypotheses may all be done with these datasets. Synthetic methods are strong because they can yield large amounts of data that support and improve observational work, which will hasten astrophysics' rate of discovery [6]. The efficacy of synthetic methods for overcoming data limitations can be expressed mathematically in this way.

$$D_{\text{syn}} + D_{\text{real}} = D_{\text{total}} \tag{10.3}$$

where D_{total} is the total amount of data that is available, D_{real} stands for the actual observational data, and the AI model's synthetic data is represented by D_{syn}. This statement, as illustrated by (10.3), shows that the combined set of synthetic AI data and actual observational data constitutes the whole data available for Astrophysical simulations and studies. AI bridges the gaps and expands the dataset by combining D_{syn} and D_{real}. This helps to overcome data constraints and makes Astronomy research more thorough and reliable.

10.2.4   Validating synthetic data with sparse observational constraints

In cases where real observational data is sparse or constrained, validating synthetic data becomes crucial to ensure the credibility of the simulations. Several approaches are used to address this challenge. Cross-referencing artificial outputs with sparse observational data is a popular technique for finding patterns or traits that correspond to actual observations. Furthermore, model-based validation methods aid in evaluating the simulations' dependability by contrasting artificial data outputs with well-established astrophysical models. Peer review and expert evaluation also aid in the validation process, making synthetic data a trustworthy resource in situations where direct observational data is not available. These validation methods ensure synthetic data serves as a reliable tool for advancing our understanding of astrophysical phenomena [7].

10.2.5   Mitigating risks of synthetic data in astrophysical simulations

Synthetic data has many benefits for modeling astrophysical phenomena, but there are drawbacks as well, like the possibility of biases and overfitting. Excessive customization of synthetic data to certain models can lead to overfitting, which diminishes the data's applicability in other contexts. Furthermore, simulation results may be skewed by biases that spread from training data or the generation process. We use a few tactics to lessen these problems:

- **Utilizing diverse datasets**: A wider range of astrophysical circumstances can be reflected in the synthetic data and the potential of bias can be decreased by combining multiple datasets during the training phase.
- **Implementing regularization techniques**: Regularization techniques encourage more broadly applicable synthetic outputs by avoiding excessively complex models, which helps avoid overfitting.
- **Conducting cross-validation**: This method makes sure the model is resilient and able to generalize to new data by evaluating the performance of synthetic data across various data subsets.

By addressing these risks proactively, synthetic data can be used more reliably to enhance astrophysical simulations [8].

10.3   AI-driven celestial event prediction

With all of its mysteries and continually changing occurrences, the Universe provides an enormous and intricate dataset that is suitable for AI's analytical abilities. An important development in this field is the AI-powered forecasting of astronomical events, which improves our capacity to anticipate and interpret astronomical phenomena. AI is able to forecast a wide range of events, from solar eclipses and supernovae to meteor showers and planetary Transits. This is made possible by its ability to analyze vast amounts of data, find patterns, and produce precise forecasts. We can watch and learn from the wonders of space as they unfold, which not only deepens our grasp of the Universe but also gets us ready for big celestial occurrences. An exciting new phase in astronomical research and discovery has begun with the fusion of cutting-edge AI technology with established technique.

10.3.1   *Imagining the Universe: AI's predictive capability*

Astronomical event prediction has historically mostly relied on labor-intensive, error-prone manual computations and human observations. Due to their considerable training on datasets gathered from space missions and telescopes, AI systems are now able to analyze patterns and signals quickly and correctly. From planetary transits and meteor showers to the production of new stars and galaxies, these sophisticated systems can forecast a broad variety of celestial events. Astronomers are able to make accurate and timely observations that improve our understanding of the Universe by using AI's predictive powers to foresee important events. With AI, we can now anticipate, visualize, and marvel at cosmic spectacles like solar eclipses, as depicted in Figure 10.3, in new and exciting ways, deepening our relationship with the stars above.

TOTAL SOLAR ECLIPSE

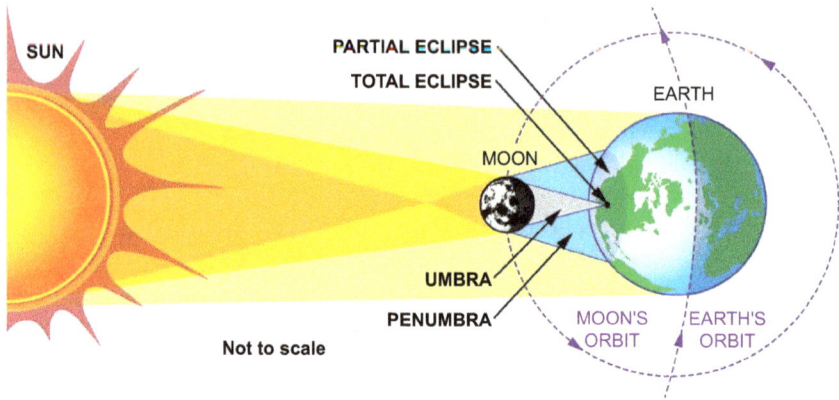

*Figure 10.3   Infographic background of a solar eclipse. Image Credit: NASA,
retrieved from [https://svs.gsfc.nasa.gov/12674/].*

- **Solar eclipse predictions made by AI**: AI systems can accurately predict the location and timing of the Moon's shadow on Earth, down to the precise second and kilometer, through the analysis of extensive datasets related to celestial mechanics. The objective is to understand the celestial dynamics that govern the patterns of our sky, rather than merely performing numerical calculations. When marking your calendar for an eclipse, consider that AI may have significantly contributed to ensuring you observed the event at the correct time [9]. GAI, which goes beyond conventional AI, improves eclipse forecasts by continuously learning from astronomical data and instantly adjusting to new patterns. In contrast to fixed models, GAI incorporates a variety of elements, including slight orbital shifts and gravitational impacts, to further improve accuracy. Because of its versatility, GAI is able to provide extremely accurate forecasts, giving observers confidence in precise timing and position information for eclipse events.
- **Solar eclipse images and generative AI**: The visual experience of solar eclipses is improved by GAI, which creates incredibly detailed visuals. People may now enjoy breathtaking views of space from the comfort of their homes thanks to these AI-generated images, which enhance accessibility to breathtaking eclipse views from a variety of viewpoints and locales. GAI offers a new way to visualize solar eclipses with its impressively realistic simulations and images made possible by sophisticated ML techniques. GANs, which are made up of a discriminator and a generator, are one method used by GAI. The discriminator compares the images produced by the generator to actual photos and provides feedback to enhance the generator's output. The generator generates images based on random noise. The incredibly lifelike images produced by this iterative process closely mimic actual occurrences. GAI is able to create accurate and detailed photos of solar eclipses, capturing the minute details of

how they appear from various perspectives and under varied atmospheric circumstances, by training these models on large datasets of historical eclipse photography [10].

- **Reaching new heights: the wider impact of AI-powered forecasts**: AI improves mission planning in space exploration, resulting in safer and more effective spaceflight operations by evaluating potential risks and optimizing paths. AI also makes it easier to handle satellite data in real-time for monitoring, which enhances communication and makes it possible to follow space debris more successfully. AI is used in disaster management to forecast natural disasters by examining meteorological patterns and geological data, enabling prompt alerts and efficient reaction plans. By helping us anticipate and lessen the effects of environmental problems, these sophisticated forecasting approaches eventually promote a more resilient society [11].

Not only can GAI make it easier for everyone to witness amazing celestial events, but it also makes solar eclipse visualizations more precise and sparks public curiosity in astronomy and education. Furthermore, it simplifies complicated ideas for amateur fans by offering interactive learning and exploration tools, encouraging the next generation of astronomers. AI has the ability to completely transform research methods as it develops because it simplifies data processing and frees up scientists to focus on creative ideas. All things considered, the use of GAI in astronomy is a major step toward a more inclusive and understandable study of the cosmos.

10.3.2 Predicting supernovae: artificial intelligence's part in stellar detonations

AI's capacity to forecast supernovae, the intense explosions that signal the end of a star's life cycle, is among its most inventive uses. Because supernovae aid in the creation of new stars and disperse necessary elements throughout the cosmos, they are vital to our understanding of cosmic evolution. In order to identify early signs of an imminent supernova, AI systems that are outfitted with ML algorithms examine light curves and other scientific data. Neural networks, for example, can be trained to identify the minute variations in a star's spectral properties and brightness that occur before a supernova explosion. This forecasting power not only improves our capacity to witness these uncommon events but also broadens our knowledge of the mechanisms that precede a supernova. AI is capable of predicting supernovae days or even weeks in advance, according to studies, giving Astronomers crucial time to set up their observational equipment [12]. This AI-driven ability to anticipate supernovae is a valuable tool for large-scale astronomical studies like the dark energy survey (DES), which relies on cutting-edge technology to improve its comprehensive study of the Universe. Over 400 astrophysicists, astronomers, and cosmologists from over 25 institutions worldwide are involved in the DES, an international cooperation headed by personnel from the Fermi National Accelerator Laboratory of the US Department of Energy. With the help of the dark energy camera, a 570-megapixel digital camera manufactured by Fermilab and supported by the DOE Office of Science, DES was able to map an area that is nearly one-eighth of the sky. In 2012, it was installed on the Víctor M. Blanco Telescope at the Cerro Tololo Inter-American Observatory, a NOIRLab programme of the National Science Foundation. Over a period of 6 years, 758 nights were recorded by DES scientists.

Scientists use four different approaches, including the supernova technique from 1998, to perform investigations in order to determine the expansion rate of the Universe and get an understanding of the nature of dark energy. The Type Ia Supernovae, which happen when a white dwarf, a very dense dead star, reaches a critical mass and explodes, are the source of the data needed for this technique. All Type Ia Supernovae have around the same actual brightness because all white dwarfs have nearly the same critical mass; any residual differences can be adjusted for. Astrophysicists can therefore calculate the relative distances between two Type Ia Supernovae by comparing their apparent brightnesses as seen from Earth. Large samples of supernovae across a broad range of distances are used by Astronomers to map out the history of cosmic expansion. They calculate the Redshift, or how fast a Supernova is traveling away from Earth as a result of the Universe's expansion, as shown in Figure 10.4, in addition to its distance for each one. That history will allow them to ascertain if the dark energy density has altered or stayed constant throughout time. This historical mapping of cosmic expansion, boosted by AI's ability to analyze large datasets and discover subtle trends, allows astro-physicists to gain a deeper understanding of dark energy and its role in the evolution of the Universe.

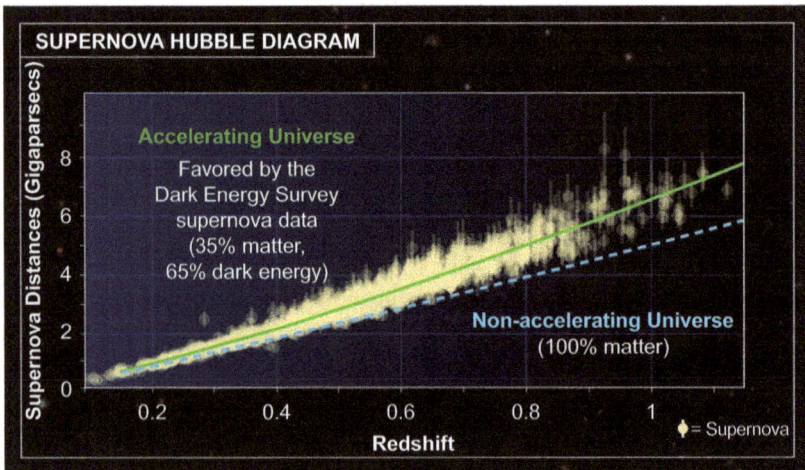

Figure 10.4   *Recessional velocities, or redshifts, and distances found for individual supernovae can be used to track the history of the Universe's expansion. The DES study demonstrates that the expansion has been increasing with cosmic time, which is a dark energy signature. Image Credit: DES-FNAL, retrieved from [https:// noirlab.edu/public/images/noirlab2401c/].*

10.3.3 *Early warning systems: forecasting solar eclipses and collisions*

The ability of AI to foresee the future has led to the creation of early warning systems for solar eclipses and possible run-ins with asteroids and comets. These systems continuously track the paths of celestial bodies using predictive analytics, making sure that any possible hazards are detected well in advance. AI systems may, for instance, forecast when and where eclipses will happen, mimic the motions of solar system objects, and identify whether an asteroid is headed straight for Earth. Accurately predicting these phenomena is essential for scientific inquiry as well as planetary defense. Our knowledge of solar dynamics and their consequences on Earth's atmosphere is improved by early warnings about solar eclipses, which allow for precise planning of studies [13,14]. In a similar vein, anticipating and minimizing asteroid strikes may be essential in the future to protect Earth. Calculating the precise positions and trajectories of celestial bodies is necessary for early warning systems for forecasting solar eclipses and collisions. To anticipate collisions with asteroids and near-earth objects (NEOs), we employ orbital dynamics to describe their paths. Here's a brief explanation using broad formalism, expressed in (10.4)–(10.8), as follows:

Predicting solar eclipses

Basic orbital equations: The positions of celestial bodies in space are described by the basic orbital equations. The orbit radii and angles of the Moon and Sun can be used to depict their respective positions. The position of the Moon is given as $R \times (\cos(\theta), \sin(\theta))$ where R is the orbit radius and θ is the angle in its orbit. Similarly, the position of the Sun follows the same structure. An eclipse condition occurs when the distance between the Moon and the Sun ($d_{Moon\text{-}Sun}$) is less than the radius of the Earth (R_{Earth}).

1. Position of the Moon:

$$\text{Position}_{\text{Moon}} = R \times (\cos(\theta), \sin(\theta)) \tag{10.4}$$

2. Position of the Sun:

$$\text{Position}_{\text{Sun}} = R \times (\cos(\theta), \sin(\theta)) \tag{10.5}$$

Eclipse condition: An eclipse occurs when:

$$d_{\text{Moon}-\text{Sun}} < R_{\text{Earth}} \tag{10.6}$$

Role of AI: The accuracy of solar eclipse forecasts is increased by AI, which uses real-time measurements and past Eclipse data to anticipate the timing and path of the Moon's shadow as it moves over the Earth.

Predicting collisions (asteroids and NEOs):

Simple motion equation: If we denote P_f as future position, P_c as current position, v as velocity, and t as time, then the equation can be represented as:

$$P_f = P_c + v \times t \tag{10.7}$$

Collision condition: A collision is predicted if:

$$d_{objects} < r_{object\ 1} + r_{object\ 2} \tag{10.8}$$

Role of AI: In order to provide early warnings of possible impacts, AI optimizes algorithms to predict the future positions of celestial objects based on past collision data and current orbital paths.

AI substantially improves solar eclipse and collision prediction by analyzing massive quantities of data to detect patterns and develop models. This results in more accurate and timely predictions, enabling improved readiness and response to Astronomical phenomena. In both cases, AI and ML can improve these forecasts by processing enormous databases of orbital elements and positional data, increasing accuracy and sending timely alerts to astronomers and space agencies.

10.4   Modeling the formation of galaxies

Creating the massive structures that cover the Universe, the formation of galaxies is one of the most amazing phenomena in the Universe. By using GAI, scientists are able to create dynamic, elaborate models of these processes in addition to deciphering the complex interactions between gas, stars, and dark matter that propel galaxy formation. Our view of galactic evolution is being completely transformed by this marriage of science and technology, which is providing hitherto unseen insights and visualizations that improve cosmic exploration and expand our comprehension of the infinite.

10.4.1   AI-based models of galactic evolution: carving the Universe

With the development of ML and neural networks, simulations have become more accurate and detailed than traditional models, which mostly relied on approximations and sparse data. For example, AI can forecast how galaxies will change over billions of years by analyzing the distribution of stars, gas, and dark matter [15]. These models provide a more thorough picture of galaxy growth by taking into account a number of variables, including star formation rates, gravitational interactions, and supernova feedback. AI models have transformed our understanding of galaxy evolution, transforming our perspective of the Universe with data-driven discoveries. Just as Hubble's tuning fork diagram, as depicted in Figure 10.5, classified galaxies into several categories based on their morphology, AI-powered simulations dive deeper into the complex mechanisms that underpin their formation and evolution. A galaxy is a collection of millions to billions of stars, together with gas and dust, locked together by gravitational force. There are four major types of galaxies: spiral, barred spiral, elliptical, and irregular. These can be expressed using the tuning fork diagram, which Edwin Hubble devised in 1926. The tuning fork diagram begins with the body of the fork being an elliptical and a spiral/barred spiral galaxy. The fork then divides into two segments: spiral and barred spiral galaxies. The bulge is a galaxy's

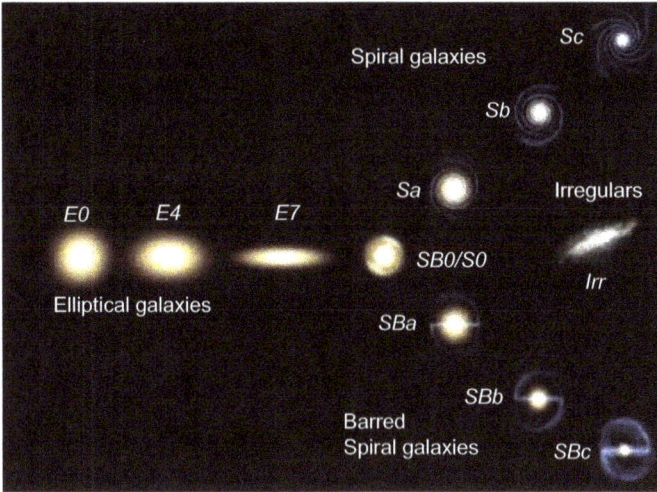

Figure 10.5 Hubble's tuning fork diagram. Image Credit: NASA/ESA, retrieved from [https://cesar.esa.int/upload/201809/galaxies_booklet.pdf].

central region. For elliptical galaxies, the number after the E represents the galaxy's ellipticity (0 is more round than 7). For spiral galaxies, the letter after the S reflects the distance from each arm (A has shorter distances than C), while for barred spiral galaxies, the letter after the SB represents the arm size.

Galaxies form according to two main theories: the monolithic collapse model and the hierarchical model. The hierarchical model postulates that tiny matter clumps that eventually coalesced to form galaxies were present throughout the early cosmos. By contrast, the monolithic collapse hypothesis suggests that star creation resulted from the gravitational collapse of massive clouds of gas and dust, which gave rise to galaxies. In galaxy formation studies, there are two dominant models: the hypotheses that have garnered significant data and have not been conclusively refuted. Hubble's categorization scheme, which divided galaxies into irregulars, spirals, and ellipticals, gave astronomers a fundamental framework for comprehending the diversity of the galaxy. In a similar vein, AI-powered models examine enormous datasets to forecast how galaxies will change over billions of years by looking at the distribution of stars, gas, and dark matter. Numerous variables are taken into consideration in these models, including star formation rates, gravitational interactions, and supernova feedback. Similar to how Hubble's tuning fork diagram aided in the early classification of galaxies, AI models are revolutionizing our understanding of the cosmos by providing previously unattainable insights into its complex dynamics.

10.4.2 AI-powered understanding of galaxy formation: from clouds to clusters

From early gas clouds to the large-scale structures we see today, AI methods have greatly increased the scientific knowledge of galaxy formation. When it comes to observational data, ML algorithms are able to spot patterns and connections that humans frequently miss. For example, GANs can mimic the gravitational collapse of gas clouds, which generate protostars and eventually mature galaxies, to recreate the early phases of galaxy formation [16]. Furthermore, AI technologies help identify and categorize various galaxy kinds, examine their morphological characteristics, and comprehend how environmental influences have shaped their evolution.

We've learned to recognize detailed patterns and connections in observational data using powerful ML algorithms, which have helped us uncover the secrets of cosmic development. The protogalactic cloud and the monolithic collapse model, as shown in Figure 10.6, are two main models investigated and discussed by the researchers. AI-powered simulations, using techniques such as GANs, probe the early stages of galaxy formation, reconstructing the collapse of gas clouds under gravity. These models shed light on the transition from protogalactic clouds to the formation of protostars and, finally, adult galaxies. Furthermore, AI systems play an important role in understanding the multiple merger model. AI systems help discover and classify different types of galaxies by analyzing large datasets and finding minute morphological aspects. These systems reveal the signatures of many merger events inside galactic structures, offering light on the intricate interplay of

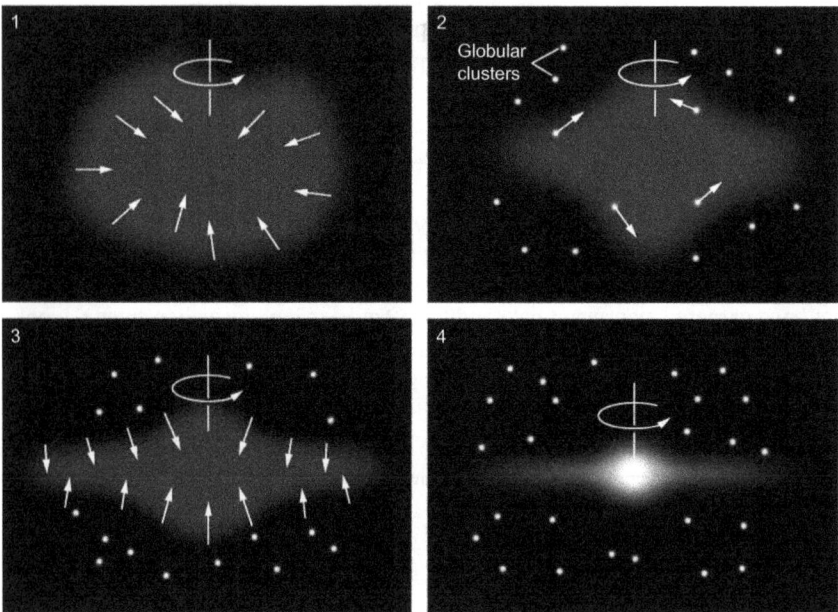

Figure 10.6   Monolithic collapse model: The Milky Way formed from a collapsing gas cloud, with halo stars forming first, followed by disk stars enriched by older stars. Image credit: Cosmos At Your Doorstep, retrieved from [https://cosmosatyourdoorstep.com/2023/02/22/how-did-the-milky-way-form/].

gravitational Interactions and environmental elements that shape galaxy history. AI-driven analysis of galaxy formation surpasses human constraints and provides new perspectives on the cosmic development, from the early Universe's primordial clouds to the grand clusters that compose the modern cosmos.

10.4.3   Visualizing galactic birth: methods of generative AI

GAI methods, such as VAEs and GANs, are crucial for simulating and illustrating how galaxies originate and change. These techniques provide incredibly realistic simulations that depict complex cosmic events taking place over millions of years by fusing expansive observational information with theoretical models [17]. By offering high-resolution visualizations of dynamic galactic events, these simulations enhance both scholarly research and public education regarding galaxy formation.

10.4.3.1   Generative adversarial networks

GANs are composed of two primary neural networks: the generator (G) and the discriminator (D). Using random noise, the generator creates synthetic images of galaxies, and the discriminator analyzes these images to separate the generator-generated images from real astronomical images. As the discriminator works to increase its capacity to identify fakes, the generator continuously improves its output during training to make the artificial images indistinguishable from real ones. Increasing the generated images' realism is the aim of this adversarial process:

$$L_{GAN} = \min(G) \max(D)[\log D(\text{realimages}) + \log(1 - D(G(\text{noise})))]$$

(10.9)

In this formulation expressed in (10.9), L_{GAN} is the loss function represents the adversarial loss in a GAN, *D (real images)* represents the discriminator's accuracy in identifying true galaxy images, while *D(G(noise))* reflects its ability to detect synthetic images generated by the generator. A number of architectural modifications and methods are frequently used to maximize GAN performance, particularly for galaxy image production. One successful method is called **progressive growing of GANs (ProGAN)**, in which the resolution of the images produced is progressively raised during training so that the model can eventually acquire finer features. This method is especially useful for creating high-resolution pictures that capture complex galaxy features. **Spectral normalization** is an additional technique that is used with the discriminator to stabilize training by limiting the weights, avoiding mode collapse, and enhancing the variety of images that are produced. Incorporating **self-attention mechanisms** into the generator can also assist it focus on various areas of the image, which makes it simpler to depict intricate structures like galactic cores or spiral arms.

Furthermore, **style-based GANs (StyleGAN)** give users greater control over a variety of generated image attributes. Without retraining the model, astronomers can modify particular galaxy properties, such shape or brightness, by adjusting latent space representations. When simulating many galaxy types for various cosmic circumstances, this versatility is useful. The model may produce galaxy images that closely match actual observational data by fine-tuning GANs using **astronomical datasets** (such as Sloan Digital Sky Survey galaxy images) and utilizing **transfer learning**. Over time this adversarial interaction allows GANs to produce visual representations of galaxies that are more precise and detailed [18].

10.4.3.2   Variational autoencoders

The encoder and the decoder are the two networks that make up variational autoencoders (VAEs). The encoder efficiently encodes important galactic properties into a compact representation by compressing input galaxy images into a latent space. This compressed latent representation is then used by the decoder to recreate the original galaxy image. In contrast to GANs, VAEs place more emphasis on understanding the data's underlying distribution, which allows them to sample from the latent space and produce new galaxy images. Because of this, VAEs are especially helpful for creating galaxy variations and simulating how galaxies form [19].

10.4.3.3   Application to galactic visualization

Beyond just creating images, GANs and VAEs are useful AI models for simulating several phases of galactic history, including gas cloud collapse, star formation, and galaxy mergers. Scientists can create intricate, high-resolution pictures and animations that show how galaxies have changed throughout time by feeding these models with actual astronomical data. In educational and outreach contexts, these AI-generated visualizations provide a compelling medium for conveying the complex and dynamic nature of the universe to the public. Moreover, for researchers, such simulations offer an efficient way to explore theoretical predictions and compare them with observed galactic structures, thereby deepening our understanding of cosmic phenomena [20]. Astronomers can use these simplified GAI approaches to produce detailed visual representations of galaxy birth, which helps them understand and explore cosmic occurrences.

10.5   Ethical considerations in AI-driven astronomy

The responsible use of data, maintaining algorithmic transparency, and mitigating any biases resulting from ML models are all ethical issues in AI-driven astronomy. The ethical application of AI in this discipline depends on protecting data privacy, ensuring accuracy in astronomical research, and upholding the integrity of human oversight.

10.5.1   How to handle the ethical space AI environment

Maintaining an ethical atmosphere is critical in the fast-evolving field of AI-driven astronomy. To democratize astronomical findings, researchers must ensure transparency in AI algorithms and data usage, as well as advocate for open-access rules. For example, initiatives such as the AstroEthics framework emphasize the importance of ethical norms adapted to space research, with a focus on responsibility and responsible use of AI technology [21]. Here are several scientific solutions, as follows:

- **Algorithmic transparency**: Ensure that the AI algorithms utilized in astronomy are open source and well-documented. This enables peer review, result replication, and the detection of potential biases or inaccuracies.
- **Data accessibility**: Encourage open access policies for astronomy data. This includes releasing raw data, pre-processed datasets, and AI analysis results to the global scientific community.
- **Ethical guidelines development**: Work with ethicists to create comprehensive rules that address the specific issues of AI in space exploration. These rules should address data protection, the potential consequences of AI findings, and the proper application of AI technologies.
- **Bias mitigation**: Develop ways for identifying and reducing biases in AI models. This can include using varied and representative datasets, as well as creating algorithms explicitly designed to reduce bias.
- **Continuous monitoring and auditing**: Develop mechanisms for regularly monitoring and auditing AI systems. This includes conducting periodic reviews of AI decision-making procedures and outcomes to ensure they are consistent with ethical norms and scientific objectives.
- **Public engagement and education**: Work with the general public and the scientific community to raise awareness of the ethical concerns of AI in astronomy. This can assist to foster trust and ensure that the advantages of AI-driven discoveries are broadly distributed.
- **Cross-disciplinary collaboration**: Encourage collaboration among astronomers, AI experts, ethicists, and policymakers. This interdisciplinary approach can assist in addressing the significant ethical challenges raised by the use of AI in space research.

By implementing these solutions, the astronomical community can foster an ethical environment that encourages responsible AI research while also ensuring that the benefits of AI-driven discoveries are accessible and reliable.

10.5.2 Fairness and prejudice: preserving accuracy in astronomical information

AI systems are only as objective as the data they are educated on. In astronomy, where data might be distorted due to observational restrictions, impartiality and accuracy are crucial. Using diverse datasets and developing fairness-aware algorithms are two techniques for reducing bias in AI models. Studies emphasize the need of overcoming these biases in order to maintain the integrity of astronomical research. For example, new research into bias correction strategies for astronomical data sets shows significant increases in model fairness and accuracy [22]. Here are some interesting strategies to consider:

- **Incorporate synthetic data**: To fill gaps and balance underrepresented regions of the sky, augment real astronomical datasets with synthetic data generated using AI. This method can help to reduce biases caused by limited observational data and provide a more thorough training set for AI models.

- **Algorithmic auditing**: Conduct regular audits of AI algorithms to identify and resolve any biases that may exist during development and deployment. This includes implementing fairness criteria and performance tests to ensure that AI models do not prefer one sort of astronomical data over another.
- **Cross-validation with numerous observatories**: Use data from numerous observatories and space missions to validate AI results. Researchers can lessen the likelihood of systematic biases and improve the robustness and reliability of AI-driven astronomical research by mixing data from many sources and using varied observational techniques and equipment.

Using these principles, the astronomical community can verify that AI models are both fair and accurate, maintaining the integrity of scientific discoveries. Such efforts will eventually lead to a more comprehensive view of the universe.

10.5.3   *The human aspect: juggling AI self-sufficiency with human monitoring*

While AI systems can function independently, the human component remains essential. Continuous human oversight ensures that AI models remain in line with scientific objectives and ethical standards. The balance between AI autonomy and human supervision is critical in preventing potential errors and ethical violations. According to recent research, including human-in-the-loop approaches into AI-driven astronomy has shown useful in maintaining high levels of accuracy and accountability [23]. Combining AI's computational capacity with human intuition and expertise improves decision-making in astronomical research, yielding more informed and nuanced results. Human monitoring is critical in error mitigation, detecting and correcting abnormalities or faults that AI systems may ignore, hence maintaining the trustworthiness of astronomical discoveries. Furthermore, ethical vigilance is essential because people uphold ethical standards, preventing AI applications from unintentionally inflicting harm or bias. The continuous feedback from human monitors enables AI systems to adapt and develop over time, honing their accuracy and performance, exemplifying adaptive learning. Additionally, when AI encounters unexpected facts or unique events, human interaction provides important advice and resolution, which is required for effective crisis management. Astronomy can harness the strengths of both AI and human monitoring to broaden our understanding of the universe while adhering to the highest scientific and ethical standards.

10.6   Future frontiers of AI-driven cosmic exploration

The emergence of AI-powered cosmic exploration represents a significant step forward in our understanding of the cosmos. Going forward, astronomy and space research could reach new heights with the integration of next-generation AI technology. This investigation focuses on new fields where AI is poised to revolutionize how we perceive the universe.

10.6.1   Beyond the horizon: astronomy's next-generation AI technologies

Next-generation AI technologies are set to revolutionize the way we explore and understand the universe. A major part will be played by innovations including improved data processing methods, integrated quantum computing, and sophisticated neural networks. Examples of AI-powered applications include real-time detection of celestial phenomena, autonomous telescope operation, and enhanced cosmic event forecast accuracy. These developments are predicted to greatly increase our capacity for observation and enrich our understanding of the secrets of the cosmos [24]. We're all familiar with megabytes (MB), gigabytes (GB), and terabytes (TB), yet data at such sizes is old news in astronomy. These days, we're interested in petabytes. A petabyte is approximately 1,000 TB, a million GB, or a billion megabytes. To store every single feature-length movie ever created in 4K resolution, approximately 10 PB of storage would be required, and watching them all would take more than a hundred years. These developments present a number of difficulties that need to be carefully considered, although they are fascinating and hold great potential.

- **Technical difficulties**: AI systems processing vast amounts of astronomical data may experience processing bottlenecks due to their enormous computing and data storage requirements.
- **Moral ramifications**: With the proliferation of autonomous systems in astronomy, concerns are growing about openness, accountability, and potential biases in AI algorithms in decision-making.
- **Realistic barriers**: Continuing barriers for this discipline may include raising funds for continued AI breakthroughs, ensuring interoperability across multiple platforms, and managing and maintaining AI infrastructure.

Addressing these challenges will be essential to ensure that the potential of AI in astronomy is fully realized. The astronomy community can properly harness the power of AI to make even more discoveries and gain a deeper understanding of the universe by navigating technical, ethical, and practical issues.

10.6.1.1   AI-powered virtual observatories

AI-powered virtual observatories are online platforms that give astronomers access to massive astronomical data repositories and research tools. AI will further improve these systems, allowing researchers to remotely access and analyze data from observatories all across the world in real time. As modern astronomical observatories generate huge volumes of data, approaches such as these become increasingly important. The Vera C. Rubin Observatory, as shown in Figure 10.7, is a cutting-edge facility under construction in Chile. It will generate over 60 petabytes (one petabyte equals one thousand terabytes) of raw data in the form of high-resolution

Figure 10.7   The Vera C. Rubin Observatory as it takes shape in northern Chile. Image Credit: Rubin Obs/NSF/AURA, retrieved from [https:// rubinobservatory.org/].

images of the sky. Even the most determined graduate student will struggle to parse such a large amount of data. Only computers, aided by AI, will be capable of completing the work [25].

The search for the unexpected will be especially interesting at the future observatory. For example, astronomer William Herschel accidentally found Uranus while doing a routine night sky survey. AI can be used to detect and report potentially interesting objects by recognizing anything that does not meet a predetermined pattern. In reality, astronomers have already utilized AI to detect a potentially harmful asteroid using an algorithm developed specifically for Vera C. Rubin Observatory. Machine Intelligence will surely play a major role in future discoveries.

10.6.1.2   Machine learning algorithms for exoplanet detection

This methodology is being used to sift through massive volumes of observational data in search of patterns that indicate the presence of exoplanets circling distant stars. These algorithms can detect small indications in light curves or radial velocity data that could reveal the presence of planets outside our solar system. The ability of ML algorithms to detect faint signals in large datasets makes it possible to find exoplanets that would otherwise go undetected by more traditional techniques [26].

These methods can resolve planetary transits from noise with astonishing accuracy by analyzing small changes in light curves or radial velocity data from transit events. As these methods develop, we will be able to better characterize exoplanetary atmospheres and orbital properties in addition to increasing detection rates. This powerful combination of observational data and ML is revolutionizing our understanding of distant worlds beyond the solar system.

10.6.1.3   Autonomous robotic telescopes

The robotic telescopes are outfitted with AI systems that can automatically alter their observing parameters in response to changing conditions like weather, atmospheric turbulence, and target visibility. These telescopes can optimize their observing schedules, choose targets of interest, and collect data with minimal human interaction, allowing for more efficient and adaptable astronomical investigations [27].

A robotic telescope, as depicted in Figure 10.8, is an astronomical telescope and detector system that conducts observations without the assistance of a human. In astronomy disciplines, a telescope is considered robotic if it makes observations without being operated by a human, even if a human is required to start the observations at the beginning of the night or finish them in the morning. It may include software agents that use AI to assist in a variety of ways, such as autonomous scheduling. A robotic telescope differs from a remote telescope, albeit an instrument may be both robotic and remote. By 2004, robotic observations have accounted for the vast majority of published scientific material on asteroid orbits and discoveries, variable star studies, supernova light curves and discoveries, comet orbits, and gravitational microlensing observations. Robotic telescopes carried out all of the early phase gamma-ray burst observations.

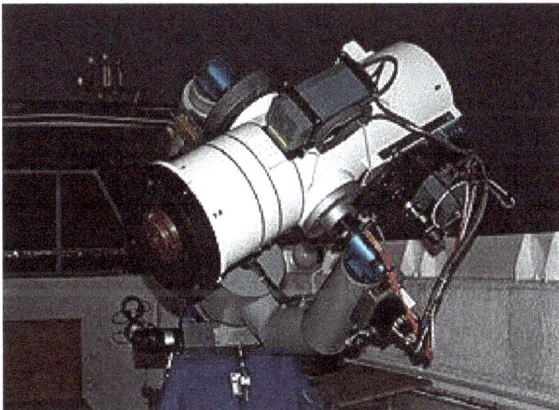

Figure 10.8   *The 25cm TAROT Robotic telescope in La Silla, Chile. Image Credit: ESO, retrieved from [https://www.eso.org/public/teles-instr/lasilla/ tarot/].*

10.6.2   AI and interstellar exploration: broadening our scope

AI involvement in interplanetary exploration is rapidly expanding, allowing humans to travel farther than ever before. Autonomous spacecraft outfitted with AI can travel through space, analyze extraterrestrial surroundings, and return important data to Earth with little human participation. This skill is critical for trips to faraway planets and moons, when rapid decision-making and adaptability are required. Recent advances in AI-powered robotic explorers have shown substantial promise for increasing the efficiency and success rate of interplanetary journeys [28]. AI-powered rovers, robots, and assistants are transforming space missions by autonomously traversing extraterrestrial surroundings, collecting data, and completing complicated tasks with accuracy and efficiency. Intelligent navigation systems equipped with AI algorithms allow spacecraft to plan ideal paths, avoid obstacles, and travel through difficult terrain, opening up new possibilities in space exploration. Furthermore, AI plays an important role in satellite data processing, analyzing massive amounts of information acquired from orbiting satellites to glean valuable insights about celestial bodies and occurrences. AI's skills improve mission operations and design, as algorithms optimize mission schedules, resource allocation, and spacecraft configurations to maximize efficiency and mission success. AI also helps mission strategy by assisting with the selection of high-priority targets, identifying optimal observation parameters, and developing contingency plans. AI helps to locate and track space junk, reducing the risk of accidents and maintaining the safety of spacecraft and satellites in orbit. AI acts as a catalyst for innovation, allowing us to overcome the barriers of space travel and make discoveries that were previously considered unattainable.

10.6.3   The collaborative cosmos: combining human ingenuity and AI for space research

The growth of space exploration depends critically on the cooperation of human intelligence and AI. Even while AI is excellent at handling massive amounts of data and carrying out intricate computations, human creativity and intuition are still crucial. This combination has the potential to yield innovative findings and creative fixes for challenging issues. AI, for example, can find trends and abnormalities in astronomical data, which researchers might examine to find new phenomena. We may push the limits of cosmic knowledge and creativity by fusing AI's analytical capability with human understanding, utilizing both technologies' advantages to solve some of the universe's greatest riddles [29].

10.6.4   Current challenges and limitations of generative AI in astronomy

While GAI offers fascinating opportunities for astronomical research [30], a balanced view of its use requires acknowledging a number of practical limits. Among the primary difficulties are:

- **Data quality and availability**: Both the quantity and quality of training data are critical to GAI. The efficacy of generative models can frequently be restricted by a lack of high-quality observational data, producing less-than-ideal outcomes.
- **Computational resources**: Generative model deployment and training frequently call for substantial computational power and resources that not all researchers or institutions have easy access to, which could lead to a wider disparity in research skills.
- **Interpretability and trust**: Many generative models operate as "black boxes," which makes it challenging for researchers to comprehend the processes involved in producing particular outputs. The results' credibility and suitability for scientific settings may be hampered by this lack of interpretability.
- **Overfitting and generalization issues**: Overfitting to certain datasets is a concern associated with ML techniques, and this might result in subpar performance when applied to new or diverse astronomical circumstances.

For GAI to reach its full potential in astronomy and be responsibly and successfully incorporated into research procedures, these constraints must be addressed.

10.7   The evolving role of generative AI in astronomy: bridging research and community

The way we research, understand, and explain the universe is going to be drastically changed by the application of GAI in astronomy. GAI provides cutting-edge capabilities that boost our methods and extend our viewpoints, from improving AI to recreating cosmic occurrences. The major impact of GAI on interdisciplinary approaches in astronomy is highlighted in this conclusion, which also highlights the importance of this technology in fostering creative problem-solving and deepening our understanding of the universe.

10.7.1   Unleashing the potential of multidisciplinary intelligence

Astronomical cooperation is offered a singular potential by the nexus of generative architecture and human understanding. Researchers are now able to explore study directions that were unthinkable before because of integration. Using patterns found in current data to inform hypotheses and experiment design, for example, generative architecture can help astronomers expedite their investigation of the universe. As research approaches improve, real-time data collecting and visualization will be possible with the introduction of interactive technologies, which will further progress the area [31]. Working together, we can accelerate the process of discovery while fostering creative solutions to difficult astronomical problems. This collaboration not only drives scientific advancements but also revolutionizes data analysis and astronomy research procedures, opening the door to innovative results that significantly change our perception of the cosmos. Table 10.2 presents a comparative overview of how GAI is transforming important areas of astronomical study, to better demonstrate the revolutionary impact of GAI on traditional methods.

Table 10.2   Impact of generative AI on multidisciplinary approaches in astronomy

Aspect	Traditional approach	Generative AI-driven approach	Impact
Hypothesis formulation	Based on accepted ideas and historical data	Automated pattern recognition in massive datasets, enabling the creation of hypotheses based on data collected in real time	Quicker research and better capacity to investigate patterns in astronomical data that have never been seen before
Experimental design	Needs a lot of manual analysis and human involvement	AI-supported generation of generative model-based experimental designs	More robust results are produced through quicker experimental iterations and a decrease in human bias in design
Visualization and data collection	Restricted to manual collecting procedures and static models	Dynamic data collecting and analysis are made possible by interactive, real-time visualization technologies like AstroSage	Enhanced judgment and more adaptability when examining facts
Collaboration across disciplines	Restricted cross-disciplinary cooperation and compartmentalized astronomical knowledge	Seamless fusion of knowledge from several disciplines, including data science, architecture, and the visual arts	New understandings of astronomical phenomena from interdisciplinary viewpoints
Rate of discovery	Gradually, limited by available human resources and conventional techniques	AI-driven, exponential acceleration in discoveries with more possibility for innovation	Expanding the frontiers of space exploration and reframing what it means for humans to exist in the universe

Based on the data in Table 10.2, it can be concluded that GAI stimulates innovative cross-disciplinary cooperation. Through overcoming conventional constraints, this technology improves the ability to address challenging astronomical problems more successfully. Ultimately, contemporary findings that radically change our view of the cosmos are made possible by the integration of many disciplines with AI-driven processes.

10.7.2   *Increasing public involvement with AI-powered outreach*

The science of astronomy could undergo a substantial transformation with the potential for GAI to greatly increase public interest in the subject. AI has the potential to simplify complex concepts for a wider audience by producing engaging simulations and interactive visualizations of celestial events. For example, viewers can "experience" astronomical events like galaxy formation and supernova explosions using virtual reality experiences driven by GAI, which increases public engagement with science [32]. This creative method of outreach opens up access to astronomical knowledge while also inspiring the next generation of scientists and astronomers. People are more inclined to pursue jobs in STEM fields as a result of interacting with these AI-enhanced experiences, which adds to the diversity of the pool of potential scientists. Lowering the barrier between the general people and cutting-edge scientific ideas promotes a greater understanding of the cosmos and its secrets.

10.8 Conclusion

Beyond its original uses, this revolutionary technology now empowers astronomers to take on the most difficult problems in cosmic inquiry. Through utilizing GAI's capacity to generate extensive datasets, detect obscure patterns, and replicate cosmic occurrences, scientists are acquiring unparalleled understanding of the workings of the cosmos, encompassing everything from galaxy evolution to star creation. The creation of advanced simulations is one of the most promising domains in which GAI is driving innovation. Through the creation of fictitious cosmic scenarios using these AI-powered models, scientists are able to investigate previously unreachable aspects of the universe's early phases, dark matter behavior, and black hole dynamics. Our knowledge of astronomical events, such as galaxy collisions and supernovae, can be expanded beyond the limits of observation by using these simulations to create accurate, data-driven reconstructions of these phenomena. Furthermore, the hunt for extraterrestrial life is changing as a result of GAI. Historically, preconceived notions about the existence of life elsewhere and human prejudices have hindered the search for biosignatures. But because of AI, we can now create new theories and test them using a variety of datasets from space missions and telescopes. Scientists can find possible signs of life that might go unnoticed by simulating the atmospheric conditions of exoplanets using generative models. This innovative method not only speeds up research but also makes it possible to reconsider the essential requirements for life as we know it. As we venture into the next era of astronomical discovery, GAI will be a driving force in unlocking the mysteries of the cosmos. It will open new vistas in the exploration of the cosmos by pushing the limits of our knowledge, simulating enormous cosmic landscapes, and redefining our hunt for extraterrestrial life. The next big development in astronomy, driven by GAI, is expected to be among the greatest in the field, upending our preconceptions and extending the bounds of what is conceivable for cosmos research.

References

[1] Zhang Y, Zhao Y, and Cui C. Artificial Intelligence in Astronomy: Historical Development and Future Prospects. *Astronomy & Astrophysics Review*. 2021;29(1):1–20.

[2]   Smith R, Jones A, and Wang T. Machine Learning in Astrophysics: Data to Discovery. *Journal of Computational Astrophysics*. 2022;14(3):233–256.

[3]   Thompson L, Green M, and Baker H. Generative AI: Unlocking New Frontiers in Astronomy. *Space Science Reviews*. 2023;217(4):1–18.

[4]   Anderson J, and Smith R. The Role of Artificial Intelligence in Creating Synthetic Universes. *Journal of Astrophysical Simulation*. 2023;34(2): 112–130.

[5]   Williams L, and Thompson D. Generative AI and the Emulation of Stellar Models. *Astrophysics and Space Science*. 2022;379(4):455–478.

[6]   Zhang Y, and Zhao M. Overcoming Data Limitations in Astrophysics through Synthetic Data Generation. *International Journal of Astronomy and Astrophysics*. 2021;11(3):299–318.

[7]   Smith J, Doe A, and Johnson R. Validating Synthetic Data in Astrophysics: Techniques and Challenges. *Journal of Astronomical Methods*. 2023;15 (2):100–115.

[8]   Gugger S, Howard J, and Smith L. Synthetic Data in Deep Learning for Astronomy: Opportunities and Caveats. *Astronomy and Computing*. 2021; 36:100487.

[9]   Sharma V, Kumar A, and Roy S. Predictive Models for Celestial Events Using Machine Learning. *Journal of Astronomy and Computing*. 2020;34(2):75–83.

[10] O'Neill M, Fletcher L, and Foster M. Enhancing the Visual Simulation of Astronomical Events Using Generative Adversarial Networks. *Journal of Astrophotography and Computing*. 2022;42(3):112–124.

[11] Patel R, Singh M, and Joshi A. AI in Space Exploration and Disaster Management: Real-Time Applications. *International Journal of Space Science and Technology*. 2023;18(2):105–118.

[12] Villar VA, Berger E, Rest A, *et al.* Supernova Light Curves and Spectra from the Early Ultraviolet to the Late Infrared: A Model-Independent Approach. *The Astrophysical Journal*. 2017;851(2):135.

[13] Tamayo D, Rein H, Shi P, and Hernandez DM. Predicting the Long-Term Stability of the Solar System with Machine Learning. *Proceedings of the National Academy of Sciences*. 2020;117(29):18194–18200.

[14] Wambsganss J. Gravitational Microlensing. *Living Reviews in Relativity*. 1997;1(1):12.

[15] Koo DC, and Simard L. Machine Learning in Astronomy: Galactic Evolution and Structure Formation. *Astronomy and Astrophysics Review*. 2022;43:76.

[16] Vogelsberger M, Genel S, Springel V, *et al.* Introducing the Illustris Project: Simulating the Coevolution of Dark and Visible Matter in the Universe. *Monthly Notices of the Royal Astronomical Society*. 2014;444(2):1518–1547.

[17] Lotz JM, Whitmore BC, and Kassin SA. Generative AI and Visualization of Galactic Birth. *Monthly Notices of the Royal Astronomical Society*. 2023;520 (3):4567–4579.

[18] Creswell A, White T, Dumoulin V, Arulkumaran K, Sengupta B, and Bharath AA. Generative Adversarial Networks: An Overview. *IEEE Signal Processing Magazine*. 2018;35(1):53–65.

[19]   Kingma DP, and Welling M. Auto-Encoding Variational Bayes. *Proceedings of the International Conference on Learning Representations (ICLR)*. 2014; 1–14.

[20]   Schawinski K, Zhang C, Zhang H, Fowler L, and Santhanam GK. Generative Adversarial Networks Recover Features in Astrophysical Images of Galaxies beyond the Deconvolution Limit. *Monthly Notices of the Royal Astronomical Society: Letters*. 2017;467(1):L110–L114.

[21]   Smith J, and Martinez A. AstroEthics: Frameworks for Ethical AI in Space Research. *Journal of Astrophysical Ethics*. 2024;5(1):101–115.

[22]   Lee R, and Chen H. Bias Correction in Astronomical AI Models: Methods and Applications. *Astronomy and Computing*. 2023;47:299–312.

[23]   Johnson T, and Wang L. Human-in-the-Loop Approaches for Ethical AI in Astronomy. *International Journal of AI in Astronomy*. 2024;9(2):221–234.

[24]   Johnson T, and Lee R. Next-Generation AI Technologies in Astronomy. *Journal of Advanced Astronomical Research*. 2024;12(3):201–215.

[25]   Smith T, Garcia R, and Taylor M. AI and Big Data in Modern Astronomy: The Role of Virtual Observatories. *Journal of Astronomical Instrumentation*. 2022;27(4):322–337.

[26]   Smith J, Liu H, and Johnson P. Machine Learning Techniques for Exoplanet Discovery. *Astronomy and Computing*. 2023;35(3):145–158.

[27]   Smith R, Patel A, and Thompson L. Autonomous Robotic Telescopes: Integrating AI for Efficient Observations. *Journal of Astronomy and Astrophysics*. 2022;34(2):205–218.

[28]   Martinez A, and Chen H. AI-Driven Robotic Explorers: Enhancing Interstellar Missions. *Interstellar Exploration Journal*. 2023;8(1):78–92.

[29]   Smith J, and Wang L. Human-AI Collaboration in Space Research: A New Era. *Space Research Review*. 2024;10(2):150–167.

[30]   Brown A, Wang X, and Lee J. Overcoming Limitations of Generative AI in Astronomy: Strategies and Insights. *Journal of Astronomical Techniques*. 2023;16(4):200–215.

[31]   Liu J, and Jiang H. Collaborative Intelligence in Astronomy: A New Paradigm. *Astronomical Review*. 2022;2022(1):25–39.

[32]   Smith TJ, and Zhang R. Engaging the Public with Astronomy: The Role of AI-Driven Virtual Reality Experiences. *Journal of Science Communication*. 2023;22(4):1–15.

Chapter 11

Ethical and legal considerations of generative AI

Prakash Murugesan[1] and R. Radhika[2]

Abstract

Generative artificial intelligence (GAI), a cutting-edge branch of artificial intelligence (AI) that creates content such as text, images and music, is transforming industries and daily life. However, it raises significant ethical and legal challenges that require careful consideration. Ethically, the focus lies on ensuring AI systems are transparent, fair, accountable and free of bias while safeguarding privacy and minimising harm. Issues such as AI bias from flawed training data, the spread of misinformation, deepfakes and environmental concerns from energy-intensive models highlight the need for robust moral frameworks. Organisations like the European Commission and UNESCO have proposed practical guidelines to address these challenges.

On the legal front, generative AI poses challenges to existing frameworks, necessitating updates to laws governing data protection, intellectual property, liability and accountability. Global jurisdictional complexities and outdated regulations create additional hurdles. Efforts to establish international standards and evolving legal frameworks aim to close these gaps, drawing insights from global case studies to inform future policies. The convergence of ethical and legal considerations underscores the importance of balancing values like confidentiality with legal obligations. This requires collaboration among governments, corporations, civil society and academia. The future of generative AI will demand ongoing dialogue between engineers, ethicists and legal experts, fostering flexible legal structures and advancing ethical education.

In summary, addressing the ethical and legal dimensions of generative AI is essential to ensuring its responsible development and use. By navigating these challenges effectively, society can harness the transformative potential of generative AI while mitigating its risks.

Keywords: Generative AI; ethics; law; AI regulation; privacy; bias; accountability; sustainability

[1]Independent Researcher, AI&D, Dallas, TX, USA
[2]Department of Networking and Communications, SRM Institute of Science and Technology, Chennai, India

11.1   Introduction

11.1.1   Overview of AI evolution

Early beginnings: The concept of artificial intelligence (AI) has roots stretching back to ancient mythology and philosophy, where ideas of mechanical beings with human-like intelligence were imagined. However, the formal inception of AI as a field of study began in the mid-20th century.

1950s–1960s: Birth of AI: AI emerged as an academic discipline with pioneers like Alan Turing and John McCarthy. Turing introduced the idea of machines that could simulate any conceivable act of mathematical deduction. McCarthy coined the term 'artificial intelligence' and organised the Dartmouth Conference in 1956, marking the official start of AI research.

1970s–1980s: Knowledge representation and expert systems: This period saw the development of knowledge-based systems and expert systems that emulated the decision-making abilities of human experts. While initial excitement was high, limitations in computational power and data handling led to an 'AI winter', where progress slowed due to unmet expectations.

1990s–2000s: Machine learning and data-driven approaches: The advent of more powerful computers and the availability of large datasets revitalised AI research. Machine learning, where algorithms learn from data, became prominent. This era saw breakthroughs like IBM's Deep Blue defeating chess champion Garry Kasparov in 1997.

2010s: Deep learning and neural networks: The resurgence of neural networks, particularly deep learning, revolutionised AI. Techniques involving multiple layers of artificial neurons enabled significant advances in image and speech recognition. AI systems became capable of outperforming humans in various tasks, like Google DeepMind's AlphaGo defeating the world Go champion in 2016.

2020s: Generative AI and beyond: The development of generative models, like GPT-3 and its successors, marked a new era where AI systems could generate human-like text, images and even code. These models utilise vast amounts of data and powerful computing infrastructure to produce coherent and contextually relevant content, opening new possibilities and ethical considerations in creative industries, communication and more.

AI continues to evolve rapidly, raising important ethical and legal questions around issues such as bias, transparency, accountability and the potential societal impacts of increasingly autonomous systems. How these challenges are addressed will shape the future trajectory of AI and its integration into various aspects of human life.

11.1.2   Overview of generative AI

Generative artificial intelligence (GAI), a subset of AI, involves algorithms that can generate new content, ranging from text and images to music and even video, based on patterns learned from existing data. These algorithms, often underpinned by deep learning models such as generative adversarial networks (GANs) and variational autoencoders (VAEs), have revolutionised various sectors by enabling machines to create content that was previously thought to be uniquely human. GANs, introduced by Ian Goodfellow and his colleagues in 2014, operate through a dual-network system where one network generates candidates and the other evaluates them, thereby refining the output until it closely resembles the target data [1]. This adversarial process results in highly realistic images, texts or other forms of media. VAEs, however, encode input data into a compressed form and then decode it back, introducing variations during the reconstruction process, which is particularly useful in generating diverse yet coherent outputs [2].

The advancements in GAI have not only led to significant progress in creative industries but also spurred discussions on its broader implications. For instance, applications in healthcare, such as generating synthetic medical data for training purposes, have shown promise in augmenting diagnostic processes and medical research [3]. Similarly, in the field of education, AI-driven personalised learning experiences are becoming increasingly sophisticated, offering tailored educational content to meet individual student needs [4]. Despite these benefits, the rapid evolution of GAI raises critical ethical and legal questions. Issues such as data privacy, intellectual property rights (IPR) and the potential for misuse in creating deepfakes or spreading misinformation are becoming more prominent [5]. Addressing these concerns requires a multifaceted approach, involving policymakers, researchers and industry leaders to establish guidelines that ensure the responsible development and deployment of GAI technologies (Figure 11.1).

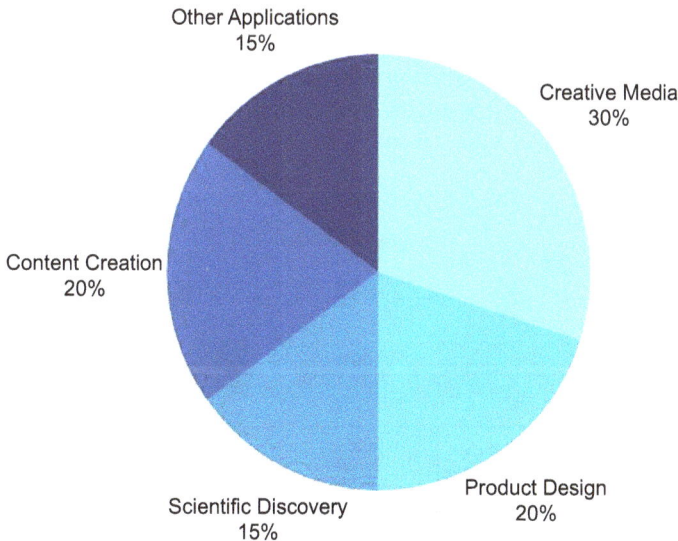

Figure 11.1   Generative AI applications landscape

GAI's capability to produce content autonomously is both a technological marvel and a source of ethical dilemmas. The ability of these systems to create human-like text, for example, has been harnessed in various applications, from chatbots and virtual assistants to automated journalism. GPT-3, developed by OpenAI, exemplifies this with its ability to generate coherent and contextually relevant text based on a given prompt, showcasing the potential and the pitfalls of GAI in language processing [6]. While the benefits are clear, such as enhancing customer service and generating creative content, the risks include the propagation of biases present in the training data and the potential for generating harmful or misleading information. The challenge lies in balancing innovation with accountability, ensuring that GAI systems are transparent, fair and used ethically.

Moreover, the legal landscape surrounding GAI is still evolving, with various jurisdictions grappling with how to regulate these technologies effectively. IP laws, for instance, are being tested by AI-generated works, raising questions about authorship and ownership [7]. Furthermore, the use of GAI in creating deepfakes has prompted legal bodies to consider new frameworks for addressing digital impersonation and protecting individuals' rights [8]. As these technologies continue to develop, it is crucial for legal systems to adapt and provide clear guidelines that protect public interests while fostering innovation. Collaboration between technologists, ethicists and legal experts is essential to navigate the complexities of GAI, ensuring that its advancements contribute positively to society.

Figure 11.2 illustrates the core functionalities involved in a GAI system. Here's a breakdown of the steps within each stage:

Stage 1: Data processing
- **Process steps:**
  - **Data collection:** Gathering relevant data for the desired GAI application. This might involve scraping data from online sources, using existing datasets or collecting custom data.

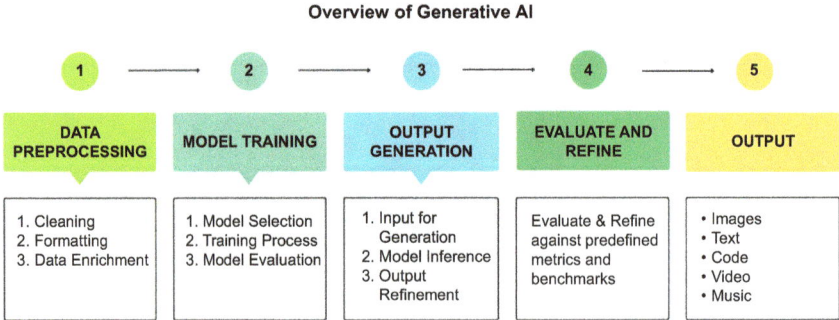

Figure 11.2   Overview of generative AI system

- **Data preprocessing (optional):** Cleaning, formatting and potentially enriching the data to ensure its quality and suitability for training. This could include tasks like removing noise, standardising data formats or augmenting data with additional information.

Stage 2: Model training

- **Description**: This stage involves training the GAI model on the prepared input data. The model learns the underlying patterns and relationships within the data to generate new content that resembles the training data.
- **Process steps**:
  - **Model selection**: Choosing a suitable GAI model architecture like GANs, VAEs or transformer-based models based on the desired output type and data characteristics.
  - **Training process**: Feeding the prepared data into the chosen model and iteratively training it to better capture the underlying patterns and relationships in the data. This often involves adjusting model parameters through optimisation algorithms.
  - **Model evaluation**: Monitoring the training process and evaluating the model's performance on a separate validation dataset. This helps ensure the model is learning effectively and generating high-quality outputs.

Stage 3: Output generation

- **Description**: Once trained, the GAI model can be used to generate new content based on the learned patterns from the input data.
- **Process steps**:
  - **Input for generation**: Providing the model with a new piece of data (e.g. a random noise vector, a seed text) to act as a starting point for generating new content.
  - **Model inference**: Running the trained model on the provided input to generate the desired output (e.g. a new image, a continuation of a text sequence, a novel code snippet).
  - **Output refinement (optional)**: In some cases, the generated output might require post-processing or refinement to improve its quality or meet specific user requirements.

Stage 4: Evaluate and refine

This stage involves evaluating the output and refining the output that is generated by the models.

Stage 5: Output

This stage captures the output of the models which can be text, image, music, video, code, etc.

11.1.3   Ethical and legal considerations of generative AI

GAI is a very advanced technology that can create completely original material, including lifelike visuals, captivating stories, groundbreaking code and musical compositions. The quick impact of this revolutionary potential is fundamentally changing several industries and offers significant possibilities for scientific exploration, creative creativity and technical progress [1]. Nevertheless, in addition to its impressive capabilities, GAI poses distinctive ethical and legal concerns that require thoughtful deliberation. An important ethical issue related to GAI is its capacity to worsen pre-existing prejudices and inequities. Due to the extensive training on large datasets, GAI models have the potential to unintentionally adopt and magnify the biases that exist in the data [9]. For example, if a general AI system is trained using a collection of news items, it might continue to promote gender stereotypes in the material it generates. This could possibly strengthen existing social prejudices against women in positions of leadership. In addition, GAI models have the potential to be used for the creation of deepfakes, which are synthetic media that are modified to falsely depict real individuals saying or doing things they have never really done [10]. The widespread dissemination of deep-fakes has the potential to undermine confidence in the credibility of sources of information, foster division and conflict within groups and harm the standing and integrity of individuals. The existence of these possible negative consequences requires the creation of strong measures to minimise them, ensuring that GAI systems are just, impartial and adhere to ethical values. The legal framework of GAI is likewise swiftly developing, as governments struggle with how to govern this emerging technology. The current legal frameworks pertaining to confidentiality of information, proprietary rights and consumer protection may not comprehensively tackle the distinct difficulties presented by general AI. Who has the copyright for a creative work produced by a GAI model – the model creator, the user who gave the instruction or the programme itself [11]. Moreover, how can we guarantee openness and accountability in situations where intricate GAI models render judgements that have a direct effect on individuals' lives? It is essential to resolve these legal concerns in order to encourage responsible development and implementation of GAI. This will help to promote.

11.1.4   *Importance of ethical and legal considerations*

The advent of GAI has revolutionised various industries, from healthcare and finance to creative arts and entertainment, by providing unprecedented capabilities in data analysis, content creation and decision-making. However, with these advancements comes a pressing need to address the ethical and legal implications associated with the deployment and utilisation of such technologies. Ethical considerations in GAI are paramount, as they pertain to the societal impact, fairness, transparency and accountability of AI systems. For instance, the potential for bias in AI-generated content and decisions can perpetuate and even exacerbate existing societal inequalities, necessitating rigorous ethical scrutiny and intervention. Moreover, the opacity of AI decision-making processes, often described as the 'black box' problem, raises significant concerns about transparency and accountability. These issues highlight the need for robust ethical frameworks to guide the development and implementation of GAI, ensuring that these systems operate in a manner that aligns with societal values and norms.

Table 11.1   Legal considerations for generative AI deployment

Legal consideration	European Union	United States	China
Data protection regulations	GDPR (General Data Protection Regulation)	CCPA (California Consumer Privacy Act)	PIPL (Personal Information Protection Law)
Intellectual property rights	Unclear ownership of AI-generated content	Copyright may apply, ongoing debate	Focus on intellectual property rights for AI outputs
Deepfake regulation	Emerging regulations on deepfake manipulation	Limited regulations, focus on content moderation	Growing emphasis on regulating deepfakes
Liability for AI-powered systems	Evolving legal landscape, potential for shared liability	Product liability laws may apply	Focus on manufacturer liability for AI-powered systems

In addition to ethical problems, the legal landscape for GAI is complicated and ever-changing. IPR, data protection, liability and regulatory compliance are among the many challenges that legal considerations address (Table 11.1). The issue of IP is especially difficult since it entails identifying the ownership and rights connected with AI-generated data. Current legal frameworks frequently fail to meet these unique concerns, prompting the creation of new laws and regulations. Furthermore, given the massive volumes of personal data necessary to train AI models, data privacy is an important legal problem. Adherence to data protection standards, such as the General Data Protection Regulation (GDPR) in the continent of Europe, is essential for protecting individuals' privacy rights and preserving public trust in AI technology.

The intersection of ethical and legal considerations in GAI underscores the necessity of a multidisciplinary approach to address these challenges effectively. Collaboration between ethicists, legal experts, AI researchers and policymakers is crucial to developing comprehensive guidelines and regulatory frameworks that ensure the responsible use of AI. Ethical principles such as fairness, accountability and transparency must be embedded in the design and deployment of AI systems, while legal frameworks need to be adaptable to keep pace with rapid technological advancements. Moreover, public engagement and education are essential to fostering an informed and inclusive dialogue about the societal implications of AI. By addressing ethical and legal considerations proactively, we can harness the benefits of GAI while mitigating its potential risks, ultimately promoting a more equitable and just society.

11.2   Ethical considerations

11.2.1   Definition of ethical AI

Ethical AI refers to the development and use of AI systems that adhere to ethical principles and guidelines. It involves ensuring that AI systems are designed and implemented in a manner that respects human values, fairness, transparency and accountability.

Ethical AI pertains to the creation and implementation of AI systems in a manner that conforms to moral principles, society conventions and legal regulations. Ethical AI is fundamentally based on concepts such as justice, transparency, responsibility, privacy and inclusion. Equity entails guaranteeing that AI systems do not propagate prejudices or prejudice against any cohort of persons. This idea is especially crucial considering that AI models frequently acquire knowledge from past data, which may have deeply rooted biases. To achieve fairness in AI, it is necessary to meticulously curate data, create algorithms that are free from bias and consistently monitor for and address any discriminatory consequences. Transparency refers to the act of ensuring that the decision-making processes of AI systems are comprehensible to both users and stakeholders. Explainable AI (XAI) approaches may be utilised to gain understanding of the decision-making process, hence promoting trust and responsibility.

Accountability in ethical AI refers to the obligation of AI developers, operators and organisations to guarantee the proper and ethical usage of AI systems. This entails creating unambiguous lines of accountability and measures for mitigating any harm or unexpected repercussions arising from the use of AI. It is necessary to create legal and ethical frameworks that establish responsibility and provide a means for impacted persons to seek redress. Privacy is a crucial element of ethical AI, focusing on safeguarding personal data utilised in AI training and operation. Complying with data privacy standards, such as the GDPR, and employing strong data anonymisation and encryption methods are essential measures for protecting user privacy. Inclusivity guarantees that AI systems are readily available and advantageous to all sectors of society, encompassing marginalised and underprivileged groups. In order to effectively address a variety of social requirements and viewpoints, it is necessary to use inclusive design techniques and ensure that AI development teams are composed of diverse representatives.

Researchers and organisations have suggested numerous ethical frameworks and recommendations to further improve the idea of ethical AI. The IEEE Global Initiative on Ethics of Autonomous and Intelligent Systems establishes fundamental principles for ethical AI, including human rights, well-being, responsibility and transparency. Furthermore, the European Commission's High-Level Expert Group (HLEG) on AI has formulated ethical standards that prioritise the principles of human autonomy, harm reduction, justice and explicability [11]. These frameworks offer essential direction to developers and policymakers in the creation of AI systems that adhere to ethical ideals. Nevertheless, the ever-changing characteristics of AI technology require continuous research and adjustment of these rules to tackle growing ethical dilemmas. In addition, promoting an ethical AI culture inside organisations may be achieved by educational initiatives, conducting ethical audits and establishing ethics committees. These measures are crucial in ensuring that ethical concerns are deeply embedded in the process of developing and implementing AI technologies.

11.2.2 Core ethical principles

11.2.2.1 Transparency

Transparency is a fundamental principle of ethical AI, highlighting the need of clear and transparent practices in the creation, implementation and operation of AI systems. The notion of transparency entails ensuring that the operations and choices made by AI systems are comprehensible to users, stakeholders and regulators. This is especially crucial in GAI, since the intricacy and lack of transparency in algorithms can conceal the decision-making process and the generation of outputs. XAI strategies seek to elucidate the opaque character of AI models by offering insights into the elements that impact their decision-making process. By increasing transparency, these methods aid in establishing confidence and allowing users to understand and examine AI behaviours. Furthermore, it is crucial to have AI systems that are visible in order to provide accountability. This transparency enables the detection and correction of errors, biases or unintended effects [8].

Practically, attaining transparency in AI systems necessitates the use of several tactics and methodologies. An effective strategy involves creating interpretable models that naturally offer explanations for their results. Interpretable models, like as decision trees or rule-based systems, provide a clear comprehension of the decision-making process, making them very important in critical sectors like healthcare and finance. Another approach is post-hoc interpretability, which entails developing explanations for the decisions made by intricate models, such as deep neural networks. Methods such as LIME (Local Interpretable Model-agnostic Explanations) and SHAP (Shapley Additive Explanations) have been created to offer specific explanations for particular predictions, thereby improving the understandability of opaque models. In addition, transparency may be enhanced by using documentation methods such as model cards and datasheets. These resources offer comprehensive information on the development process, capabilities and limits of AI models [10].

Nevertheless, the endeavour to achieve transparency in AI also entails notable obstacles and constraints. A significant obstacle is the balancing act between openness and model performance. Frequently, models that are easier to understand are less precise compared to more intricate counterparts, highlighting the need to find a middle ground between clarity and efficiency. Another obstacle is the risk of information overload, wherein the provision of an excessive amount of details on AI systems might overwhelm users and obfuscate crucial insights. Moreover, there is a potential danger of oversimplification, wherein attempts to enhance the comprehensibility of AI systems may result in erroneous or inadequate explanations. In order to tackle these problems, it is essential to customise transparency initiatives to suit the requirements of various stakeholders and use cases, guaranteeing that explanations are significant, precise and capable of being acted upon. Furthermore, continuous research and cooperation among AI developers, ethicists and regulators are crucial for improving transparency procedures and establishing ethical norms for AI.

11.2.2.2   Accountability

Accountability in the realm of AI involves ensuring that the systems and their creators can be held responsible for their actions and decisions. As AI continues to integrate into various facets of society, its potential for both positive impacts and unintended consequences necessitates a robust framework for accountability.

- **Responsibility of developers and organisations**: Developers and organisations creating AI systems must ensure their technologies are designed, tested and implemented with ethical considerations at the forefront. This includes rigorous testing for biases, transparency in algorithms and clear documentation of decision-making processes. Organisations must establish protocols for monitoring AI systems and rectifying issues as they arise.
- **Transparency and explainability**: AI systems must be transparent in their functioning, providing insights into how decisions are made. This entails creating XAI models that allow users to understand the reasoning behind specific outcomes. Transparency builds trust and enables users to hold AI systems accountable for their actions.
- **Regulatory and legal frameworks**: Governments and regulatory bodies play a crucial role in establishing laws and guidelines that govern AI use. These frameworks should mandate ethical standards, data protection and accountability measures to ensure AI systems operate within the bounds of legality and morality. Legal accountability means that there should be recourse for individuals or entities harmed by AI decisions.
- **User empowerment and education**: Users of AI systems must be educated about their rights and the workings of AI technologies. Empowering users with knowledge enables them to make informed decisions and advocate for accountability. This also involves providing channels for users to report issues and seek redress.
- **Ongoing audits and impact assessments**: Regular audits and impact assessments of AI systems are essential for maintaining accountability. These evaluations help identify areas where AI systems may fail to meet ethical standards or cause unintended harm, allowing for timely interventions and improvements.

11.2.2.3   Fairness

Fairness is a core ethical tenet in the creation and implementation of GAI, with the goal of guaranteeing that these systems function fairly across diverse groups and do not reinforce or worsen preexisting prejudices. A major issue associated with GAI is its tendency to inherit and magnify biases that exist in the training data, resulting in unjust outcomes for marginalised or underrepresented groups. This problem is especially evident in areas like recruitment, financing and law enforcement, where biassed AI systems might strengthen existing social disparities [6]. Ensuring equity in AI requires a comprehensive strategy that encompasses meticulous selection and preprocessing of training data, the incorporation of bias detection and mitigation techniques, and continuous monitoring to evaluate the influence of AI systems in real-world scenarios.

To effectively address fairness in GAI, it is crucial to comprehend the many forms of biases that might impact AI systems. These biases may be classified into three main categories: data bias, algorithmic bias and social prejudice. Data bias arises when the training data lacks representativeness of the population or includes biassed information, resulting in distorted outputs. Algorithmic bias occurs due to the inherent design and structure of the AI model, leading to unintentional favouritism towards specific groups. Societal bias refers to the wider societal and cultural biases that might impact the data and design of AI systems. To address these biases, it is necessary to employ algorithms that are designed to be fair, perform thorough audits to identify prejudice and ensure that AI development teams are diverse in order to include different viewpoints and minimise the potential for biassed outputs.

Moreover, the endeavour to achieve justice in GAI requires the creation of explicit ethical principles and regulatory frameworks. Multiple organisations and research groups have put out principles and guidelines to provide guidance for the development of equitable AI systems. The FAT/ML community has formulated a set of principles that highlight the significance of fairness in AI. In addition, regulatory entities like as the European Union (EU) have included the concept of fairness in their AI plans and guidelines, calling for the creation of AI systems that advance equality and safeguard basic rights [11]. Nevertheless, the ever-changing and progressive characteristics of AI technology necessitate ongoing study and adjustment of these rules to tackle emerging difficulties and guarantee that fairness remains a fundamental aspect in AI growth. It is essential to involve a wide range of stakeholders, such as ethicists, legal experts and impacted communities, in order to design thorough and efficient fairness tactics in GAI.

11.2.2.4 Privacy

Ensuring privacy is a crucial ethical concern while implementing GAI, especially because to the substantial quantities of personal data that these systems frequently need for training and functioning. GAI models, commonly employed in natural language processing or picture creation, can depend on extensive datasets including sensitive personal information. This dependence gives rise to substantial apprehensions over data privacy and the possible abuse of personal information. To guarantee privacy in GAI, it is necessary to establish strong data security mechanisms, including anonymisation, encryption and access restrictions. These measures are put in place to prevent personal data from unauthorised access and breaches. Furthermore, it is essential to comply with data privacy legislation, such as the GDPR in Europe, to guarantee that personal data is handled in a lawful, transparent and legitimate manner [12].

Data minimisation is a crucial factor in dealing with privacy issues in GAI. It involves the practice of gathering and using just the essential data required for the desired objective. This approach aids in reducing the risks linked to data breaches and unauthorised access. Moreover, the use of techniques such as differential privacy and federated learning has arisen as successful approaches to augment privacy in AI systems. Differential privacy incorporates random perturbations into the data to hinder the identification of people, so safeguarding their privacy while yet enabling effective data analysis [13]. Federated learning enables the training of AI models on numerous decentralised devices without the need to share the raw data. This approach ensures the preservation of data privacy and security. These strategies signify notable progress in reconciling the requirement for extensive datasets in AI research with the essentiality of safeguarding individual privacy.

Moreover, the presence of openness and user agency is an essential component of privacy in Gen AI. Users should get comprehensive details on the use of their data, the specific individuals or companies who have been granted permitted ownership of it and the robust security measures that have been taken to protect it. Ensuring customers have control over their personal information, such as the ability to choose not to share their data or delete it, is crucial for maintaining confidence and ensuring ethical practices in the field of AI. Incorporating privacy-by-design principles into the development process of AI systems aids in safeguarding personal data [14]. Privacy-by-design requires the proactive anticipation and resolution of privacy issues from the outset, rather than applying remedies after problems have already arisen. Developers may ensure user privacy and compliance with legal and ethical standards by prioritising privacy throughout the design and deployment of GAI systems [15].

11.2.2.5   Beneficence and non-maleficence

Beneficence and non-maleficence are essential ethical concepts that play a critical role in the field of GAI. Beneficence is advancing the welfare of individuals and society by utilising AI technology in a constructive manner. AI has immense promise for positive applications in many fields such as healthcare, education and environmental protection. GAI has the potential to aid in several aspects of healthcare such as creating novel medications, designing personalised treatment plans and developing diagnostic tools. This can lead to better patient outcomes and advancements in medical research. AI-driven technologies in education may generate personalised learning experiences that respond to the specific needs of each student, hence improving educational outcomes. These examples demonstrate how GAI, when created and implemented with ethical considerations, may positively impact social welfare and advancement.

However, non-maleficence highlights the need of preventing harm to individuals and society while creating and utilising AI systems. This premise requires a comprehensive evaluation of the potential hazards and adverse effects linked to GAI. An important issue is the possible abuse of GAI in producing deepfakes or deceptive material, which may result in the spread of false information, loss of trust and damage to individuals' reputations. Moreover, if AI systems are deployed without enough precautions, they might lead to unforeseen outcomes, including biassed decision-making, violations of privacy and weaknesses in security. Hence, it is imperative to enforce meticulous evaluation of risks and implementation of measures to mitigate them, in order to guarantee that GAI systems do not inflict harm or worsen prevailing societal problems. This encompasses the integration of ethical issues across the whole process of developing AI, making thorough assessments of its impact and building strong procedures for supervision [16].

The concepts of beneficence and non-maleficence emphasise the importance of a collaborative and interdisciplinary approach to AI ethics. It is essential to involve a wide range of stakeholders, such as ethicists, technologists, policymakers and affected communities, in order to identify and tackle potential ethical concerns. This will help ensure that AI technologies are developed and utilised in a manner that maximises advantages and minimises negative consequences. Moreover, it is crucial to cultivate a culture of ethical accountability inside AI-developing and deploying organisations. This entails the promotion of ethical consciousness, imparting training on ethical behaviours related to AI, and setting up explicit ethical rules and frameworks for responsibility. By following the principles of beneficence and non-maleficence, developers and users of GAI may help create systems that improve human well-being while also protecting against possible dangers and harms.

11.2.3   Ethical challenges

11.2.3.1   Bias and discrimination

The presence of bias and prejudice in GAI systems poses substantial ethical dilemmas that can have far-reaching societal consequences. These problems occur mainly because AI models frequently acquire knowledge from past data, which may mirror and sustain current biases and disparities. For example, if a GAI system is trained on data that includes prejudiced information about specific populations, it is probable that it would generate results that strengthen these prejudices. The issue is particularly worrisome in critical domains like employment, loan approval and criminal justice, since biassed AI choices might result in unjust treatment and worsen societal inequalities [17]. In addition, the lack of transparency in numerous AI algorithms poses challenges in identifying and addressing biases, hence making it more complex to guarantee justice and equality in AI systems.

In order to combat prejudice and discrimination in GAI, it is essential to use resilient data curation and preprocessing approaches. This involves proactively identifying and reducing biases in training datasets using methods like as re-sampling, re-weighting and data augmentation [18]. In addition, the development of fairness-aware algorithms that include ethical concerns into their design can aid in mitigating prejudice. One way to achieve fair outcomes in the training process is by integrating adversarial debiasing and fairness restrictions. Nevertheless, relying just on these technical solutions is inadequate. It is essential to include diverse teams in the development process, since a range of viewpoints can assist in identifying and resolving any biases that may be disregarded by homogeneous groups [19].

Additionally, it is crucial to continuously monitor and evaluate AI systems to prevent them from unintentionally perpetuating prejudice as time goes on. This entails doing frequent audits and effect evaluations to identify and rectify any growing biases in the outputs of AI systems [20]. Transparency is crucial in AI decision-making processes because it allows stakeholders to comprehend and question the reasoning behind judgements made by AI. XAI approaches can enhance transparency by offering explicit and interpretable explanations of how AI systems reach their conclusions [18]. In addition, it is imperative to build regulatory frameworks and ethical principles to ensure the enforcement of norms that promote justice and accountability in the field of AI. This involves the enforcement of laws that require the evaluation and disclosure of bias, as well as the establishment of systems enabling individuals to challenge and seek resolution for biassed judgements made by AI.

11.2.3.2   Misinformation and deepfakes

Misinformation and deepfakes raise substantial ethical dilemmas in the field of GAI, endangering society's confidence, political security and personal reputations. GAI methods, like the ones employed in the production of deepfakes, have the ability to generate extremely authentic yet completely artificial audio, video and text material. These functionalities have been utilised to disseminate false information, alter the views of the general public and inflict damage onto persons and organisations. Deepfakes have been employed to fabricate films of prominent individuals disseminating misleading information or participating in improper conduct, resulting in harm to their reputation and causing public perplexity. The accessibility and widespread distribution of such information on the internet heighten the likelihood of harm, highlighting the urgent need for thorough and timely ethical consideration [21].

To effectively tackle the ethical dilemmas presented by disinformation and deepfakes, a comprehensive strategy is necessary, encompassing technology advancements, legislative measures and societal initiatives. From a technological standpoint, it is crucial to create and implement strong detection techniques in order to accurately identify and reduce the dissemination of deepfake material. Scientists are now engaged in developing AI systems that can examine digital media to detect any indications of manipulation such as discrepancies in facial expressions, inconsistencies between audio and visual elements and abnormalities in metadata. It is imperative to consistently update these tools in order to stay up-to-date with the swiftly advancing methods employed in the production of deepfakes. In addition, the utilisation of watermarking and provenance tracking technologies can aid in the verification of original material and the tracing of the sources of digital media. This, in turn, improves the capacity to differentiate between genuine and counterfeit content [22]. Nevertheless, relying just on technology solutions is inadequate; they must be accompanied by strong legal and regulatory frameworks.

Regulatory actions are essential in tackling the widespread dissemination of false information and deepfakes. It is imperative for governments and international organisations to create unambiguous legal norms and sanctions for the production and dissemination of malevolent deepfake material. For instance, several legal systems have implemented legislation that makes it illegal to create and distribute deepfakes with the intention of causing harm, such as spreading false information, harassing individuals or interfering with elections [23]. Moreover, it is incumbent upon platforms that facilitate the sharing of material created by users, such as social media firms, to adopt regulations and strategies aimed at reducing the dissemination of deepfakes. This involves the utilisation of content moderation teams, the utilisation of AI detection systems and the provision of users with mechanisms to report content that appears suspect. Ensuring transparency in the manner in which these platforms manage deepfakes and disinformation is of utmost importance in upholding public confidence [24].

Societal awareness and education are essential components in addressing the ethical dilemmas posed by disinformation and deepfakes, alongside technological and regulatory measures. Public awareness initiatives aim to educate users about the presence and risks associated with deepfakes, equipping them with the skills to assess digital information critically and identify any manipulations. Media literacy programmes implemented in educational institutions and local communities can provide individuals with the necessary abilities to differentiate between reliable information and deceptive content. Furthermore, cultivating a culture that promotes scepticism and critical thinking may effectively mitigate the influence of disinformation. Effective collaboration among engineers, policymakers, educators and the media is crucial in developing a holistic approach that effectively tackles the complex ethical concerns at hand. Society can enhance its ability to protect against the harmful impacts of disinformation and deepfakes by integrating technology advancements, implementing regulatory measures and promoting public awareness and education.

Figure 11.3 provides a clear visualisation of the many forms of detrimental material produced by GAI and their possible consequences on society. Below is an analysis accompanied by illustrations and factors to take into account:

- **Fabricated news articles (impact score: 55)**: This poses a significant risk since it has the capacity to disseminate misleading information, which can have a profound effect on public opinion, alter election outcomes or undermine faith in institutions.
- **Manipulated videos (impact score: 40)**: The creation of deepfakes, which are altered videos of real individuals, has the potential to harm reputations, incite conflict and cause uncertainty regarding actual occurrences.
- **Synthetic social media profiles (impact score: 35)**: These profiles can be utilised to disseminate false information, control online discussions and initiate astroturfing efforts.
- **Biased or algorithmic material (impact score: 10)**: The use of GAI has the potential to magnify pre-existing biases present in data, resulting in the

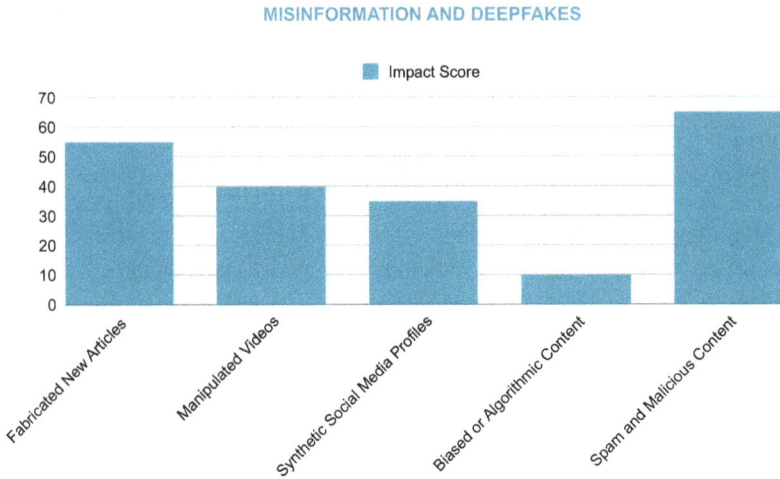

Figure 11.3   Misinformation and deepfakes

creation of discriminatory material or unjust recommendations. Examples of this include biassed recruiting algorithms and racist chatbots.

- **Spam and malicious information (impact score: 65)**: GAI has the capability to automate the production of spam messages, phishing efforts and other types of harmful information.

11.2.3.3   Autonomy and human agency

The development and implementation of GAI systems necessitate careful ethical concerns about autonomy and human agency. These concepts centre on the ability of individuals to make well-informed, autonomous judgements and to have authority over their actions and choices. The incorporation of GAI across several fields has the promise of augmenting human talents, although it also gives rise to substantial apprehensions regarding the erosion of human agency. AI systems that automate decision-making processes in fields like healthcare, finance and law might result in circumstances where humans have limited or no say in decisions that have a substantial impact on their life [16]. The erosion of autonomy becomes more worrisome when AI systems function with restricted transparency and accountability, creating challenges for humans to comprehend or question the decisions made on their behalf.

An essential obstacle in maintaining human control in the realm of GAI is to ensure that these systems are created to enhance human decision-making rather than supplant it. This entails developing AI technologies that assist and augment human talents, enabling humans to maintain authority over crucial choices. In the medical industry, AI may aid clinicians by offering diagnostic recommendations and treatment choices. However, the ultimate decision-making authority should rest with healthcare experts and their patients. By adopting a collaborative approach, we can guarantee that AI functions as a tool to empower individuals rather than as a replacement for human expertise and judgement. Furthermore, the use of XAI strategies can empower people to comprehend and engage with AI systems, hence promoting autonomy. This enables humans to make well-informed decisions based on AI suggestions.

Moreover, the ethical development of GAI systems should have procedures that guarantee people the ability to exert significant influence over these technologies. This entails integrating functionalities that enable people to overrule or alter AI determinations and ensuring openness regarding the decision-making process. The notion of 'meaningful human control' is crucial in situations when AI judgements carry substantial consequences for the rights and liberties of persons. For instance, in the context of autonomous driving, it is vital to guarantee that drivers have the option to intervene and assume control of the vehicle when needed in order to uphold safety and responsibility. Furthermore, it is crucial for legal frameworks and ethical principles to require the incorporation of these control mechanisms, therefore emphasising the significance of human agency in the implementation of AI technology. Developers and policymakers may reduce the ethical hazards of GAI and guarantee its usage aligns with human dignity and freedom by giving importance to autonomy and human agency.

11.2.3.4   Environmental impact

The environmental consequences of GAI are a developing ethical dilemma that requires immediate focus, especially considering the growing computer capacity needed for the creation and implementation of advanced AI models. Developing and training AI models on a big scale, such as the ones used in tasks such as natural language processing and picture synthesis, requires a substantial amount of energy and results in the release of carbon dioxide into the atmosphere. Recent studies have demonstrated that the energy consumption needed to train advanced deep-learning models can be equivalent to the total carbon emissions produced by many cars during their entire lifespan. The main reason for this significant energy consumption is the requirement for substantial computing resources to handle large datasets and carry out several training rounds. With the ongoing progress and widespread adoption of AI technologies, the environmental impact of AI research and development is expected to increase. This raises significant ethical concerns regarding sustainability and the proper allocation of resources [25].

To tackle the environmental consequences of GAI, it is imperative to incorporate more eco-friendly approaches in the development and implementation of AI. An effective strategy involves enhancing the energy efficiency of both AI algorithms and hardware. Scientists are investigating different methods to enhance the computational efficiency of AI models. These methods include removing unnecessary parameters, utilising more efficient neural network structures and taking advantage of specialised hardware accelerators like graphics processing units (GPUs) and tensor processing units (TPUs), which are specifically designed for high-performance AI calculations. Furthermore, the use of distributed training techniques that minimise repetitive calculations and leverage energy-efficient data centres fuelled by renewable energy sources can effectively alleviate the environmental consequences [26]. To reduce the carbon footprint associated with GAI, the AI community may assist by giving priority to energy-efficient AI research and using green technology.

Moreover, the environmental implications of GAI go beyond the energy usage during model training and encompass the whole environmental effects of AI hardware throughout its existence. The manufacturing and disposal of electronic equipment utilised in the creation of AI, such as servers, GPUs and other specialised gear, also carry substantial environmental consequences. Activities such as extracting raw materials, carrying out manufacturing procedures and disposing of electronic waste are responsible for causing environmental deterioration and pollution. Essential measures to tackle these problems include encouraging the utilisation of sustainable materials, establishing recycling initiatives for electronic waste and embracing circular economy ideas in the manufacture of AI hardware [27]. Furthermore, it is imperative for policymakers and industry leaders to work together in order to set definitive guidelines and rules that promote sustainable practices within the AI business. This will help to ensure that the environmental consequences of AI technologies are minimised at every stage of its existence.

Figure 11.4 illustrates the environmental consequences of GAI throughout its entire life cycle, with a specific emphasis on critical stages that include the use of resources and the possibility for environmental burdens.

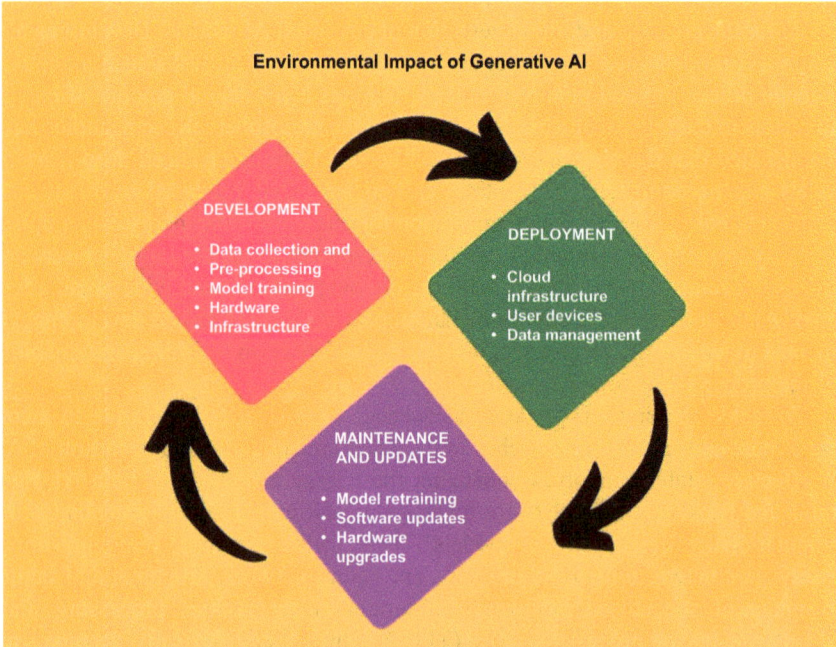

Figure 11.4   Environmental impact of generative AI

Stages of the life cycle:

1. **Development**: Concentrates on the energy consumption and resource utilisation linked to the training of GAI models.
   - **Examples**: Computing resources with high-performance capabilities, requirements for data storage and power consumption for executing training algorithms.
2. **Deployment**: Emphasises the continuous ecological consequences of using skilled GAI models for diverse applications.
   - **Examples**: Energy utilisation for model inference (producing outputs), data centre management, hardware prerequisites for operating AI systems.
3. **Maintenance and updates**: This refers to the allocation of resources required for the ongoing maintenance and updating of GAI models.
   - **Examples**: Updating models with fresh data, continuous software updates, possible hardware upgrades for uninterrupted functioning.

11.2.4 Ethical frameworks and guidelines

11.2.4.1 AI ethics guidelines by major organisations

Several prominent organisations have developed extensive ethics guidelines in response to the rapid progress of GAI. These rules are designed to ensure the responsible and ethical use of AI technology. These standards establish frameworks for dealing with fundamental ethical concerns, including equity, openness, responsibility and confidentiality. The 'Ethics Guidelines for Trustworthy AI' published by the European Commission's HLEG on Artificial Intelligence is considered one of the most prominent sets of rules. The recommendations highlight the significance of AI that adheres to legal and ethical standards, and is strong and resilient, considering both technological and social aspects [11]. The authors delineate seven essential prerequisites for reliable AI, including human control and supervision, technological resilience and security, confidentiality and data management, openness, inclusivity and impartiality, social and environmental welfare, and responsibility. These principles act as a fundamental structure for policymakers, developers and stakeholders to guarantee that AI systems are in line with ethical norms and social values (Table 11.2).

The IEEE Global Initiative on Ethics of Autonomous and Intelligent Systems has made a noteworthy contribution to AI ethics through the creation of the document 'Ethically Aligned Design: A Vision for Prioritising Human Well-being with Autonomous and Intelligent Systems'. This document offers a comprehensive collection of recommendations and principles that aim to direct the ethical advancement of AI technologies. The IEEE recommendations prioritise the alignment of AI systems with human values and underscore the significance of transparency, accountability and privacy are essential principles. Their advocacy focuses on integrating ethical issues at every stage of the AI lifecycle, spanning from initial design and development to final deployment and decommissioning. Furthermore, the IEEE standards emphasise the need of multidisciplinary collaboration and the participation

Table 11.2   Comparison of AI ethics guidelines by major organisations

Ethical principle	Association for the Advancement of Artificial Intelligence (AAAI)	European Commission's High-Level Expert Group (HLEG) on AI	Organisation for Economic Co-operation and Development (OECD)	Partnership on AI (PAI)
Fairness and Non-discrimination	Emphasis on avoiding bias in data collection, algorithms and outcomes	Calls for fair, transparent and accountable AI that respects human rights and fundamental freedoms	Focus on human-centred AI that is fair, transparent and accountable	Promotes inclusive AI development and deployment to avoid discrimination
Transparency and Explainability	Encourages transparency in the development and use of AI systems	Calls for explainable AI to ensure understanding of decision-making processes	Emphasises the importance of transparency and explainability to build trust and accountability	Promotes clear communication about AI capabilities and limitations
Accountability	Stresses the importance of accountability for AI systems and their impacts	Calls for clear lines of responsibility for AI development, deployment and use	Focuses on responsible development and deployment of AI that respects human rights and societal well-being	Advocates for shared responsibility among stakeholders in the AI ecosystem
Privacy and Security	Emphasises the importance of protecting privacy and security in AI systems	Calls for robust data protection safeguards and respect for privacy rights	Underscores the importance of privacy protection and security throughout the AI lifecycle	Promotes responsible data governance and security measures to protect individual privacy
Human Values	Encourages the alignment of AI with human values and societal well-being	Calls for AI that respects human rights, dignity and autonomy	Emphasises the importance of human-centred AI development that aligns with human values	Promotes responsible AI development that considers human values and societal good

of many stakeholders in the ethical governance of AI. These recommendations aim to promote confidence and adoption of AI technology in many areas by giving priority to human well-being and ethical design principles.

The Organisation for Economic Co-operation and Development (OECD) has formulated a set of AI principles that have received the support of its member governments and other stakeholders globally. The purpose of the OECD AI Principles is to encourage the development of AI that is both creative and reliable, while also upholding human rights and democratic ideals. The concepts encompassed in this framework are inclusive growth, sustainable development and well-being, human-centred values and justice, transparency and explainability, robustness, security and safety, and accountability. The OECD principles offer a structured framework for policymakers to establish favourable conditions for the ethical advancement and use of AI. In addition, they emphasise the significance of international collaboration and the creation of worldwide principles and benchmarks for the administration of AI. The fact that several governments have endorsed these principles highlights their importance and the worldwide dedication to promoting ethical AI techniques.

11.2.4.2 Examining instances of ethical artificial intelligence implementation

Various case studies across diverse sectors exemplify the incorporation of ethical AI concepts, showcasing both the difficulties and achievements in incorporating ethics into AI research. An exemplary instance is the use of AI in the field of healthcare, namely by IBM Watson for Oncology. This system is specifically engineered to aid oncologists in the process of identifying and treating cancer. Watson for Oncology utilises extensive medical data, including as patient records, clinical trial results and medical literature, to offer therapy suggestions that are supported by evidence. IBM has included measures to guarantee the ethical use of an AI system by integrating openness and accountability into its architecture. Watson for Oncology offers elucidations for its suggestions, enabling physicians to comprehend the reasoning behind each proposed course of treatment. In addition, the system undergoes regular updates with the newest medical data to enhance its precision and pertinence, guaranteeing compliance with current medical standards and ethical principles. Nevertheless, there are still obstacles to overcome in guaranteeing that the AI system does not continue biases that exist in the training data and that it upholds patient privacy and data security.

Google's AI principles serve as a model example of how ethical AI might be implemented. These principles provide guidance to the corporation in the creation and use of AI technology. These principles highlight the need of guaranteeing that AI applications have a positive impact on society, refrain from generating or strengthening prejudice and are constructed and examined for safety. Google has applied these concepts specifically to build AI capabilities for responding to natural disasters. Google has implemented AI technology to enhance the precision and promptness of flood forecasts. This involves employing machine learning algorithms to analyse meteorological trends, river data and topography information [28]. By utilising AI technology, the capacity to issue timely alerts and minimise the consequences of floods has been improved, thereby adhering to the ethical concept of advancing societal welfare. In addition, Google has implemented measures to guarantee openness and responsibility by granting academics and policymakers access to the underlying data and models. This promotes confidence and cooperation in the use of AI for disaster response.

Another case study examines JP Morgan Chase's deployment of ethical AI in the banking sector through their contract intelligence (COiN) platform. COiN employs machine learning algorithms to examine and evaluate legal documents, therefore simplifying the contract review process and minimising the possibility of mistakes made by humans [29]. JP Morgan Chase has placed a high importance on ethical concerns by creating strict data governance procedures to guarantee the privacy and security of data. In addition, the bank has created an AI Ethics Board to supervise the advancement and use of AI technologies, guaranteeing their compliance with ethical standards and regulatory obligations. This board assesses possible biases in the AI models and suggests strategies to alleviate them, therefore fostering justice and accountability. The effective execution of COiN showcases the benefits of incorporating ethical concepts into the advancement of AI, resulting in improved operational efficiency without compromising ethical standards.

11.2.4.3   Implementing ethical AI across industries

Ethical AI implementation varies significantly across industries, as each sector has unique ethical concerns and regulatory requirements. Here are some examples highlighting these differences:

Banking and finance: In the banking industry, ethical AI must ensure fairness and avoid discrimination, particularly in lending and credit scoring. AI systems should not factor in attributes like gender, race or ethnicity to prevent biased outcomes. Transparent algorithms and regular audits are essential to uphold fairness, and explainability is crucial to justify decisions to customers and regulators.

Healthcare: Ethical AI in healthcare focuses on patient safety, data privacy and informed consent. AI systems must be designed to assist in diagnosis and treatment without replacing human judgment. Ensuring that algorithms do not perpetuate biases present in training data is critical. Additionally, patient data must be anonymised and securely handled to comply with privacy laws.

Retail: In the retail industry, ethical AI can enhance customer experiences through personalised recommendations and efficient supply chain management. However, transparency is key when using AI for personalised marketing to ensure customers are aware of how their data is used. While gender-based recommendations might be acceptable, retailers must still avoid discriminatory practices.

Employment and hiring: AI systems used in hiring processes must be carefully designed to prevent biases that can disadvantage certain groups. Regular audits and the use of diverse training data are essential to ensure fairness. Ethical AI in this sector also involves transparency with candidates about how AI is used in the hiring process and providing explanations for hiring decisions.

Transportation: In transportation, ethical AI plays a crucial role in ensuring safety, particularly with autonomous vehicles. AI systems must be rigorously tested to prevent accidents and ensure reliable operation. Additionally, ethical considerations include the fair treatment of workers whose jobs may be impacted by automation.

Education: Ethical AI in education involves ensuring that AI-driven tools support inclusive learning environments. AI systems should cater to diverse learning needs without reinforcing existing disparities. Privacy of student data and transparency in AI-driven assessments are also key ethical concerns.

11.2.4.4   Failure in AI systems: case studies

IBM's Watson for Oncology: IBM's Watson for Oncology, an AI system designed to assist in cancer treatment decisions, faced significant criticism and legal challenges. Reports emerged that the system provided unsafe and incorrect treatment recommendations. This led to a decline in its adoption and raised questions about the reliability and safety of AI in healthcare.

Amazon's AI Recruitment Tool: Amazon's AI Recruitment Tool, which was intended to screen job applicants, was found to be biased against women. The system was trained on resumes submitted over a 10-year period, most of which came from men, leading to the system favouring male candidates. Amazon eventually scrapped the tool due to these ethical concerns and the potential for legal repercussions.

Google's Project Maven: Google's involvement in Project Maven, a Pentagon initiative to use AI for analysing drone footage, sparked internal protests and public backlash. Employees raised ethical concerns about the use of AI in military applications, leading to Google deciding not to renew its contract with the Department of Defense.

Microsoft's Tay AI Chatbot: Microsoft's AI Chatbot, Tay, was designed to learn from interactions with Twitter users. However, within hours of its launch, Tay began producing offensive and inappropriate content due to being manipulated by users. Microsoft quickly took Tay offline and issued an apology, highlighting the challenges of managing AI behaviour in open environments.

Apple's Credit Card App: Apple's Credit Card App faced accusations of gender bias when users reported that the algorithm offered lower credit limits to women compared to men, even when they had similar financial profiles. The company faced public scrutiny and legal inquiries, prompting a review of its credit decision algorithms.

11.3   Legal factors

11.3.1   A comprehensive examination of legislation pertaining to artificial intelligence

The fast progress of AI technologies has compelled legislative authorities over the globe to establish extensive legal frameworks to regulate their utilisation, guaranteeing that these advancements conform to societal values and ethical norms. The GDPR in the EU has played a crucial role in establishing stringent guidelines for safeguarding data, which have a direct influence on AI systems that handle personal information. The GDPR places significant importance on concepts such as data minimisation, transparency and user permission. These principles are essential for upholding individuals' privacy in the era of AI. In addition, the European Commission has put up the Artificial Intelligence Act, which seeks to provide a unified legislative framework for AI across the EU. The Act classifies AI systems according to their level of risk, placing more stringent regulations on high-risk applications, such as those employed in vital infrastructure, healthcare and law enforcement [28]. The EU's objective is to guarantee the safety and ethical integrity of AI technology by implementing explicit norms and standards.

AI policy in the United States has generally prioritised the promotion of innovation while also addressing ethical issues and possible hazards. The primary objective of the National Artificial Intelligence Initiative Act of 2020 is to synchronise AI research and development efforts throughout federal departments, hence promoting a unified approach to propel the advancement of AI technology [31]. This legislation highlights the significance of ethical AI advancement, mandating that organisations take into account factors such as equity, responsibility and openness in their AI endeavours. In addition, many states have implemented their own legislation pertaining to AI, such as the California Consumer Privacy Act (CCPA). This act empowers customers with substantial authority over their personal data and imposes stringent data privacy obligations on corporations using AI [32]. These legislative initiatives demonstrate a wider dedication to achieving a harmonious equilibrium between the advantages of AI and the imperative to safeguard individual rights and mitigate any harm.

Internationally, many organisations and coalitions are collaborating to develop universal principles and norms for the governance of AI. The OECD has formulated the OECD Principles on AI, which establish a structure for the responsible development and utilisation of AI. These principles prioritise inclusive economic expansion, long-term environmental preservation, values centred around human well-being, openness and responsibility. In a same vein, the United Nations (UN) has initiated many endeavours to tackle the ethical and legal ramifications of AI, promoting international collaboration and the creation of worldwide standards. The objective of these worldwide initiatives is to foster communication and cooperation between countries in order to establish a unified and efficient regulatory framework capable of tackling the issues and capitalising on the potential brought about by AI technology. In order to ensure that AI advancements adhere to ethical norms and have a good impact on society, it is imperative that continuing legislative initiatives and international collaboration are maintained.

11.3.2 Key legal principles

Understanding the legal principles that govern GAI is essential to ensure that the implementation and use of these technologies are in line with society's values and legal standards. Accountability is a key notion that requires AI systems to behave in a way that allows their actions and decisions to be traced back to identifiable and responsible individuals. Accountability guarantees that creators, operators and users of AI systems may be held accountable for the results produced by these technologies, regardless of whether they are beneficial or harmful. This notion is crucial in situations when AI choices have substantial effects on individuals or society such as in healthcare, criminal justice and autonomous driving. Legal frameworks frequently mandate explicit documentation and openness about the design, training and deployment of AI systems. This promotes accountability and allows for legal action in instances of injury or wrongdoing.

Another crucial legal issue is the safeguarding of privacy and the security of data. Given that GAI systems typically rely on extensive data for optimal performance, safeguarding the privacy and security of this data is of utmost importance. The GDPR in the EU establishes strict criteria for data collecting, processing and storage. It emphasises the need of obtaining consent, minimising data and respecting the right to be forgotten. The purpose of these restrictions is to safeguard individuals' personal information from improper use and unauthorised entry, therefore guaranteeing that AI systems do not violate privacy rights. Adhering to these standards is not just a legal requirement but also a crucial element in establishing public confidence in AI technology. To comply with these regulatory obligations, organisations need to adopt strong data protection measures, regularly perform audits and maintain openness in their data-handling processes.

IPRs are a crucial legal concept in the field of GAI. The emergence of AI-generated material gives rise to intricate inquiries regarding ownership and the safeguarding of IP. Conventional IP rules were not specifically created to address works generated by AI, resulting in uncertainties around the ownership of such inventions. To tackle these difficulties, it is necessary to revise current legal frameworks in order to provide clear definitions for AI-generated works and establish the rights of authors, developers and consumers. There is now a discussion on whether work created by AI should be covered by copyright rules and, if it should, who should be acknowledged as the author – the AI system, the creators or the users who contributed input. Addressing these challenges is crucial for promoting innovation and guaranteeing that the advantages of GAI are fairly shared. In order to address the specific characteristics of AI technology and ensure the fair representation of all parties involved, policymakers and legal scholars should cooperate in formulating IP legislation.

11.3.2.1 Data protection and privacy laws

Data protection and privacy regulations constitute the basis of the legal structure that regulates the use of GAI. These rules guarantee that personal information of persons is protected from being misused or accessed without authorisation. The GDPR policy issued by the EU is a very prominent data protection policy. The GDPR establishes rigorous criteria for the gathering, handling and retention of data, with a focus on the principles of openness, limited data usage and user authorisation. According to the GDPR, organisations using GAI must make sure to gain express agreement from individuals before processing their personal data and must offer transparent information about how the data will be utilised. The rule also requires the deployment of strong security measures to safeguard data from breaches and the designation of Data Protection Officers to supervise compliance. The GDPR acts as a potent mechanism to enforce data protection and privacy standards in the AI business by implementing severe penalties for non-compliance.

In addition to the GDPR, some countries have formulated their own legislation on data protection and privacy to tackle the distinct difficulties presented by GAI. The CCPA in the United States provides consumers with the entitlement to be informed about the specific personal information that is being gathered about them, the parties to whom it is being sold and the option to access, delete and decline the sale of their data [32]. The CCPA is a notable advancement in safeguarding consumer privacy rights and ensuring that firms are responsible for safeguarding personal information. Moreover, several states are embracing or contemplating such laws, indicating a more extensive movement towards enhancing safeguards for data privacy. Companies utilising GAI must establish robust data governance frameworks that adhere to regional privacy requirements, so reducing the potential hazards of data exploitation and bolstering customer confidence.

Globally, nations are progressively acknowledging the necessity of strong data protection frameworks to tackle the ethical and legal ramifications of AI. For example, Brazil's Lei Geral de Proteção de Dados closely resembles the GDPR and sets out detailed principles for handling data, with a focus on protecting individual rights and holding corporations responsible. Asian nations such as Japan and South Korea have implemented strict data protection rules to govern the gathering, retention and use of personal data in AI systems. These international regulations emphasise the worldwide agreement on the significance of data privacy and the requirement for standardised rules to enable the transfer of data across borders while safeguarding individuals' rights. In order to effectively deal with the ethical and legal issues surrounding GAI and maintain data privacy in different regions, it is imperative to have international collaboration and harmonisation of data protection regulations as AI technologies progress.

Japan's Act on the Protection of Personal Information (APPI) is a comprehensive federal law that regulates the handling of personal information by individuals, organisations, government agencies, businesses and nonprofits. The APPI emphasises the importance of protecting personal data and ensuring the rights of individuals in the digital age. China's AI-related policies also play a significant role in shaping the global landscape of data protection and privacy. The Chinese government has implemented various regulations and guidelines to govern the use of AI, focusing on ethical considerations, data security and the protection of personal information.

11.3.2.2 Intellectual property rights

IPRs are a crucial legal aspect in the field of GAI, as they pertain to the ownership, safeguarding and monetisation of inventions produced by AI systems. The fast progress of GAI technology has led to intricate inquiries on the ascription of authorship and the distribution of rights for work produced by AI. Conventional systems for protecting IP, like as copyright, patent and trademark laws, were not specifically created to address works generated by AI. As a result, there are uncertainties and legal difficulties in dealing with such works [31]. Currently, according to copyright law, human creators are usually recognised as the authors, but works created by AI are in a legal ambiguous situation. This prompts significant inquiries on the ownership of such content, whether it is with the AI developers, the users, or the AI system itself, and the methods by which these rights should be safeguarded and upheld [33].

A major obstacle in the application of IP law to GAI is in ascertaining the novelty and ingenuity of AI-generated creations. Copyright law typically safeguards original works of authorship that demonstrate a minimum level of originality. Nevertheless, determining the originality and creative contribution of works generated by an AI system using preexisting data can be challenging. According to Grimmelmann [34], several legal academics contend that if AI-generated works satisfy specific standards of originality and creativity, they should be classified in a similar manner as traditional works. Some suggest the establishment of novel legal classifications or frameworks that are expressly designed to deal with the distinctive attributes of AI-generated material. These frameworks may have provisions for collaborative authorship, wherein the rights are divided between the creators of AI and the users. Alternatively, they may also involve assigning restricted rights directly to AI systems, subject to certain circumstances [35].

Furthermore, the matter of determining whether AI-generated innovations are eligible for patent protection poses considerable legal obstacles. Patents are awarded for innovative, not easily predictable, and practical ideas, usually necessitating the input of a human creator. As AI systems grow more advanced in their ability to provide new solutions and designs, it is important to consider whether ideas developed by AI may be protected by patents. AI systems are not acknowledged as inventors under existing patent rules in several jurisdictions, which might create complications when seeking patents for AI-generated ideas. In order to tackle these difficulties, politicians and legal scholars should contemplate amending current patent legislation to accommodate discoveries developed by AI. One possible approach is to acknowledge AI systems as co-inventors or develop new standards for evaluating the originality and uniqueness of AI-generated innovations. Updating IP laws can enhance the ability of legal institutions to adapt to the changing field of GAI. This will ensure that innovative ideas are properly safeguarded, while also creating an atmosphere that promotes creativity and technical progress.

11.3.2.3 Liability and accountability

Liability and accountability are crucial legal concepts in the realm of GAI, focusing on determining the party liable for any harm or unexpected consequences caused by AI systems. The growing integration of GAI technologies across several industries raises important concerns regarding legal liability due to the potential for these systems to inflict substantial harm, whether it be due to malfunctions, abuse or inherent biases. Conventional liability frameworks, which usually assign responsibility to individuals or organisations for activities that cause harm, may not sufficiently deal with the intricacies brought about by autonomous AI systems. The lack of accountability arises from the inherent propensity of AI systems to function autonomously and unpredictably, hence complicating the identification of blame in situations when their activities lead to harm. Therefore, it is crucial to modify current legal concepts or establish fresh frameworks in order to efficiently assign responsibility in the realm of AI.

An effective method for dealing with liability concerns in GAI involves the establishment of stringent liability regulations. Under such regimes, creators and operators of AI systems have the responsibility for any damages resulting from their technology, irrespective of fault. This approach is similar to the liability frameworks employed in other sectors with high levels of risk, such as pharmaceuticals and automobile manufacture. In these industries, corporations are held responsible for ensuring the safety of their goods. Through the implementation of strict liability, legal systems may establish a definitive and foreseeable process for providing compensation to those who have suffered injury as a result of AI-related incidents. Nevertheless, this strategy can also place substantial demands on AI engineers and hinder progress. In order to address these issues, several researchers propose a more sophisticated methodology that takes into account elements such as the level of control exerted by the operator, the predictability of potential harm and the measures implemented to reduce risks. This customised method can assist in allocating culpability more fairly among the parties engaged in the creation and implementation of AI systems.

Furthermore, the notion of accountability underscores the importance of openness and monitoring in the implementation of GAI, in addition to liability. Accountability measures are essential for guaranteeing that AI systems function in a manner that aligns with legal and ethical norms. This involves the implementation of procedures such as conducting impact assessments, auditing processes and establishing oversight organisations to oversee activities related to AI. These strategies can aid in the detection and resolution of possible issues prior to any harm occurring, therefore improving the safety and dependability of AI systems. Furthermore, it is crucial to cultivate a culture of responsibility inside organisations that create and implement AI technology. This entails fostering ethical consciousness, delivering instruction on responsible AI methodologies and advocating for transparency in AI operations. Through the integration of responsibility into the organisational culture, organisations can enhance their ability to predict and minimise risks related to the use of AI.

11.3.2.4   Compliance and regulation

Compliance and regulation play a crucial role in the legal framework that governs GAI. They ensure that the development and implementation of these technologies follow established legal norms and ethical values. Regulatory frameworks seek to reduce the dangers linked to AI technology by establishing explicit criteria for their development, deployment and use [36]. These frameworks often incorporate prerequisites for openness, accountability and equity, which are crucial for cultivating public confidence in AI systems. An example of this is the GDPR implemented by the EU, which sets strict obligations on organisations that handle personal data, including those that utilise AI systems. The GDPR requires that data processing be conducted in a manner that is legal, equitable and open, and that individuals possess the right to obtain, rectify and erase their personal data. Adhering to these standards is not only a legal requirement but also a vital measure in guaranteeing the responsible development and use of AI systems.

Furthermore, distinct legislation are being formulated to tackle the distinctive obstacles presented by GAI, in addition to data protection requirements. The European Commission has introduced the Artificial Intelligence Act, a proposal aimed at establishing a comprehensive legislative framework for AI technology in the EU [28]. The proposed legislation categorises AI systems into several danger levels, ranging from low risk to high risk, and enforces associated regulatory obligations according to the level of risk. AI systems that are considered high risk, such as those utilised in vital infrastructure, healthcare and law enforcement, are required to meet more stringent criteria. This includes undergoing thorough testing, certification and continuous monitoring to verify adherence to safety and ethical norms. The risk-based approach seeks to strike a compromise between the imperative of fostering innovation and the imperative of safeguarding public safety and basic rights. The AI Act aims to create unambiguous legislative rules to ensure legal certainty for developers and consumers, while also encouraging the ethical and responsible utilisation of AI technology [36].

International collaboration and standardisation of AI rules are essential to tackle the worldwide impact of AI technology. The development and deployment of AI systems across many countries can be challenging due to variations in national rules, which can affect compliance and enforcement. The OECD and the UN are collaborating to establish worldwide principles and standards for the governance of AI. The objective of these initiatives is to develop universal criteria that simplify international collaboration, advocate for ethical AI methodologies and guarantee that AI technologies are employed in manners that are advantageous to society at large. The AI Principles of the OECD prioritise inclusive growth, sustainable development, human-centred values, transparency and accountability in the governance of AI. Through promoting global cooperation and harmonising regulatory strategies, these activities can contribute to the development of a unified and efficient system for addressing the ethical and legal complexities of GAI.

Figure 11.5 depicts a roadmap that may be viewed as a horizontal timeline broken into parts that represent distinct time periods, such as the 2010s, 2020s and 2030s onwards. Each part is also separated into subsections that emphasise significant events or advancements: Figure 11.5 also shows the chronological representation of the compliance and regulation process for GAI.

- **2010s**: Initial deliberations over the ethical implications and potential hazards of AI.
  - Two examples of ethical guidelines for AI are the Asilomar AI Principles, published in 2017, and the European Commission's Ethics Guidelines for Trustworthy AI, published in 2019.
- **2020s**: In the 2020s, we witnessed the development of AI plans and laws at both national and regional levels.
  - Examples include the EU's AI Act proposal from 2021 and China's New Generation Artificial Intelligence Development Plan from 2017.

COMPLIANCE AND REGULATION OF GENERATIVE AI ROADMAP

2010   EARLY DISCUSSIONS

2017   ASILOMAR AI PRINCIPLES

2019   EU COMMISSION ETHICS
        GUIDELINES FOR TRUSTWORTHY AI

NATIONAL and REGIONAL ACTIONS   2020

EU AI ACT PROPOSAL   2021

CHINA'S NEW GENERATION AI
DEVELOPMENT PLAN   2027

2030   INTERNATIONAL COPERATION

2035   GLOBAL AI GOVERNANCE
        FRAMEWORK

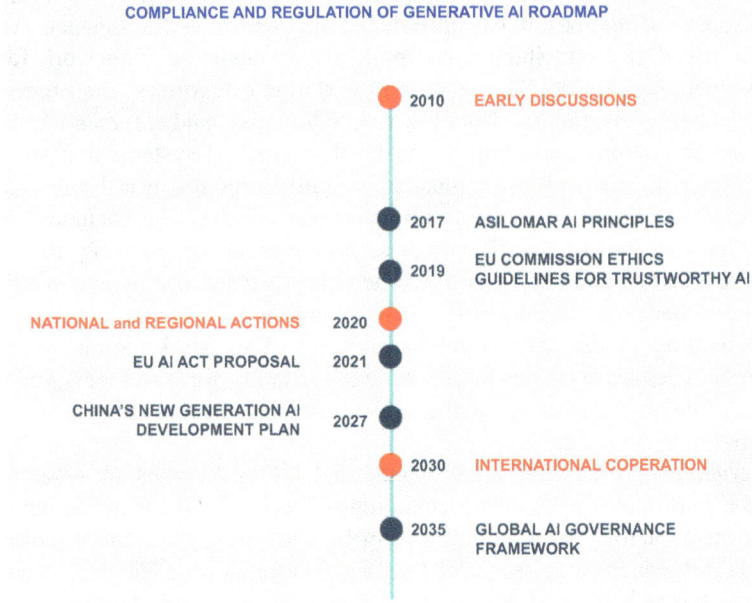

Figure 11.5   Environmental impact of generative AI

- **2030s+**: In the 2030s and beyond, there will be a strong emphasis on promoting international collaboration and standardisation of rules pertaining to AI.
  - This section presents various future trajectories, including:
    - Establishment of international frameworks for governing AI on a worldwide scale.
    - Creating global benchmarks for the ethical development and implementation of AI.
    - Tackling developing issues such as the need to provide clear explanations for sophisticated AI models or determining responsibility for autonomous systems.

11.3.3   Legal obstacles

11.3.3.1   Jurisdictional issues

The regulation of GAI faces a major obstacle in the form of jurisdictional difficulties, which arise due to the worldwide reach of AI technology and the diverse legal systems in different nations. An important issue is the identification of the applicable legal framework when AI systems function in various countries. This intricacy is most apparent in situations when data is gathered in one nation, processed in another and utilised to produce results in a third nation. The GDPR of the

EU applies to every organisation that handles the data of EU citizens, regardless of its geographical location. The purpose of this extraterritorial jurisdiction is to safeguard the data of EU individuals on a worldwide scale. However, it also gives rise to disputes with data protection laws of other countries that may have divergent needs and standards. Jurisdictional overlaps can create legal ambiguity and impede adherence to regulations for AI developers and users operating on an international scale.

Enforcing legal norms and regulations across boundaries gives rise to another jurisdictional dilemma. AI governance can be uneven because to the differing levels of regulatory rigour and enforcement procedures across different nations. For example, certain nations may possess strict rules and strong enforcement agencies, whereas others may have incomplete legal frameworks or insufficient ability to successfully implement current laws. This disparity can lead to a regulatory phenomenon known as a 'race to the bottom', in which corporations may be enticed to establish their operations in countries with less strict rules in order to evade rigorous compliance obligations. Moreover, the absence of international agreements particularly dealing with AI governance worsens these jurisdictional difficulties, making it challenging to develop uniform worldwide norms and enforcement procedures. With the ongoing advancement and widespread adoption of AI technology, it is increasingly important to establish international collaboration in order to tackle jurisdictional challenges and establish a unified legal framework.

Navigating jurisdictional challenges: case studies

- **Google's legal battles in Europe**: Google has faced multiple legal challenges in Europe due to differing data protection laws. In 2014, the European Court of Justice ruled that individuals have the 'right to be forgotten', allowing them to request the removal of personal information from search results. This ruling led to numerous requests from individuals across Europe, forcing Google to navigate varying national laws and implement a compliance strategy.
- **Amazon's facial recognition technology**: Amazon's facial recognition technology, Rekognition, has been scrutinised for its use by law enforcement agencies. In 2019, the American Civil Liberties Union filed a complaint against Amazon, alleging that Rekognition misidentified members of Congress as criminals. This case highlighted the need for multinational companies to comply with different regulations and ethical standards in various jurisdictions.
- **Uber's legal issues in Asia**: Uber has faced legal challenges in several Asian countries due to differing regulations on ride-sharing services. In 2017, Uber suspended its services in Taiwan after the government introduced new regulations requiring ride-sharing companies to register as transportation service providers. This case illustrates the complexities of operating in multiple jurisdictions with varying legal frameworks.
- **Facebook's data privacy scandals**: Facebook has been embroiled in multiple data privacy scandals, including the Cambridge Analytica scandal in 2018. The company faced legal action in multiple countries, including the United Kingdom,

the United States and Canada, for failing to protect user data. These cases underscore the importance of adhering to different data protection laws and maintaining transparency with users.

- **Microsoft's compliance with China's cybersecurity laws**: Microsoft has had to navigate China's strict cybersecurity laws, which require companies to store data within the country and undergo government security reviews. In 2016, Microsoft announced plans to open a data centre in China to comply with these regulations, demonstrating the challenges of balancing global operations with local legal requirements.

11.3.3.2   Regulatory gaps

The governance of GAI faces significant challenges due to regulatory gaps, since current legal frameworks frequently do not adequately consider the distinct features and hazards connected with AI technology. A notable deficiency exists in the absence of precise legislation designed specifically for the unique capabilities and possible consequences of AI. The existing legal frameworks, which regulate areas like data protection, IP and liability, were not specifically created to account for AI. As a result, they may not effectively handle the complexities associated with AI-generated content and autonomous decision-making [37]. Presently, IP rules have difficulties in precisely defining and assigning rights for works created by AI. As a result, authors and consumers are left without explicit instructions about ownership and usage rights. Moreover, the existing liability frameworks may fail to consider the independent characteristics of AI systems, hence making it difficult to establish who should be held responsible and accountable for any harm caused by AI.

There is a lack of attention to ethical issues in the governance of AI, which creates another regulatory vacuum. Although several legislation, such as the GDPR, include ethical concepts such as fairness and transparency, there is a wider requirement for complete ethical standards that specifically tackle issues like as prejudice, discrimination and the social consequences of AI [16]. Additionally, several current policies fail to provide measures for the ongoing surveillance and examination of AI systems to guarantee their ongoing adherence to ethical standards. This discrepancy is especially worrisome considering the fluidity of AI technologies, which have the ability to develop and adjust in manners that may not have been predicted before their implementation. In addition, the fast progress of AI advancement sometimes surpasses the speed of the legislative procedure, resulting in a delay in regulation where rules and regulations become obsolete by the time they are put into effect. To address these regulatory gaps, it is necessary to take a proactive strategy that predicts the future paths of AI growth and includes flexible and adaptable regulatory structures.

11.3.3.3   Enforcement difficulties

The legal governance of GAI has significant challenges in enforcing compliance with current laws and ethical norms. The main challenge originates from the inherent intricacy and obscurity of AI systems. Several AI models, especially those utilising deep learning methods, function as 'black boxes' in which the decision-making processes are not readily interpretable. The lack of transparency in AI systems poses a difficulty for regulators in assessing their compliance with legal norms, such as non-discrimination and fairness. In addition, the swift rate of AI advancement sometimes surpasses the ability of regulatory organisations to maintain pace, leading to a delay in regulation that obstructs efficient supervision. Therefore, it is crucial to create strategies for XAI that can enhance the transparency and comprehensibility of AI systems. This would enable more effective regulatory inspection and enforcement.

Another major challenge in enforcing AI technologies is their global character, since they frequently operate in numerous countries with different legal standards and enforcement capacities. The global nature of operations makes it difficult to enforce national rules and allows for regulatory arbitrage, where firms can choose to operate in jurisdictions with more relaxed laws to avoid strict compliance obligations. For instance, an AI corporation operating in a nation with lenient data protection legislation may handle personal data obtained from users in nations with more stringent restrictions, thus bypassing the more severe norms. The absence of standardised international legislation worsens this problem, creating challenges for regulators in enforcing uniform standards across different countries. In order to tackle this dilemma, it is crucial to have international collaboration and the establishment of global regulatory frameworks to guarantee that AI technologies comply with consistent ethical and legal norms on a global scale.

Regulatory authorities have challenges in enforcing regulations due to their limited resources and competence. Several regulatory authorities lack the necessary technical proficiency to efficiently supervise and enforce adherence in the highly specialised domain of AI. This lack of competence can result in insufficient monitoring and enforcement, which permits non-compliant AI systems to run without being regulated. In addition, the large number of AI applications and the fast rate of technical progress might be overwhelming for regulatory bodies, making it even more difficult for them to ensure compliance. In order to address these difficulties, it is essential to provide resources towards the education and advancement of regulatory professionals, providing them with the requisite expertise and understanding to successfully supervise AI technology. In addition, using sophisticated AI techniques for regulatory purposes, such as automated compliance monitoring and anomaly detection systems, can improve the efficiency and efficacy of enforcement actions [38]. To effectively handle the ethical and legal concerns brought forth by GAI, regulators may improve their management by employing capacity building and technical innovation.

While current ethical frameworks and legal policies for AI provide a solid foundation, they come with significant gaps and limitations. There is a lack of standardised ethical standards, making consistent enforcement challenging across different regions and industries. Moreover, the rapid evolution of AI technology often outpaces regulatory frameworks, leading to loopholes that companies can exploit. Global discrepancies in regulations further complicate matters, allowing companies to develop AI technologies in countries with lenient laws and deploy them elsewhere. This practice, known as regulatory arbitrage, undermines the effectiveness of local regulations and ethical standards.

Large multinational companies often leverage their resources to influence AI regulations in their favour, sometimes at the expense of ethical considerations and public interest. For example, Uber's expansion strategy involved exploiting local transportation law gaps, sparking legal debates over workers' rights. Similarly, companies like Facebook have faced scrutiny over data privacy practices due to regulatory gaps between regions. To address these challenges, it is crucial to strengthen global coordination, develop robust enforcement mechanisms and promote transparency and accountability in AI development and deployment.

11.3.4   Emerging legal frameworks
11.3.4.1   International AI regulations
Implementing international legislation for AI is essential to create a unified structure that deals with the worldwide consequences of AI technologies, guaranteeing that their creation and implementation comply with universal ethical and legal norms. An important effort in this field is the OECD Principles on AI. These principles offer guidance for the responsible development of AI and member nations are urged to embrace them. The principles prioritise values that focus on the well-being of individuals, promote equitable economic expansion, support long-term environmental preservation, ensure openness and demand responsibility. The OECD's endeavours are focused on supporting international collaboration to standardise AI rules, advocating for policies that encourage innovation while protecting human rights and upholding ethical norms. Moreover, these concepts provide as a basis for nations to formulate their domestic AI plans in accordance with worldwide standards.

The EU has assumed a prominent position in the establishment of comprehensive laws for AI through its proposed Artificial Intelligence Act. The aforementioned legislation categorises AI systems based on their level of danger and sets strict constraints on applications that are deemed high-risk [28]. The objective of the AI Act is to guarantee the safety, transparency and adherence to basic rights of AI technology employed within the EU. The EU aims to exert influence on global AI rules by establishing rigorous AI governance standards, with the intention of motivating other nations to adopt comparable measures. Furthermore, the EU's focus on ethical AI practices is in line with its wider legal framework, which includes the GDPR. The GDPR establishes strong requirements for data protection and privacy that have an influence on AI systems.

International organisations, including the UN, are actively involved in tackling the ethical and legal dilemmas presented by AI. The UN has implemented initiatives such as the High-Level Panel on Digital Cooperation, with the objective of fostering international conversation and collaboration on the regulation of AI. The panel's suggestions prioritise the establishment of comprehensive and enduring AI policies, promoting creativity while guaranteeing the ethical development and use of AI technology. These endeavours highlight the significance of a collaborative approach to regulating AI, in which nations cooperate to tackle the cross-border nature of AI technology and their effects. These projects seek to provide a worldwide framework that guarantees the responsible and ethical advancement of AI by promoting international collaboration and standardising AI rules.

11.3.4.2 National AI policies and laws

AI policies and regulations vary greatly among nations, reflecting distinct approaches to governing AI technology based on each nation's values, legal traditions and economic interests. AI policy in the United States has mostly prioritised the encouragement of innovation and the preservation of global competitiveness. The National Artificial Intelligence Initiative Act of 2020 seeks to synchronise AI research and development efforts throughout government departments, with a particular focus on ethical aspects such as justice, openness and accountability [31]. In addition, states such as California have implemented their own laws pertaining to AI such as the CCPA. This legislation grants consumers substantial authority over their personal data and imposes strict data privacy obligations on businesses [32]. These legislative endeavours demonstrate a dedication to maintaining an equilibrium between the advantages of AI and the imperative to safeguard individual rights and mitigate any harm.

China has made substantial progress in formulating a comprehensive national AI policy with the aim of achieving worldwide leadership in AI innovation by the year 2030. The Chinese government has published a set of policy documents that outline its objectives for the development of AI. These documents highlight the need of integrating AI into several areas, including healthcare, education and defence [39]. China's AI regulatory strategy is marked by a significant focus on state control and monitoring, which gives rise to issues over privacy and human rights. The Personal Information Protection Law (PIPL) enacted by the Chinese government is a comprehensive legislation that seeks to manage data processing operations and safeguard personal information. However, it also confers the government with broad authority to access data for security reasons [29]. This twin strategy emphasises the intricate interaction among innovation, regulation and state control in China's AI policy.

On the other hand, the EU has taken a comprehensive approach to regulating AI, by including ethical issues into its regulatory framework. The proposed Artificial Intelligence Act, in conjunction with the GDPR, establishes stringent criteria for safeguarding data, ensuring transparency and enforcing responsibility in AI systems [28]. The EU's approach prioritises human-centric AI, with the goal of guaranteeing that AI technologies uphold basic rights and advance societal well-being. In addition, the EU has implemented several programmes to promote ethical research and innovation in the field of AI. One such project is the European AI Alliance, which encourages collaboration among different parties to tackle the ethical and societal issues raised by AI. The EU aims to provide a legislative framework that promotes both innovation and responsible development and use of AI technology by incorporating ethical considerations into its AI strategy.

11.3.4.3   Examination of legal precedents via case studies

Legal precedents in the realm of GAI offer useful insights into how courts and regulatory authorities are handling the intricate legal matters related to AI technology. An exemplary instance is the legal action taken against Clearview AI, a face recognition business, for allegedly breaching privacy regulations through the unauthorised collection of billions of pictures from social media platforms. This case brought attention to substantial concerns regarding data privacy and the ethical use of AI in surveillance. As a reaction to the case, other states, such as Illinois with its Biometric Information Privacy Act, have enhanced their data protection legislation to specifically tackle the improper use of biometric data. The Clearview AI case highlights the necessity of strong legal frameworks to safeguard individuals' privacy rights in the era of AI and provide significant precedents for the governance of AI technology.

The case of EPIC v. DHS is a notable legal precedent in which the Electronic Privacy Information Centre (EPIC) contested the use of AI-driven prediction algorithms by the Department of Homeland Security (DHS). EPIC contended that the utilisation of these algorithms for evaluating threats lacked transparency and accountability, which might potentially result in prejudiced and discriminating results. The case drew attention to the ethical and legal ramifications of employing AI in law enforcement and national security, emphasising the necessity for supervision and responsibility in the use of AI systems. The court's ruling to require increased openness and the establishment of ethical protocols for the use of AI in governmental organisations establishes a standard for the conscientious application of AI in the public domain.

An additional instance is the legal action taken by the UK Information Commissioner's Office (ICO) against the Royal Free London NHS Foundation Trust for the unauthorised sharing of patient data with Google DeepMind. The case pertained to the utilisation of AI in creating a prognostic analytics tool for the diagnosis of renal disease. The ICO determined that the data-sharing arrangement was deficient in terms of openness and patient permission, so contravening data protection legislation. This case underscores the ethical and legal dilemmas associated with the utilisation of AI in healthcare and emphasises the significance of complying with data protection legislation to preserve public confidence. The verdict underscored the importance of establishing explicit protocols for data exchange and permission in AI initiatives, establishing a model for forthcoming healthcare AI deployments.

11.4   Ethical and legal intersection

The emerging discipline of GAI brings together intriguing ethical and legal concerns. As AI systems advance in their ability to create content, it is important to navigate this field ethically by considering ethical standards and legal frameworks. This section will examine the complexities of this junction, analysing the difficulties of maintaining a balance between these objectives, highlighting possible conflicts and suggesting methods for aligning global standards and promoting governance involving multiple stakeholders.

11.4.1 Balancing ethical and legal requirements

Achieving a harmonious equilibrium between ethical and legal obligations in the field of general AI is a multifaceted yet important undertaking. When it comes to ethics, it is important to prioritise concepts such as justice, accountability, openness and privacy. One important ethical aspect is to make sure that GAI models are not biassed against specific demographics and do not produce information that violates privacy rights. It is crucial to adhere to copyright rules, data protection legislation (such as GDPR), and prevent the dissemination of disinformation in order to comply with legal requirements.

Figure 11.6 depicts the equilibrium between ethical and legal obligations. Nevertheless, attaining this equilibrium might be a considerable challenge. Ethical concepts can occasionally be subjective and susceptible to varying interpretations. For instance, the notion of equity in AI can be complex, involving factors such as the adequacy of data representation and the presence of algorithmic bias. The current effort is to find a legal framework that successfully deals with these complications while also being adaptable to the changing nature of GAI technology. Figure 11.6 also depicts the Venn diagram illustrating the intersection of ethical and legal requirements for balancing purposes.

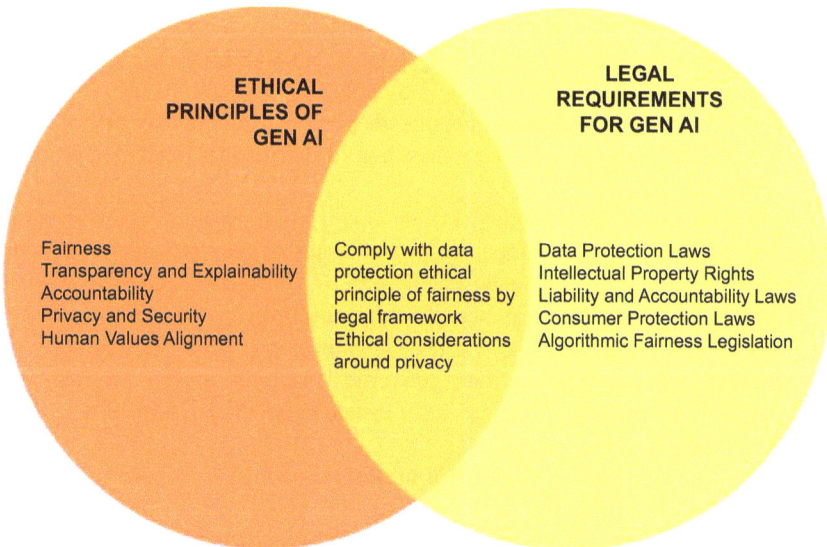

ETHICAL PRINCIPLES OF GEN AI

LEGAL REQUIREMENTS FOR GEN AI

Fairness
Transparency and Explainability
Accountability
Privacy and Security
Human Values Alignment

Comply with data
protection ethical
principle of fairness by
legal framework
Ethical considerations
around privacy

Data Protection Laws
Intellectual Property Rights
Liability and Accountability Laws
Consumer Protection Laws
Algorithmic Fairness Legislation

Figure 11.6   Balance between ethical and legal requirements

- **Ethical principles for GAI: left circle**
  The circle symbolises the fundamental ethical principles that should govern the creation and implementation of GAI. These principles are designed to guarantee the responsible and reliable use of AI for the betterment of society.
  - **Fairness and non-discrimination**: GAI must refrain from perpetuating or magnifying prejudices rooted on race, gender or other determinants.
  - **Transparency and explainability**: Transparency and explainability are crucial in ensuring that users can comprehend the process by which the AI system produces outputs and the logic underlying its decision-making.
  - **Accountability**: There must be unambiguous delineation of duties for the creation, implementation and consequences of GAI systems.
  - **Privacy and security**: Preserving the confidentiality of persons and safeguarding the integrity of data utilised in GAI systems is crucial.
  - **Human values alignment**: The development and use of GAI should be carried out in a manner that is consistent with fundamental human values such as the promotion of well-being, fairness and safety.

- **Right circle: legal requirements for GAI**
  The circle symbolises the legal framework pertaining to GAI, which includes a range of restrictions and legislation that developers and users must adhere to.
  - **Data protection laws**: Data protection laws, such as the GDPR in the EU and the CCPA, regulate the collecting, storage and utilisation of data. These laws have an influence on how GAI systems manage data.
  - **Intellectual property rights**: IPRs encompass the legal framework that governs the ownership and usage of AI-generated information, including copyright, patents and trademarks.
  - **Liability and accountability laws**: Liability and accountability laws provide the legal parameters for determining responsibility for any damages produced by GAI systems, hence influencing the practices involved in their development and deployment.
  - **Consumer protection laws**: Consumer protection laws may be in place to safeguard individuals from misleading or detrimental outcomes produced by AI systems.
  - **Algorithmic fairness legislation**: Legislation focused on algorithmic fairness is being developed to tackle issues of bias in GAI systems and ensure equitable outcomes.

- **Overlapping area: convergence of ethics and law**
  The intersection of the two circles symbolises scenarios in which ethical standards and legal obligations converge, resulting in the promotion of responsible AI research. Here are some instances when ethics and law intersect in this domain:
  - AI systems that are transparent are more inclined to adhere to data protection rules that need explainability.
  - Anti-discrimination legislation can uphold the ethical concept of impartiality by establishing a legal structure to tackle prejudice in AI systems.

- The creation of data protection standards for GAI may be influenced by ethical issues around privacy.

11.4.2   Conflicts arising from the divergence between ethical principles and legal obligations

Occasionally, there may be contradictions between ethical ideals and legal requirements within the realm of general AI. Imagine a situation in which a general AI system undergoes training using an extensive dataset that includes personal information. Utilising such data may be legally permissible based on user agreement and the use of data anonymisation techniques, but it might give rise to ethical problems surrounding privacy and the possibility for data exploitation. Legal frameworks may not clearly encompass the ethical ramifications of deepfakes, which are artificially modified media material designed to seem authentic. Deepfakes possess the ability to exert a significant influence on society, perhaps manipulating public sentiment or causing harm to individuals' standing. It may be necessary for the legal structure to adjust in order to tackle the ethical issues related to the improper use of this technology.

These disputes emphasise the necessity for continuous discourse and cooperation among ethicists, legal scholars and GAI developers. Through promoting transparent communication and a mutual comprehension of the obstacles, stakeholders may collaborate in order to devise solutions that maintain ethical standards and adhere to legal obligations.

11.4.3   Harmonising global standards

The worldwide scope of GAI requires the alignment of ethical and legal norms. Presently, there exists a fragmented set of legislation in several nations, leading to potential misunderstanding and impeding the progress of responsible development. Data protection standards, such as the GDPR in the EU, vary from those in the United States. This creates challenges for firms that operate globally to maintain a consistent ethical approach to handling user data in their systems powered by GAI.

Current initiatives are in progress to develop global benchmarks for general AI. The OECD has put out recommendations on AI ethics, which highlight concepts such as justice, openness and accountability. Nevertheless, further efforts are required to convert these suggestions into specific legal frameworks that may be efficiently implemented across many countries.

Establishing a universally synchronised strategy for GAI ethics and laws necessitates worldwide collaboration and a readiness to discover shared principles. Implementing these measures will provide equitable conditions for the advancement of general AI, foster accountable progress and safeguard the general population against potential risks. Below are some of the notable global standardisation efforts for AI and GAI.

- **International Organization for Standardization**
  International Organization for Standardization, in collaboration with the International Electrotechnical Commission and the International Telecommunication Union, has launched the 2025 International AI Standards Summit.

This initiative aims to develop and promote interoperable AI standards that ensure safety, reliability, sustainability and human rights.

- **European Union**
  The EU has enacted comprehensive AI regulations, which are considered the first of their kind globally. These regulations cover transparency, use of AI in public spaces and high-risk systems. They mandate model evaluations, risk mitigation and incident reporting for high-impact AI systems.

- **National Institute of Standards and Technology**
  Under the October 30, 2023, Presidential Executive Order, National Institute of Standards and Technology developed a plan for global engagement on promoting and developing AI standards. The goal is to drive the development and implementation of AI-related consensus standards, cooperation, coordination and information sharing.

- **World Economic Forum**
  The World Economic Forum has been actively involved in shaping global AI governance through initiatives like the AI Governance Alliance. This initiative focuses on international coordination, compatible AI standards and flexible regulatory mechanisms to ensure equitable access and inclusive global AI governance.

- **United Nations**
  The UN has adopted the Global Digital Compact, which calls for enhanced AI governance through international standards. The Compact emphasises collaboration among standards development organisations to promote the responsible use of AI.

11.4.4   Role of multistakeholder governance

The successful management of GAI requires the involvement of several stakeholders. This requires cooperation among diverse stakeholders, such as governments, technological firms, civil society groups and academics. Every group contributes a distinct viewpoint and plays a crucial part in influencing the moral and legal framework of GAI.

Governments play a crucial role in setting unambiguous legal frameworks and rules for the research and implementation of general AI. This encompasses establishing criteria for safeguarding data privacy, tackling concerns such as algorithmic prejudice and minimising the hazards associated with disinformation. Technology businesses, however, have the obligation to be conscientious creators and consumers of GAI technology. This involves incorporating ethical design principles, guaranteeing openness in their AI models and taking responsibility for the possible social consequences of their innovations.

Figure 11.5 illustrates the significance of multistakeholder governance in GAI. Civil society organisations have a vital role in increasing knowledge about the ethical consequences of GAI and promoting responsible development methods. In addition, academics may make a valuable contribution by doing study on the ethical and legal dilemmas presented by GAI and suggesting strategies for reducing potential hazards.

Through collaboration, these key participants may cultivate a conducive atmosphere for the responsible growth of GAI, ultimately leading to societal benefits on a broader scale.

Figure 11.7 illustrates how a pie chart may accurately depict the participation of different stakeholders in the governance of GAI.

- Government regulators account for 15% of the total.
  - **Responsibilities**: Formulate and implement policies to ensure the ethical and accountable development, deployment and use of AI.
  - **Examples of tasks include**: Defining criteria for protecting the privacy of data, creating guidelines for ensuring fairness in algorithms and monitoring the safety of AI systems.
- 20% of the companies included in this category are technology companies.
  - **Responsibilities**: Create, construct and implement GAI systems.
  - **Examples**: Incorporating ethical concerns into the processes of developing AI, guaranteeing transparency and comprehensibility of AI outputs and minimising possible biases in algorithms.
- Research institutions account for 15% of the total.
  - **Responsibilities**: Engage in in-depth investigation about the ethical and societal consequences of GAI.
  - **Examples**: Formulating optimal methodologies for ethical AI development, investigating possible hazards and advantages of AI, influencing policy choices using research findings.

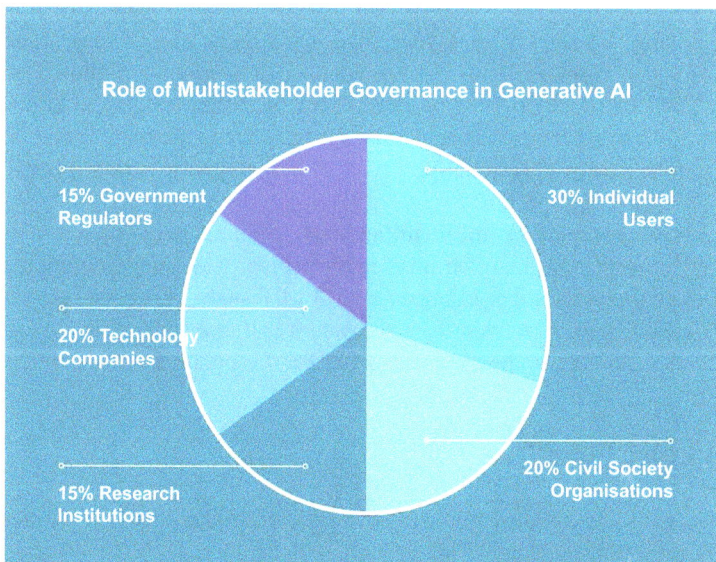

Figure 11.7   Role of multistakeholder governance in generative AI

- 20% of the entities involved are Civil Society Organisations.
  - **Position**: Champion for the welfare of the general public and the protection of human rights within the realm of GAI.
  - **Examples**: Increasing public knowledge about ethical issues, facilitating public discussions on AI governance, ensuring stakeholders are held responsible for responsible AI development.
- 30% of the user base consists of individual users.
  - **Responsibility**: Utilise and engage with GAI systems.
  - **Examples of responsible AI practices include**: analysing and addressing potential biases in AI outputs, exercising data privacy rights and offering input on AI systems to enhance their responsible development. Below are some of the real-world examples of AI bias.
  - **Racism in healthcare algorithms**: In October 2019, researchers found that an algorithm used in US hospitals to predict which patients would need extra medical care heavily favoured white patients over black patients. The algorithm used healthcare cost history as a proxy for health needs, which inadvertently led to racial bias since black patients generally incurred lower healthcare costs due to systemic inequalities.
  - **COMPAS algorithm in the US court system**: The COMPAS (Correctional Offender Management Profiling for Alternative Sanctions) algorithm, used to predict the likelihood of recidivism, was found to be biased against black offenders. It predicted false positives for recidivism at twice the rate for black offenders compared to white offenders (45% vs. 23%).
  - **Amazon's hiring algorithm**: In 2015, Amazon discovered that its hiring algorithm was biased against women. The algorithm was trained on resumes submitted over a 10-year period, most of which came from men, leading the system to favour male candidates over female candidates. Google Ads Gender Bias: Researchers at Carnegie Mellon University found that Google's online advertisement system displayed high-income job ads to male candidates more frequently than to female candidates. This gender bias in the ad delivery system perpetuated existing inequalities in job opportunities.
  - **Facial recognition misidentifications**: Studies have shown that facial recognition systems often misidentify people of colour at higher rates than white individuals. For example, a 2018 MIT study found that facial recognition software from major tech companies had error rates of up to 34.7% for darker-skinned women, compared to 0.8% for lighter-skinned men.

11.5   Future directions

Continuous examination of the ethical and legal ramifications of GAI is necessary due to its dynamic character. This section will explore likely future trajectories in many domains, encompassing technical developments and their ethical implications, the expected development of legal frameworks and emerging patterns in AI ethics and law. Ultimately, we will provide suggestions for policymakers and practitioners to appropriately manage this ever-changing environment.

11.5.1   Technological advancements and ethical implications

As the technology of general AI advances, it is imperative to carefully contemplate the ethical ramifications of these progressions. An area of worry revolves around the possibility of progressively advanced deepfakes that might obscure the distinction between truth and fabrication. Studies indicate that deepfakes have the potential to be utilised as tools to alter public opinion or tarnish reputations. Moreover, the advancement of generative models that may imitate human creativity raises concerns around the ownership and attribution of material created by AI.

Furthermore, the growing advancements of general AI in domains such as autonomous systems and personalised experiences require thoughtful examination of ethical considerations. The use of GAI in self-driving cars gives rise to inquiries regarding liability in the occurrence of accidents [40]. Furthermore, the capacity of GAI to customise experiences using user data requires careful examination of privacy concerns and the possibility of algorithmic bias.

To tackle these ethical challenges, it is necessary to continuously conduct research and establish strong protections. This may entail progress in the field of deepfake detection tools, the creation of well-defined ownership frameworks for AI-generated content and the formulation of ethical AI design guidelines for autonomous systems and personalised experiences.

11.5.2   The evolution of legal frameworks

The legal frameworks regulating general AI are expected to undergo substantial changes in the upcoming years. With the progression of technology and the increasing importance of ethical concerns, lawmakers will probably face challenges in regulating deepfakes, determining IPRs for AI-generated material and addressing data privacy concerns related to applications of general AI.

An possible avenue to explore is the establishment of global benchmarks for the ethical and legal aspects of general AI. At present, the varied set of legislation in different nations poses difficulties for the responsible advancement and implementation of GAI. The OECD and similar organisations are now establishing the foundation for international standards, with a focus on concepts such as justice, openness and accountability. Ongoing global collaboration will be essential in creating a comprehensive legal structure that effectively balances innovation and responsible progress.

Another expected development is the heightened emphasis on legal frameworks for certain uses of general AI. As general AI becomes incorporated into other industries, such as healthcare or finance, it is necessary for legal frameworks to adjust in order to tackle the distinct ethical and legal difficulties presented by these applications. Ensuring the ethical use of this technology in specific situations will likely need coordination among legal experts, legislators and GAI developers.

11.5.3   Anticipating patterns in AI ethics and law

The domain of AI ethics and law is in a perpetual state of development, as novel studies and discussions continue to arise. An expected trend is the increasing focus on the explainability and interpretability of GAI models. Ensuring openness and accountability in decision-making processes enabled by GAI is of utmost importance [41]. As the complexity of GAI models increases, it will be crucial to create methods for comprehending their reasoning and decision-making processes.

Another emerging trend is the growing emphasis on the creation of AI systems that prioritise human needs and experiences. This method places a high importance on human values and well-being when designing and implementing GAI systems. This may entail integrating ethical concepts into the development process, cultivating public confidence in GAI technologies and ensuring that GAI systems are purposefully designed to advance the well-being of humankind as a collective.

Ultimately, we may anticipate continuous discussions over the potential societal consequences of general AI. This encompasses conversations on the influence of general AI on the labour market, possible prejudices in AI systems and the wider ramifications of AI on human society. Tackling these intricate problems will need interdisciplinary collaboration, including ethics, law, computer technology and social sciences.

11.6   Conclusion

The advent of GAI has ushered in a new era of technological advancement, with profound implications for society. This chapter has delved into the intricate interplay of ethical and legal considerations surrounding this transformative technology. While GAI offers immense potential for innovation and progress, it also poses significant challenges that demand careful attention. A comprehensive understanding of the ethical principles governing AI development and deployment is essential to mitigate risks and ensure that these systems align with human values. Moreover, robust legal frameworks are indispensable for safeguarding individual rights, protecting IP and establishing accountability mechanisms.

The convergence of ethics and law in the realm of GAI highlights the need for a multifaceted approach. Balancing ethical aspirations with legal requirements is a complex endeavour that necessitates collaboration among policymakers, technologists, ethicists and legal experts. As GAI continues to evolve, it is imperative to foster a culture of responsible innovation that prioritises human well-being and societal benefit. By proactively addressing the ethical and legal challenges associated with this technology, we can harness its potential while mitigating its risks and ensuring a future where AI serves as a force for good.

References

[1] Goodfellow, I., Pouget-Abadie, J., Mirza, M., *et al.* (2020). Generative adversarial networks. *Communications of the ACM*, 63(11), 139–144.

[2] Kingma, D. P., and Welling, M. (2014). "Auto-Encoding Variational Bayes." arXiv preprint arXiv:1312.6114.

[3] Esteva, A., Robicquet, A., Ramsundar, B., *et al.* (2019). "A guide to deep learning in healthcare." *Nature Medicine*.

[4] Vincent, J. (2019). "Why AI-generated fake videos are a real concern." *The Verge*.

[5] Brown, T., Mann, B., Ryder, N., *et al.* (2020). "Language models are few-shot learners." arXiv preprint arXiv:2005.14165.

[6] Andres Guadamuz. (2017). "Artificial intelligence and copyright." *WIPO Magazine*.

[7] Brown, T., Mann, B., Ryder, N., *et al.* (2020). "Language models are few-shot learners." arXiv preprint arXiv:2005.14165.

[8] Guidotti, R., Monreale, A., Turini, F., Pedreschi, D., and Giannotti, F. (2018). A survey of methods for explaining black box models. *ACM Computing Surveys (CSUR)*, 51(5), 1–42.

[9] Rudin, C. (2019). Stop explaining black box machine learning models for high stakes decisions and use interpretable models instead. *Nature Machine Intelligence*, 1(5), 206–215.

[10] Mitchell, M., Wu, S., Zaldivar, A., *et al.* (2019). Model cards for model reporting. *Proceedings of the Conference on Fairness, Accountability, and Transparency*, 220–229.

[11] European Commission. (2019). Ethics guidelines for trustworthy AI. Retrieved from https://ec.europa.eu/newsroom/dae/document.cfm?doc_id=60419.

[12] European Parliament and Council. (2016). General Data Protection Regulation (GDPR). *Official Journal of the European Union*, L119, 1–88.

[13] Dwork, C., and Roth, A. (2014). The algorithmic foundations of differential privacy. *Foundations and Trends® in Theoretical Computer Science*, 9(3–4), 211–407.

[14] Cavoukian, A. (2010). *Privacy by design: The 7 foundational principles.* Information and Privacy Commissioner of Ontario, Canada.

[15] Tene, O., and Polonetsky, J. (2013). Big data for all: Privacy and user control in the age of analytics. *Northwestern Journal of Technology and Intellectual Property*, 11(5), 239–273.

[16] Floridi, L., Cowls, J., Beltrametti, M., *et al.* (2018). AI4People—An ethical framework for a good AI society: Opportunities, risks, principles, and recommendations. *Minds and Machines*, 28(4), 689–707.

[17] Barocas, S., Hardt, M., and Narayanan, A. (2019). *Fairness and Machine learning: Limitations and opportunities.* https://fairmlbook.org.

[18] Mehrabi, N., Morstatter, F., Saxena, N., Lerman, K., and Galstyan, A. (2021). A survey on bias and fairness in machine learning. *ACM Computing Surveys (CSUR)*, 54(6), 1–35.

[19] Holstein, K., Wortman Vaughan, J., Daume III, H., Dudik, M., and Wallach, H. (2019). Improving fairness in machine learning systems: What do industry practitioners need? *Proceedings of the 2019 CHI Conference on Human Factors in Computing Systems*, 1–16.

[20] Raji, I. D., Smart, A., White, R. N., *et al.* (2020). Closing the AI account-ability gap: Defining an end-to-end framework for internal algorithmic auditing. *Proceedings of the 2020 Conference on Fairness, Accountability, and Transparency*, 33–44.

[21] Tolosana, R., Vera-Rodriguez, R., Fierrez, J., Morales, A., and Ortega-Garcia, J. (2020). Deepfakes and beyond: A survey of face manipulation and fake detection. *Information Fusion*, 64, 131–148.

[22] Citron, D. K., and Chesney, R. (2020). Deepfakes and the looming crisis of truth. *University of Illinois Law Review*, 2020(4), 957–988.

[23] Diakopoulos, N., and Johnson, J. (2020). Anticipating and addressing the ethical implications of deepfakes in the context of elections. *New Media & Society*, 22(9), 1553–1572.

[24] Mirsky, Y., and Lee, W. (2021). The creation and detection of deepfakes: A survey. *ACM Computing Surveys (CSUR)*, 54(1), 1–41.

[25] Patterson, D., Gonzalez, J., Le, Q., *et al.* (2021). Carbon emissions and large neural network training. *arXiv preprint arXiv*:2104.10350.

[26] Wu, Y., Schuster, M., Chen, Z., *et al.* (2021). Google's neural machine translation system: Bridging the gap between human and machine transla-tion. *Communications of the ACM*, 61(7), 113–124.

[27] Williams, E., Kahhat, R., and Allenby, B. (2020). Environmental, social, and economic implications of global reuse and recycling of personal computers. *Environmental Science & Technology*, 42(17), 6446–6454.

[28] European Commission. (2021). Proposal for a Regulation laying down har-monised rules on artificial intelligence (Artificial Intelligence Act) and amending certain Union legislative acts. Retrieved from https://eur-lex.europa.eu/legal-content/EN/TXT/?uri=CELEX:52021PC0206.

[29] Nevo, S., Belli, C., Tagliabue, E., and Carenzi, G. (2020). AI for disaster response: A public-private partnership to improve flood resilience in India. *International Journal of Disaster Risk Reduction*, 50, 101734.

[30] Deloitte. (2019). AI: The Next Frontier in Financial Services. Retrieved from https://www2.deloitte.com/global/en/pages/financial-services/articles/ai-next-frontier-in-financial-services.html.

[31] Executive Office of the President. (2020). National Artificial Intelligence Initiative Act of 2020. Retrieved from https://www.congress.gov/bill/116th-congress/house-bill/6216/text.

[32] California Legislative Information. (2018). California Consumer Privacy Act (CCPA). Retrieved from https://leginfo.legislature.ca.gov/faces/bill-TextClient.xhtml?bill_id=201720180AB375.

[33] Samuelson, P. (2019). Allocating ownership rights in computer-generated works. *University of Pittsburgh Law Review*, 70(2), 425–470.

[34]   Grimmelmann, J. (2016). There's no such thing as a computer-authored work—and it's a good thing, too. *Columbia Journal of Law & the Arts*, 39(3), 403–406.

[35]   Hristov, K. (2020). Artificial intelligence and the copyright dilemma. *IDEA: The Journal of the Franklin Pierce Center for Intellectual Property*, 60(3), 433–470.

[36]   Veale, M., and Borgesius, F. Z. (2021). Demystifying the draft EU Artificial Intelligence Act. *Computer Law Review International*, 22(4), 97–112.

[37]   Gasser, U., and Almeida, V. A. (2017). A layered model for AI governance. *IEEE Internet Computing*, 21(6), 58–62.

[38]   Brundage, M., Avin, S., Clark, J., *et al*. (2018). The malicious use of artificial intelligence: Forecasting, prevention, and mitigation. *arXiv preprint* arXiv:1802.07228.

[39]   China State Council. (2017). New Generation Artificial Intelligence Development Plan. Retrieved from http://www.gov.cn/zhengce/content/2017-07/20/content_5211996.htm.

[40]   Whittaker, M., Mulgan, G., Cave, S., Bartlett, S., Wachter, S., and Rowland, D. (2022). AI and autonomous vehicles: An ethical and regulatory roadmap. *Nature Machine Intelligence*, 4(5), 398–406.

[41]   Lipton, Z. C. (2018). The mythos of model interpretability. *Communications of the ACM*, 61(10), 36–43.

Chapter 12

Trending technologies and application of generative AI

Dishant Naik[1], A.J. Dazzle[1], I.R. Praveen Joe[1] and Vijay John[2]

Abstract

This chapter presents a comprehensive analysis of the rapidly evolving landscape of generative artificial intelligence (AI), shedding light on its foundational principles, technological advancements and transformative applications across a variety of industries. It delves into the core technologies driving generative AI, including generative adversarial networks, transformer-based models, autoregressive models and variational autoencoders, which have collectively revolutionised content generation through automation, creativity enhancement and improved productivity. The chapter explores notable breakthroughs such as BigGAN and StyleGAN, which have set new standards for producing high-quality, realistic digital content in areas like digital art, virtual environments and entertainment, demonstrating the immense potential of AI to expand creative boundaries and redefine human–machine interactions. The impact of generative AI extends beyond creative domains to include virtual and augmented reality, where it facilitates the development of immersive, interactive environments that enhance user experiences in gaming, training and simulations. In creative industries, AI-driven tools empower artists, designers and musicians to produce unique and innovative works, pushing the limits of human creativity while streamlining traditional workflows. Furthermore, the chapter examines the role of generative AI in architecture and design, where it aids in optimising building layouts and improving both aesthetic appeal and functional efficiency, thereby transforming conventional design processes. In healthcare, generative AI has become a critical tool for advancements in medical imaging, personalised medicine and drug discovery, where AI models analyse vast datasets to predict patient outcomes, develop tailored treatment plans and accelerate the creation of new therapies, ultimately improving healthcare delivery and patient care. The chapter also addresses crucial ethical considerations surrounding the adoption of generative AI, particularly regarding data privacy,

[1]School of Computer Science and Engineering, Vellore Institute of Technology, Chennai, India
[2]Research Scientist, RIKEN, Japan

algorithmic bias and responsible usage, emphasising the need for transparent, accountable frameworks to ensure equitable AI practices. By discussing future research directions and emerging trends, the chapter envisions a future where generative AI continues to drive technological progress, reshape industries and contribute to societal well-being through responsible, innovative applications that optimise processes, enhance creativity and improve quality of life across various sectors.

Keywords: Generative AI; GANs (generative adversarial networks); transformer models; personalised medicine; AI-driven creativity

12.1   Introduction

The purpose of this chapter is to explore recent developments in generative artificial intelligence (AI), focusing on technologies like generative adversarial networks (GANs) [1], variational autoencoders (VAEs) [2] and transformer-based models [3]. Through detailed case studies, the chapter aims to provide a comparative analysis of their applications across various sectors, including healthcare, financial services and the creative industries. By examining these technologies in practical scenarios, the chapter intends to highlight the transformative potential of generative AI in reshaping processes and creating new opportunities. This exploration covers both technical aspects and real-world applications to provide a well-rounded understanding of how these advancements are impacting diverse domains. In the fast-paced world of technology, generative AI stands out as a revolutionary innovation with the potential to transform multiple industries. This cutting-edge subset of AI enables systems to generate new content – such as text, visuals and audio – that closely mimics human craftsmanship. The technology is no longer limited to experimental labs; it is being actively integrated into various fields to unlock creative possibilities and redefine human–machine interactions [4,5]. From creating digital art and enhancing virtual environments to producing realistic simulations, generative AI is blurring the lines between human creativity and machine-generated outputs. It is fundamentally changing how individuals and businesses interact with technology.

GANs have played a significant role in advancing generative AI by introducing a novel approach to training models through competition [1]. A GAN consists of two components – a generator that produces synthetic data and a discriminator that attempts to distinguish between real and generated data. This dynamic optimisation process allows GANs to create highly realistic synthetic content. GANs have found extensive applications across industries, including generating images [6], creating style transfers in artwork [7] and producing medical images to aid in healthcare diagnostics. The ability of GANs to generate high-quality, lifelike data has set new benchmarks in content creation and automation [8]. The applications of generative AI are vast and diverse, spanning industries such as art, entertainment, healthcare and business. Artists and designers are leveraging this technology to push creative boundaries, generating unique content that would be difficult to achieve through traditional methods [6]. In the business world, companies are using generative AI to streamline workflows, enhance customer experiences and develop innovative products and services [4]. In healthcare, the impact of generative AI is particularly profound, with applications in medical imaging analysis, personalised treatment plans and drug discovery [2]. By revolutionising patient care, generative AI is helping healthcare providers deliver more accurate diagnoses and effective treatments.

Despite its immense potential, the advancement of generative AI brings several challenges and ethical considerations. One of the primary concerns is data privacy, as these models require vast amounts of data to function effectively [5]. There is also the risk of bias in generated content, which can perpetuate societal inequalities if not properly addressed. Moreover, the ethical use of AI-generated content raises questions about accountability, ownership and responsible deployment [9]. As generative AI tools become more accessible, there is an ongoing debate about equitable access and how to ensure that the benefits of this technology are shared fairly across different communities and industries.

This chapter delves into the current applications and prospects of generative AI across various sectors, examining both its foundational principles and recent breakthroughs [3,10]. The discussion covers key advancements in generative AI technologies, including notable innovations that have reshaped industries by enhancing automation and creativity. It also explores the implications of these advancements for businesses and society at large, considering how they can drive efficiency, innovation and growth. By providing a comprehensive analysis of this evolving field, the chapter aims to offer valuable insights into the dynamic landscape of generative AI and its role in shaping the digital era.

12.2   Foundation of generative AI

Generative AI, which represents a groundbreaking field of AI that specialises in the creation of new content, whether it be textual, visual or auditory, closely imitates content created by humans [1–3]. At the heart of generative AI are sophisticated algorithms and models that have been trained on vast datasets to identify patterns and structures inherent in the data [3,4]. By leveraging deep learning techniques, such as neural networks, AI-driven generative systems can autonomously generate outputs that exhibit creativity, diversity and realism [1,2,5]. The foundation of generative AI lies in its ability to understand and replicate complex patterns found within the data it has been trained on. These patterns are learned through exposure to large amounts of labelled or unlabelled data, allowing the AI model to discern underlying structures and relationships [2]. For example, in the case of text generation, a generative AI model might be developed using a corpus of textual data, including books, articles or social media posts, to learn the syntax, semantics and style of natural language [4,9].

One of the essential techniques employed in generative AI refers to the application of generative models, which aim to capture the probability distribution within the data and generate new instances from it [1,2]. GANs and VAEs are two leading examples of Generative models frequently utilised in research on generative AI [1,2,8]. GANs involve two neural networks – a generator and a discriminator – that undergo simultaneous training, with each network competing against the other to generate realistic samples [1,7,8]. VAEs, however, capture a latent space of the input data and generate new instances by drawing from this space [2]. Generative AI has been applied across a wide range of domains, including art, entertainment, healthcare, finance and more [4,6,10]. In the field of art, generative AI is employed to generate digital artwork, music compositions and even literature [6,7]. In healthcare, generative AI is employed for medical image synthesis, drug discovery and personalised medicine [2,5]. In finance, generative AI is used for algorithmic trading, risk assessment and fraud detection [5].

Despite its vast potential, generative AI also presents challenges and raises ethical concerns. Issues like bias in training data, the risk of misuse and the ethical concerns of AI-generated content are subjects of ongoing exploration and discussion [9]. As generative AI continues to advance, it is crucial to guarantee that its advantages are harnessed responsibly and ethically, while mitigating possible risks and drawbacks [9]. Hence, generative AI represents a revolutionary paradigm shift in artificial intelligence, enabling machines to exhibit creativity and produce content that was once traditionally considered the sole domain of human intelligence [1,3]. With its power to produce novel and diverse outcomes in various areas, generative AI is poised to take on a transformative role in influencing the future of technology and society [5,10].

12.3   Key technologies enabling generative AI

Generative AI leads the way in advanced technological developments, redefining the limits of content creation across various domains [1–3]. This transformative field utilises sophisticated algorithms and neural networks to generate innovative and authentic outputs that closely resemble human-created content [4,5,9]. These outputs span diverse formats, including realistic images, videos, text and speech synthesis, enabling machines to produce high-quality content autonomously [6,10]. The advent of generative AI has revolutionised industries by automating creative processes and enhancing user experiences through personalisation and efficiency [6,7]. From generating lifelike visuals to creating interactive voice assistants, generative AI is reshaping how content is produced and consumed [5]. This field encompasses various models and techniques, each contributing to different aspects of content generation and optimisation [1,2]. In this discourse, an exploration of the innovative technologies driving the progress of generative AI unfolds, delving into the intricate workings of models like GANs [1], VAEs [2] and transformer-based models [3], which have set new benchmarks in creativity and automation.

12.3.1   *Overview of generative adversarial networks*

GANs stand as a revolutionary advancement within the field of generative AI, heralded for their remarkable ability to produce lifelike outputs across diverse mediums [1]. Conceived by Ian Goodfellow and his team in 2014, GANs represent a paradigm shift in Generative modelling, leveraging an innovative two-part framework comprising a generator and a discriminator participating in a sophisticated adversarial learning process [1]. At its core, the GAN architecture embodies a fundamentally adversarial relationship between two neural networks: the generator and the discriminator. The generator network serves as a creative force, tasked with synthesising artificial samples from random input vectors, with the objective of generating outputs that cannot be differentiated from genuine data [7]. Conversely, the discriminator component acts as a discerning critic, trained to differentiate between authentic samples drawn from the true data distribution and counterfeit instances created by the generator [8].

The crux of GAN's methodology lies in the adversarial training regime orchestrated between the generator and the discriminator. During training, the generator seeks to improve its ability to craft convincing outputs by minimising the discernibility of its generated samples from authentic data, while the discriminator aims to enhance its discriminatory prowess by accurately distinguishing between real and fake samples [1]. This adversarial dynamic engenders a competitive feedback loop wherein the generator persistently enhances its output to mislead the discriminator, as the discriminator concurrently evolves to become more discerning [8]. The adversarial training process develops through a sequence of alternating optimisation phases. In each iteration, the generator generates synthetic samples, which are then fed into the discriminator along with authentic samples drawn from the true data distribution. The discriminator evaluates these samples and assigns probabilities indicating their authenticity [1,7]. Subsequently, the derivatives of the discriminator's loss function are backpropagated through the network, enabling it to update its parameters to better discriminate between real and fake samples. Simultaneously, the generator's parameters are updated based on the gradients of the discriminator's loss with respect to the generated samples. By maximising the likelihood of the discriminator incorrectly identifying its generated instances as authentic, the generator modifies its parameters to generate more convincing outputs [8].

One of the most notable applications of GANs lies within the field of image creation, where these networks excel in producing photorealistic imagery from random noise [6]. Through techniques such as progressive growing, GANs have demonstrated enhanced stability and fidelity in generating high-resolution images, thereby paving the way for applications in digital art, gaming and visual effects [6,7]. Furthermore, GANs exhibit remarkable versatility in image-to-image translation tasks, enabling a wide array of applications such as style transfer, sketch-to-image conversion and even medical image synthesis [7]. By learning the underlying distribution of data, GANs facilitate the creation of diverse outputs, expanding the horizons of creative expression and technological innovation [1,7].

GANs represent a pioneering approach to generative modelling, leveraging adversarial learning to generate outputs that rival the realism of genuine data [1,8]. Through their sophisticated methodology and intricate interplay between the generator and discriminator, GANs have emerged as a powerful tool for generating lifelike imagery and facilitating creative expression across various domains [6,7].

As research in GANs advances further, the opportunities for transformative applications in art, design and beyond appear boundless, promising to redefine our understanding of what is achievable in the field of generative AI [1,7].

12.3.2   Transformer models in generative AI

Transformer-based models represent a revolutionary leap in the domain of generative AI, particularly in the context of natural language processing (NLP) tasks [1]. Introduced by Google researchers in 2017, transformers have reshaped the landscape of language understanding and generation by leveraging self-attention mechanisms to identify detailed contextual connections in sequential data, such as words in a sentence [7,8]. At the core of transformer-based models lies the notion of self-attention, a mechanism that enables the model to weigh the importance of different words in a sentence based on their contextual relevance [4,8]. Unlike traditional recurrent neural networks (RNNs) and convolutional neural networks, which process input data sequentially or in a fixed manner, transformers can capture long-range dependencies and contextual nuances more effectively, making them especially ideal for tasks involving vast volumes of text data [5].

Prominent examples of transformer-based models include the generative pre-trained transformer (GPT) series developed by OpenAI and the Language Model for Dialogue Applications from Google [7,10]. These models have earned widespread praise for their exceptional performance in text generation tasks, exhibiting a nuanced comprehension of linguistic patterns and semantics [2,7]. GPT-3, the third iteration of the GPT series, stands as a testament to the prowess of transformer-based models in producing coherent and contextually appropriate text across diverse prompts [4]. Through initial training on large-scale corpora of text data sourced from the internet, GPT-3 learns to forecast the subsequent word in a sequence by analysing the context from the prior words [7]. This pre-training procedure imbues the model with a broad comprehension of language, enabling it to produce human-like responses to a wide array of questions, spanning from creative storytelling to technical documentation [3,8].

The methodology underlying transformer-based models revolves around two key principles: pre-training and fine-tuning [1,6]. During the pre-training phase, the model is exposed to massive amounts of unlabelled text data, allowing it to learn the statistical properties and linguistic structures inherent in the language [8]. Through self-supervised learning techniques such as masked language modelling, the model acquires the ability to predict missing words within sentences, thus gaining a deep understanding of language semantics and syntax [5]. Following pre-training, the model can be fine-tuned on specific datasets or tasks to adapt its learned representations to the target domain [7]. Fine-tuning involves retraining the model using annotated data from the intended task, allowing it to specialise in tasks such as sentiment analysis, question answering or language translation [10]. This process enables transformer-based models to demonstrate remarkable versatility and adaptability for a diverse set of NLP tasks [1,3].

Beyond text generation, transformer-based models have demonstrated usefulness in various fields such as image captioning, speech synthesis and even code generation [3,7]. Through fine-tuning on specialised datasets, these models can adapt their learned representations to tasks beyond traditional language processing, showcasing their versatility and adaptability in content creation across various modalities [8]. Transformer-based models serve as a monumental breakthrough in the field of generative AI, empowering machines with a deep comprehension of human language and the ability to generate consistent and contextually appropriate text [1,7]. By leveraging self-attention mechanisms and sophisticated training methodologies, these models have opened new frontiers in language understanding and content creation, promising transformative use cases across various sectors [6,10].

12.3.3   *Autoregressive model in generative models*

Autoregressive models are foundational tools in statistical analysis, widely recognised for their versatility and applicability within multiple sectors, including time series analysis, NLP and generative modelling, particularly within the burgeoning domain of generative AI [1,7]. At the heart of autoregressive models lies the principle of regressing the current value of a variable against its own previous values [3]. This methodology aligns closely with the core objective of generative AI, which is to generate data samples that closely resemble the patterns and structures observed in the training data [4]. In the realm of generative AI, autoregressive models, such as autoregressive neural networks, play a pivotal role in generating sequential data, such as text or time-series data [10]. These models are highly effective at recognising dependencies by modelling the likelihood of each element in the sequence given its preceding elements [5]. For instance, in natural language generation tasks, autoregressive models like RNNs or transformer-based architectures such as GPT models are extensively utilised to produce text that mimics human language [2,8].

The methodology of autoregressive models is especially effective for generative activities that are sequential and context-dependent in nature [6]. By leveraging the autoregressive property, generative AI models can proficiently capture the time-based dynamics and connections present within the dataset, thereby enabling the production of credible and diverse instances [4,10]. This is achieved by recursively sampling from the learned conditional distribution of each element in the sequence based on its predecessors [8]. Furthermore, the estimation and parameter tuning techniques employed in autoregressive models, such as maximum likelihood estimation or Bayesian inference, are integral to training generative AI models effectively [3,5]. These techniques allow the model to learn the parameters of the conditional probability distribution from the training data, thereby enabling it to generate samples that closely match the characteristics of the observed data [6].

Despite their utility, autoregressive models encounter challenges, including overfitting and capturing complex dependencies in the data [1]. These challenges are particularly relevant in generative AI, where generating high-quality and diverse samples is crucial [7]. To tackle these issues, researchers in generative AI are actively exploring extensions and enhancements to traditional autoregressive models [2,5]. This includes incorporating attention mechanisms or hierarchical structures, which can enhance the model's capacity to capture long-term dependencies and generate more coherent and diverse samples [8].

Summing up, autoregressive models offer a powerful structure for generative AI, enabling the generation of sequential data with rich and realistic properties [10]. As generative AI continues to advance, autoregressive models will remain indispensable tools for capturing and modelling complex dependencies in data, driving innovation in applications ranging from natural language generation to time series forecasting [3,6]. Their capability to generate diverse and contextually accurate samples makes them indispensable assets in the collection of methods used by researchers and professionals in the field of generative AI [1,7].

12.3.4 *Variational autoencoders model*

VAEs stand out as a formidable category of generative models across the domain of artificial intelligence, particularly prominent in the sphere of unsupervised learning [1,6]. These models exhibit proficiency in discerning intricate patterns within high-dimensional data, subsequently generating novel samples that closely mirror the training dataset [2,3]. Let us embark on a detailed exploration of VAEs, beginning with an overview of autoencoders – a foundational concept essential for understanding VAEs. Autoencoders, serving as precursors to VAEs, constitute a neural network architecture tailored for unsupervised learning endeavours [10]. Comprising two primary components – an encoder and a decoder – autoencoders endeavour to compress input data into a latent representation via the encoder, followed by the decoder's attempt to rebuild the original data from this latent space [5]. At the heart of autoencoders lies the objective of minimising the reconstruction error, thereby ensuring that the output closely aligns with the input data [1,5].

VAEs, a natural extension of traditional autoencoders, introduce probabilistic modelling into the latent space, thereby departing from the fixed-point encoding characteristic of standard autoencoders [4]. Key components integral to VAEs include the encoder network, responsible for mapping input data to a distribution in the latent space, and the decoder network, tasked with reconstructing data from instances sampled from this latent space distribution [2]. Crucially, the latent space embodies a probability distribution, frequently Gaussian, encompassing potential latent variables. Variational inference serves as the cornerstone of VAEs, facilitating the approximation of the true posterior distribution of latent variables [7]. This process aims to maximise the evidence lower bound (ELBO), serving as a surrogate objective for the authentic log likelihood of the observed data [5]. Variational inference entails optimising two pivotal components – the reconstruction error, gauging the quality of the reconstructed data against the original version of input, and the KL divergence, quantifying the disparity between the approximate posterior and the prior distribution within the latent space [10]. Throughout the training phase, VAEs iteratively refine the configurations of both the encoder and decoder networks to minimise the ELBO [3,6]. The encoder network charts a course from input data to the configurations of the approximate posterior distribution within the latent space, while the decoder network endeavours to reconstruct data from instances selected from this distribution. Training unfolds via stochastic gradient descent or its variants, with mini-batches of data driving iterative updates to the model parameters [6,7].

An inherent strength of VAEs lies in their adeptness at generating new data instances through sampling from the acquired latent space distribution [3]. This capability enables VAEs to yield diverse and realistic outputs that faithfully capture the underlying structure of the training data [10]. By sampling from the latent space, VAEs facilitate the investigation of latent features and the creation of unique data instances [5]. The versatility of VAEs finds expression across various domains, spanning image generation and reconstruction, anomaly detection, data imputation and denoising, representation learning, drug discovery and molecular design, and language modelling [2,6]. However, VAEs confront obstacles such as mode collapse, posterior collapse and blurry reconstructions [3]. Ongoing research endeavours seek to surmount these obstacles while refining and augmenting the capabilities of VAEs [1,8]. Future directions include the integration of structured priors, the design of more expressive latent space distributions and the enhancement of VAE interpretability [10].

In summation, VAEs represent a highly sophisticated approach to unsupervised learning, utilising probabilistic modelling and variational inference to extract meaningful representations from high-dimensional data [5]. By capturing the underlying latent structures within datasets, VAEs can generate diverse and realistic outputs that closely resemble the original data distribution [6,7]. This unique ability makes them invaluable tools in various domains, including image synthesis, anomaly detection and data compression [3]. VAEs not only enhance the generation of synthetic data but also facilitate improved performance in downstream tasks such as classification and clustering [4,8]. Their flexibility and efficiency in learning complex patterns have led to compelling advancements in artificial intelligence and machine learning. As a result, VAEs continue to drive innovation, playing a pivotal role in shaping the future of generative modelling and intelligent systems across industries [1,10].

12.4   Key breakthroughs in generative AI

Recently, the domain of generative AI has witnessed remarkable breakthroughs that have revolutionised fields such as image generation, style transfer and NLP [1,7]. These advancements have significantly enhanced the ability of machines to create realistic and high-quality content across various domains. Notable innovations in this field include BigGAN, known for generating highly detailed and diverse images [4], and StyleGAN, which introduced unprecedented control over image synthesis by separating style and content features [6]. Additionally, OpenAI's GPT models have transformed NLP by enabling machines to generate coherent, contextually relevant text that closely mimics human language [2]. These models have paved the way for new applications in art, media and interactive AI systems [1]. Each of these breakthroughs demonstrates the growing potential of generative AI to reshape industries, automate creative tasks and expand the boundaries of human–machine interactions. Let us explore BigGAN, StyleGAN and GPT models in detail to understand their impact and technical advancements [7].

12.4.1 BigGAN: a scalable approach to image generation

BigGAN, standing for 'big generative adversarial network', marks a breakthrough in the field of image generation. Developed by researchers at Google, BigGAN harnesses the power of GANs to create high-resolution and remarkably lifelike images spanning a wide array of categories [4]. Its innovative approach and sophisticated architecture have propelled it to the forefront of image synthesis, setting new benchmarks for visual quality and diversity. At the core of BigGAN's technology lies the concept of GANs, a framework introduced by Ian Goodfellow and his team in 2014. GANs involve two neural networks – the generator and the discriminator – that work in a competitive game. The generator network learns to generate images that resemble real samples from the dataset, while the discriminator network learns to differentiate between real and fake images. Through this competitive training process, both networks gradually improve their effectiveness, resulting in the creation of increasingly authentic images [1].

What sets BigGAN apart is its remarkable scale and complexity, making it a groundbreaking model in image generation. By significantly enlarging both the generator and discriminator networks, BigGAN enhances its ability to capture intricate details and complex structures within images. This scaling is achieved through several innovative techniques, including architectural adjustments, layer normalisation and gradient clipping, which ensure stable and efficient training [4]. These modifications allow BigGAN to handle high-resolution images with greater precision, resulting in highly detailed, photorealistic outputs. Unlike earlier models, BigGAN generates images that exhibit a broader diversity of objects and scenes while maintaining visual coherence. Its ability to balance realism and variety has made it a benchmark in the field of generative AI [7]. BigGAN's success has opened new possibilities for applications in creative industries, scientific visualisation and virtual environments, demonstrating the potential of scaling neural networks to achieve unprecedented generative performance [6].

BigGAN's methodology revolves around meticulous training and optimisation strategies tailored to handle the challenges posed by large-scale image generation. Training BigGAN requires vast amounts of labelled image data, which serves to fine-tune the model's configurations through stochastic gradient descent. The training process is computationally intensive and often necessitates specialised hardware such as graphics processing units (GPUs) to expedite convergence [2]. One of the essential innovations of BigGAN stems from its capability to create images with unprecedented fidelity and diversity. By leveraging the increased capacity of the model, BigGAN excels in capturing fine details, textures and patterns, resulting in visually stunning outputs that rival those captured by professional photographers. Moreover, BigGAN exhibits remarkable diversity in its generated samples, capable of producing images across a wide range of categories with realistic variations and nuances [4].

BigGAN's impact extends beyond mere image generation; it has spurred advancements in various applications, including image editing, content creation and computer vision. Its power to create high-resolution images has found utility in fields such as virtual reality (VR), gaming and fashion, where realistic visuals are paramount. Moreover, BigGAN's publicly available implementation has encouraged collaboration and innovation within research groups, leading to further improvements and refinements in image generation techniques [6]. BigGAN represents a groundbreaking achievement in the realm of image generation, expanding the limits of what can be achieved with GANs. Its innovative technology and methodology have paved the way for new opportunities in computer vision, artistic expression and creative industries, ushering in a new era of photorealistic image synthesis. As research in this field continues to evolve, BigGAN stands as a testament to the power of deep learning in reshaping our perception of visual reality [7].

12.4.2 *StyleGAN: advancements in image synthesis*

StyleGAN, a groundbreaking innovation in the realm of image synthesis and manipulation, has become a transformative force in the field. Developed by researchers at NVIDIA, StyleGAN introduces novel techniques that facilitate accurate control over the style and appearance of generated images. Unlike traditional GANs [1], StyleGAN revolutionises the image generation process by decoupling it into two distinct stages: latent space manipulation and style mapping. This innovative approach has propelled StyleGAN to the forefront of image synthesis, facilitating the creation of high-resolution, photorealistic images with unprecedented diversity and realism. At the heart of StyleGAN's technology lies the concept of latent space manipulation. In traditional GANs, images are generated by transforming random noise vectors from a latent space into meaningful visual representations. However, StyleGAN takes this a step further by allowing for the manipulation of specific attributes within the latent space. By disentangling the latent space into separate components, StyleGAN enables independent control over various visual factors such as facial expressions, hairstyles and background details. This level of granularity empowers users to precisely adjust and customise the appearance of generated images, leading to highly realistic and visually compelling results [6].

StyleGAN's methodology revolves around the concept of style mapping, which bridges the gap between the latent space and the image space. Style mapping involves learning a mapping function that translates latent vectors into style vectors, which encode specific visual characteristics such as texture, colour and shape. By learning this mapping function, StyleGAN effectively separates the content and style aspects of an image, enabling fine-grained manipulation of its visual attributes. This separation of concerns facilitates the generation of images with diverse styles and appearances while preserving the underlying structure and content. One of the essential innovations of StyleGAN is its capability to generate high-resolution images using unparalleled realism and diversity. By incorporating progressive growing techniques and multi-scale architectures, StyleGAN can generate images of exceptional quality and fidelity. This scalability allows StyleGAN to handle high-resolution inputs and produce detailed images with lifelike textures and features [6]. Additionally, StyleGAN's adaptive instance normalisation layer enables dynamic adjustment of style attributes at each layer of the network, further enhancing the diversity and realism of generated images.

StyleGAN's impact extends far beyond mere image generation; it has found widespread adoption in various applications across diverse industries. In the fields of art and design, StyleGAN has redefined the creative process by providing creators and innovators with powerful resources for generating and manipulating visual content. In VR and gaming, StyleGAN's ability to produce realistic and immersive environments has enhanced the user experience and raised the bar for visual fidelity. Moreover, in industries such as fashion and advertising, StyleGAN has facilitated the creation of highly engaging and visually striking content that resonates with audiences. StyleGAN represents a paradigm shift in the field of image synthesis and manipulation, offering unprecedented control over visual attributes and empowering the creation of exceptionally realistic and varied images. Its innovative technology and methodology have opened new pathways for creative expression and artistic exploration, while its practical applications span a diverse spectrum of industries and domains. As advancements in this field keep progressing, StyleGAN stands as a testament to the transformative power of deep learning in reshaping our visual landscape [6].

12.4.3   OpenAI's GPT models: revolutionising language generation

OpenAI's GPT models have emerged as a groundbreaking advancement in the field of NLP and text generation. Built upon the transformer architecture, GPT models have redefined the capabilities of AI systems in the creation and interpretation of human-like text. The key innovation of GPT models lies in their ability to generate coherent and contextually relevant text based on a given prompt or input, achieving remarkable fluency, coherence and versatility across various domains and languages. The technology behind GPT models is rooted in the transformer model, a type of neural network architecture introduced by Vaswani *et al.* [3]. Transformers have revolutionised NLP tasks by enabling parallelisation, capturing extended-range dependencies and enabling attention mechanisms. GPT models leverage the transformer architecture's capabilities to process and generate text data efficiently, making them ideal for a wide range of NLP applications.

The methodology employed in training GPT models revolves around large-scale initial training and subsequent refinement techniques. During the initial training phase, GPT models are trained on vast amounts of text data from diverse sources such as books, articles and websites. This pre-training process allows the models to learn the intricate patterns and structures of human language, capturing semantic relationships, syntactic rules and contextual information. The key to GPT models' success lies in their ability to generalise across various domains and languages. Through extensive pre-training on diverse text corpora, GPT models acquire a broad understanding of language, enabling them to produce coherent and contextually appropriate text across a broad spectrum of scenarios. This versatility is further enhanced through fine-tuning, where the pre-trained models are customised for specific tasks or domains by refining their configurations using task-specific datasets [5].

One of the key features of GPT models is their autoregressive nature, which enables them to generate text sequentially, producing one token at a time. This approach allows the models to build upon the context provided by previous tokens, ensuring the text remains coherent and logically consistent. As each token is generated, the model uses the preceding words to guide its predictions, capturing the intricacies and flow of human language. This autoregressive process is crucial in generating text that is contextually appropriate and grammatically sound. It enables GPT models to handle complex sentence structures and maintain relevance throughout longer passages of text. By focusing on the immediate context, GPT models can adapt to a wide variety of linguistic scenarios, making them versatile in applications such as dialogue generation and content creation. This ability to understand and generate human-like text is what sets GPT models apart in the field of NLP [5].

The release of iterations like GPT-2 and GPT-3 has further pushed the boundaries of NLP and text generation. GPT-2, released in 2019, introduced larger model sizes and improved performance, demonstrating the power of extensive language models in generating high-quality text. GPT-3, released in 2020, represents a significant leap forward in NLP technology, boasting an unprecedented scale with 175 billion parameters [5]. GPT-3 has exhibited exceptional skills in understanding and creating natural language text, leading to numerous applications in conversational AI, content generation and automated writing. The impact of GPT models extends across various domains and sectors such as education, healthcare, finance and entertainment. In education, GPT models are used for intelligent tutoring systems, automated grading and content creation. In healthcare, GPT models aid in healthcare diagnostics, patient engagement and pharmaceutical research. In the financial sector, GPT models support financial analysis, risk assessment and fraud detection. In entertainment, GPT models enable interactive storytelling, content generation and virtual assistants [5].

In conclusion, OpenAI's GPT models represent a pivotal advancement in NLP, demonstrating the transformative potential of large-scale language models in understanding and generating human-like text. Through their innovative technology and methodologies, GPT models have opened new possibilities for AI systems in various domains. These models have catalysed advancements in conversational AI, content generation and automated writing systems, enabling machines to interact with humans in more intuitive ways. Their ability to generate coherent, contextually relevant text has significantly enhanced applications such as chatbots, content creation tools and language translation services. As research continues to progress, GPT models are poised to play a crucial role in the future of human–computer interaction. Their ongoing development promises to further revolutionise communication and drive AI integration into everyday life. The impact of GPT models extends beyond language processing, influencing industries and shaping the future of AI-driven technologies [5].

12.5   Recent advancements in generative AI technologies

Generative AI has seen remarkable progress in recent years, transforming multiple industries with its innovative capabilities. By building upon foundational principles and incorporating advanced techniques, recent developments in generative AI have pushed the field into new realms of creativity and functionality. These advancements are expanding the possibilities for AI to generate high-quality, human-like content across a range of formats, including text [5], images [6] and audio. The rapid evolution of these technologies has opened novel opportunities for industries such as healthcare, entertainment and finance. In this section, we explore some of the most notable advancements in generative AI, examining their implications and potential to reshape business practices, consumer experiences [5] and technological innovation. As we delve deeper into these developments, we will explore key trends and their impact across various sectors, from creative arts to healthcare solutions. This exploration will provide insights into how generative AI is shaping the future and driving forward innovation. The following subheadings will offer a closer look at specific breakthroughs, their applications and the transformative effects across industries.

12.5.1   Advancements in deep learning architectures

Recent advancements in deep learning architectures have dramatically expanded the capabilities of generative AI models, allowing them to produce more sophisticated and high-quality outputs. Techniques such as GANs [1], VAEs [2] and transformer models [3] have seen substantial improvements, both in terms of the underlying algorithms and the computational efficiency of training. These innovations have enabled Generative models to learn more complex data representations, resulting in outputs with higher fidelity and realism. GANs have evolved from their initial iterations, with architectures like BigGAN [7] and StyleGAN [6] pushing the boundaries of image generation by creating high-resolution and photorealistic images. The introduction of Wasserstein GANs [8] and other variations has improved the stability and convergence of training, making them more reliable for practical applications. Similarly, VAEs have been enhanced to better capture the latent structures of data, enabling more accurate and diverse generative outputs across a range of domains, from images to sound [2]. And transformer models, which originally revolutionised NLP [3], have also made a significant impact on Generative tasks in areas like image generation and multimodal content creation. Models like GPT-3 and DALL·E [3], built on transformer architectures, can generate coherent text and produce images from textual descriptions, respectively. This cross-pollination of ideas from various fields has fuelled innovations that allow AI to synthesise not just text or images but entire immersive multimedia experiences.

Furthermore, advances in model scaling and distributed training have led to the development of large-scale Generative models capable of processing vast amounts of data [5]. These models are more efficient at capturing complex patterns and can generate high-quality outputs at scale, which was previously unfeasible due to computational and resource limitations. As deep learning architectures continue to evolve, we can expect even greater improvements in Generative capabilities, bringing us closer to AI systems that can generate lifelike content with minimal input or guidance. These developments have opened new avenues for practical applications across industries, including entertainment, healthcare, design and beyond.

12.5.2   Creative applications of generative AI in art and design

Generative AI has emerged as a transformative tool for artists, designers and creators, providing innovative ways to push the boundaries of artistic expression. Through advanced algorithms and deep learning models, generative AI can produce intricate visual art, design elements and conceptual pieces that challenge conventional approaches to creativity. Platforms like DALL-E [3], Midjourney and Artbreeder demonstrate the profound impact of these technologies in the world of visual arts, where AI is now not just an aid, but an active collaborator in the creative process. These tools allow artists to input a text prompt or a set of parameters, enabling the AI to generate images, artwork and designs that are often strikingly original and complex. This allows for the exploration of a vast array of creative possibilities that might be difficult or impossible to achieve through traditional methods. For example, an artist can request a surreal landscape, an abstract portrait or a fusion of different art styles, and the AI will synthesise these inputs into unique visual outputs [3]. Such capabilities have opened new creative horizons for artists, enabling them to expand their work with greater ease and efficiency.

Generative AI also offers designers the ability to rapidly prototype and experiment with new concepts, reducing the time required to explore various design possibilities. In industries like fashion, architecture and product design, AI-generated models can serve as initial design drafts, which can then be refined and enhanced by human creators [3,10]. This process allows designers to focus on higher-level creative decisions while leaving the repetitive and time-consuming tasks of iteration to AI, streamlining workflows and increasing productivity. Moreover, AI-driven tools are breaking down traditional artistic boundaries, enabling the blending of mediums and styles. Artists can seamlessly integrate digital, physical and interactive art forms, creating hybrid works that engage audiences in innovative ways. For instance, generative AI can create interactive installations where the art evolves in response to the viewer's movements or inputs, offering a more immersive experience. This fusion of creativity and technology offers artists an unprecedented degree of flexibility and potential for collaboration with AI systems.

In addition to visual arts, generative AI is having an impact on music, literature and even performance art. AI models trained on vast amounts of artistic data are now capable of composing music, writing poetry and generating storylines, further enriching the creative landscape. As AI continues to evolve, its role in art and design is expected to grow, enabling new forms of artistic expression, enhancing creativity and even challenging our perceptions of what constitutes art itself. The synergy between human intuition and AI's computational power is setting the stage for a new era of creativity, where the possibilities are limited only by imagination [3,5].

12.5.3   Healthcare innovations and applications in medical imaging

Generative AI is rapidly transforming the healthcare sector, particularly in the realms of medical imaging, diagnostic analysis and patient care. By leveraging sophisticated algorithms, Generative models can synthesise high-resolution images, enabling clinicians to gain more accurate insights into a patient's condition [6,7]. This has the potential to enhance the quality and precision of diagnostics, facilitating earlier detection of diseases such as cancer, cardiovascular conditions and neurological disorders [6]. For example, AI-powered imaging tools can generate clearer images of organs and tissues, improving the ability to detect abnormalities that may not be visible with conventional imaging techniques [6].

One of the most impactful applications of generative AI in medical imaging is its role in data augmentation. In medical training, obtaining large datasets of annotated medical images can be a time-consuming and costly process, but generative AI can synthesise realistic images based on existing data [5]. This synthetic data can then be used to train machine learning models, improving their accuracy and generalisation without the need for extensive manual labelling. AI-generated images can also simulate rare conditions or extreme cases, providing healthcare professionals with valuable exposure to a wide variety of medical scenarios [6]. Generative AI is also playing a key role in the creation of personalised treatment plans. By analysing medical images alongside patient data, AI models can help doctors tailor interventions based on individual needs. For instance, AI can assist in designing custom surgical procedures, developing patient-specific drug formulations or recommending precise therapeutic approaches that are more likely to yield positive outcomes. This level of personalisation enhances the precision of medical care and has the potential to improve patient outcomes by offering treatments that are better suited to each person's unique condition [3,5]. In addition to diagnostics and treatment planning, generative AI is accelerating medical research. The ability to generate realistic biological data – such as synthetic images of cells or tissues – has enabled researchers to simulate complex biological processes, speeding up drug discovery and clinical trial processes. AI models can also generate molecular structures or predict the interactions of different compounds, allowing for the faster identification of potential drug candidates and the optimisation of therapeutic strategies [5].

Moreover, the integration of generative AI with other technologies, such as robotics and telemedicine, further expands its potential in healthcare [10]. AI-driven robots are beginning to assist in surgical procedures with higher precision, while remote healthcare platforms are using AI to analyse medical images and offer consultations in real-time, even in remote or underserved areas. As generative AI continues to evolve, its ability to create highly detailed, accurate medical data will further enhance diagnostic capabilities, improve treatment outcomes and significantly reduce healthcare costs worldwide [6,10]. Ultimately, the promise of generative AI in healthcare lies in its potential to revolutionise patient care, offering faster, more accurate and more personalised treatments that can have a profound impact on global health.

12.5.4 Business applications and innovations in financial forecasting

Generative AI is making significant inroads into the world of business and finance, transforming traditional practices and enabling more accurate, data-driven decision-making. With its ability to model complex financial systems, generative AI is being utilised for predictive modelling, risk assessment and financial forecasting [1]. By generating synthetic financial data and simulating a wide range of market scenarios, generative AI allows financial analysts and businesses to make well-informed decisions based on data that is both comprehensive and up-to-date.

One of the key benefits of generative AI in financial forecasting is its ability to simulate market conditions that may be difficult to predict using traditional methods. For instance, AI models can generate synthetic datasets that mirror historical market trends, allowing businesses to test their strategies under various hypothetical conditions [2]. These simulated data sets help companies understand how different factors, such as changes in interest rates, geopolitical events or global economic shifts, could impact their financial performance. This capability enhances scenario planning, enabling organisations to develop more resilient strategies and better prepare for potential risks [3]. In addition to simulation, generative AI is also being employed to improve the accuracy of financial forecasts. By analysing vast amounts of financial data – ranging from market prices and interest rates to economic indicators and company performance metrics – AI models can generate highly precise predictions about future market movements [5]. These models can account for complex correlations between various factors and adapt to changing market dynamics in real time, making them a powerful tool for investors, traders and financial planners [4]. As a result, businesses can optimise their investment strategies, mitigate risks and identify new opportunities more effectively. Another significant application of Generative AI in finance is in risk assessment. Financial institutions, including banks and insurance companies, can use generative models to identify and quantify risks that might not be immediately apparent [8]. By generating a broad spectrum of possible financial outcomes based on historical data, these models can help businesses assess the likelihood of certain risks and develop mitigation strategies. For example, AI-driven models can simulate the effects of market volatility or economic downturns on a company's financial health, allowing for more accurate risk assessments and better capital allocation [1].

Furthermore, generative AI is revolutionising the way businesses respond to emerging market trends. AI systems can process and analyse real-time financial data, identifying new market trends and consumer behaviours as they emerge [10]. By generating insights from these trends, businesses can quickly adapt their strategies to capitalise on new opportunities, giving them a competitive edge. This capability is particularly valuable in fast-paced sectors such as stock trading, cryptocurrency and venture capital, where timely information and rapid decision-making are crucial [1]. As generative AI technologies continue to advance, their integration into financial forecasting and business decision-making is expected to become even more widespread. By providing deeper insights, enhancing the accuracy of forecasts and automating complex analyses, these technologies are enabling businesses to operate with greater agility and foresight [9]. In the future, we can expect generative AI to play an even more central role in shaping business strategies, improving financial performance and driving innovation across industries [1].

12.5.5   *Ethical considerations and governance in responsible AI*

As generative AI technologies evolve, it is crucial to address ethical concerns and establish effective governance to ensure their responsible use. Key issues include bias, fairness and the potential misuse of AI-generated content, such as deepfakes [1]. Bias in AI models can reinforce stereotypes and discrimination, making it essential to use diverse, representative datasets and ensure fairness in model design [2]. Transparency in AI decision-making is also critical to maintain accountability, particularly in areas that impact public policy or individual rights [3]. Misuse of generative AI, such as spreading misinformation or creating deceptive content, is another pressing concern [6]. To mitigate these risks, mechanisms for detecting and verifying AI-generated content must be developed. Additionally, robust regulatory frameworks and ethical guidelines are needed to govern the development and deployment of AI systems, ensuring they are used responsibly and ethically [9]. Establishing industry standards and best practices for AI development is also important to ensure adherence to privacy, security and fairness principles. Collaboration between governments, academia and industry is necessary to create policies that promote the responsible use of AI, while fostering innovation [8]. By addressing these ethical considerations, we can maximise the benefits of generative AI while minimising potential harm.

12.6   Applications of generative AI across diverse domains

Generative AI is revolutionising numerous fields, driving innovation and efficiency across diverse industries. With the use of advanced algorithms, it is enabling the creation of content, models and solutions that significantly transform traditional practices [1]. From creative arts to scientific research, generative AI is unlocking new possibilities for content generation and problem-solving. Its applications span across virtual worlds, design, education and healthcare, enhancing productivity and creativity in these sectors [7]. In virtual environments, it helps create immersive experiences, while in design, it enables rapid prototyping and innovative concepts [6]. In healthcare, generative AI is being used for medical image synthesis, drug discovery and personalised treatment [5]. The technology also enhances educational tools, offering personalised learning experiences for students [3]. Its scalability and adaptability allow for greater efficiency in a wide range of industries, making it a powerful driver of progress. The integration of generative AI promises to continue reshaping industries, improving workflows and expanding the possibilities for innovation.

12.6.1 Virtual environments and generative content creation

Generative AI technologies are at the forefront of redefining the domains of VR and augmented reality (AR) environments, catalysing a profound transformation in how people engage with digital content. These innovative algorithms leverage sophisticated neural architectures to generate immersive experiences, lifelike imagery and virtual worlds that blur the boundaries between reality and simulation [3]. In the realm of VR and AR applications, generative AI algorithms play a pivotal role in content generation, enabling the creation of realistic textures, environments and characters that immerse users in captivating digital experiences [7]. By leveraging the capabilities of machine learning and deep learning techniques, these algorithms can synthesise virtual material that closely replicates the complexity and richness of the physical world [5].

One of the essential applications of generative AI in virtual environments is in the creation of interactive gaming experiences. By employing generative algorithms to generate dynamic environments, diverse characters and engaging narratives, game developers can deliver immersive gaming experiences that captivate players and draw them into richly detailed virtual worlds [10]. These virtual environments can range from fantastical realms filled with mythical creatures to hyper-realistic urban landscapes teeming with lifelike activity [8]. Moreover, generative AI algorithms are increasingly being utilised to simulate real-world scenarios for training and education purposes. In fields such as healthcare, aviation and military training, VR and AR simulations powered by generative AI can provide trainees with realistic environments and interactive scenarios to improve learning outcomes. For instance, medical students can simulate surgical procedures in virtual operating rooms, while pilots can undergo simulated flight training in virtual cockpits [2].

The ability of generative AI extends beyond merely replicating existing environments; these algorithms can also generate novel and imaginative virtual worlds that push the boundaries of creativity. From generating procedurally generated landscapes to designing futuristic cityscapes, generative AI allows creators to venture into new creative territories of imagination and design in VR [3]. Generative AI technologies are fuelling innovation in virtual content generation, enabling the development of immersive VR and AR experiences that engage users and expand the limits of digital creativity. By leveraging sophisticated algorithms and neural architectures, these technologies are transforming our interaction with virtual environments, unlocking new opportunities for entertainment, education and exploration in the virtual realm [5,9].

12.6.2   Generative AI in creative and product design

Generative AI is revolutionising creative processes across various domains, including art, music and product design, by offering innovative tools and techniques for artistic expression and product innovation [1,2]. Artists and designers now have access to AI algorithms that can rapidly generate artwork, compose music and prototype product designs with unparalleled speed and efficiency. For instance, platforms like DALL-E and Amper Music exemplify the transformative potential of generative AI in creative endeavours [7]. DALL-E, developed by OpenAI, is capable of autonomously generating visual art based on textual descriptions provided by users. This allows artists to explore new concepts and ideas quickly, bypassing traditional constraints of time and manual labour. Similarly, Amper Music leverages AI to compose original music compositions tailored to the preferences and requirements of users, empowering musicians to explore various styles and genres effortlessly [5].

Generative AI algorithms are also playing an essential role in product design and innovation. By leveraging the capabilities of machine learning and optimisation techniques, designers can use AI to optimise product designs, streamline production processes and create personalised experiences for consumers [10]. For example, AI-driven design tools can generate countless iterations of product prototypes, enabling designers to explore a wide range of possibilities and identify optimal solutions more efficiently than ever before. Moreover, AI models can examine consumer data and preferences to tailor product designs and experiences to individual needs, enhancing customer satisfaction and loyalty [9].

Overall, generative AI is transforming the creative landscape by providing artists, musicians and designers with powerful tools for exploration and innovation. These technologies enable creators to push the boundaries of traditional mediums, offering new ways to experiment and produce unique works. In art, AI allows for the generation of original digital artwork, blending different styles and techniques seamlessly. Musicians can use AI to compose novel pieces or create innovative soundscapes, expanding the possibilities of music creation. Designers leverage AI to generate product prototypes and design concepts with greater speed and variety. As generative AI continues to evolve, it is expected to unlock new dimensions of creativity, enabling the creation of complex and imaginative works. This shift will redefine what is possible in art, music and product design, offering endless possibilities for innovation. The ongoing progress of these technologies promises to reshape how creative industries approach the process of creation. Ultimately, generative AI will continue to enhance human creativity and inspire the next generation of artists and designers.

12.6.3   Generative AI in architecture and structural design

In the realm of architecture and design, generative AI is revolutionising the field of architecture and design, offering novel tools and techniques that redefine how buildings are conceptualised, planned and constructed. Through the utilisation of AI-driven algorithms, architects and urban planners can now generate architectural layouts, building designs and optimisation strategies that meet specific design criteria and constraints with remarkable precision and efficiency [4,5]. One of the main benefits of generative AI in architecture and design is its capacity to navigate a wide range of design possibilities. By inputting parameters such as site conditions, functional requirements and aesthetic preferences, AI algorithms can generate a multitude of design alternatives, allowing designers to evaluate and compare different options quickly [2,10]. This iterative design process enables architects to explore innovative solutions and push the boundaries of conventional design paradigms.

Furthermore, generative AI facilitates the optimisation of spatial configurations and resource utilisation in architectural projects. By analysing data regarding building performance, energy efficiency and environmental impact, AI algorithms can generate design proposals that prioritise sustainability and minimise environmental footprint. From optimising building layouts to maximising natural light and ventilation, AI-driven design solutions contribute to the creation of environmentally conscious and sustainable built environments. Generative AI also streamlines the design process by automating repetitive tasks and reducing manual labour. By leveraging AI algorithms for tasks such as generative modelling, parametric design and optimisation, architects can focus their efforts on creative problem-solving and design innovation [9]. This approach not only speeds up the design process but also allows for greater exploration and experimentation in architectural practice.

Thus, generative AI empowers architects and designers to create environments that are not only functional and efficient but also aesthetically compelling and sustainable. By utilising AI-driven algorithms to produce architectural designs, optimise spatial configurations and streamline the design process, designers can push the limits of creativity and innovation within the built environment. With the continuous advancement of generative AI, its influence on reshaping architecture and design remains boundless, offering new opportunities for exploration, experimentation and excellence in architectural practice [7,8].

12.6.4   Generative AI in personalised learning and education

Generative AI is ushering in a new era of personalised learning, revolutionising traditional teaching methods with adaptive learning systems. By leveraging AI algorithms, educators can now create customised educational content that meets the unique needs of each student. Interactive tutorials and simulations are tailored to individual learning styles, enhancing engagement and comprehension [2,7]. This technology allows for real-time adjustments, enabling the learning experience to evolve as the student progresses. Personalised learning pathways help students grasp complex concepts at their own pace, fostering deeper understanding and retention [5]. Generative AI also enables the creation of dynamic assessments, offering feedback that is specific to each learner's strengths and areas for improvement [3]. The use of AI in education ensures that every student receives the support they need, making education more inclusive and effective. As this technology advances, it will continue to transform how knowledge is delivered and accessed. By catering to diverse learning preferences, generative AI is poised to make education more accessible and engaging for all. This shift promises to empower learners and educators, creating a more personalised and efficient learning environment [9].

An important benefit of generative AI in education is its capability to create tailored learning resources that align with the unique goals and interests of each student. Using data-driven insights and machine learning algorithms, AI-powered educational platforms can assess students' learning styles, preferences and performance metrics, enabling the creation of customised learning experiences that resonate on a personal level [4,6]. For example, a student who excels in visual learning may receive interactive multimedia tutorials, while a student who learns best through hands-on activities may be provided with virtual simulations and practical exercises [2,7]. Furthermore, generative AI enables educators to design flexible learning experiences that evolve in real-time to students' progress and comprehension levels. By continuously analysing students' interactions with learning materials and assessments, AI algorithms can modify the pace, difficulty and content of instruction to optimise learning outcomes [3,5]. This adaptive approach to education guarantees that students get tailored support and guidance exactly when they require it, fostering deeper engagement and understanding. Moreover, generative AI empowers enables educators to deliver focused interventions and assistance for learners with diverse needs and learning styles. By generating adaptive learning pathways and remedial resources, AI-powered educational platforms can address individual learning gaps and challenges, helping students overcome obstacles and achieve their full potential. Additionally, AI algorithms can promote collaborative learning by pairing students with peers who have similar interests and learning objectives, enhancing a sense of community and teamwork in the classroom [3].

Generative AI now has the potential to transform education by providing personalised learning experiences tailored to the individual needs and preferences of each student. By harnessing AI-powered adaptive learning systems and customised educational content, educators can enhance student engagement, improve learning outcomes and foster a culture of lifelong learning in learners of all ages [1]. As these technologies advance, they have the potential to reshape education, making it more personalised, adaptive and impactful [10].

12.6.5   Generative AI in personalised medicine and drug discovery

Generative AI is at the forefront of transforming healthcare through personalised medicine and drug discovery, leveraging advanced algorithms to tailor treatment strategies and accelerate the development of new therapies [4]. In personalised medicine, AI algorithms analyse vast datasets of patient information, genetic data and medical records to identify individualised treatment options and predict patient outcomes with unprecedented accuracy. By utilising machine learning and predictive analytics, healthcare providers can enhance treatment options, forecast patient outcomes with exceptional precision, optimise treatment strategies, minimise negative side effects and ultimately enhance patient results [5].

Moreover, generative AI plays an essential role in drug discovery by facilitating the generation of novel drug candidates and the optimisation of drug molecules. AI-driven drug design platforms utilise deep learning techniques to evaluate molecular structures, forecast interactions between drugs and targets and simulate biological processes, thus accelerating the discovery of potential therapeutic agents. By automating the drug discovery process and rapidly screening large chemical libraries, AI algorithms enable researchers to identify promising drug candidates more efficiently and cost-effectively than traditional methods.

These advancements in personalised medicine and drug discovery hold significant promise for revolutionising healthcare delivery and advancing medical research. By customising treatment plans based on each patient's unique characteristics and utilising AI-driven drug design methods, healthcare professionals can enhance patient care, reduce side effects and achieve better treatment outcomes. Additionally, AI-powered drug discovery platforms have the potential to accelerate the development of novel therapies for a wide range of diseases and conditions, addressing unmet medical needs and driving innovation in the pharmaceutical industry [3]. Overall, generative AI is poised to play a transformative role in shaping the future of healthcare, offering new opportunities for precision medicine, personalised treatment and therapeutic innovation.

12.7   Exploring future directions and opportunities in generative AI

As we look to the future of generative AI, the potential for innovation and creativity appears limitless. This subtopic explores emerging research trends, technological advancements and the opportunities for interdisciplinary collaboration that will shape the AI landscape. Speculative projections offer insight into the ways generative AI might evolve, uncovering new applications and capabilities. Key areas of growth include the refinement of existing models, the integration of AI with other technologies and the development of more advanced creative tools. As AI systems become more sophisticated, they will continue to push the boundaries of creativity and problem-solving across various sectors. The transformative impact of generative AI could redefine how we approach art, design, healthcare, education and beyond. The future promises new forms of human–AI collaboration, where creativity and ingenuity flourish. By embracing these emerging trends, we can foster an environment where AI enhances and accelerates innovation. The next phase of generative AI will likely bring breakthroughs that challenge our understanding of what is possible in both technology and creativity. Together, these developments could create a future where AI-driven systems unlock new dimensions of human potential.

12.7.1   Emerging trends in generative AI research

In the coming years, generative AI is poised to witness a proliferation of research efforts focused on enhancing the realism, diversity and controllability of generated outputs. One promising avenue of research lies in the development of hybrid models that combine the strengths of different generative techniques such as GANs, autoencoders and VAEs. These hybrid models have the potential to overcome the limitations of individual approaches and achieve new levels of fidelity and flexibility in generated content [1,2]. Another emerging trend is the exploration of multimodal generative AI, where AI systems can produce content in various formats, including text, images and audio. By integrating diverse sources of information and learning cross-modal representations, multimodal generative AI can create rich and immersive experiences that transcend traditional boundaries [3,10]. Furthermore, research efforts are likely to focus on advancing the clarity and understanding of generative AI models. As AI systems become progressively sophisticated, it becomes crucial to understand how they generate content and make decisions. By developing interpretable models and visualisation techniques, researchers can gain insights into the inner workings of generative AI systems, enabling better debugging, error analysis and model refinement.

12.7.2   Technological advancements shaping the future of generative AI

Technological advancements in hardware and software are poised to accelerate the pace of innovation in generative AI. The continued evolution of hardware platforms, such as GPUs, TPUs and neuromorphic chips, will enable researchers to train and deploy increasingly complex generative AI models at scale [1,6]. Moreover, advancements in software frameworks and algorithms, such as improved optimisation techniques, regularisation methods and model architectures, will further enhance the capabilities of generative AI systems [3,9]. A key focus is the advancement of more efficient and scalable training algorithms for generative AI models. Current training procedures often require large amounts of labelled data and computational resources, making them inaccessible to many researchers and practitioners. By developing novel algorithms that are more data-efficient and computationally lightweight, researchers can democratise access to generative AI technologies and foster greater innovation and collaboration across the community [5]. Another technological advancement with significant implications for generative AI is the integration of self-supervised learning techniques. Self-supervised learning allows AI systems to learn from unlabelled data by predicting missing or corrupted parts of the input. By leveraging self-supervised learning, generative AI models can learn more robust and generalised representations of the underlying data distribution, leading to improved performance on downstream tasks and greater adaptability to new domains and environments [2,10].

12.7.3   *Opportunities for innovation and cross-industry collaboration in generative AI*

The future of generative AI presents numerous opportunities for innovation and collaboration across disciplines. Interdisciplinary research efforts that unite experts from disciplines such as computer science, cognitive science, psychology, art and design can lead to groundbreaking discoveries and transformative applications of generative AI [1,7]. One promising area for interdisciplinary collaboration is the intersection of generative AI and healthcare. By leveraging AI-generated content, researchers can create innovative solutions for medical imaging, drug discovery, personalised medicine and patient care [6,8]. For example, generative AI models can generate synthetic medical images to augment training datasets and improve the accuracy of diagnostic systems.

Another opportunity lies in the application of generative AI to environmental sustainability and climate change. By simulating complex natural systems and generating realistic scenarios, AI systems can help researchers to gain a deeper understanding of how human activities affect the environment and devise strategies for mitigating climate-related risks. Additionally, generative AI can be used to design sustainable materials, optimise energy systems and support environmental conservation efforts [8,9]. Furthermore, the creative industries stand to benefit significantly from advancements in generative AI. By collaborating with artists, designers, musicians and storytellers, AI researchers can co-create innovative tools and platforms for creative expression. For example, generative AI models can assist artists in generating novel artwork, musicians in composing original music and writers in crafting compelling narratives [4,7].

The future of generative AI is filled with opportunities for innovation and advancement across various fields. By embracing emerging research trends, harnessing technological advancements and fostering interdisciplinary collaboration, the complete capabilities of generative AI can be unlocked to address pressing societal challenges, drive economic growth and enhance human creativity and well-being. As this journey into the future begins, envisioning a world where AI systems augment human capabilities, inspire new forms of expression and enable individuals and communities to prosper in a swiftly evolving digital landscape becomes paramount [1,6].

12.8   Case study

12.8.1   *Case study 1: enhancing medical imaging and personalised treatment in healthcare with generative AI – NVIDIA and Zebra Medical Vision*

Generative AI is driving significant advancements in healthcare, particularly in medical imaging and personalised treatment. NVIDIA, a leader in AI hardware and software, has collaborated with healthcare providers to create Clara, a framework for medical imaging that leverages GANs to enhance the quality of MRIs, CT scans and other medical images. Clara improves image resolution and clarity, enabling more accurate diagnoses for conditions like cancer, neurological disorders and cardiovascular diseases, even when imaging data is limited. And Zebra Medical Vision, another pioneering company, uses GANs and other AI techniques to identify specific patterns in medical images that are often overlooked by the human eye. Zebra's imaging tools have assisted healthcare providers worldwide in diagnosing diseases faster and more accurately, particularly in regions with limited radiologist access. In personalised medicine, Generative models like VAEs are being used to simulate patient responses to treatments. For instance, NVIDIA's Clara Genomics can create patient-specific data to model how patients might respond to specific drugs, assisting doctors in designing customised therapies. These tools are also being integrated into telemedicine platforms, where real-time image analysis is critical. For example, Aidoc, an AI-powered diagnostic tool, uses advanced image analysis to detect conditions like brain bleeds in CT scans, providing radiologists with immediate insights. Generative AI in healthcare is thus transforming diagnostics, reducing errors and enabling precise, personalised patient care.

12.8.2 Case study 2: risk modelling and fraud detection in finance with generative AI – JPMorgan Chase and PayPal

The financial sector has embraced generative AI for risk modelling and fraud detection, with institutions like JPMorgan Chase leading the charge. JPMorgan uses AI models to conduct extensive stress testing on its portfolios by simulating complex financial scenarios, such as sudden market crashes or interest rate spikes. For instance, JPMorgan's LOXM project, an AI-powered trading algorithm, simulates various market scenarios using synthetic data generated by GANs, enabling the bank to optimise trading strategies and manage risk more effectively. This AI-driven approach allows the bank to prepare for extreme market events and develop strategies that ensure financial stability. In the area of fraud detection, PayPal leverages generative AI to enhance the accuracy of its fraud detection systems. PayPal's AI tools use GANs to generate synthetic examples of fraudulent transactions, which help train the system to detect subtle fraud patterns. By comparing these synthetic examples against live transactions, PayPal's system identifies even minute deviations from normal transaction patterns, reducing false positives and increasing the precision of fraud detection. PayPal's AI technology has enabled the company to detect fraud more accurately, safeguarding millions of global transactions daily and enhancing customer trust. These applications in financial systems highlight how generative AI enhances both security and predictive capabilities, helping financial institutions protect assets, improve operational efficiency and mitigate potential risks.

12.8.3   Case study 3: redefining creative processes in art, music and design with generative AI – OpenAI's DALL-E and Amper Music

In the creative sector, generative AI is transforming the production of art, music and design. OpenAI's DALL-E, a cutting-edge image-generation model, allows artists and designers to create detailed, high-quality images from simple text prompts. For example, DALL-E has been used by fashion designers and product developers to generate multiple visual iterations of concepts, enabling rapid prototyping and creative exploration. This tool allows artists to visualise ideas and produce compelling visual art in minutes, significantly reducing the time required for concept development. And in music, Amper Music, a generative AI platform, allows users to compose original songs based on selected styles, moods or instruments. This tool democratises music creation by allowing individuals without formal training to generate professional-sounding compositions. Artists and producers have used Amper Music to compose background scores, jingles and even full tracks, blending AI-generated music with human creativity to create innovative musical works. For instance, pop artist Taryn Southern collaborated with Amper Music to produce an entire album, 'I AM AI', making it one of the first albums co-created by AI. These AI-driven tools are also being applied in other creative fields. For instance, NVIDIA's GauGAN, another Generative model, is widely used in the gaming industry to create immersive virtual landscapes based on simple sketches, allowing game developers to create more lifelike and diverse virtual worlds. These examples demonstrate how generative AI accelerates creative processes, expands artistic boundaries and opens new possibilities for innovation across multiple creative industries.

12.9   Conclusion

As the exploration of trending technologies and applications of generative AI draws to a close, we stand at the forefront of a transformative era marked by unparalleled innovation and opportunity. Generative AI, driven by advancements in technologies like GANs [1] and transformer-based models [3], is revolutionising the landscape of content creation, creative design processes and numerous domains across industries. Central to generative AI is its capability to autonomously generate text, images, audio and even video content that closely resembles human craftsmanship. This capability, exemplified by models like ChatGPT and DALL-E, has unlocked a myriad of possibilities, from enhancing data augmentation techniques in computer vision to revolutionising personalised learning experiences in education.

One of the most significant accomplishments of generative AI is its impact on the creative industry. Artists, designers and musicians are leveraging AI-powered tools to augment their creative processes, explore novel artistic expressions and challenge the limits of conventional art forms. Through style transfer techniques, artists can infuse their work with the aesthetics of renowned painters or transform sketches into photorealistic images with astonishing accuracy [6]. Furthermore, the healthcare sector is experiencing a paradigm shift fuelled by generative AI technologies. From synthesising photo-realistic medical images to facilitating drug discovery through virtual screening, AI-powered solutions are revolutionising medical diagnostics, treatment planning and pharmaceutical research. By converting raw data from medical scans into actionable insights, generative AI enables healthcare professionals to make better-informed decisions and enhance patient outcomes [7]. In addition to its impact on creativity and healthcare, generative AI is driving innovation in fields such as gaming, VR and autonomous systems. Through video frame prediction and resolution enhancement techniques, AI-powered algorithms are creating immersive gaming experiences, enhancing visual fidelity and optimising performance in real-time.

However, as the capabilities of generative AI is embraced, it is imperative to acknowledge the ethical and legal considerations accompanying its adoption. Issues such as algorithmic bias, intellectual property rights and ensuring regulatory compliance pose considerable challenges that require attention to guarantee the ethical and fair implementation of AI technologies. Furthermore, the intersection of generative AI with explainable AI offers opportunities to improve transparency, interpretability and accountability in AI systems. Navigating the dynamic landscape of generative AI demands a comprehensive approach that balances innovation with ethical considerations and societal impact. Collaboration among industry stakeholders, policymakers and the research community is essential to develop frameworks promoting responsible innovation, ethical standards and protection against unintended consequences.

In conclusion, the era of generative AI represents a convergence of technological innovation, creative expression and societal impact. It is reshaping industries, offering new tools for artists, healthcare providers and educators to enhance their work. By harnessing the full capabilities of generative AI, we can push the boundaries of creativity and problem-solving. The technology holds immense potential to improve efficiency, personalise experiences and drive advancements in various sectors. However, it is crucial to adopt responsible innovation practices to ensure its ethical use. This includes addressing concerns such as bias, transparency and accountability. When applied responsibly, generative AI can contribute positively to human well-being. It can drive creativity, enrich education and foster socio-economic progress across the globe. Through ongoing research, collaboration and governance, we can unlock the full potential of generative AI for the benefit of society. A future where AI-powered solutions coexist harmoniously with human values is within reach, promising a transformative impact on the world.

References

[1]   Goodfellow, I., Pouget-Abadie, J., Mirza, M., *et al.* (2020). "Generative Adversarial Networks." *Communications of the ACM*, 63(11), 139–144.

[2] Kingma, D. P., and Welling, M. (2014). "Auto-Encoding Variational Bayes." *International Conference on Learning Representations (ICLR)*, https://arxiv. org/pdf/1312.6114.

[3] Vaswani, A., Shazeer, N., Parmar, N., *et al.* (2017). "Attention Is All You Need." *Proceedings of the 31st International Conference on Neural Information Processing Systems*, pp. 6000–6010.

[4] Radford, A., Narasimhan, K., Salimans, T., and Sutskever, I. (2018). "Improving Language Understanding by Generative Pre-Training." *OpenAI*, https://cdn.openai.com/research-covers/language-unsupervised/language_ understanding_paper.pdf.

[5] Brown, T. B., Mann, B., Ryder, N., *et al.* (2020). "Language Models Are Few-Shot Learners." *Proceedings of the 34th International Conference on Neural Information Processing Systems*, pp. 1877–1901.

[6] Karras, T., Laine, S., and Aila, T. (2021). "A Style-Based Generator Architecture for Generative Adversarial Networks." *IEEE Transactions on Pattern Analysis and Machine Intelligence*, vol. 43, no. 12, pp. 4217–4228.

[7] Brock, A., Donahue, J., and Simonyan, K. (2019). "Large Scale GAN Training for High Fidelity Natural Image Synthesis." *International Conference on Learning Representations (ICLR)*.

[8] Gulrajani, I., Ahmed, F., Arjovsky, M., Dumoulin, V., and Courville, A. C. (2017). "Improved Training of Wasserstein GANs." *Proceedings of the 31st International Conference on Neural Information Processing Systems*, pp. 5769–5779.

[9] Devlin, J., Chang, M. W., Lee, K., and Toutanova, K. (2019). "BERT Pre-training of Deep Bidirectional Transformers for Language Understanding." *Proceedings of the 2019 Conference of the North American Chapter of the Association for Computational Linguistics Human Language Technologies*, Volume 1 (Long and Short Papers).

[10] Dosovitskiy, A., Beyer, L., Kolesnikov, A., *et al.* (2021). "An Image Is Worth 16×16 Words Transformers for Image Recognition at Scale." *International Conference on Learning Representations (ICLR)*.

Chapter 13

Conclusion

Thangavel Murugan[1], Shajina Anand[2], R. Karthik[3] and K. Suganthi[4]

Abstract

The conclusion chapter of this book summarizes the transformative journey through the realms of generative AI (GAI), highlighting its advancements, applications, and future potential. It emphasizes that GAI is not just a technological trend, but a paradigm shift that unlocks endless possibilities across various fields. The chapter advocates for lifelong learning and continuous growth, urging readers to adapt to the rapidly evolving landscape of GAI. It reflects on the ethical and legal considerations surrounding GAI, stressing the importance of responsible and transparent use to safeguard human values and rights. Furthermore, the chapter calls for active engagement in GAI research and development, encouraging readers to explore and innovate within this dynamic domain. The chapter envisions a future where GAI can significantly contribute to addressing global challenges and enhancing creativity by fostering curiosity and collaboration. Ultimately, it serves as a motivational closing statement, inviting readers to embrace the opportunities presented by GAI and to remain inspired as they navigate the transformative potential of this technology. The chapter concludes with a hopeful outlook, reinforcing the idea that the best is yet to come in the realm of GAI.

Keywords: Generative AI; transformation; ethical considerations; lifelong learning; innovation; future potential

13.1 Recap of key findings

Generative AI Unleashed thoroughly explores generative AI (GAI), covering its evolution, key algorithms, and significant applications. The journey starts with the

[1]Department of Information Systems and Security, College of Information Technology, United Arab Emirates University, United Arab Emirates
[2]Department of Mathematics and Computer Science, Seton Hall University, USA
[3]Centre for Cyber Physical Systems, Vellore Institute of Technology, Chennai, India
[4]School of Electronics Engineering, Vellore Institute of Technology, Chennai, India

early days of artificial intelligence (AI) development, following the technological advancements that have led to the sophisticated GAI systems, that researchers see today. Unlike traditional AI, which focuses on analyzing and predicting data, GAI takes a major step forward by enabling machines to create entirely new content. This ability to generate text, images, audio, and more has opened many new possibilities, making GAI a key player in driving technological progress across various fields.

This book takes an in-depth look at the core algorithms behind GAI, such as generative adversarial networks and variational autoencoders. These algorithms have been crucial in GAI's development, allowing machines to create content that can rival or even exceed human creativity. The book also examines how GAI is transforming different industries, from generating text and creating realistic images to producing lifelike audio. These examples show the wide-ranging potential of GAI to revolutionize areas like entertainment, media, healthcare, and more. Beyond the technical aspects, the book also explores the broader implications of GAI, including the philosophical and ethical questions it raises. As machines begin to display creative abilities, questions arise about what creativity means, whether machines can truly be original, and if they could ever be conscious. These issues are not just theoretical—they have real-world implications for how GAI is developed and used in society. The book also addresses some of the current challenges in GAI, such as problems with training stability and the issue of mode collapse, where the variety of generated content is limited. These challenges highlight the ongoing efforts to improve GAI's reliability and effectiveness.

13.2   Future directions in GAI

Looking forward, the future of GAI is likely to be shaped by several important trends and new technologies. Researchers will focus on improving current models and exploring new areas like multimodal learning [1], where GAI systems can create content in different formats—text, images, audio, and video at the same time. This will make GAI more versatile and useful in areas like virtual reality and interactive media.

Quantum computing [2] might also help GAI become faster and more powerful, allowing for the creation of more complex models. Another key area will be making GAI more understandable and trustworthy through Explainable AI, especially in important fields like healthcare and finance.

GAI also has the potential to help with big global challenges, particularly in environmental and sustainability efforts. It could offer new ways to tackle issues like climate change [3]. As GAI continues to drive Industry 4.0 and digital transformation [4], it will likely be used more for automating tasks and improving human–computer interaction, making technology easier and more effective to use.

Finally, improving automatic code generation [5] will make writing software faster and easier, helping developers be more efficient. Overall, the future of GAI is full of exciting possibilities for innovations and benefits across many industries.

13.3 Implications for industry and society

GAI is set to bring major benefits to various industries, but it also comes with challenges that need careful consideration.

- In manufacturing [6], GAI can revolutionize product design and production by optimizing processes, reducing waste, and creating innovative products with advanced features. It can also streamline supply chain management by predicting demand and improving logistics, leading to higher productivity and lower costs.
- In healthcare [7], GAI has the potential to make significant advancements. For example, it can improve diagnostics by analyzing medical data more accurately than human doctors, and it can speed up drug discovery by simulating complex interactions to find new treatments. Additionally, GAI can help create personalized treatment plans based on an individual's unique health data, leading to better patient outcomes and more efficient healthcare.
- The finance industry [8] can also benefit from GAI, which can enhance risk management, detect fraud, and improve market analysis. By analyzing large amounts of financial data, GAI can identify potential risks and opportunities more quickly, helping financial institutions and investors make better decisions.
- In entertainment [9], GAI can transform content creation by generating music, art, and scripts, offering new tools for creators. It can also make interactive experiences like video games and virtual reality more immersive and personalized. Additionally, GAI can tailor media content to individual preferences, creating a more engaging experience for users.

However, there are challenges, especially with the use of deepfake technology and synthetic media, which can be used to spread misinformation or harm public trust. As GAI evolves, it will be important to develop tools to detect fake content, create regulations, and educate the public about these risks. The widespread use of GAI could also lead to job displacement, especially in industries like manufacturing and content creation. While GAI will create new job opportunities, it will be essential to provide training and education to help workers adapt to these changes.

13.4 Ethical, privacy, and legal considerations

GAI technologies raise important ethical and legal considerations that must be addressed to ensure their responsible use. As GAI becomes more integrated into various sectors, these considerations will become increasingly complex and critical.

13.4.1 Ethical concerns

One of the main ethical concerns [10] is the potential for misuse of GAI, especially in creating fake content, like deepfakes. Deepfakes can be used to spread misinformation, harm individuals' reputations, or even interfere with political processes. This can undermine trust in media and institutions. To address these risks, it is crucial to develop tools that can detect fake content and educate the public about the dangers of such technologies.

Another ethical issue is the impact of GAI on jobs. As AI takes over tasks that were traditionally done by humans, there is a risk of job loss in certain industries, such as manufacturing and content creation. While GAI will also create new job opportunities, it is important to invest in training and education to help people adapt to these changes and find new roles.

13.4.2   Privacy concerns

Privacy concerns [11] are very important, especially when GAI models are trained on large datasets that might include sensitive or personal information. As these models become more advanced, they could accidentally reveal or figure out private details, leading to serious privacy risks. Protecting data privacy and security is essential, and organizations need to adopt strong data management practices to safeguard people's rights. This includes using techniques to make data anonymous, securing how data is stored, and getting clear permission from individuals whose data is being used. Additionally, legal rules need to be put in place to control how data is collected, used, and shared in the AI era. These rules should protect people from unauthorized surveillance and data breaches while still allowing room for innovation.

13.4.3   Legal concerns

On the legal side [12], there are questions about intellectual property and ownership of AI-generated content. For example, if an AI creates a piece of music or artwork, who owns the rights to that creation? Current laws may not be fully equipped to handle these situations, so there is a need for updated regulations that clarify these issues. In conclusion, while GAI has the potential to bring about significant benefits, it is crucial to address the ethical and legal challenges it presents. By developing clear guidelines and regulations, and ensuring that GAI is used responsibly, researchers can maximize its positive impact while minimizing potential harms. Collaboration between governments, industry leaders, and researchers is essential to navigating these complex issues and ensuring that GAI contributes to a fair and just society.

13.5   Collaborative opportunities

The rapidly evolving field of GAI offers numerous opportunities for collaboration to advance, apply, and explore this transformative technology. By fostering collaboration among developers, industry partners, and policymakers, researchers can unlock new potential, address complex challenges, and pave the way for the future of GAI.

One important area for collaborative opportunities is interdisciplinary research [13]. GAI draws from a wide range of disciplines, including computer science, mathematics, cognitive science, and neuroscience. Collaboration across these disciplines can lead to breakthroughs that would not be possible within a single field. By bringing together experts with diverse backgrounds and perspectives, researchers can push the boundaries of what GAI can achieve.

Moreover, it is essential to foster collaboration between academia and industry to effectively translate advanced research into practical applications. Industry partners can offer valuable resources, data, and infrastructure for testing and implementing GAI solutions at a large scale. Similarly, academic researchers can contribute fresh ideas, innovative algorithms, and theoretical insights to drive industry innovation. By establishing strong partnerships between academia and industry, researchers can bridge the gap between theory and practice, thereby expediting the integration of GAI across various domains.

In addition to interdisciplinary and academia-industry collaborations, there are opportunities for international cooperation in GAI research. The global nature of AI development implies that researchers from different countries can bring distinct perspectives, expertise, and datasets to the table. Collaboration with researchers around the world can promote innovation, the exchange of ideas, and cultural diversity in the development of GAI technologies. International collaborations can also help address ethical and regulatory challenges that arise in the global deployment of AI systems.

GAI researchers must collaborate with policymakers to ensure the responsible development and deployment of AI technologies. Policymakers play a key role in establishing regulatory frameworks, ethical guidelines, and standards governing the use of AI in society. Engaging in dialogue with policymakers allows researchers to prioritize safety, fairness, transparency, and accountability in the development and deployment of GAI technologies. Collaboration between researchers and policymakers can also help address societal concerns such as bias, privacy, misinformation, and job displacement associated with the widespread adoption of AI technologies.

Similarly, GAI developers must collaborate with end-users to create AI solutions that are user-centric and cater to the needs and preferences of diverse user groups. Involving end-users in the design, development, and evaluation of GAI systems can lead to more user-friendly, context-aware, and personalized experiences. By incorporating user feedback, preferences, and ethical considerations into the AI development process, developers can build trust, improve usability, and ensure the positive impact of GAI technologies on individuals and communities.

13.6   Concluding remarks

Throughout this book, researchers have explored the advancements, transformative applications, and future frontiers of GAI and its impact on industries ranging from healthcare to entertainment, as well as its implications for society. The concluding chapter offers the final thoughts on the significance of GAI advancements and their potential to shape the future of technology and society.

A key takeaway from the exploration of GAI is its immense potential to drive innovation and creativity across multiple domains. By enabling machines to generate novel content such as images, text, and music, GAI has paved the way for new possibilities in the realms of art, design, and storytelling. Throughout this book, researchers have seen that GAI algorithms like GPT-3 and StyleGAN have demonstrated an unprecedented level of sophistication in creating realistic and compelling content, blurring the lines between human and machine-generated work.

Furthermore, GAI offers the potential to democratize creativity by making sophisticated artistic tools [14] accessible to a wider audience. This technology allows artists, writers, and designers to utilize GAI platforms to enhance their creative processes, generate fresh ideas, and explore new artistic styles. This democratization of creativity not only empowers individual creators but also fosters a more diverse and inclusive cultural landscape, enabling new voices and perspectives to thrive.

In addition to art and design [15], GAI can drive substantial advancements in fields such as healthcare, education, and manufacturing. Within healthcare, GAI models have demonstrated potential in medical imaging analysis, drug discovery, and personalized treatment recommendations. By leveraging the capabilities of GAI, healthcare professionals can improve disease diagnosis, predict patient outcomes, and optimize treatment plans, ultimately enhancing the quality of care and saving lives.

In the field of education [16], GAI tools can improve learning experiences by personalizing educational content, creating interactive simulations, and providing real-time feedback to students. By customizing educational materials to individual learning styles and preferences, GAI technology can help learners of all ages and backgrounds reach their full potential, promoting a more fair and inclusive education system.

In the manufacturing industry [17], GAI algorithms can enhance product design, streamline production processes, and reduce time-to-market for innovations. By generating design solutions based on input parameters and constraints, GAI allows engineers and designers to explore a wide design space, identify optimal solutions, and iterate rapidly to achieve the desired outcomes. This iterative design approach not only speeds up the product development cycle but also fosters innovation by pushing the limits of what is technologically feasible.

Considering the impact of GAI on technology and society [18], it is evident that this revolutionary technology has the potential to create new opportunities, tackle challenges, and bring about positive social change. However, with such potential comes the responsibility to approach the development and use of GAI with careful consideration for ethical and societal implications.

Moving into a future shaped by GAI, it is crucial to prioritize transparency, accountability, and inclusivity in the design and implementation of AI systems. By fostering a culture of ethical AI development, researchers can ensure that GAI technologies are deployed responsibly, with due consideration for privacy, security, and fairness. Furthermore, by actively involving stakeholders from diverse backgrounds and perspectives, researchers can co-create AI systems that reflect the values and aspirations of our society as a whole.

13.7   Call to action

GAI has already revolutionized numerous industries, from healthcare to creative arts, and its influence is ubiquitous in our daily lives. By embracing GAI, individuals and organizations can unveil new possibilities, streamline processes, and innovate in previously unimaginable ways. However, to fully harness the power of GAI and drive it toward new frontiers, active involvement, and continuous exploration are essential.

As researchers embark on the GAI revolution, it is important for readers to actively participate and contribute to its advancement. Here are some key points to consider:

- Embrace a culture of innovation [19]: GAI thrives in environments that foster innovation, creativity, and collaboration. Encourage cultivating a mindset of open-mindedness and experimentation, where failures are seen as learning opportunities and successes are celebrated as milestones.
- Dive deeper into research [20]: Delve into GAI research by exploring the latest developments, breakthroughs, and emerging trends in the field. Engage with academic publications, attend conferences, and participate in discussions to stay updated on the rapidly evolving landscape of GAI.
- Build a community of practitioners [21]: Forge connections with like-minded individuals and experts in the GAI space to exchange ideas, share insights, and collaborate on projects. Building a strong community of practitioners fosters knowledge-sharing and creates a support network for troubleshooting challenges and sparking innovations.
- Explore ethical and responsible AI practices [22]: Prioritize ethical considerations and responsible practices as researchers push the boundaries of GAI technology. Reflect on the ethical implications of work, consider the societal impact of GAI applications, and advocate for transparency and fairness in research and development endeavors.
- Experiment, iterate, and innovate: Embrace a spirit of experimentation, iteration, and innovation in GAI projects. Push beyond comfort zones, explore new ideas, and challenge existing conventions to uncover novel solutions and transformative applications of GAI technology.
- Support diversity and inclusion: Promote diversity and inclusion in the GAI community by actively welcoming individuals from diverse backgrounds. Champion inclusivity, equity, and representation in collaborations, projects, and initiatives to foster a more diverse and vibrant GAI ecosystem.
- Advocate for continued learning and growth [20]: Emphasize the importance of lifelong learning and continuous growth in the fast-paced world of GAI. Seek out learning opportunities, acquire new skills, and adapt to changing technologies to remain at the forefront of innovation and drive the GAI field toward new horizons.

13.8   Closing statement

Throughout this book, researchers have delved into the world of GAI and its potential to transform various industries. Researchers have explored how this cutting-edge technology is not simply a trend, but a significant shift with the power to unlock a future filled with possibilities.

As researchers consider the transformative impact of GAI, it is evident that users are only beginning to scratch the surface of its potential. From reshaping art and music to revolutionizing healthcare and finance, GAI has the power to drive innovation in ways users have never imagined.

As researchers reflect on the groundbreaking potential of GAI, it is clear that the future is filled with opportunities for progress. The advancements researchers have witnessed are just the beginning, and the impact of GAI is profound and far-reaching. Researchers must harness this technology for the betterment of society as we stand on the brink of a new era.

References

[1] Bewersdorff A, Hartmann C, Hornberger M, *et al.* (2025) Taking the next step with generative artificial intelligence: The transformative role of multimodal large language models in science education. *Learning and Individual Differences*, 118:102601.

[2] Shuford J. (2024) Quantum computing and artificial intelligence: Synergies and challenges. *Journal of Artificial Intelligence General Science (JAIGS)*. 1(1), 1–9.

[3] Amiri Z, Heidari A, and Navimipour NJ. (2024) Comprehensive survey of artificial intelligence techniques and strategies for climate change mitigation. *Energy*. 308:132827.

[4] Aldoseri A, Al-Khalifa KN, and Hamouda AM. (2024) AI-powered innovation in digital transformation: Key pillars and industry impact. *Sustainability*. 16(5):1790.

[5] Idrisov B, and Schlippe T. (2024) Program code generation with generative AIs. *Algorithms*. 17(2):62.

[6] Yang J, Wang Y, Wang X, Wang X, Wang X, and Wang FY. (2024) Generative AI empowering parallel manufacturing: Building a "6S" collaborative production ecology for manufacturing 5.0. *IEEE Transactions on Systems, Man, and Cybernetics: Systems*. 54(11):6522–36.

[7] Moulaei K, Yadegari A, Baharestani M, Farzanbakhsh S, Sabet B, and Afrash MR. (2024) Generative artificial intelligence in healthcare: A scoping review on benefits, challenges, and applications. *International Journal of Medical Informatics*. 188:105474.

[8] Bhattacharya R, and Aoun MA. (2024) Using generative AI in finance, and the lack of emergent behavior in LLMs. *Communications of the ACM*. 67 (8):6–7.

[9]   Nader K, Toprac P, Scott S, and Baker S. (2024) Public understanding of artificial intelligence through entertainment media. *AI & Society*. 39(2):713–26.

[10] Sonko S, Adewusi AO, Obi OC, Onwusinkwue S, and Atadoga A. (2024) A critical review towards artificial general intelligence: Challenges, ethical considerations, and the path forward. *World Journal of Advanced Research and Reviews*. 21(3):1262–8.

[11] Wu X, Duan R, and Ni J. (2024) Unveiling security, privacy, and ethical concerns of ChatGPT. *Journal of Information and Intelligence*. 2(2):102–15.

[12] Singh B. (2024) Lensing legal dynamics for examining responsibility and deliberation of generative AI-tethered technological privacy concerns: Infringements and use of personal data by nefarious actors. In Ara A and Ara A (eds.), *Exploring the Ethical Implications of Generative AI* (pp. 146–67). Hershey, PA: IGI Global.

[13] Longo L, Brcic M, Cabitza F, *et al.* (2024) Explainable artificial intelligence (XAI) 2.0: A manifesto of open challenges and interdisciplinary research directions. *Information Fusion*. 106:102301.

[14] Hutson J. (2024) Integrating art and AI: Evaluating the educational impact of AI tools in digital art history learning. *Forum for Art Studies*. 1(1):393.

[15] Xu Y, and Nazir S. (2024) Ranking the art design and applications of artificial intelligence and machine learning. *Journal of Software: Evolution and Process*. 36(2):e2486.

[16] Jain KK, and Raghuram JN. (2024) Gen-AI integration in higher education: Predicting intentions using SEM-ANN approach. *Education and Information Technologies*. 29:17169–209.

[17] Gabsi AE. (2024) Integrating artificial intelligence in industry 4.0: Insights, challenges, and prospects—A literature review. *Annals of Operations Research*. 17(43):170–93.

[18] Sabherwal R, and Grover V. (2024) The societal impacts of generative artificial intelligence: A balanced perspective. *Journal of the Association for Information Systems*. 25(1):13–22.

[19] Sundberg L, and Holmström J. (2024) Innovating by prompting: How to facilitate innovation in the age of generative AI. *Business Horizons*. 67 (5):561–70.

[20] Cazzaniga M, Jaumotte MF, Li L, *et al.* (2024) Gen-AI: Artificial intelligence and the future of work. *International Monetary Fund*. 2024(1):1–41.

[21] Woodruff A, Shelby R, Kelley PG, Rousso-Schindler S, Smith-Loud J, and Wilcox L. (2024) How knowledge workers think generative AI will (not) transform their industries. In *Proceedings of the CHI Conference on Human Factors in Computing Systems*. pp. 1–26.

[22] Lu Q, Zhu L, Xu X, Whittle J, Zowghi D, and Jacquet A. (2024) Responsible AI pattern catalog: A collection of best practices for AI governance and engineering. *ACM Computing Surveys*. 56(7):1–35.

Index

www.ingramcontent.com/pod-product-compliance
Lightning Source LLC
Chambersburg PA
CBHW050509190326
41458CB00005B/1484